SATURDAY
AND THURSDAY MORNING

A Year in the Life of a
Lower Division Football Fan

by Dave Espley

JCA Publishing

First published in 1997
by JCA PUBLISHING

ISBN: 0-953-1833-00

A catalogue record for this book is available from the British Library

Printed and bound in Great Britain by
Kendall Press, Trafford Park, MANCHESTER

JCA PUBLISHING
PO Box 10
STOCKPORT
Cheshire
SK2 5FB

Main cover photo & inset top: Dave Espley
Inset bottom: Chris Hill, Stockport Express Advertiser

Front cover design: Dave Humphrey

*For Anna,
Julia, Christopher and Andrew*

CONTENTS

CONTENTS

INTRODUCTION

Monday June 17th 1996

When does the football season start? Cynics might be forgiven for thinking that, with a major championship - European or World - every other year, and close-season innovations such as the Intertoto Cup, the football season doesn't start, as such, because it doesn't actually finish. This is, of course, complete crap, and such cynics can go and take a running jump (as can anyone, indeed, who cannot recognise the attractions of the beautiful game). The start of the football season is a moveable feast, but will usually fall around the second week of August.

Or at least that's when the actual points gathering begins. For me and thousands of others, the actual football season starts with the publication of the fixtures in mid-June. This, frankly, is when you can start planning a large part of your leisure time for the nine months beginning in August. This year, for instance, will start with a short trip to Crewe for the opening game, easing me into the season nicely. Wrexham on Boxing Day could be worse, and the home fixture on New Year's Day (York) compares favourably with last year's ridiculous trek to Brighton. However, the Football League's fixture computer - cheeky scamp! - has decreed that the greater part of Easter Monday will be spent travelling to and from Bournemouth, and the first two away games of 1997 will be the longest of the season, at Plymouth and Gillingham, on successive Saturdays. That'll take some domestic negotiation.

People who aren't afflicted by the madness that is supporting a lower division team, in person, home and away, will wonder, in view of problems such as these, why? Why bother? What's the point? I wish I could give you an answer. Looked at from a purely footballing perspective, Stockport County, realistically, are never, ever, going to win a major trophy. It's probably only slightly less likely that they will ever even play in the Premiership. To do so would involve an ascent almost as dramatic as Wimbledon's from 70s Southern League to 90s Premiership, but, logically, the very fact that Wimbledon did it reduces the chances that County will follow suit (there's a lot that people blame Wimbledon for, but, surely, holding them responsible for reducing Stockport County's logical chances of playing at the pinnacle of English football is a first). The chance that I will see my team play in the top division in England at some point during my lifetime is, therefore, infinitesimal. Sobering thought, that.

So, then, why follow a team condemned to the eternal damnation that is lower division football? I offer in my defence only that I was first taken to County by my dad - also a lifelong fan - and that they are my home-town team. In this regard, it annoys me intensely that there are thousands - literally - of Stockport-bred football fans, however, that take a different view. It annoys me equally intensely that were County to draw either Manchester City or Manchester United in cup competition, the cars, buses and trains heading back to Stockport would have a majority of either red or light blue colours being sported. But what annoys me most of all is that, should County lose, the majority of Stopfordians disembarking from train, bus or car and making their way into their Stockport homes would be feeling the warm glow of victory, and saying smugly to themselves "well, I wonder who *we* will get in the next round. Not "they" - "*we*".

Paranoia aside, this book will, in many respects, describe a large part of the leisure time of a perfectly normal person. I don't have any pre-match rituals, as I consider myself well-enough adjusted to know that wearing a certain colour of underpants, or driving a particular way to the ground, will not have any bearing whatsoever on the result (the fact that if I step on a pavement crack with my left foot, I need to step on the next dozen or so with my right in order to balance out the feelings in both feet need not concern us here, as that is a complex psychological obsession wholly unconnected with football, and more to do with the fact that I am probably a bit of a prat).

My trouble is that I recognise the inherant absurdity of what I do. And, make no mistake, it *is* absurd. To travel thousands of miles and to spend hundreds of pounds, watching eleven men - who, let's be honest, couldn't give a toss about *me* - play a game against a similar group, in the name of the town where I happen to have been born is, let's face it, pathetic. It's almost as pathetic as feeling preposterously proud (of them? of the town? of *myself?*) when they win.

Recognising that I have a problem is one thing, however; curing it is something I am neither willing, nor, if the truth be told, able, to do.

AUGUST

NATIONWIDE LEAGUE DIVISION TWO

	P	W	D	L	F	A	Pts
BLACKPOOL	0	0	0	0	0	0	0
BOURNEMOUTH	0	0	0	0	0	0	0
BRENTFORD	0	0	0	0	0	0	0
BRISTOL CITY	0	0	0	0	0	0	0
BRISTOL ROVERS	0	0	0	0	0	0	0
BURNLEY	0	0	0	0	0	0	0
BURY	0	0	0	0	0	0	0
CHESTERFIELD	0	0	0	0	0	0	0
CREWE ALEXANDRA	0	0	0	0	0	0	0
GILLINGHAM	0	0	0	0	0	0	0
LUTON TOWN	0	0	0	0	0	0	0
MILLWALL	0	0	0	0	0	0	0
NOTTS COUNTY	0	0	0	0	0	0	0
PETERBOROUGH UNITED	0	0	0	0	0	0	0
PLYMOUTH ARGYLE	0	0	0	0	0	0	0
PRESTON NORTH END	0	0	0	0	0	0	0
ROTHERHAM UNITED	0	0	0	0	0	0	0
SHREWSBURY TOWN	0	0	0	0	0	0	0
STOCKPORT COUNTY	**0**	**0**	**0**	**0**	**0**	**0**	**0**
WALSALL	0	0	0	0	0	0	0
WATFORD	0	0	0	0	0	0	0
WREXHAM	0	0	0	0	0	0	0
WYCOMBE WANDERERS	0	0	0	0	0	0	0
YORK CITY	0	0	0	0	0	0	0

Saturday August 17th 1996. Crewe Alexandra (away).

The 9 month, God-knows-how-many miles odyssey begins today with one of the shortest journeys of the lot (discounting the 3 or so miles from my house to Edgeley Park, which, although an integral part of the odyssey, is hardly comparable to the Twelve Labours). Whilst it's true to say that following a team - any team - for a minimum of 50 games in nine months, represents quite a trip, however, I don't really expect to meet man-eating giants at Turf Moor, or goddesses promising immortality if only I agree not to continue on my quest to Deepdale. Neither do I expect to return home after an arduous journey to Plymouth to find my wife (who in any case is called Anna, not Penelope) surrounded by suitors bent on seduction whilst simultaneously trashing my house.

Nonetheless, an odyssey, albeit in a purely metaphorical sense, it most certainly is. An average of just over a game a week, each and every week, August to May, is not a commitment to be undertaken lightly. Neither is the expense of such devotion. I estimate that by the time the season is finished (and not including possible playoffs, which, being at the expensive dump that is Wembley, represent a second mortgage in themselves), my bank balance will be lighter to the tune of well over a grand.

But such details lie ahead. For today, there is only the thought of this afternoon's match with Crewe Alexandra to concern us, and the happy feeling which the first game of the football season engenders. All teams are equal when the whistle goes in a couple of hours or so, for the first and only time in the 46-game marathon. No matter what successes and failures concerned us during the football season which ended a mere 15 weeks ago, we are now on equal terms with all our rivals, and we view the coming year with the anticipation of children who've just seen the pile of presents on Christmas morning.

It's a sunny day, of course - the first Saturday of the football season always is (and people wishing to plan successful barbecues would do well to bear this in mind). As I am picking up fellow supporter Tom, in the Reddish area which lies to the north of Stockport, I elect to travel on the longer, but quicker, motorway route. As we trundle down the M6 as quickly as my 950cc Ford Fiesta will go, we discuss the forthcoming game, and season, with genuine optimism. Whilst Tom regales me with tales of last night's Man City v Ipswich match (being one of the large number of "bisexual" County fans whose allegiances are split between Maine Road and Edgeley Park, he attended in person), and how neither team would have given County much of a game, I inform him that should County and Newcastle both win their respective leagues, I will be richer to the tune of £518.25, thanks to the generosity of William Hills in offering 25-1 for County to win the Second Division title.

Saturday Night and Thursday Morning

There is some justification for such positive thoughts. County's pre-season friendlies were an unqualified success, with the side losing only twice, both in a pre-season tour of Portugal, and both defeats mitigated; one by the fact that County fielded a team of Portuguese triallists, and the second because the Portuguese team they were playing were pretty good (mitigation, in my eyes). We also beat Tranmere 3-2 at Prenton Park, and Birmingham at Edgeley, 4-0, with goals from Andy Mutch, Alun Armstrong (2) and captain Mike Flynn. Birmingham didn't have new strikers Paul Furlong and Mike Newall playing, but the rest of their side was strong enough for County to take heart from the victory, containing as it did recent Premier League stars Barry Horne, Gary Ablett and Steve Bruce. Bruce in particular was unimpressive, being left sat on his arse after Armstrong turned him to score County's second, and I would imagine that more than a few of the Birmingham fans dotted around Edgeley Park's Railway End must have harboured doubts about the coming season. The County fans had no such reservations, however, as *"you're so shit it's unbelievable"* made its first appearance of the season. It's boorish and crude, of course, but I do so hope it's not the last.

That said, it's dangerous to attach much significance to pre-season games. Indeed, the pre-season friendly itself is a peculiar beast. Ostensibly to provide teams with valuable match practice before the season proper starts (or continues, for those who think the football season never actually finishes, but, rather, pauses for a quick breather), pre-season games serve a far more complex purpose. There is, of course, the chance for the fans to get their first sightings of the squad - the new signings, who's put on the most weight during the summer, who looks the most tanned. Friendships are renewed in the stands (in fact, I myself have friendships which exist wholly and exclusively within the confines of Edgeley Park), and whilst the game itself, with up to a dozen substitutes freely rotated by both sides, is hardly the most competitive of encounters, it's football all the same, and there's something tremendously relaxing about watching your chosen pastime whilst reclining languidly in the stands, fully aware that even if County score, you're not expected to celebrate with anything more arduous than a cheer (an ironic one at that, if it's the 14th goal against local team Offerton Corinthians) and a desultory round of applause. Serious goal-celebrating comes later in the season - for now, it's time to enjoy the unique experience of watching football whilst wearing a t-shirt and sunglasses (pre-season friendlies are also *always* played in blazing sunshine).

One of the most memorable of County's pre-season games occurred at Morecambe in 1990 - a celebrated occasion of mass democracy, when the crowd provided themselves with far more entertainment than that which the professionals and semi-pros had managed to serve up.

The size of the County following had been seriously underestimated, with the result that about 500 County fans were "policed", if that's the right word for such an inadequate performance, by a lone copper and his dog. The half time score was 0-0, and the match had been less of a spectacle for the fans than an opportunity for the usual social gathering. However, the boredom of the game was only partially dissipated, and it was clear that something more was needed. That something turned out to be an impromptu kick-around between a group of spectators and a couple of brightly coloured plastic footballs, newly acquired from the shop fronts of Morecambe. This spontaneous game soon became far more enjoyable than the real thing, with more and more spectators entering the field of play - so much so that, sensing the possibility that friendly football supporters might be about to start enjoying themselves on a large scale, the authorities decided to clamp down. As the stewards attempted vainly to clear the pitch, one man and his dog decided it was time to round up some troublemakers.

Trouble was, the two teams contesting the game were by now so big that the copper could only chase small groups of fans at any one time, while the game continued around them. As soon as the dog's attention turned to another group, therefore, the previous "chasees" rejoined the game. The dog was getting more and more frantic, as indeed was the copper, as they realised they were fighting a losing battle. Then it happened.

One fan, a member of the small group being chased at the time, unfortunately lost his footing and fell to the floor. Rover, seizing his chance with both paws, pounced, and sank his teeth into the posterior of the poor unfortunate, before recommencing the chasing of another small group. The bitten fan, his pride undoubtedly hurt - as well as his rear end - got to his feet, calmly dusted himself down, trotted to where the dog was currently chasing, and booted it up the arse as hard as he could. Exit Rover, pitch left, yelping.

The copper, realising he was seriously outnumbered without his injured canine pal, beat a hasty retreat, and the game continued. Even the pinching of one of the balls by a steward who, presumably, proudly related his triumph to Mrs Steward over the cocoa that night *("I dived in and nicked their ball, I say, nicked their ball. That stopped 'em!")* didn't halt proceedings, as the game merely continued with the other ball, only stopping when County and Morecambe emerged for the second half.

The "real" game ended 1-1, with full-back Lee Todd scoring County's goal. History doesn't record who scored the County fans' winner in the half-time game. As a postscript, however, about 10 minutes into the second half, the cavalry approached in the form of lots of coppers, who seemed to have arrived expecting a riot. All they found was a rather boring pre-season friendly, and a police dog with a sore bum.

Back in 1996, we arrive in Crewe, and at the main roundabout before the ground, clogged with pre-game fan-traffic, I perform the experienced queue-jumpers' routine of ignoring the jam which wants to go ahead to the ground in the left hand lane and joining the lane to ostensibly turn right. I zoom along this empty boulevard to the roundabout, drive gaily right round its circumference, and, with a cheery wave to the seething mass I have just trumped, join the exiting traffic for the ground. We park up in a side street just off Gresty Road, and head for the away turnstiles.

Crewe Alexandra's ground has undergone major redevelopment in recent seasons, although it remains one of the smallest of lower division grounds. Away fans get the Gresty Road end - once a tiny terrace, and now an equally tiny stand, a mere 10 or so rows deep (indeed, in the equivalent game last season, with County holding on desperately to a 1-0 lead late on, and deep in their own half, there was a frenzied cry from a fan of "put it in row Z, Mike!" "They haven't got a row Z!" countered another. *"Well put it in row fucking E then!"*). Sadly, the rest of the ground remains in proportion, with an even punier stand behind the opposite goal, a marginally bigger "Popular" Stand to our left (if that's "popular", I'd hate to see "unpopular", arf, arf, arf), and the old wooden Main Stand to our right. Towering over the Popular side is a massive British Rail building (this being Crewe, after all), the windows of which would seem to give a splendid view of the game. Indeed given the relative size of the two buildings, it's probable that the BR windows would accommodate slightly more spectators than the stand.

It might be an uncharitable thought, but if the extent of Crewe's ambition lies in home attendances of, at most, 5,500, it seems that they - or at least their Board - seem happy for Division 2 to represent the pinnacle of their aspirations. That said, it could be argued that they are simply being realistic, and will build or relocate if and when they progress up the league. It remains true that most supporters of lower league teams remain ridiculously optimistic concerning their own sides. Ask them about future elevation to the Premiership, and the vast majority will say that it is a question of "when", rather than "if". This opinion flies in the face of all the statistics, of course, but it doesn't help their delusions when teams like Carlisle, Northampton and Wimbledon (the worst offenders, as not only did they make the top flight, they were ridiculous enough to stay there) actually climb to the top of the greasy pole. It does make far more sense, though, in view of the facts, for teams like Crewe (and County?) to accept their limitations, build cheaply enough to accommodate their average home attendance, and accept that on the relatively rare occasions that they draw a big team in one of the cups, they'll disappoint a few fair-weather supporters.

In that case, Gresty Road represents a smart, modern, lower division ground (although despite what the marketing types would have you believe, I still cannot use the word "stadium" to describe such a place). Try telling that to either home or away supporters, however, and you'd get extremely short shrift. *"Shit ground, no fans"* puts in an early appearance from the County support (unintentionally ironic, in view of our own still-recent history), and one can almost sense the home fans, whilst seething, thinking, en masse, "well, they have got a point".

Sweltering inside, the fact that County have sold out their quota of 1,200 tickets seems to have taken the stewards by surprise, and there is no attempt at ensuring fans sit in the seats allocated. I actually find my row - away from Tom, who bought his ticket separately - but, as I cannot see any spaces, let alone on the 30th seat along, where I should be sitting, and do not fancy the prospect of struggling past 29 hot and sweaty fans to debate the issue with whoever's sitting in seat 30, I flop into the vacant space at the end of the row, and hope against hope that whoever's seat *I've* sat in is already situated elsewhere.

I am disappointed to discover, however, as I sit down - and here is just one of the reasons, albeit a fairly trivial one, why the all-seater utopia is often shown up for the myth it is - that I am sitting next to a person who is not only fat, and sharing his BO with the rest of us, but cannot - or chooses not to - sit, as he should, within the confines of the width of his seat, but rather sits with legs splayed akimbo, crassly invading my space. Even seizing the opportunity to re-establish my territory when he swivels in his seat to share a joke with his cronies, by means of whipping my legs swiftly and firmly to the extent of *my* domain has no effect, as he simply forces his knees against mine, and wins the battle of wills which ensues - neither of us actually pushing, but my resolution breaking first, as I'm disgusted by the feeling of a fat and sweaty male knee squashing up against mine. I consider for a moment doing what animals do in these situations, and urinating freely to mark out my territory, but discard the idea, on the basis that I do actually want to watch the match, and watch it, moreover, through unblackened eyes.

The game starts with the traditional roar from the crowd that greets all kick-offs, enhanced by it being the first such opportunity of the season. It soon becomes clear, however, that the teams are too evenly matched, and - perhaps it is the heat of the day - all 22 players seem to be struggling to find any rhythm.

The pretty boys of Crewe (a not altogether unfair description, as they are and remain media darlings due to the fact that their team consists of many young players, and their passing game causes otherwise streetwise local sports reporters to drool uncontrollably) spray the ball around liberally, as usual, and quickly move to support each other, but lack any kind of penetration; they have a number of shots from 20 yards or so, none of which cause us any disquiet. County, meanwhile, have a couple of decent breakaways, but lack any firepower up front, with twin strikers Armstrong and Mutch receiving little support from the midfield. Half time is thus greeted with something approaching relief, there having been no incidents of note to take the mind off how hot it is.

Amusingly, I am told later that an overflow of County fans, who have been seated in the old wooden Main Stand can quite clearly hear manager Dave Jones berating winger Kieron Durkan - a mid-season signing from Wrexham last year, who has signally failed to live up to his promise - in no uncertain terms. The hot and sweaty County fans in our end, meanwhile, packed together and perspiring under the low roof, debate the first half. *"Fuckin' hell, that was shit, wasn't it?"* *"Where's our attack?"*, *"Durkan's playing crap"*, *"We definitely need a new striker"*. It's almost as if, having come to the match prepared to let off steam - as do most football fans - with passion and noise, and having been prevented from doing so by events on the pitch being so torpid, they feel the need to make up for it at half time.

The second half starts marginally better for County than the first, as we have a twenty minute spell of pressure, during which we are unlucky not to score. However, following such frenzied excitement, the match resumes its previous pace, and the only interest for me is in listening to a group of County fans sitting in the aisle to my right (none of them finding their allocated seats, and not even bothering, like me, to find an unallocated seat) discussing arrangements for their trip to Moldova in a couple of weeks to watch England. There is some confusing talk of visas, which concludes with one fan revealing that he is actually going to travel to Brussels in person after Tuesday's game with Chesterfield, in order to pick up his passport, duly authorised that he can then fly to Moldova a week or so later. Such dedication is by no means unusual. I work with Alan, a man who is planning trips to Italy, Poland, and possibly Georgia to see England's World Cup qualifiers. He's not a shaven-headed, tattooed hooligan, and has no intention of going to these places to cause trouble. On the contrary; when he travels abroad to follow England, or his own club, Leeds United (all too rare an experience of late), he deliberately arranges to stay for a couple of days either side of the game, thus allowing him to experience many of Europe's most beautiful cities. I know for a fact he is not alone in such arrangements, yet because he is a football fan, he and his travelling companions will be looked down upon and reviled by people whose idea of "abroad" is a fortnight in Torremolinos (or even a summer in Tuscany).

The game looks to be meandering to a 0-0 draw (and both teams were lucky to get nil, Brian, hur, hur, hur). A point on the first day of the season, away from home, isn't a bad return, although considering the pre-game optimism, when a win was almost taken as read, a draw would be a disappointment. What would be unthinkable, however, would be an 88th minute slip up by County's full back, new signing Damon Searle, allowing the Crewe right winger to swing in a cross to the far post where Tierney would be waiting, unmarked, to power a header into the net. The goal is all the more painful for me, sitting behind the opposite end, from where it can be seen that County's poor marking has left such a wide expanse of goal that even I could have nodded the ball in. The worst sound in the world for away football fans - the roar of the home support washing in on a time-delay from three sides of the ground - announces Crewe's winner, for although County immediately go into a speeded-up, Benny Hill "let's press for an equaliser quickly" routine, a winner it is, and one which gives County their first opening day defeat in nine years.

The ride home is filled with recriminations and aftermath. It's made worse by the fact that the weather by now is much more bearable, and the drive - through the early evening sun-drenched Cheshire countryside, rather than along the motorway - would have been well nigh perfect. What is worst of all, however, is that, even whilst we discuss County's depressing lack of penetration up front, we both of us know that this has completely fucked-up Saturday night. Following a County win, you are buoyant for the rest of the evening. Down the pub, at the pictures, even "Match of the Day" in your dressing gown with a bottle of Grolsch - the feeling a win provides is akin to that you experience as a child on the evening of Christmas Day. Suddenly remembering, as you sit doodling with your Etch-a-Sketch, that your Auntie Eileen also bought you that game of Mousetrap that you've wanted for ages brings a lovely warm glow. Suddenly remembering, as you think to yourself that there must be something better than "Casualty" on, that earlier in the day you beat Wrexham 3-2 with a late winner, to go third in the table, has a similar effect. Moreover, this feeling can even last until well into the following week, depending on whom the opponents were. All that a 1-0 defeat at Crewe brings is bellyache.

To make matters even worse, the first league table shows us at the bottom, alphabetically last of those teams which lost and didn't score (number of goals scored, rather than goal difference, decides placings in the Nationwide League) and, ridiculous as it is to even produce a table after one game, it only adds to the depression. The only note of optimism is offered by the fact that the defeat can be excised as early as three days hence, when County play their first home game of the season, in the Coca Cola Cup. Roll on Tuesday.

Tuesday August 20th 1996. Chesterfield (home) (Coca Cola Cup R1).

The League Cup - or Coca Cola Cup, or Littlewoods Cup, or Milk Cup, as its various sponsored incarnations over the years have lead it to be known, and apologies if I've missed any benevolent, philanthropic, football-supporting company out - has provided County with the majority of their giant-killing exploits. Apart from an incredible near-miss against Manchester United at Old Trafford in 1978 (of which more later), we've beaten (old) First Division West Ham at Edgeley, (old) First Division Crystal Palace at Selhurst Park, (old) Second Division Crystal Palace at Edgeley a year later, and, last year, (new) First Division Ipswich Town over two legs. Back in 1980, however, came arguably the biggest upset ever.

County had just won a fairly rare place in the second round of the plain old League Cup, by virtue of beating the mighty Chester over two legs. I eagerly bought a copy of the Manchester Evening News on the day the draw was made, to see who we had landed... Sunderland. Crap! Big club? Well yes, in the sense that they were well supported and riding fairly high in the (old) First Division at the time, but they were hardly the sort of glamour team we had hoped to get. They had no star names, yet would probably be good enough to give us a sound beating, without being enough of a draw to attract a big crowd, which would thus cushion the blow with decent gate receipts.

Such fears were realised, to a certain extent, when the crowd for the home leg proved to be only around 6,000. County started well, however, and went in at half time 1-0 up, thanks to a Dave Sunley goal, the result of a sweeping move which culminated in a great cross field ball to the left wing, a first time cross from record £15,000 signing Tony Coyle, and a stooping header from Sunley, which flew into the Cheadle End net.

An indication of the small crowd was given by the fact that I was able to change ends at half time, and thus saw the Sunderland equaliser from behind the Railway End goal. Ah well, we all thought as we made our way home, at least we held them to a draw, and now we can (all together) "concentrate on the League" (or, more realistically in those days of re-election, concentrate on trying to avoid being thrown out of it).

I wasn't able to travel up to Roker for the formality of the second leg, being still an impecunious 6th Form College student at the time. I had the trusty radio, however, and, amazingly for them, Manchester's Piccadilly Radio had a reporter at the game, one Doug Weatherall, who was obviously freelancing, as he also wrote the report in the following morning's "Daily Mail". He was also as completely unbiased a Geordie as the next Sunderland fan.

When the inevitable first Sunderland goal was reported as having gone in, I debated whether or not to end the agony by turning the radio off, and doing some homework. It was no contest, really, as I never did any homework anyway, just debated whether or not to. That night, as ever, it was a pretty one-sided debate. I was lying on my bed, filled with spotty teenage angst, therefore, when the ridiculous jingle that was used on Piccadilly at the time to announce that goals had been scored, rent the air. The pre-recorded, manic "It's a GOALLLL!" screech broke into the record that was playing at the time, and, with the sixth sense granted to all radio-listening football fans, I instantly knew that it was County who had scored. Sure enough, wor Doug came on air to relate through his tears how Dave Sunley had scored his second of the tie.

The nine o'clock news started, and the newsreader glibly reported the day's events, inconsiderately deciding not to give a score flash from Roker Park between each story. She did recap the night's scores at the end of the bulletin, however, and after reading details of inconsequential games involving Man United, Bolton, Bury, et al, uttered the words I will never forget as long as I draw breath, "... and up at Roker Park where the score is Sunderland one, Stockport County (pause) *two*, now". She could hardly keep the note of surprise out of her voice, but went on to read the bloody weather, oblivious to the shouts of joy that were heading along the A6 from the direction of Stockport.

The sports presenter put us out of our misery when the programme rejoined him in the studio, however. No messing, "straight up to Roker Park, now, and Doug Weatherall..." Dougie could hardly contain his woe, but told us back home how Tommy Sword had buried the penalty that had set County on the way to the victory which was duly confirmed ten minutes or so later.

I can't remember much of the rest of the programme, switching off the radio at full time so I could bask, gloriously, in the magnitude of the result. Amazingly, it wasn't the lead story on News at Ten, so I went to bed early, willing tomorrow to come quickly, like a little kid on Christmas Eve.

The next day, I bought all the newspapers I could afford, including the Manchester Evening News in the afternoon. The fact that Tommy Sword scored the winner probably had most of Fleet Street's sub-editors weeping with delight the previous evening, as their job had virtually been done for them: "Roker Put To The Sword"; "The Sword Killer"; "Tommy's Pork Sword" (Okay, I made the last one up).

I revelled in the papers, but couldn't really gloat at college. I'd finished at St Augustine's, an all-boys' Grammar school, in the June, where every major football match was analysed ad nauseam (had it not been a Grammar school, with compulsory Latin, the matches would probably have been analysed over and over), and, as the only County fan (the school was in Manchester), I'd have been in my element. Aquinas 6th Form College, however, was half full of people with curves, and soft squashy bits, and football was, fairly understandably, far from being the main topic of conversation. Even my male friends had only a passing interest; it was most frustrating - if only the game had happened a year earlier.

Not to worry, though. We were in the draw for the next round, and we had luck this time, being drawn out immediately prior to Arsenal. We again made the back pages of the tabloids the following day, chiefly because some desperate photographer had persuaded Tommy Sword to pose outside the Railway End with a plastic sword brandished over his head. To make matters infinitely worse, he apparently did it without being paid.

The attendance for the Arsenal game was much better, as the Stockport public proved, not for the first time, how adept they are at woodwork-vacating when the big boys are in town. There were around 13,000 packed in, as I recall, and, to my mind, the writing was on the wall after an awesome display of warming-up (yes, warming-up!) from Arsenal. Willie Young in particular looked sharp, at one point sending a header bulleting into the top corner of the net, pausing only to stop, breath on his nails, and then polish them on his shirt. It didn't stem the constant cries of *"Willie Young is a homosexual!"* (to the tune of the evergreen classic *"You're Going To Get Your Fucking Head Kicked In"*), that reverberated throughout the game, however.

Sure enough, Arsenal then cruised to a comfortable 3-1 win, after our keeper, ex-Evertonian "star" Dave Lawson, had picked up his usual big-game injury, this time when desperately trying to get out of the way of a John Hollins blast that put the visitors 1-0 up. The match had a couple of incidents that made it worthwhile, however. The first was when Kenny Sansom scored what I'm convinced must have been the best goal of his career, a thirty-five yard blob of a shot that almost burst the net in the Railway End goal. The look on his face as he ran triumphantly across the field, only to see a linesman standing smugly with upraised flag, was something to treasure forever. An Arsenal player had apparently been standing in an offside position when he ducked to avoid being decapitated. It was one of the most unfair decisions I'd ever seen, and therefore also one of the funniest.

The second incident occurred when County scored their consolation goal. 3-0 down, and County striker Les Bradd ambled tokenly after a ball that was bouncing gently back to George Wood in the Arsenal goal. The defender who was shepherding it back, however, suddenly decided that, for a bit of sport, he'd run crashing into George, leaving Bradd to tap the ball gleefully into the empty net, and George on the floor needing treatment. Oh how we laughed.

Tonight's game is not without interest, as, during the close-season, Chesterfield signed one of County's longest-serving players, Chris Beaumont; one of the last links with the team ex-manager Danny Bergara built which launched us on our recent upward surge. In addition, yesterday County re-signed, albeit on loan from Sunderland, another member of that team, and one of our most prolific goalscorers of recent seasons, Brett Angell. Whether County will smash their existing transfer record of £150,000 (paid to Preston North End for current captain Mike Flynn) in order to make the move permanent (Sunderland reportedly want £200,000) will probably be dependent on him performing at least as well as he did in his previous spell at Edgeley Park for the three months he is with us now.

I decide to buy a ticket for the Vernon Building Society stand - the one opposite the Main Stand which runs the length of the pitch. This is not so much for aesthetic reasons as for the fact that the County Board decided that the Cheadle End Stand - a 5,000 seater monstrosity behind one of the goals - would cost the same this season as the Vernon stand: £9 (it had previously been a pound cheaper). Although there are disadvantages to sitting there - the main one being no fewer than five roof support stanchions - you do therefore get a side-on view for the same price as behind-the-goal.

However, it is clear that I am in a minority, as most of the paltry crowd of 3,088 prove to be creatures of habit, and decide to remain in the Cheadle End; the Vernon Stand thus has the echoey, deserted air of a reserve game. Nonetheless, this allows me not only to pick and choose which seat I wish to sit in, but also to change ends at half-time, the age-old ritual which virtually disappeared with the arrival of seats.

County seem solid enough, and control the early exchanges. Bottle-blond striker Armstrong is playing well, with his flicks and knock-ons a class apart - which means that a lot of them are wasted by team-mates not attuned to his abilities. Nevertheless, Andy Mutch opens the scoring in the 21st minute, gleefully hammering home after Armstrong has headed forward Sean Connelly's free kick. There is no more scoring in the first half, although the way County are playing lifts the spirits slightly after Saturday. Chesterfield were ahead of County for much of last season, and only missed out on a play-off place late on because of fixture congestion. They were never going to be a walkover, therefore, and County can thus take a certain degree of heart from being ahead (the fact that the same arguments can also be said to apply to Crewe, defeated in the playoffs last season, hardly matters. County were so pisspoor on Saturday that it would have been disheartening even had the opposition been AC Milan).

I spend half time glancing at the one match programme I will buy all season. Despite County's publication being one of the best examples of the genre, the fact remains that programmes (or "Matchday Magazines", to give them their full, pathetic, title) are, to be frank, crap. They contain hardly anything worth reading, most of it being tediously formulaic and predictable (ghost-written "Manager's notes", "commercial corner", how the reserves/youth team are doing, which sad local company is offsetting the cost of a matchball against their tax this week...) What is stranger still is the buying of away programmes. Fans who do so for every away game in any given season presumably want to read, as well as those riveting items mentioned above - only less interesting, if that were possible, as they concern a club with whom you have no affinity whatsoever - exactly the same pen-pictures of their heroes 23 separate times.

I bought a copy of tonight's programme simply to see how the traditional annual redesign has gone. It proves amusing, however, to try and spot the various misprints, and typos that the printers have introduced (and equally amusing to try and spot which ones are simply grammatical errors by the various contributors that have remained uncorrected). The funniest misprint concerns a letter from a woman on the rather fatuous ladies page (called *"No Mans' Game"*, ho, ho, ho), which raves about how sexy defender Matthew Bound is. The same letter is inadvertently reprinted over the page, in the children's section (*"Not Kidding"* - KID-ding, geddit?), where it forms a bizarre counterpoint to letters from 5 and 6 year olds concerning their favourite player, and what they do at school and how they liked their first visit to Edgeley Park. That said, I suppose it's possible that the letter may have indeed belonged on the children's page rather than the previous one, and County are producing some particularly sexually precocious young fans.

The second half starts, and the sense of optimism and general well-being (it should actually be passionate and frenzied support, but the low-key nature of the game, emphasised by the lack of atmosphere produced by the sparse crowd means that optimism and general well-being is the order of the day) is heightened early on, when Mutch gets a second. It's an amusing goal too - one of the best kind, as all fans appreciate - as the Chesterfield keeper allows a well-directed but weak header to squirm under his body.

County are cruising at this point, but in the 64th minute, a Chesterfield striker bursts through towards the away fans in the open Railway End to my right. County's Matthew Bound seems to get in a good, ball-winning tackle, but the referee, about forty yards behind play but catching up as fast as his little legs will allow, blows for a foul, a penalty and a sending off. It would be interesting to be party to the referee's thought-processes at this point, as he makes his decision despite being forty yards away from the incident, and despite his linesman - nearer, better sighted, but merely a bit-part player in the drama that is "I'm In Charge", starring Graham Frankland, from Chester - not flagging for an infringement.

Some near me trot out the line that as it was deemed a foul, Bound had to go.

That's as maybe, but it seems to me that even assuming, in the face of all the evidence, that the referee was right, and Bound *didn't* get the ball, it seems hellishly unfair that, having genuinely attempted to, he receives the same punishment as he would had he rugby-tackled the forward, ripped his head off and flobbed down the hole. Well, okay, he would probably have been prosecuted as well in that case, but you get my point. Surely a penalty is enough punishment in such circumstances? Chesterfield score, it's 2-1, and they're back in the game.

County regroup, with Jim Gannon replacing winger Kieron Durkan to shore up the defence, and manage to weather the inevitable storm that the confidence which surges through the Chesterfield team as a result of the goal engenders. In the 77th minute, Brett Angell makes his re-appearance to a loud ovation from the County fans, and misses a great chance a couple of minutes later, heading over when he should have scored, following another brilliant cross from John Jeffers. County manage to hold on for a win, despite Chesterfield hitting a post late on.

It's the kind of result that will make for a competitive, not to say nail-biting, second leg in two weeks' time. Despite the European-qualifying teams being given a bye to the third round this year, this competition, seeded as it is from round 2 onwards, represents the chance of a big pay-day for clubs like County, which, despite the fact that it is the supporters that will be ripped-off to provide that pay-day, we are constantly told is good news.

As well as all that, of course, it's a win, and that means shiny happy people, at least until Saturday.

Saturday August 24th 1996. Notts County (home).

I'm looking forward to today's game slightly more than usual, as it's been a good week on the domestic front. Whilst it's true that good results for one's team cascade happiness into life away from football, it's not widely recognised that the opposite is also the case. Good news, or happy events, in your non-football-following life makes you approach the next game with a spring in your step, a smile on your face, and a song in your heart. That said, of course, a bad result pisses you right off again.

Nonetheless, the news which has left me feeling illogically optimistic about this afternoon's game concerns the GCSE results, which came through on Thursday. As well as my brother Martin gaining 8 good grades, my dad managed, at the age of 62, to gain an A pass in French. His five kids probably feel as proud about this result as he or my mum did about any of our exam results, at any level, despite the fact that Martin's four older siblings have got four degrees and any number of O and A levels between us. My share, after enduring God knows how many exams from the age of 16, was 8 O levels, 3 A levels and a degree in Economic and Social Studies from Manchester University. I'd like to bet, however, that for no one exam did I study as hard as my dad has done this last year for his, and that none of my grades was as well-deserved as his A.

It absolutely lagged it down last night, which a a few seasons ago would have meant the game would have been called off at first light. However, County took the decision a year or two ago to install a new playing surface at the cost of a couple of hundred grand (or, to be cynical, a goalscoring striker), with the result that the pitch is now one of the best in the Second Division, with commensurately good drainage.

Edgeley Park itself has also been transformed over the past ten or so years into what it is now - a smart lower division ground with a stand at one end so huge that, unlike Gresty Road, it can just about be called a "stadium" without irony (in fact a full house at Gresty Road could just about fit, en masse, into County's Cheadle End). The "Main" Stand is, paradoxically, the second smallest area, especially as its old wooden bench seats were replaced over the close season with the ubiquitous modern plastic. Opposite is the Vernon Building Society Stand, lately the pre-sponsorship Barlow Stand, and even more lately the Popular Side. It was the Popular Side when terraced, but had seats installed a few years ago under the existing roof. This had the effect of reducing capacity in that area by around 50%, but, of course, allowed the club to charge more.

The massive Cheadle End is the ground's piece de resistence. Constructed over the summer of 1995, at a reported cost of £1.5M, it holds almost 5,000 people. It is also so high that the back rows offer superb views over the west side of Stockport, towards the Peak District. The catering concourse, with recently installed bar selling stupidly highly priced beer at £1.90 a pint, is on the second floor, which means that things can get quite crowded at half time. However, it also means that the ground floor of the stand can be developed as club offices and a new club shop. The stand was originally planned as an even higher 6,000 seater, but local opposition (which was also noisily exploited by councillors during the election campaign which coincided with the start of construction) ensured that it's not quite as huge as it might have been. Nevertheless, at least part of the ground now towers over the terraced houses in the vicinity - a feature of a football ground which fans, if not the local residents over whose houses the ground towers, always appreciate.

The crowd - five and a half thousand odd - is bigger than Tuesday's for the obvious reason that this is the first home league game of the season, and the Coca Cola Cup first round is never much of an attraction, but also because County, these days, give away up to a couple of thousand tickets free to local schools. This is part of the club's efforts in the "Community" - that obligation which some clubs treat purely as a PR exercise, but which County, to their credit, take seriously - but also part of a conscious drive to attract kids back. We have always suffered from living in the shadow of the Manchesters United and City, and the fact that we were consistently crap for much of the 70s and 80s, at a time of generally falling football attendances, meant that a whole generation of kids missed out on the dubious attractions of Stockport County (whether or not they would have become regulars at that time had either County been a good team, or United and City not been so geographically close, is debateable).

Doing my own bit for the youth drive, I am accompanied to the game by my daughter, Julia, aged 7. It's not her first game; indeed since making her debut last season (at age 6, a full two years younger than I was when I went to *my* first game), she's been to a dozen or so matches. Sadly, her attendance last year coincided with one of the worst home seasons in living memory, and, as she hasn't been to any away games yet, she has a somewhat jaundiced view of the attractions of watching County.

Not to worry - it will stand her in good stead for the future if she doesn't come to expect too much. I made my own debut during the worst period in the club's history: for the first 15 years of my watching them, they only finished in the top half of the Fourth Division twice, and it wasn't until I had been a County regular, home and, sometimes, away for 17 years that I actually saw them promoted. As a result, although I can appreciate the success of the past few years (in fact, can appreciate it far more than any of the johnny-come-latelys, who seem to almost *expect* County success these days), I am well aware of just how bad things can get at Edgeley Park. In case I was about to forget this, however, what transpires this afternoon reminds me, with a vengeance.

The game is crap. Not just crap crap, but CRAP. Not "United fan walking away from Old Trafford after a stuffy 1-0 win and thinking, well, that wasn't one of our better performances" crap, but incredibly, inconceivably, preposterously crap. If games were comedians, this one would have been Syd Little. If games were quiz shows, this one would have been "Pets win Prizes". If games were international cricket teams, this one would have been England. Do I make myself clear? Bad, poor, pathetic, wretched, unsatisfactory, substandard, deficient, inept, and here my thesaurus runs out, expires and halts. Crap, poo, shit.

As a result, I feel incredibly sorry for Julia. Like many kids, she loves the whole experience of attending professional football, probably more than watching the game itself. She joins in with *"Davy Jones' Blue and White Army"* with gusto, arms flung wide in salute just like all the men around her, and dutifully keeps quiet, apart from the sniggering, at *"Where's your father, where's your father,*

17

where's your father, referee? Haven't got one, never had one, you're a BAS-tard,
referee" (to the tune of *"My Darling Clementine"*, in case you're interested).

The trouble is, as I said above, she has not seen many good games. Her first
ever was a 3-1 drubbing of Crewe, and it has been downhill ever since. Whether
today's match represents the nadir is debateable only in as much as she may still
yet see a worse one, difficult as it is to envisage. If I were superstitious, I might
think it was her fault, in fact. I'm not superstitious - quite the opposite, as I find
the fact that horoscopes are so prevalent in this country almost as depressing as
the popularity of "Neighbours" - but the fact that she's not coming next Tuesday
is a relief in more ways than one.

What is shown up all too clearly today is that County desperately need a
goalscorer. Angell makes another disappointing substitute appearance, and it's only
partial mitigation that the rest of the team are equally bad. It goes without saying
that a team which hasn't scored a league goal since April needs to find someone,
and quickly, who knows how to put the ball into the net. The pre-season optimism
is evaporating with each goalless minute; a lot of the poor play from the rest of
the team could be excused - and might disappear anyway following the surge of
confidence which would surely flow through the team - if only we could score.

Despite this, in the last few minutes - as, strangely, often happens in these
circumstances - both teams press for the winner with slightly more urgency than
they've shown for the previous hour and a half. Perhaps they realise that scoring
now would absolutely guarantee three points, whereas an earlier goal would mean
that they would have to get their arse in gear and actually earn their inflated wages
defending their lead. Whatever. It's painfully clear that neither team would score
today if the match was played until midnight, and, as the announcement of Sean
Connelly's capture of the Man of the Match award is made, a man behind me says,
to no-one in particular, "says it all when your full-back wins Man of the fucking
Match, dunnit?". Man Of The Fucking Match. Now there's a thought.

Tuesday August 27th 1996. Bournemouth (home).

Bournemouth, pre-season, were thought by many to be the whipping-boys-
elect of the Second Division (a bizarre image - that of whipping-boys actually
being elected: "Vote for Cabin Boy Jack - His Babysoft Skin Won't Let You
Down!"). On the way to tonight's match, the overriding thought is one of desperate
hope that this will be so. The league table published in the Sunday papers made
depressing reading, despite it being, after only two games, hardly a representative
indication of the teams' strength this year, with Burnley sitting on top after two
wins, and County now experiencing the dizzy heights of fifth from bottom, thanks

to Saturday's point. I'm feeling sorry in anticipation for the 50 or so Bournemouth fans who will, thanks to the stupidity of whoever programs the Football League's fixture computer - or, to be pedantic, whoever checks and approves its output - have made the long trek north on a Tuesday evening. That said, if their team wins, sod their long trek north. I'll be wishing them all manner of plagues, pestilence and petrol-leak on their way back down the M6.

What made last Saturday's game most depressing of all was the sense of déjà vu. Last season, County won a mere 8 games at home compared with 11 away. If it hadn't been for performances away from home, we would have been fighting a battle against relegation; as it was, we entered the last game, away at champions Swindon, with an outside chance of scraping into the play offs. A 0-0 draw, combined with results elsewhere, meant that we slipped to ninth in the final reckoning, but many fans thought that the team were at last beginning to play well at home. The problem which had been solved, it seemed, was that the team were formidable opponents at other sides' grounds because they played the type of game - solid defence, quick on the break - which was tailor-made for pinching results away from home. Their problems arose because lack of adaptability meant that they also played that way at Edgeley Park, with the results that goals didn't exactly flow, the crowd got restless, and confidence drained away.

I'm again sitting in the Vernon Stand tonight, this time with my dad, who's overcome his misgivings about last Saturday's result and come along. He does not suffer from County as badly as I do, and is thus able to say "sod 'em" and not go if he thinks they are playing poorly enough to not be able to guarantee 90 minute's entertainment. Presumably, therefore, he also thinks that the previous two league results were an aberration, and all will be well tonight.

Brett Angell makes his first start, and great things are expected. This is not merely desperation; he was a regular goalscorer in his first spell at the club, getting 33 goals in 73 games. His final season with us was 1989-90, in which we reached our highest final position for years. Although clumsy looking, he had the knack of being in the right place at the right time, and as a result scored 23 goals in that final season before he upped and left for Southend for a hotly-disputed £100,000 fee.

The fee was decided by tribunal, Angell being out of contract, and County wanted £250,000: not unreasonable in view of his record, and the fees being paid for similar players at this level. Southend, bending the rules of the game of Tribunal to their maximum elasticity, offered £5,000 for a player who had cost us, as an unknown reserve from Derby County, £25,000 less than 18 months previously. He had then gone on to become the most prolific striker in the Fourth Division, and here was Southend claiming that his value had decreased by 80%.

Saturday Night and Thursday Morning

It's a wonder they weren't charged with bringing the game into dispute; instead, their strategy worked, and the tribunal set a "split the difference" figure of £100,000. The only consolation was the sell-on clause which gave us 40% of any future profit, and which kicked-in following Angell's move to Everton for over half a million a year or two later. A County wag commented at the time that the space in the programme reserved for "record fee received" should therefore read "Brett Angell, Southend to Everton, £300,000"

Angell, however, is disappointing, as are - again - the rest of the team. It can, I decide, only be confidence. There can be no other reason why a side recognised as one of the most talented County have ever assembled, and one which was soundly beating higher division opposition a couple of weeks ago - albeit in friendlies - should now be playing like a bunch of arseholes. Bournemouth's goal, after half an hour, has a depressing air of inevitability about it. Their keeper punts a long ball downfield, and their lively black striker, on the edge of the County area and with his back to goal, executes an athletic leap, and, after a fashion, an overhead kick which loops over Paul Jones in the County goal.

It's a superbly taken goal, and a large number of County fans respond with generous applause, which actually makes more noise than comes from the sparsely-populated and unroofed Bournemouth end. I don't join in. It might seem petty and small-minded, but, to me, applauding other teams' goals means you don't care enough. I have never, I am proud to say, applauded another team's goal, because, quite simply, it doesn't matter how good the execution, a goal scored against County is a goal scored against County, and I don't invest hundreds of pounds of my own money and God knows how much of my own time in order to see goals scored against County. Simple as that. Okay, if pushed, I might give a cursory clap if County's opponents should score a brilliant 35-yard consolation in reply to our seven earlier scores, but that's about it. Sadly, there seem to be far too many fans without my hard resolve, who remain all too willing to applaud opposition goals.

There are two distinct circumstances in which this practice is manifested. Firstly, there is simply patronising your opponents, where which a fairly good opposition goal is scored, late on, in reply to your team's five or six. The feeling of benevolence, which the demolition job your team has just performed on those helpless saps engenders, justifies a rousing round of applause, and a "good goal" to no one in particular. Had Ipswich managed to score during their 9-0 defeat at Old Trafford a couple of seasons ago, an example of such a situation would have been... well, no it wouldn't would it? We're talking United fans here, aren't we? *Every* goal scored against the Reds is, of course, an outrageous act, and an affront to human dignity. I'm sure you get the picture, anyway.

The second instance is simply politeness, and can be encountered under any circumstances, although most irritatingly when the opposition team has just scored a spectacular 85th minute winner, and there are, unbelievably, idiotic sods in the home support who applaud. These people are invariably smug, self-satisfied types, who consider themselves "fair-minded". The fact that no one in the ground - supporters, players, linesmen, even the police, gives a toss about their fair-mindedness seems irrelevant to them, viewing their magnanimity, as they do, as something akin to a charitable act, when it is, in fact, simply rank hypocrisy.

The most humorous instance of applauding away team's goals was demonstrated at an Aston Villa - Leicester game a few seasons ago. Villa were 4-1 up, late on, when Leicester scored. It wasn't a good goal, yet the odd spectator could be seen patronisingly applauding, amongst the home support. Then Leicester scored again, and the number applauding diminished sharply, as panic began to set in. When Leicester equalised in the 90th minute, there was only one person left clapping, smugness personified as he wallowed in his self-satisfied "fair-mindedness". The rest of the Villa fans then beat the shit out of him.

That Bournemouth's goal will be the winner becomes increasingly clear as the second half brings no improvement from County. When I used to come to County as a kid, I would, with the peculiar logic of childhood, be almost pleased if County went in at half-time 1-0 down. Presumably having had my imagination caught early by someone's claim that "well, they'll get a right old rollicking now" on a day when County came back in the second half to win, I thus for years considered the ubiquitous "half time team talk" as akin to a magical ceremony which invested the players with almost superhuman powers (*"Faster than a speeding bullet! Able to leap tall buildings with a single bound! Can string more than three passes together without falling over! Is it a bird? Is it a plane? No, it's the County forward line!"*)

Towards the final whistle, when it's clear we are not going to equalise, people are talking of a relegation battle. Football fans are known to be fickle, but as we're only in August, this is bloody ridiculous. Or is it? The pre-season optimism, reinforced by friendly performances (and yes I know that friendlies don't mean anything, but you've got to be able to draw *some* bloody conclusions, surely?) has dissipated in the space of 270 goalless minutes. Even worse, by racking my brain, I can only remember two, possibly three, goalscoring chances in that whole period. A season or two ago, we'd have been disappointed to have so few chances in the first half hour of a game; to have so few in three complete games beggars belief.

Our depression as we troop away is only slightly lifted as we walk past the gleaming new Adidas-sponsored shop which was set into the Cheadle End stand during the summer. The shop is so clean, and its windows so shiny, that a customer - a young lad in his early 20s - mistakes one of the front windows for a door, and fetches himself a resounding whack against the plate glass. The sight of him thudding into the window with upraised leg as he stepped into what he thought was the shop, and then staggering in through the *actual* door, clutching his nose in genuine pain would normally have had hundreds of County fans rolling about the floor in hysterics. All it raises now is a few smiles and a desultory "no, you want the door, mate" from one wag. Yes, we're that depressed.

Saturday August 31st 1996. Bristol Rovers (away).

Martin rang up for the result after Tuesday night's game, leaving me in two minds where I would prefer to be: at home paying good money to watch the crap County have been serving up, or with him in Ibiza. Actually, there's no genuine comparison to be drawn, as being on holiday during the football season is, as any true fan will tell you, a nightmare.

I have only transgressed the unwritten law of Football Fan Booking Holiday once, but boy was it a serious violation. Following the disappointment of play off defeat in 1989-90, County had, under Danny Bergara, launched a bid for promotion the following season which had seen them rarely out of the top three. Come the back end of the season, there was a single weekend, in which we had two successive home games - on Friday and Monday - which could have seen us virtually secure a promotion place. However, I was absent. Yes, and here I don the sackcloth and ashes, I actually arranged to be in Portugal the momentous week in April 1991 in which County played Aldershot (H) and Torquay (H).

I was staying, strangely enough, in the Portuguese villa owned by Bruce Grobbelaar, who is a friend of my brother-in-law. Now, as readers will be aware, it's not every day you get offered the chance of a cheap week in a luxury apartment on the Algarve, is it? Well no, but it's not every season County look like they'll get promoted. Yes, but you won't miss the last games, will you - you'll be back for them. I know, but I've been to every home game this season. Well you can make up for it by going to Blackpool and York, can't you? Look, why don't *you* go and I'll st... **Don't you dare even *think* it!** Okay, okay, okay...

Yes, gentle reader, I KNEW COUNTY WERE PLAYING TWO OF THE MOST IMPORTANT GAMES FOR TWENTY YEARS, AND STILL AGREED TO GO ON HOLIDAY! Disgraceful, I know, but they do say confession is cathartic.

For the Aldershot game, we were able to get Sky News in the apartment, so I was able to follow the regular score updates from County's, and the handful of other teams' Friday night games that were taking place. The Aldershot game finished 3-2, and although we were expected to win, I later discovered that we almost made a balls of it, only scoring a late winner after letting Aldershot back into the game. I wasn't to know that, however, and consumed the Portuguese lager in blissful ignorance, and the satisfaction that we had gained three more points towards promotion.

Come the Monday, and we had been informed that the link to the town which beamed satellite pictures to the Grobbelaars' apartment was knackered. I thus resorted to the familiar holiday making football fan's standby - the phone call home. I can still vividly recall standing in shirt sleeves by a telephone on a dusty Praia de Rocha dirt track, the sun setting a deep scarlet red over the Mediterranean sea, and the background hum of chirruping crickets combining with the distant excited murmuring of the holiday town to make the only sound which disturbed the hot silence, and being told by Martin that County had won 2-1, after being 1-0 down for most of the game, and "Andy Kilner scored a good goal" (later voted County's Goal of the Season). Bliss it was in those days to be alive. But to be a County fan was very heaven. I was then arrested for only wearing shirt sleeves (© Spike Milligan, 1964).

Today is the first away game of any distance, and one that has necessitated a coach booking. I could have driven, of course, or caught the train, but the one method is far too painful in a 950cc Fiesta, and the other too expensive and involved (there was no direct train from Stockport to Bristol, and waiting for connecting trains at the best of times is a pain in the arse; with an immoveable 3 o'clock appointment, it would be a nightmare). Loaded up with - as well as Walkman and reading material - sandwiches, drinks and crisps, it's hard to avoid feeling like a complete anorak. However, one has to eat, and with prices the way they are in grounds, it's either bring your own nosh these days, or get ripped off.

The coach is one organised by the Independent County Supporters' Club, an organisation which operates out of the Fingerpost pub, a mile or so from my home. They started running coaches a few years ago, realising that not only was there a demand, but also that County, like any other club, viewed the business of providing travel for their supporters to away games as an opportunity for more fleecing, rather than the providing of a much-needed service.

Needless to say, they operate a far better service than County - cheaper *and* more reliable (County have been known, in the past, to cancel their own coaches when demand was not exactly overwhelming, and recommend to the disgruntled punters that they try the Fingerpost). Sadly, however, no amount of organisation can prevent certain inconveniences, and mine today involve legroom and smell. The legroom is tiny, which necessitates constant position changing, from which follows, inexorably, a numb arse. The problems with smell relate to the dense fug caused by some punters smoking (I have yet to hear of a football coach being made non-smoking), and certain others clearly being of the opinion that the concept of personal hygiene encompasses a whole range of options, from a cursory fsplash of water every few days at one end of the scale, to sleeping in your clothes, and not owning a bar of soap, still less deodorant, at the other.

Such privations aside, however, it's still childishly exciting to be setting out. Coach journeys, in my experience, almost always commence with such exhilaration. This is because presumably, and unlike car or train journeys, coach trips - dating back to school days, and hence the description of the excitement being "childish" is probably not too far wide of the mark - invariably involve setting out to somewhere nice, somewhere you want to be (as opposed to somewhere you *have* to be, which is often the case with other modes of transport). The mood of the rest of the coach is also upbeat, presumably for similar reasons, and even though County's crap performances are the main topic of conversation, there don't seem to be many glum faces.

Sadly, I seem to have been adopted by the coach saddoe; his plaintive "is anyone sitting here?" as he points to the seat next to me doesn't fill me with confidence for the next three or four hours. He asks me if I'm going next Monday? My blank look by way of reply is countered with an "FA Youth Cup replay. Bury". A negative response is followed by a "Tuesday?". Yes, I'm going to Chesterfield on Tuesday. He falls silent and I take the opportunity to get the Guardian out. "Wednesday?" Blank look. "Reserves." Oh. No. No, I'm not. If this is his idea of conversation, I'm not interested. I pointedly open my paper, although I soon have to give up with the broadsheet sections, when I realise that to turn each page would involve most of the rear section of the coach having to stand in unison. I glance at my watch: 10.45. Time to eat my lunch.

Today's game represents a long-awaited return to their home city for Rovers, 10-year squatters at non-League Bath. Twerton Park was a ground I never got to see, despite once being on a work-related training course in the city when Bristol were playing Tranmere in the old Division Three, on the same evening that Spurs were playing Liverpool live on telly. I was thus left with a dilemma: did I watch the genuinely live game ("live" in the sense of being there, and not sat on my arse in the hotel room), or the TV one? Sadly, and to my eternal shame, the TV won, and it serves me right that I missed a classic top-of-the-table clash at Twerton, in which Rovers came from 2-0 down to win 3-2 in front of a packed ground. (The telly game was crap, Paul Stewart getting the only goal, late on, for Spurs).

The game was in doubt as late as yesterday morning, as Bristol Council's safety inspectors refused to grant a certificate for the rugby club's Memorial Ground (where Rovers will be playing now for some years to come). I find it strange that the rugby club had no such problems in receiving a certificate; they obviously get smaller crowds, football - that is, proper football, the game played primarily with the *feet* - being a far more popular game than chase-the-egg; but surely the capacity of the ground is what matters? Unless vast swathes of previously closed terracing have been opened just for football, I find it difficult to accept that different standards should apply. The safety certificate was eventually granted on Friday, however, after the club had appealed for fans to help clear loads of crap from the ground (so they evicted the rugby club, ho ho ho).

I realise, not for the first time, that The Guardian's "Weekend" magazine - the only section small enough to read on board a coach - is as boring as hell, and resort to my Walkman instead. Staring blankly out of a coach window whilst travelling 180 or so miles down a motorway is not exactly guaranteed to make time fly, but the journey is made surprisingly bearable by music. Oasis, REM and The Lightning Seeds should see us nicely to the outskirts of Bristol. I'm *just* too late to get the headphones on, however.

"Long way, Bristol, isn't it?"

"Mmm, yes."

"Not as long as Bournemouth."

"No."

"Or Plymouth."

"No... no, you're right." I realise that he's measuring distance in terms of away games, and award myself one and a half seconds of fun by trying to guess what's coming next. Gillingham, I'd say.

"Or Carlisle". Damn!

We eventually approach, after a journey that has lasted several millennia, the outskirts of Bristol, and, with Rovers' recent roamings in mind, a salutary reminder of their problems is provided as we pass their old ground, Eastville. It seems to still have one stand in place, but looks neglected and dog-eared - appropriately enough, as greyhound racing and speedway are the only events which still take place there. From here, it's a 25 minute trundle to the ground, the last part of which is through a densely packed shopping street. We seem to be viewed by the locals as exhibits in a mobile zoo, as they stare, slack-jawed and drooling, at us passing through. A plump girl in an extremely short mini skirt draws a chorus of sickening wolf whistles from the moron element on board - sadly, the majority, it seems. The guy sitting in front of me says, to the coach in general, "what *has* she got on - not much!" In case any of us don't immediately grasp his ready wit, the ugly, obnoxious fatso laughs for himself. Thankfully, we are almost at the ground, so that this crap doesn't have to be endured for too long.

It's clear that today is a celebration, as the ground seems packed. Balloons and banners are everywhere, the car park is full, and a godawful karaoke rendition of "Goodnight Irene" - Rovers' unofficial club song - is being sung at full blast by Tony Tonedeaf over the tannoy (a clincher, that one - you can always tell when a club is returning to its home town after a 10-year exile - the idiot singing "Goodnight Irene"). If the local residents' campaign against Rovers' groundsharing plans had been based around not wanting to listen to this idiot on the first day back, they'd never have been able to leave Twerton Park.

I get off the coach, join in the communal stretching which makes up look like workers about to start the morning shift at a Nissan factory, and head for the away turnstiles

"Is it all-ticket for them, d'you think?"

Christ, he's still next to me! "Er, yeah, I should think so"

"I'llll seeeee you innn my dreeeeeeamssss"

"Oh."

"Goodniiightt Irennneee, Goodniiightt Irennneee......"

"It's all-ticket for us, isn't it?"

"Er, yeah"

"Goooodniiiiighttt Irennnnneeeee......"

"Have *you* got a ticket?"

"Yes."

"GOOOOOOOD-NIIIIIIIGGGGGHHHTTTT!!!!!!" There is a stunned silence throughout Bristol.

"Does he do that every week, do you think?"

Thankfully, the away turnstiles prevent me having to answer, and I nip through, resolving to keep an eye on matey boy, and making sure I stand elsewhere. Luckily, he slopes off down to the right somewhere, and I take my place on the small away terrace, which is filled with a reasonable Stockport following.

The ground is clearly being upgraded as fast as possible, with a new stand being built on the opposite side of the pitch to where we are situated. Most of the home support is crammed onto a small terrace behind the goal to our right, with those who like to sit being in the cantilever stand next to us. The other goal has naught but a fence to stop wayward shots, although the goal line is fully twenty yards away, on the other side of the rugby "try" area. There is thus room for a nice little stand here too, although the rugby club might be a touch upset if their new tenants went ahead and built it, thereby preventing the landlords from actually playing their daft game.

The teams emerge from double decker portakabins just off one corner of the pitch (County, as the away team, are placed upstairs), and, after a short ribbon-cutting ceremony from a lady mayor who is roundly, and gratifyingly, booed ("gratifyingly", because the council were one of the major reasons behind Rovers' exile, and the home fans, like me, are sickened at the sight of two-faced, two-bit, local politicians seeking photo-opportunities), the two sides actually take the field.

County manager Dave Jones has rung the changes, understandably, and started with a back five - a formation which he has stated publicly he doesn't like as much as 4-4-2. This is clearly a sign of panic, although, as a fan of the sweeper system, I find myself comforted by the format.

The game starts, and there are early signs that the referee is one of those fussy types, who make you wonder whether it was a choice between refereeing or Akela-ing when it came to an adolescent hobby. I am roused from such thoughts, however, when Bristol score. Their left winger exploits space which has been left by the confusion in County's ranks caused by the unfamiliar formation, and sends in a good cross, which is headed in off the underside of the bar. The ball bounces close to the goal line, and, whilst it seems to me to have actually been well over, the awarding of the goal is enough to mean that the linesman on the near side is subjected to constant barracking for the rest of the match.

It doesn't help, either, that his colleague in the middle is such a prat, poncing about in the new kit design which makes Nationwide League refs look as though they have fallen over on the touchline, and smudged the markings all over their back. It wouldn't be so bad if he was a competent referee, but his control of the game, fussing and preening for all he's worth, is firm only in the sense that a fresh, steaming cowpat is firm. At one point a Rovers player, frustrated at a decision, pushes him in the chest. Rather than a sending off (or a public execution, as demanded by the County fans around me), he is subjected to nothing more than a ticking-off, which heralds a rousing chorus of "How much have you paid the ref?" (to the tune of The Pet Shop Boys' "Go West" - surely the most ubiquitous of modern football melodies). I almost expect him to start dishing out lines, or detention, rather than yellow cards.

County, struggling with the formation and a chronic lack of confidence, are as dire as ever, and half time thus comes as a blessed relief, although the analysis which breaks out from all sides is more wearying than instructional. We have hardly been able to string two passes together, Rovers are quicker to every loose ball, and it is only their wayward finishing which has kept the score to 1-0.

Towards the end of half time, when the queue has died down a bit, I buy a Cornish pastie from the tea hut. Having eaten my sandwiches early, and with a four hour journey ahead, I realise that sustenance is needed, whatever the cost. I am actually pleasantly surprised to find that the pasties are only £1.10, and - even more surprising - not merely edible, but tasty. It makes a refreshing change not to be ripped off in a football ground - indeed, it is probably a unique experience, and quite cheers me up for the second half.

I'm not sure whether pasties were on the menu in the dressing rooms at half time, but it must be either that or a tongue sandwich which County have been fed, as the second half is a revelation. Jones has reverted to 4-4-2 and brought on Gannon and Armstrong for Bound and Angell, and County immediately start looking dangerous. We begin to dominate the midfield, and, following the early introduction of fullback Lee Todd as a makeshift winger in place of Luis Cavacao, we go close time after time, as I realise - not by any means for the first time - that clutching one's head in one's hands is not merely an affectation.

Thankfully, our pressure is finally rewarded in the 70th minute, when John Jeffers gets hold of the ball outside the area, switches feet, and crashes a 25-yarder into the top corner of the net. Mayhem. It's our first league goal of the season, late on in the fourth game, and the celebrations of the County fans, tightly packed on the small away terrace, reflect the euphoria, and - let's be honest - the relief.

Following the goal, we continue to press, and although Rovers have chances of their own, County could well have pinched it late on, when Todd's shot is blocked on the line. It would have been an injustice if we had scored, but who gives a shit? Since when has a strong sense of justice been a prerequisite for supporting a football club? Since never, is when.

The players receive the warm ovation appropriate in these circumstances, and it's back on the coach. One of the major pluses of taking the coach to away games is the ease of departure. Parked right outside the turnstiles, you can stroll on board, then smile beatifically at the departing fans - perhaps even giving the odd regal wave - as the police escort whips you through the post-match traffic to the motorway. You can almost ignore what this implies - that they are metaphorically washing their hands of you, running you out of town like the undesirables you are - especially when you've had a result. Almost, but not quite. The coppers take us right up to the motorway slip road - to ensure we don't double back and start trashing Bristol, presumably - before biking back to the ranch. This anti-football-fans attitude always bugs me, so, like the hero I am, I fight back with a lip-curled "piss off" mouthed through the window, which I figure won't be seen (especially as I aim it at the copper who isn't looking) - unlike two fingers, which would probably get the coach stopped, and me arrested.

Thankfully, I am absolutely knackered on the return journey, and am thus able to grab some sleep - with "some" being the operative word. Andrew has recently decided that one in the morning is the screaming hour, and gave his lungs a good workout on Thursday night. As is the way of things when you have a baby in the house, your body clock tends to be somewhat off beam, with the result that the lack of sleep is only really catching up with me this afternoon. I make sure that my headphones stay in whilst I'm slumped against the window, to ward off any attempted "conversation" should my dear friend see my eyes open.

I need relaxation too, as it's one of those "weekends" (i.e., those that last well into the following week) made for football addicts like me: those with Sky TV. There was live football (Plymouth v Preston) last night; I'll be at a game today; Bolton v QPR tomorrow will be followed by England v Moldova; Monday night will bring surprise Premiership leaders Sheffield Wednesday v Leicester City; and on Tuesday, I'll be travelling across to Chesterfield for the second leg of the Coca Cola Cup tie, followed by Wolves v Swindon live on Sky on Wednesday. Thursday I've got pencilled in for rest.

SEPTEMBER

NATIONWIDE LEAGUE DIVISION TWO

	P	W	D	L	F	A	Pts
PLYMOUTH ARGYLE	4	3	1	0	10	6	10
BRENTFORD	4	3	1	0	9	3	10
BURY	4	3	1	0	8	2	10
CHESTERFIELD	4	3	0	1	4	2	9
MILLWALL	4	2	1	1	7	5	7
SHREWSBURY TOWN	4	2	1	1	6	6	7
BLACKPOOL	4	2	1	1	3	4	7
YORK CITY	4	2	0	2	6	6	6
BURNLEY	4	2	0	2	6	7	6
BOURNEMOUTH	4	2	0	2	5	5	6
WATFORD	4	2	0	2	4	5	6
BRISTOL ROVERS	3	1	2	0	2	1	5
PETERBOROUGH UNITED	3	1	1	1	4	4	4
PRESTON NORTH END	4	1	1	2	4	5	4
CREWE ALEXANDRA	4	1	1	2	4	6	4
GILLINGHAM	4	1	1	2	4	6	4
NOTTS COUNTY	3	1	1	1	2	2	4
BRISTOL CITY	4	1	0	3	7	8	3
LUTON TOWN	4	1	0	3	4	10	3
WYCOMBE WANDERERS	4	0	3	1	2	3	3
WREXHAM	2	0	2	0	5	5	2
STOCKPORT COUNTY	**4**	**0**	**2**	**2**	**1**	**3**	**2**
ROTHERHAM UNITED	4	0	1	3	3	6	1
WALSALL	3	0	1	2	2	4	1

Tuesday September 3rd 1996. Chesterfield (away) (Coca Cola Cup R1).

I've been full of a streaming cold since Saturday, which I must have caught when that odd window thing that all coaches have in their roof was opened for most of the return journey, causing cold air to blow around the rear of the vehicle *(a doctor writes:* the common cold is a virus, and cannot be caught, contrary to popular belief, from exposure to cold air). It's actually bad enough for me to justify going home from work at half ten, and back to bed for a couple of hours. Thankfully, this seems to do the trick, as, come five o'clock, I'm ready, and raring to go.

My better health reinforces the feelings of optimism which have been building since the second half on Saturday. County outplayed Rovers for a large part of that period; indeed, they were almost back to their best, and, in the circumstances, one could almost believe the old footballing cliché about a draw being nearly as good as a win. Almost.

I set out early, expecting heavy rush-hour traffic, and what also is helping make me feel good is the fact that I've managed to blag the Cavalier for the journey, Anna agreeing with my logical reasoning (abject grovelling, if the truth be known) that she won't need it for tonight. The difference between a big-engined, new(ish) car and my crappy old C-reg Ford Start-You-Bastard is incredible; the radio works, the engine is quiet and powerful, and the seats are comfortable. In addition, traffic is surprisingly light, and the drive is made more enjoyable by the new dual carriageway just past New Mills. This road was, of course, designed years ago purely for my benefit, the architects and planners conspiring, in endless smoky meetings, to fashion the layout in such as way as to maximise my pleasure, even arranging, via a climatic sub-committee, for the evening weather to be particularly pleasant on the day I would make this journey, all those years in the future.

Many people, especially from the south, who have only the vaguest idea of the location of Stockport will, no doubt, conjure up images of bleak industrial mills with soot-blackened walls, row upon row of terraced houses, and a Fred Dibnah chimney stack on every corner. Get stuffed. My image of ooh, let's say Esher, for example, is a stinking cess-pool, with people defecating freely from upstairs windows into drainage troughs set roughly into the pavements below.

Devastating satire about the nature of people's preconceptions aside, my point is that in reality - and despite the fact that it is indeed oop north - Stockport is a pleasant enough town, with a well nigh perfect geographical position: close to a major international airport and the motorway network, yet situated on the edge of the beautiful Peak District National Park. With a range of affordable housing, Stockport is the ideal place to relocate *your* business. Er, ahem. Sorry.

Saturday Night and Thursday Morning

Although it was one of the many northern towns whose "wealth" was based on cotton, it has coped better than most with recession and redevelopment. In addition, from the dead centre of town, 15 minutes' drive can see you in the heart of some of the best countryside in England, either east or south into Cheshire, or west towards the Pennines or the Peak District. The drive I make tonight - south-west, via Disley and Chapel-en-le-Frith (which literally means "Chapel in the Frith"), into the Peaks - is one of the best.

Typical, then, that once I've passed through the quaintly named village of Sparrowpit (you wouldn't think it was quaint if you was a bleedin' sparrow, mate) and started the climb over the tops, I should get stuck in a convoy of traffic which is chugging along behind a fully-laden, quarry-bound lorry doing a breathtaking 2 mph on the steep bits. Luckily, I can break the monotony because I find myself, following a couple of manic overtaking manoeuvres, directly behind the official supporters' club coach. I can thus enjoy a game of face-pulling with the cheeky, replica-shirt wearing scamps who are kneeling on the back seat. Trouble is, there's always one who spoils it all by sticking two fingers up, and, sure enough, that's precisely what I do as I pull out to pass the coach on a rare straight bit.

I finally get past the lorry (it turning left helped), and drop down into Chesterfield. Arriving near the ground, I park up on the main road with the car facing home; a trick all experienced football-travellers will recognise. Indeed, this can be an amusing way to spot away match virgins - car facing the way they drove in, and trying desperately to turn against the heavy flow of post match traffic. Spending a moment or two manoeuvring the car for a quick getaway now can save, ooh, literally minutes later on. Okay, expressed that way, worrying about car positioning can seem an extremely stupid thing to concern yourself with, but those ten minutes can feel like hours when you're fighting with other cars to be on your way home - especially after a defeat. Also, if you're unlucky, you can get well and truly gridlocked: I once spent 40 minutes trying to inch out of the car park at Rotherham - try telling me it's not worth pointing back over the Pennines at Millmoor! Huh!

Chesterfield's Saltergate ground is showing its age; like many another ground whose owners harbour dreams of relocating, as do Chesterfield, it's being left to rot. The away end, however, behind a goal, is a decent enough terrace, if a little shallow, and the fact that County have only brought a couple of hundred fans means there's plenty of room to find a crush barrier to slouch against.

The first half of the game continues this season's fine tradition of good cup performances by County, as they dominate, and are unlucky not to take the lead, hitting the bar on two occasions, and missing a number of other chances. Although the scores are level at the break, therefore, there is no great despondency in the away end, as we are confident that the 2-1 aggregate lead can be at least defended.

Half-time is enlivened by Chesterfield's club mascot. Rather than simply dressing some poor sap in whichever animal costume was on offer in the local joke shop that week, the club have actually put some thought into their choice, and opted for having someone wear a "fat Geordie" costume as they announce the half time raffle winners, in an amplified voice that causes me to check my ears for bleeding. It comes as quite a shock when he leaves the pitch via an exit quite near me to see that it isn't, in fact, someone dressed in a "fat Geordie" costume, but an actual fat Geordie who wobbles past. The choruses of "who ate all the pies?" - from the home support - should, I suppose, have given me a clue.

Tearing myself away from this fascinating spectacle, I go to get a brew from the tea hut. On the way there, I bump into Louie, one of the main organisers from the Fingerpost. He's got a joke for me. It's a mark of my dealings with him that whenever we meet, which is fairly often, given the general size of the County away following, he seems to feel it's his duty to tell me his latest joke. Occasionally, these are of a disgracefully racist nature, and I feel the fixed smile on my face slowly assume the solidity of granite. I know what I *should* do in these circumstances - remonstrate with him, argue, walk away. To do this, however, would make an enemy of Louie, which I don't want to do, as he is an essentially nice man: the liberal's dilemma. As I am a coward, therefore, I simply don't laugh as heartily as I would otherwise; I grunt a few hur-hurs, which I assume pass muster, as he continues to tell me jokes each time we meet. Tonight's, thankfully, is not racist, although it is a prime example of the genre "Louie's Jokes":

There's a Scouser who's walking down the street when he sees a magic lamp. So he rubs it and out pops the genie. "I can give you three wishes," says the genie, "but with a difference. Anything you wish for, your wife will get three times as much."

"Okay", says the man, "I'll have a lottery win."

"You're wife'll get three of them," the genie warns.

"Don't care," says the man, "second, I want a fucking big house."

"You're wife'll get one three times as big..."

"I don't care. I've got one wish left, yeah?"

"Yes"

"Right, I'll have a slight heart attack."

Precisely why the main character was a Scouser, I decide not to enquire. All I can say is that it's a good job the score's 0-0.

The first 45 minutes have sown seeds of hope, but it's actually Chesterfield who start the second half well, and a sustained period of pressure is rewarded when Beaumont feeds a great through ball - of the type we've been crying out for all season, and *we* sold Beaumont to Chesterfield, arrrrgh - into the path of the home centre-forward, who clips it confidently over the diving Jones.

This causes elation on the home terraces for a few minutes, understandably, and the Chesterfield fans decide to express their joy in a rather curious way - by demonstrating geographical ignorance: *"you're the shit of Manchester"*. The County chanters respond with *"We don't come from Manchester"*, followed by the simple, yet moving, *"Chesh-i-yure, Chesh-i-yure, Chesh-i-yure.."* investing the word with three syllables in order to fit the tune ("Here we go, here we go..." etc). I consider for a moment starting my own one-man chant of *"The Metropolitan County of Greater Manchester actually, so you're both wrong"*, but decide against it on the grounds that I cannot make it scan with any of the existing football chant tunes, and there isn't time to compose another.

The best way to shut up taunting, of course, is to score, and this we duly do, thanks to a superb 25-yarder from midfielder Paul Ware that restores our advantage on the hour. The tie is then virtually killed off 10 minutes or so later, when, in an incident hysterically similar to that in the first leg, the keeper lets another Andy Mutch header squirm over the line. Now we can relax, and, indeed, we are so comfortable that there is even time for Alun Armstrong to flick the ball against the post, from where it rebounds, agonisingly, straight back into the goalkeeper's arms.

Towards the end, I sidle across to the exit, ready to start running as soon as the final whistle sounds. I see Andy Gosling, an old friend from Keele University, and we both agree that it seemed County's season started at half time on Saturday. God, I hope so: getting promotion will be hard enough this year in a division containing Millwall and Watford without giving everyone a ten point start. The whistle goes; we've won, 4-2 on aggregate. 4 goals! From County! Against a single set of opponents! In one tie! Okay, it was added up over two games, but so many goals! Counting them, you'd almost run out of fingers!

Despite my self-proclaimed expertise in the game of parking-to-get-away-quickly, I realise, as I jog to the car, that I've miscalculated just how far away I have parked, and the jog soon becomes painful. However I finally make it, and my experience has paid off, as I've gained that all-important five minutes at the cost of a pounding heart, wheezing chest and wobbly legs. Physical discomfort will soon ease, however; we won, which means great mental comfort for the next few days.

An away win, and a speedy drive home on the fast, straight roads through the evening beauty that is the Peak District, in a quiet, comfortable car, with the other results on Radio Five Live, followed by The Lightning Seeds at full blast on the stereo. It's a sad reflection on my life that I feel it probably doesn't get very much better than this.

Saturday September 7th 1996. Watford (away).

The big news of the week is that on Thursday County drew Sheffield United in the Coca Cola Cup round 2, for the second time in three years. And on Wednesday, Christopher, my eldest son, started school.

I would not like you to think that the order in which those two items was reported represents any weight attached, by me, to their significance. I am fully aware of the relative importance in my life of my family and County. In fact, I am aware of it to the tune, today, of twelve quid.

The Fingerpost were charging £13 for the coach, but with Watford being on a direct rail line from Stockport, there was an alternative; an alternative, moreover, which left at 11.38 as opposed to 9.30, and got me back in Stockport at 20.15 rather than at about ten past 21. However, the cheapest ticket - Super Apex Red Saver Weekend Special, or some such - was £25, leaving me with a simple choice: cheap and cheerful, or £12 extra for 2 hours more with the kids. As I always feel exceptionally shameful anyway when leaving my family behind whilst I swan off around the country watching football, it was a small price (well, a middling price) to pay to assuage my guilt.

I like travelling on trains. This does not necessarily mean that I am a sad individual (I say "necessarily", as I am fully aware that the jury is out regarding my degree of sadness in a football-following sense), as many other people also enjoy the pleasure without feeling the need to write down engine numbers in a little exercise book. Does BBC2 run a hugely popular, celebrity-presented programme called "Great Railway Platforms of the World"? I think not. Train journeys are quick, efficient and comfortable, with legroom (especially if you can blag a table to yourself) to make grown men weep.

Like many another immature person, however, rail travel tends to bring out the adolescent in me, which manifests itself, as far as I'm concerned, in performing silly pranks. I was once on a train pulling out of Manchester's Piccadilly station, which was travelling next to another train, at a similar speed and in the same direction (pulling out of a major station is probably the only part of British Rail where you would experience this). We were thus able, my friend Mike and me, to act out, for the benefit of the busy commuter train at the side of us, that scene from the Agatha Christie film, where someone gets strangled in a railway carriage.

I was also once on a local station platform when an express rushed through, with the terrifying speed which you never appreciate when you are actually travelling on one. I raised a laugh from the schoolkids on the opposite platform by quickly, as the train thundered through, lying down on the bench, pulling my shirt out of my trousers, ruffling my hair and putting one leg over the armrest, with both arms flailing, so that, when it had passed, it looked as though I had been blown into that position by the turbulence caused by the train (I fully accept that they *may* have been laughing because they thought I was a prick).

Perhaps strangely, however, I have never mooned, which omission from my repertoire of juvenilia I can only assume to be because I have never found myself in a completely empty carriage: a prerequisite, for me at least, to dropping my trousers. I have *seen* the manoeuvre performed on a train, however, by a couple of lads with no such inhibitions (the cans of super-strength lager they had been consuming may have been a contributory factor); the marks their bare arse-cheeks left on the carriage windows faded slowly, like the Cheshire Cat's grin, remaining clearly visible for ages after they themselves had disembarked.

The only stunt I try today is the cowards' one, where you catch the eye of a person waiting on the platform as your train slowly pulls out. You hold their gaze for a couple of seconds, then (and timing is critical here) pull the most grotesque face you can - eyes boggling, gaping mouth, lolling tongue - *just* as they pass from your view. I score satisfying hits at Macclesfield, Stoke and Milton Keynes, only just avoiding adding two fingers at Stoke.

It is another beautiful late summer's day; the autumnal colours of the fields as we thunder through are superbly illuminated by the delicate sunshine, as are the satellite dishes spotted around the walls of the bleak Midlands high rise flats. The train is filled with people heading for London; it doesn't feel as though I'm going to a football match at all. I pick up snatches of conversation from people whose fun-packed, metropolitan lives put my own hick existence to shame, or at least I assume that's the impression they're trying to give. By heck, lad, if Julie Christie were on this train, you wouldn't catch *me* poncing off down t'platform for a carton o' milk. Gazing out of the window at the residential areas (which are much more interesting than the countryside, as people's back garden secrets are revealed: tents, pools, ponds - I'm sure I even spotted a gazebo at one point) makes my eyes heavy. I'm tired again (take another bow, Andrew) so I doze off, to the sound of a woman sitting behind me loudly discussing with a friend, via a mobile phone, the shortcomings of her London boyfriend.

We arrive at Watford just after 14, and three of us share a taxi to the ground (it comes, unluckily for the driver, to exactly three quid, so it's a quid each and no tip, matey). Vicarage Road is a splendid looking ground from the outside, and it's amazing to think that the club were non-league 20 years ago. That said, access to the away fans' entrance is down a passageway at the side of the ground, along which you pass what was obviously the "main" stand in non-league days, and which is, incongruously, still the formal entrance for players and officials - a rickety and run down looking area which contrasts with the three fantastic stands on the other sides of the ground.

Sadly, and presumably due to the fact that today's crowd is expected to be a small one, we are allowed to cut across behind the quaintly named Rookery stand to our entrance, and thus miss out on the famous walk around the allotments. Apparently, when the away following is large enough to justify it, fans have to follow a narrow path around a massive set of allotments which back onto the ground; a ten minute hike during which you actually lose sight of the stands, but not the local horticultural enthusiasts, glaring at you from their one eye, and growling "you bain't be from rewnd these year paaarts, be you?" as they chew their corn, pluck their banjos, and marry their sisters (I believe John Denver once wrote a song about them).

There is a shock waiting for me at the turnstiles. Not the price - £11 is, whilst a disgusting rip-off, hardly unexpected - but at a rotund, balding old man whose face seems vaguely familiar. It's only when he introduces himself as an old friend from Aquinas 6th Form College that I realise, with a thrill of horror, that he is, like me, only 32. I know I can't possibly have aged as badly in the 14 years since I saw him last, but it's a disturbing moment nonetheless. "We'll have a chinwag inside," he says affably. We fucking won't, I think, as I hold back, pretending to fumble with my turnstile money, and knowing that I'll now be depressed for the rest of the week.

Almost as worrying as seeing such a ghost is the fact that early signs indicate County's 1½ match revival may be a flash in the pan. Once again, the team is playing like 11 strangers, and although the defence is as solid as ever - restricting Watford, like Crewe, to shots from distance - we don't create a single chance in the first half.

Not that this seems to bother certain County fans. There are, I realise, having seen the phenomenon at other away games, people for whom the whole business of following County around the country is a massive, long-term social event. There are a group of them today, for example, who come in late from the pub, and, standing in the concourse directly behind me, hardly bother to watch the match, preferring to talk about their pre-game session in the pub, and to make their travel arrangements for the next away game. I once heard one of them describe their County-following as a sort of nine-month holiday, a comparison which gives pause when you realise what kind of conventional holiday you could afford with the money shelled out on County: a world cruise at the very least.

Ears flapping, I hear talk of aggressive and unnecessary pre-game policing, with the well-known head bobby of the Stockport hooligan squad making a conspicuous show of noting down names in one of the pubs in which County fans were drinking. This tallies with an event I saw on Vicarage Road before the match: the mass herding of a group of County fans towards the turnstiles, during which I was able to observe that police posturing seemed as much a part of the game both groups were playing as any yobbish behaviour from the fans. I'm not an apologist for football violence; far from it, as some of the behaviour I saw in the 70s and 80s - from moronic groups of individuals whose common link was that the total number of brain cells each possessed was in single figures - was quite sickening. I just wish that certain policemen - certain whole forces in some cases - would realise that initiating the aggressive posturing towards tanked-up young lads is probably not the best way to ensure trouble-free Saturday afternoons.

The second half opens to more Watford pressure, which spurs the home fans into life. This heralds a bout of strong-accented chanting, which I have always found something of a rarity at football grounds. In the same way that pop singers tend to sing in a mid-Atlantic accent, football crowds tend to chant in an accent which would presumably be described as middle-England (not that any of them ever start up the cry *"well, tax-and-spend is no longer an option in a modern market economy, and hasn't that Mr Blair got a nice smile?"*). Thus it is that a massive cry of "AYN-BOW!" in the 58th minute, following a penalty-area clash between County keeper Paul Jones and a Watford striker, leaves no doubt. The referee points to the spot, and, effectively, to another County defeat. Despite a late flurry, the home fans are thus able to take great delight in informing us that "yer gowin' dahn wiv ver Lu'on", and, on current evidence (Lu'on, having started the season even worse than us, are the only team keeping us off the bottom), it's hard to disagree.

Walking back to the station, I discover another reason - apart from the obvious one about heads and their increased likelihood of getting fucking kicked in - for not wearing County colours, as I slow down and fall in step with a group of Watford lads behind me who are oblivious to the fact that I'm a County fan. Their discussion is depressing, especially in the light of our own pre-season 'optimism, as we ourselves should be promotion material; *we* should be having this conversation.

"Cowse, Stockpowt are the toipe of teaym we gotta beat if we're gonna get aht o'vis division." Fack off.

"Yeah, bat oi fowt we did jast enaff. Thiy were never in it, really" Fack. Off.

"Yeah, wew'll be two divisions aparwt next season."

FACKOFFACKOFFACK OFFACKOFFACKOFF!!

At least I'm not sardined onto a coach for the return journey, and can thus slouch across the table foursome I've managed to grab (it being a Super Apex Red, etc, ticket, there is a seat reserved for me somewhere on the train, but I'm buggered if I'm going to try and find it). Headphones help pass the journey back, as does counting the number of passes the crap-collector makes. This is a poor sod whom BR (or whoever it is these days) employs to constantly roam the train, armed with a bin bag, and picking up litter wherever they see it. Although the net effect is a nice, shiny, clean carriage, I can't help but feel sorry for those people obliged to take such a job; at least all I've got to bother me is a football match defeat. The minimum wage promised by a Labour Party odds on to win an election sometime before the season ends next May will be some consolation for people trapped in crappy jobs such as this, however. I just hope that they don't find a way to ditch that particular policy along with most of the other policies that gradually, as I became politically aware, made me a socialist rather than a selfish bastard, and the steady abandoning of which made me cancel my membership of the Labour Party 18 months or so ago.

As we pull into Stockport station, I reflect on where today's result leaves us. The bare facts are that we have now scored only one league goal in the first five games, and gained a mere two points; this has been reflected in our league position. Excuses (such as playing two tough away games on the trot) can be offered, but no matter how you look at it, if you're at the bottom of the table after five games, it's beginning to look as though you deserve to be. If the season genuinely started at half time at Bristol, it was a bleeding short season.

Tuesday September 10th 1996. Wrexham (home).

Today is the nadir. We cannot get any worse (and you'll note the absence of any qualifying "surely" or "possibly" in that last sentence).

The bare facts are that we lose 2-0, with Wrexham's goals from Watkin - a tap-in after Wrexham broke down one of our rare attacks and sped upfield - and, just after half time, Skinner, who hammers home after his first shot is blocked by Jones in the County goal. Late on, County's arch snapper, Chris Marsden, is sent off for a second booking. He throws the ball away in disgust following a free kick to Wrexham (the linesman had indicated a throw-in to County), and, realising he has already been booked, starts the long walk off the pitch. This isn't good enough for the referee, a Mr P Dantic from Fussyville, who insists Marsden walks all the way back over to him so that he can indulge himself in his dual-card displaying ceremony. Two minutes after Marsden's dismissal, Wrexham's Phillips is also sent off after a scuffle with County's Jeffers.

Bare facts, however, do not even begin to think about starting to approach the outskirts of the hinterland of the full story. In a season which commenced with such optimism - and it wasn't false optimism, we really *were* good in the warm up - this result makes people angry, truly angry, rather than depressed; the team are deservedly booed off at half-time and full time.

What compounds the depression is the fact that ex-County players Martyn Chalk and Peter Ward both play superbly well for Wrexham (although *I* could probably have put in a half-decent display against County tonight). Ward's performance is expected, as he was one of our better players, but Chalk was almost universally deplored just before he left, in exchange for Kieron Durkan, midway through last season. He had started his career well at County, but being forced to calm down following a series of bookings which culminated in a sending off at Huddersfield seemed to take the wind completely out of his footballing sails, and he was eventually offloaded to the Taffys - swopped for Durkan and some money. Typical, then, that he should rediscover his form against his old club.

It's difficult to explain, with any degree of accuracy, quite how bad County are tonight. More than once I hear reference to the "old days", as in "even in the old days, it wasn't as bad as this". These "old days" are actually fairly recent - the 70s and early 80s, in fact, which was when County were at their lowest. We were stuck in the old Fourth Division for 20 years, finishing above halfway only three times in the 18 years between my terrace debut in 1972-73, and promotion in 1991. However, for those few hardy souls who watched County in those dark days, there was no expectation of success. We were, indeed, to coin a phrase, shit, and we knew we were. That wasn't why we followed them. Being a County fan in those days was to be a member of an exclusive club, with shared disappointment, sorrow and very occasional joy. I regard with pride the fact that I was one of the 1,039 fans who endured County's worst-ever attended league game - a 1-2 defeat by Southend United on 15th February 1985

Whilst the last few years of County's relative success have been very welcome, they have thus tended to raise people's expectations. So it is that performances such as tonight's anger and depress rather than provoke nothing more than a shrug of the shoulders. We've left the dark days behind us, so what are we doing playing like this?

County cannot get worse. That is fact. They can, however, be equally bad. If so, if we bump along the bottom like this for a few weeks more, the rot will probably have set in, and we'll end up being relegated. Never mind all the pre-season hype, all the assurances from the management in the local press that we've got the best squad in years. They said Nottingham Forest were too good to go down in Cloughie's last season, and Dave Jones is no Brian Clough.

The only - very slight - relief of the night is provided at half time, when the tannoy announcer reads out a dedication to a certain "Don Kiddick", apparently from "the rest of the stewards". The announcer falls for it hook, line and sinker, reading the name out twice, in a typical bout of cheesey football-tannoy-announcer sincerity ("so that's a nice dedication there for Don Kiddick from your mates, the stewards"). One smile, lots of anger.

Saturday September 14th 1996. Plymouth Argyle (home).

The collective sigh of relief after today's game measures 9 on the Beaufort Scale, and causes ships in the North Sea to list alarmingly.

Pre-game, however, the mood is greatly different. Following the mid-week catastrophe, I spoke to someone who had been in the pub after the game with Martyn Chalk and Peter Ward, Wrexham's two ex-County players (in much the same way as I understand Eric Cantona and Ryan Giggs often pop into the Stretford pubs for a quick pint with the fans after United's home games). They had been of the opinion that the County squad was one of the strongest in the division, reinforcing many people's belief - my own included - that confidence, not lack of ability, is at the root of our current problems. However, certain others seem to be of a different opinion. Two anonymous first team players were also in the pub, and were criticising Dave Jones to high heaven. *"He claims to have an FA coaching badge - well I'd like to see it"*, and *"it takes more than a sharp suit and a mobile phone to be a fucking manager"* were just two of the reported comments. I begged for names, but my friend was unrepentant, presumably believing - not unreasonably - that should he spill the beans, he was unlikely ever to be vouchsafed such confidentialities again.

Outside Edgeley Park before the game, I bump into the GMR reporter, Paul Rooney, whom I know casually; he asks me what I think of Jones' chances of survival, presumably so that he can invest his later reports with a "the word on the terraces is..." preface. I tell him what I have both told, and been told by, at least twenty odd fans with whom I have discussed the matter: that if we lose today, I wouldn't expect Dave Jones to still have a job come Monday night. I don't mention the players' pub comments from Tuesday, preferring to think that *not* stirring the shit might help the club more than otherwise. Although I myself am not convinced by Dave Jones' managerial skills, in a strange way I would prefer him to be sacked - if that is indeed to be his fate - because of results rather than a whispering campaign; a campaign I don't really want to become part of, however insignificantly.

The feeling is that Brett Angell is also drinking at the last chance saloon. Although he is reportedly not fully match fit, having not played for Sunderland, due to injury, for months before his loan spell, he is also - again "reportedly" - on big wages, said to be (okay then, "reportedly") not unadjacent to two grand a week.

There is a bonus before the game, as I meet up with a friend whose son is currently walking the Pennine Way. This in itself is not the good news (not that I want to belittle a such noble and character-forming venture, oh no); rather the fact that his dad thus has his season ticket going spare, and only wants a fiver for today's token, a price I am more than happy to pay. I am thus breaking club rules, due to the fact that season tickets, as it clearly states inside the book, ARE NOT TRANSFERABLE. Interesting one, that. Why, exactly, are they not transferable? If someone has paid up front for a seat in the ground, and cannot make it themselves, why is it such a heinous crime to allow a friend to sit there? I must remember to ask next time I'm in the "Question Time" audience.

Dave Jones has rung the changes after apparently, according to informed rumour (ie terrace speculation), having been given a "win or else" ultimatum by Chairman Brendan Elwood. He is therefore more relieved than most when County receive the best start possible following their first attack, which forces a corner. The ball is sent across to the far post, where Jim Gannon, one of County's longest serving players, who normally weighs in with half a dozen goals or so a season, opens his account for this year by hammering the ball past Bruce Grobbelaar, who is, this season, turning out for Plymouth (I must remember to thank him for the Portuguese villa if he comes near me to get the ball). The sense of the confidence flowing through the side is almost tangible, and we get a deserved second goal ten minutes later, again from Jim Gannon, who heads a free kick past Grobbelaar. Two quick goals, the advantage well and truly with County, and the team begin to play in a manner which we all knew they were capable of. However, a season which, even at this early stage, has provided us with some disgracefully incompetant refereeing, Plymouth are helped back into the game by the bastard in the black, when he awards them a penalty.

It's yet another truly appalling decision, along with the penalty at Vicarage Road (which, the referee confirmed after the game, was for a foul, not an "an-bow"), and the penalty and sending off against Chesterfield. Indeed, this decision is remarkably similar to that which led to Bound's dismissal, with the ref again giving the foul from a position thirty or so yards behind the play. What is clear, though, is that Gannon won the ball. Sitting again in the Vernon Stand, I can clearly see the ball being toe-ended back to keeper Jones who boots it clear. Gannon should be receiving applause for a great saving tackle, not wondering whether he's taking the long walk, having let Plymouth back into the game.

The referee doesn't, in fact, send Gannon off, which, although a relief, annoys me even more: if it was a foul on a player bearing down on goal, why wasn't he, like Bound, dismissed? Gannon isn't even booked, and although it could be argued that there a sort of justice thus served, it's the kind of justice that saw the Birmingham Six merely imprisoned for years instead of hanged.

Half time arrives with the consensus amongst those I talk to that the next goal will probably prove crucial. Thankfully, it's County who score, when Alun Armstrong gets his first of the season, winning a header deep into the Plymouth half, and reacting more quickly than the defence as he lobs it over the onrushing Grobbelaar. 3-1, game over, and all that remains is for the kiddies in the free seats to taunt the Plymouth fans with a high-pitched "3-1, 3-1" chant. Highly amusing, and, no doubt, as irritating as hell to the Plymouth fans.

A performance like today's leaves us wondering whether we have turned the relegation corner (the one at the junction of Bottom-of-the-table Boulevard and Season-of-struggle Street, deep in the heart of Cliché Town). It'll take more than one good performance to confirm that we're back to our best, but, hey, every revival has to start somewhere (did I not mention, I was actually born in Cliché Town?).

The result has certainly brightened up the County fans' lot, so much so that later on, watching Zaragoza v Valencia on Sky (I must emphasise here that I'm *not* sad - there was nothing else on, honest), I keep wanting to tell Anna things, pathetic things, as they occur to me: *"Alun Armstrong took a quick free kick, but Durkan held on to it too long"; "just after we scored our third, Jeffers beat two men and swung in a really good cross for once, but there was no one on the far post"*. I don't actually go as far as to open my mouth - the thoughts just pop unannounced into my mind as I chill out in front of the telly (Anna would probably not be bothered if I did, but although she's used to my obsessions, she might worry why, instead of descriptions of the goals, I preferred to remember pitifully inconsequential incidents like these). It doesn't matter that I keep the thoughts to myself; it's enough that I actually remember these things - not only the sign of a good win, but of the relief which a good win following a poor spell brings. A loss of the type County have been serving up of late tends to induce localised memory loss - an hour and three quarters between three and quarter to five. (Incidentally, I fully accept that the phrase "poor spell" rather understates the issue. What County have been experiencing is the kind of poor spell Merlin once produced when King Arthur asked to be entertained, and he responded with "pick a card - any card").

I'm like this when they win: it really sets up Saturday night. Anna and I have had an arrangement ever since Julia was born - both liking our sleep, we alternate the 6.30 am kid-shift at the weekend, one of us staying in bed until ten whilst the other feeds, clothes and changes nappies (occasionally, when it's my turn, I even perform each of those tasks on the correct child). A perfect Saturday is therefore one like tonight: a good win on a weekend when it's my turn for the Sunday lie-in. I can't even allow myself to be fazed by the fact that the jingoistic, flag-waving bullshit that is bloody "Last Night of the Proms" overruns so that Match of the Day is five minutes late.

Tuesday September 17th 1996. Sheffield United (home) (Coca Cola Cup R2).

My God, we've done it for not one, not one and a half, but two - count 'em! - *two* whole games on the trot! Even better than the bare statistical evidence that we beat First Division Sheffield United 2-1 is the fact that we played, if anything, even better than Saturday.

It's not the first time County have played the Blades at this stage of the League cup. Indeed, we drew them the season before last, when a battling 1-0 defeat in the second leg at Bramall Lane was not quite enough to cancel out the 5-1 first leg loss. That was a strange game. Sheffield took an early lead, before weathering all kinds of County pressure (by all kinds of County pressure, I mean, of course, left wing crosses, right wing crosses, shots from outside the area, etc. I wouldn't like you to think that County had resorted to mental torture, or anything (*"Those stripey shirts are really naff - everyone's looking at you, you know"*)). Early in the second half, we equalised through Kevin Francis and then set about Sheffield with a vengeance. It was slightly against the run of play, therefore, that United got a second, and ridiculously against the run of play that they also got a third, a fourth and a fifth, all in the last five minutes, as the County fans' jaws dropped lower and lower.

Tonight's game, therefore, represents something of a revenge match, and County play superbly well, creating a number of good early chances, one of which is converted when Mike Flynn rises to head home a corner. Even better, 15 minutes later County double their lead following good work by Durkan on the left wing, and a low whipping cross that Tom Bennett sidefoots home. Just before half-time, Armstrong misses a good chance, but it's two-nil, we're dominating a First Division team, and our season really has started.

Early in the second half, however, ex-Man City player Michel Vonk heads home and for a short spell, United take control. County rally, though, and have chances to score more before the final whistle. However, 2-1 it remains, and, as I remark to my dad, it seems unfair that Sheffield were only a goal away from a completely undeserved draw. This is quite the best County have played in a long long time, and a 4 or 5-1 final score would not have been undeserved. However, we've secured not only our third 2-1 Coca Cola Cup win on the trot, but our second win of any description on the trot. That's almost a run! Unfortunately, 2-1 could well not be enough for the return leg at Bramall Lane in a week's time.

Saturday September 21st 1996. York City (away).

My last trip to York City passed without incident - County gaining a 0-0 draw in the first leg of the play-off semi-final of 1994 - and thus helped partially erase some painful memories.

Back in 1982, I started studying PPE at Keele University. For those unacquainted with the world of academic abbreviation (and doesn't it give the rest of us a nice warm feeling of superiority?), this stands for Philosophy, Politics and Economics (though not necessarily in that order). For me, it might as well have stood for Piss off, you won't Pass your Exams, as, due to a combination of laziness and a failure to get to grips early on with three subjects I had never before studied, I was "sent down" (I believe is the official term) at the end of my second year. Purely due to the deep upset I knew this caused my parents - for both of whom, schooled as they were in post-war working class Stockport, the prospect of going to University was as remote as that of going to the moon - this was probably the worst period of my life.

My University failure was exacerbated by the fact that Anna was at Hull College of Higher Education, having gained a place on a Business Studies HND course. I was thus in the habit of travelling up there for weekends which hardly deserved the description, lasting as they did from about tea-time on Thursday to mid-morning on Monday. By a stroke of good fortune, the nature of which all true football fans will recognise ("oh look dear, I told you it was worth waiting until October to come to Devon - the boys are playing at Torquay tomorrow. What luck!"), County were due at York on the Saturday of one such weekend.

Such was Anna's delight at the prospect of my company for yet another weekend, she readily agreed to accompany me to the game. The train journey from Hull to York was an uncomplicated one, made all the more attractive by dual possession of student railcards. It was thus decided that train was the mode of transport we would employ, and we duly rose early (about 11 o'clock), on the Saturday, and made our way to Hull's peculiarly named Paragon Station. After buying our tickets, we approached the barrier, and asked the guard which was the York train. He struck me initially as a - dare I say it? - typical Yorkshireman: salt-of-the-earth, bluff, dour - a real humourless git, in fact. I couldn't have been more wrong. The man's face lit up as he gaily responded to our query, with a delighted "that one", as he indicated the train which had, in the seemingly deliberately prolonged interval between our request and his reply, started up, and was now rapidly departing from platform three. There was no chance of running after it, or rather, to be pedantic, every chance of running after it, but ball-all of catching it. I turned in dismay to the worthy, whose demeanour suggested that he hadn't had so much fun for a very long time, "what time's the next one?"

"To York?"

"Yes, to York."

"What time do you have to be there?"

"Er, well, about half past two at the latest, really."

"Twenty to three, platform six." He turned on his heel and walked away, doubtless to seek out his workmates, so they could all roll about hysterically on the floor for a few moments. I had obviously made his day, if not his week. Possibly his life.

The next couple of hours passed interminably slowly as we mooched around Hull City Centre (well, I mooched anyway - I suspect Anna was slightly less bothered about the disaster). I spent most of this period desperately working out the revised timetable. Arrive in York at 3.20, 10 minutes to the ground, might catch a bit of the first half...

We eventually boarded the 2.40 train, whose driver had evidently decided it was going to be the 2.44 train (simple minutes had by this time assumed an almost obscene importance in my life). Nevertheless, in due course we were approaching the cathedral city, and I fancied I saw the floodlights, presumably not far away from the station. It was at this point that Fate decided to join the Hull guard in having a damn good belly-laugh at my expense, by sending one of those endearing little on-line pauses that make British Rail what it is - shit. This particular example lasted for about ten minutes that seemed like hours, before, with nothing apparently changed on the track, the train started up again, and trundled the hundred or so yards into York station. I stole a look at my watch; just gone twenty five past. Still time to see all the second half as long as the ground, like so many others, was close to its town's railway station. Any readers amongst you who are acquainted with York's environs will, I imagine, be doing a passable impression of the guard at this moment. We rushed out of the station, and stopped the first person we saw - "where's the football ground, mate?"

"Well, let me see, it's... er, no, hang on, if you go..."

"Thanks" I snapped. We decided to dash in what we thought was the general direction of the ground. Amazingly enough we got it right, as turning a corner, we saw the floodlights about a mile away. Great! I revised my mental itinerary: it was 3.34 - we might even catch the end of the first half at this rate. As we trotted on, we lost sight of the ground, but I was confident my bodily compass was in good working order - unlike my body itself, which was knackered. However, we then came to a junction in the road which necessitated a decision. Left or right? Never had there been such a choice to be made. Did we take the money, or open the box? Whether we saw any of the first half depended on this decision, and, God help us, there was a difference of opinion. "Look, I'm sure it's left - it has to be". Using the logic of the desperate, I was trying to convince myself as much as anyone else. My willpower prevailed, and we set off to the left, me trying to ignore the smug looks coming from my side. We had travelled a worryingly long distance towards what I had hoped would be the ground, when, at last, it loomed in front of us. The trouble was, it loomed tinily, in the distance, approximately a mile and a half further away. We were standing outside the National Railway Museum.

At this point I, understandably enough, I feel, lost control. "Aaaaarrggggfffffghhhhhuckkkkkinnnnaaaaarrrrggghh!!!" Anna was tactful - or sensible - enough not to say "I told you so", as we speedily retraced our steps, desperation granting us second - or, more accurately, about eighth - wind. We reached the point where I had made the fateful, ie wrong, choice, and set off again, this time to the right. A bus had stopped ahead of us, and it seemed to be pointing the correct way. We jumped on board, and asked the driver whether, gasp, he went, pant, anywherenearBoothamCrescent. His reply - "well, not really" - was enough. At that point, I would gladly have boarded a pensioners' outing to South Shields, on the grounds that it was heading in the general direction of Bootham Crescent. We paid our fare, and sat eagerly awaiting his promised call, which came a disappointingly short time after we had got on - about 300 yards travel, to be precise.

After gasping our way for ten minutes or so in the direction which the saintly driver had indicated, we then espied the floodlights what seemed a reasonably short way off. As if to confirm things, we then happened upon the entrance to... Bootham bloody Crescent! I fell to my knees and offered a short prayer of thanks. It must have been missed. For those of you who've never been to York City's ground, the following information may be of use in planning any future journey: allow half an hour extra for your journey, as Bootham fucking Crescent is enormous. It took us what seemed an age to stagger down its length, and collapse, sobbing and weeping, at the visitors turnstile. The time was seven minutes past four, and the turnstile was closed.

After what we'd been through, however, we were buggered if a little thing like that was going to stop us. We made our way to the home fans' end, where a solitary turnstile remained open, presumably to cater for idiots like us who were unable to arrive at the ground until the game was two thirds over. We paid our half-price - possibly the one ray of sunshine in a day of deluge - and entered the ground.

I can't remember much of that tiny portion of the game we saw. I think County were already two down when we arrived, pulled one back, but let in a third at the end. You'd never have guessed, but, seemingly, no sooner had we arrived than the match was over. It didn't really matter. I was, by then, a broken man.

Now, as you will appreciate, the foregoing would have been bad enough in itself. But my hate affair with that wonderful county's administrative city had not been dimmed by the passage of time when we made our way across the Pennines for the last away game of 1991. It was a vital game in the climax of our promotion season, so I, along with hundreds of other County fans, had decided to make the trip. I also, along with tens of other map-illiterate County fans, didn't leave the good old A64 until a junction too late. And I, along with bloody millions of day trippers, got caught in the longest traffic jam in the history of vehicular transport. The match had originally been scheduled for Friday night, presumably due to the fact that it was a Bank Holiday weekend. However, a few months earlier, it had been moved back to the Saturday, with no explanation given. If I had the individual in front of me now who decided to make the switch, I'd attempt to explain to him the frustration experienced by one who, with a three o'clock appointment to make, doesn't move an inch between 2.10 and 2.25. I'd explain to him that the appointment I was hoping to keep was, quite simply, one of Stockport County's most important games for over twenty years. I'd attempt to explain to him with what childish anticipation I'd set off that morning. And then I'd hit the bastard.

At around 2.40, we eventually inched into York, my brother Martin and me, having started the ten mile crawl about eighty minutes previously. I had, despite my previous experience of the city, no idea whatsoever where the ground lay. Luckily, I spotted the County fan's car (identified by the scarf hanging out of the window) I had been tailing turn purposefully into a side street. Thank God! I turned into the street as well, and parked up behind them, following on foot at a respectful distance. At last, I thought, I was going to see the whole game. It was at this point that the man we were following turned and uttered the fateful words - **to us!** - "d'y'know where the ground is, mate?" At this, I wept.

Martin was slightly more resourceful, and urged us towards a bus offering open top tours of the city. "Good idea," I said, "at least we'll have something to show for the trip"

"Not a tour - the driver'll be bound to know where the ground is."

"Oh yeah, good idea"

Thankfully, the driver did indeed know where the ground was, and gave us directions only slightly complicated by his devotion to his job necessitating him sending us on the scenic route. It was at this point that the real evil genius of the fixture-shifter came into its own, as we then had to battle through hundreds of Bank Holiday shoppers in order to reach Bootham Crescent, which was humorously situated on the far side of the main shopping precinct. Soon, however, we were free, and cruising. Five to three, and only Bootham Crescent itself to negotiate. Bootham Crescent!! Arrrrghhhh!!! I prefer to draw a veil over our progress down that particular road, forever etched in my memory with feelings of exhaustion, nausea and frustration. Suffice to say that we reached the ground and passed through the turnstiles at the precise moment the match kicked off, proof if any were required of the existence of a malicious force called Fate, toying with our lives for her own sick amusement.

We won 2-0, though, which made it alright.

I've got the Fiesta today, and have my dad and Martin as passengers. Three fully grown people (well, not exactly, but our extra weight balances out the fact that Martin is only 17, so it averages out at three fully grown people) sharing a noisy 950cc car on a lengthy motorway-and-moor trip is not an experience I would particularly recommend, and, despite the car doing its best, the journey gets a touch wearisome. It doesn't actually help that the car's "best" is pitiful. Indeed, when I once got a speeding summons, I was quite affronted. I considered for a time putting, in the area on the summons reserved for mitigating circumstances, a comment along the lines of, "yeah, like how?", but thought better of it.

News of the week is that ex-County manager Danny Bergara was appointed at Rotherham in the week. He was sacked from County following an alleged punch-up with the Chairman at a sponsors' function at a local hotel. Makes a change from receiving a vote of confidence, I suppose.

We approach York in good time, and, despite some frustrating roadworks on the ring road, we arrive in enough time to park close to the ground (and facing back the way we came, of course). Entering the ground, it seems as though County have brought a decent following, but it's clear as I move along the terrace that the fans have, as always happens, simply gathered on that part of the terrace closest to the entrance. Moving along, we find a crush barrier with ample room, right behind the goal.

Bootham Crescent is a small, compact ground, and one which I like immensely. The away fans' position is close to the pitch, and there are trees visible over the roofs of one of the stands, which adds a nice touch (not that they were planted deliberately to please the aesthetic sensibilities of away supporters, I suppose). The terraces also afford a reasonable enough view, despite the presence of the fences which York still, sadly, deem necessary.

Home fans stand in the David Longhurst Stand - a roof built over the old terrace in memory of the York City player who died on the pitch, aged 25, in September 1990. I still remember clearly the shock I felt when I heard the news of his death on Grandstand that particular Saturday, even though I had no affinity whatsoever with either him or York City. For me (and, I'm sure, many others), a regularly-attending football supporter, the thought of a player actually collapsing and dying on the pitch was a grotesque and hideous one. Grandstand rolled their end-credits in silence, without the usual jaunty music, that day.

The feeling amongst County fans is that, as York have just gained a draw at Goodison Park in the Coca Cola Cup, we might catch them cold. It certainly happened to us, last year, in similar circumstances, when heroic exploits at Goodison (2-2 draw, should have won) and the Edgeley Park replay (3-2 defeat, with Everton's winner coming in the last minute, seconds after we had equalised through Alun Armstrong) were followed by more prosaic home defeats by, respectively, Bradford City (1-2) and Walsall (0-1).

As well as being a pleasant ground to look at, Bootham Crescent is also a good ground on which to barrack goalkeepers. York's makes the mistake, when feinting to take a goal kick, of screeching a frantic, "hey!" in an attempt to alert a full-back to his idea of a quickly taken short pass. Immediately, a group of County fans behind the goal mimic him: "Hey!" "Hey!" "Hey!" "Hey!" "Hey!" "Hey!" The cry is soon taken up by more and more people, until it reaches the stage that whenever he's about to take a goal kick, there is an increasingly loud chorus of rapid and high-piched "hey!"s, rising to a crescendo as he strikes the ball. "Is he a Scouser, then, or what?" someone shouts.

Our confident start seems to reinforce the view that we'll catch York on the rebound, and we have the better of a generally quiet first half, with a couple of shots cleared off the line. The team are playing well together, as the confidence gained from 2 successive wins - and good wins at that - means that they aren't scared of trying things - long crossfield passes, ambitious runs, shots from distance. After one of these has just missed the post, the York keeper prepares to take the goal kick. "Hey!" "Hey!" "Hey!" "Hey!" "Hey!" "Heyheyheyheyheyheyhey.....HEY!!" There is a short pause. "MR GRIMSDALE!"

Half time arrives with no goals, confident play from County, a chorus of "hey"s at the departing keeper, and a murmuring from the sparse home support which is more reminiscent of a theatre interval than a football half-time. I get out my Merimate® Dandelion & Burdock Flavour Drink, purchased from the tea-hut. I like that "flavour" - as though they couldn't use genuine dandelion and burdock (*"Do you know how difficult it is to process real dandelions? And as for burdocks..."*). The drink is in a tiny plastic bottle - one of the rules of football grounds these days being that fans can't bring cans in (missiles, d'you see? Animals, some of these football fans, animals). The bottle has a picture of a jaunty cartoon lion on it, a lion which is presumably supposed to be a dandy (although it doesn't seem to be wearing monocle, cane and spats). Presumably it was a straight choice for the illustrator, and he shied away from trying to draw a burdock.

I go for a slash in York's bogs, which are a classic example of lower division facilities - a rough concrete trough around the foot of a brick wall in an unroofed six foot square building, lying at the bottom of a slight slope made up of grainy sand. At least we can all build sandcastles later if we get bored.

Just after half time York score when Tolson heads in a left wing cross right in front of us (how dare he! Right in front of us!), and such is the perceived fragility of our recent revival that this event, despite County's first half pressure, is greeted with foreboding. This is clearly the winning goal. Except that it isn't. Brett Angell at last reinforces his recent good form by scoring a mere two minutes later, when he turns on Mike Flynn's long throw to prod home. Even better, a minute or so after that, he runs through a York defence that has so much wide open space a group of ramblers are staging a mass trespass, and scores a second. Three goals in four and a half minutes gives County yet another win, for although we have further chances, and York stage a late flurry, that's the end of the scoring.

Just before the end, I go to rid myself of the final traces of dandelion and burdock, noting, to my delight, that there is indeed someone building sandcastles on the slope down to the bogs, using a discarded plastic cup. It's a little girl, admittedly, rather than a fully-grown County fan, but it shows that someone at least was prepared to make their own entertainment today. "Look dad," she shouts excitedly, as she reveals a cup-shaped "castle". "Mmm," her dad grunts. Keep playing on that muddy, piss-sodden sand, love, I'm watching the football.

Three wins on the trot, a pleasant ground, and a trip home that even the car seems to appreciate more than this morning's effort. One of the more enjoyable of away games.

Tuesday September 24th 1996. Sheffield United (away) (Coca Cola Cup R2).

It's a ridiculous £13 (£7 for kids) tonight, which will have the effect of guaranteeing a pitifully small crowd for a game that, with the home side facing a 2-1 deficit, deserves better. At least Sheffield are not charging the even more amazing £14 that they expected people to pay last time we played here, two seasons ago. The tie was already over, after the first leg 5-1 thrashing, yet still the idiots who decide admission prices were too inflexible, or too stupid, to cut the charge. The final attendance was a pathetic 5,065.

It never ceases to amaze me that football club administrators can be so thick. We all know that they need to maximise their revenue, and, to a certain extent, if they pitch the price right then they will make more money from a half-empty ground than they will from a full one. It's a sad fact that, in those circumstances, such a match - played in an echoey, half-empty stadium - will be regarded as a "success" by the money men. However, I refuse to believe that overall revenue could not be increased in a lot more cases by slashing admission where interest in the match is hardly immense. Leeds and Huddersfield are just two clubs who have shown in recent years that attractive yet sensible pricing (in other words, what seems bleedin' obvious to your average fan) puts bums on seats. If there were a few less bums on the seats in the Boardroom, we might see such ideas at a few more clubs.

I've got my dad and Martin with me again tonight. Martin would have come anyway, but my dad's attendance is slightly unusual. He's a postman, which entails a 4.20am start on weekdays. This would normally mean that he would have to think twice about attending a County game at Edgeley Park, let alone one at Sheffield with a 7.45 kick off which, assuming there's no extra time, will get him home at around 10.45. However he's on his two week "summer" (unlucky in the ballot) holiday at the moment, so late nights hold no terrors for him.

I decide to take a somewhat offbeat route - through Edale and the Peak District rather than over the more direct Snake Pass, as I've been advised there's less traffic this way. However, I begin to wonder whether this is such a good idea in the Fiesta (Anna has taken the kids to her mum's in the Cavalier), as it struggles, to put it mildly, climbing the hills. The engine screams in third gear, but a rapid change up brings a depressing chugging and immediate loss of speed. I'm therefore subjected to ten miles or so of frantic gear changing, with the convoy of traffic behind me getting increasingly frustrated. Sorry folks, but it's a shit car - what can I do? (Does the Highway Code contain a hand gesture for that?)

We arrive at Bramhall Lane in good time, and I see a friend, Martin Frost, outside the ground. I mention that I won't be too upset if we lose tonight, although this is for no reason other than my own twisted logic, which, as I explain to him, states that if we were to win tonight, then to win on Saturday, at home to Gillingham - and being a league game, a victory then would be far more important than tonight, as we all know - would mean that we would then have to extend our winning sequence to five straight games, which, knowing the fragility of the side's confidence, I think is beyond us.

It makes sense to me, anyway. Smiling fixedly, however, Martin starts to back away, like a man who has just caught sight of a newspaper hording over the shoulder of the pleasant, if rather wide-eyed, stranger he has been talking to, which reads "**Escaped Axe-murdering Lunatic Latest - Engages Strangers In Conversation About His Bizarre Footballing Theories**". We say our goodbyes, and I head for the turnstiles.

Inside the ground, the first thing I see is a portakabin containing a temporary bookies. It's almost kick off, and I really should be taking my seat, but I cannot resist the strange lure of football bets. This is not to say that I am a regular gambler - sometimes I don't even bet on the Grand National, which makes me, apparently, less of a gambler than many British housewives - but football bets are a particularly attractive form of gambling, appealing as they do to the supporter's sense of vanity. Forecasting football results? Pah, I go to games regularly, you know. Thus it is that, despite the fact that the cumulative odds on a string of correct forecasts are in the tens of thousands to one, it feels as though it is genuinely a test of skill rather than a gamble ("all I've got to do is forecast seven games correctly, and I pick up fifteen grand!"). I usually go for a seven game perm (any five from seven, any six from seven and all seven: 29 bets at 10p, £3.16, tax paid - see, I even know the lingo), which means that five correct games more or less gives me my money back. The fact that I have only ever got five correct on one occasion doesn't deter me one little bit. One day I'll get all seven, and who'll be laughing then, eh?

As it is quite late, I content myself with a "who will score the first goal" quid on Jim Gannon, who, I figure, following his pair against Plymouth, is on a roll. The bookies obviously don't agree, rating him at 28-1, and even, in a show of contempt for what they consider to be his chances, scrawling his name and price on the nearby whiteboard, next to "Armstrong 8-1", and "Angell 9-1", in a "look, you can even put silly bets on if you like" manner.

The Bramall Lane Stand, in the top tier of which the County fans are situated, is quite the steepest I have ever sat in. Squeezing past a couple of blokes who sullenly move their legs only the merest fraction to let us by, I am struck by the feeling that if I were to slip and fall, I would probably end up on the pitch, such is the sheer drop.

Our position makes for a tremendous view, however, and we can thus appreciate the way County start. Picking up where they left off in the first leg, they dominate the first 15 minutes, and it is no great surprise, or injustice, when they go ahead. Chris Marsden floats a free kick in from the right which sails over everyone's head to the far post, where Jim Gannon manages to head home from the tightest of angles. Bedlam all around me. That's 3-1 on aggregate, and we've cancelled out their away goal (away goals count double in the Coca Cola, but only after extra time). They'll thus need to score two to force penalties, and three on the night to put us out direct. County's defence don't often concede two goals in a... JIM GANNON! Get in! Twenty-eight quid!! If there is a state beyond euphoria, I've just reached it. It's not so much the money - although it wipes out tonight's expense at a stroke, and then some - as the fact that it's immediate confirmation of my footballing knowledge. No WAY was that a fluke - I've told you, I go to football. I *know*. I bet the lad who took my bet is open-mouthed right now, thinking, just who was that handsome dark stranger? HE certainly knew his football. And I bet the Ladbroke's manager is smacking him round the head, saying "I told you not to write Gannon's price on that bloody whiteboard, you arse!"

County don't sit on their lead and, amazingly, their pressure pays off five minutes later, with another goal from Alun Armstrong, who is playing like the Premier League star he will surely one day be. John Jeffers chases a lost-cause ball and just manages to pull it back from the touchline. Armstrong controls the ball and dummies the covering defender in one movement before waiting for the keeper to dive and placing the ball into the corner of the net. There wasn't another player on the pitch - County or United - who would have had the ability to score in the same manner. More bedlam. Immediately, the mental calculators tell us that it's now 4-1 on aggregate, but, even better, we've now got more away goals. Sheffield's task is now to score 4 - at least three in normal time. Let's face it, we're in round three.

That may be so, but, as if to make certain, the lads still continue to dominate, and to pour forward in numbers. Just two minutes after Armstrong's goal, a left-wing cross is flapped out to Tom Bennett, whose shot is blocked by the keeper. The rebound falls straight back to Bennett, however, and he buries it. Right in front of the County fans. Three goals in eight minutes. I'm not sure if pandemonium is a strong enough word to describe what ensues twenty or so feet above the now bulging net, but in the absence of a professor of linguisitcs (never one around when you need one, have you noticed?), it'll do.

This is genuinely unbelieveable, as are the shouts of "easy, easy" now directed at the home support. *"We can see you sneaking out"*. Incredibly, with a mere 30 minutes gone, there are a number of Sheffield fans leaving. Thirteen quid for half an hour of misery is a high price to pay for all but the most maso of sado-masochists *"Cheerio, cheerio, cheerio. Cheerio, cheerio, cheer-ee-o-ho. Cheerio, cheerio, cheerio. Cheerio-ho, CHEER-EE-O!"* we sympathise. The aggregate score is now Sheffield United 1, Stockport County 5 - a scoreline as reminiscent of that game at Edgeley two seasons ago as tonight's three goal burst is of the way United took us apart in the last few minutes on that night. Rare, indeed, are the occasions when footballing revenge is so complete, or so swift.

It may be the breathless emotion, it may be the combination of nerves and adrenaline, or it may be the fact that I'm a complete and utter mard arse, but I find myself gulping for air and frantically blinking back tears. *That's* the way football gets to you. Since I was a young kid, I've cried at the birth of each of my kids, and at football moments like this. And on no other occasion.

Thankfully, Sheffield immediately pull one back, which has the dual effect of helping me get a grip on myself and planting, absurdly, the tiniest seed of doubt, despite the aggregate score of 5-2 and Sheffield's need for another four goals to put us out. "You only need another four, lads," I shout at the home fans, more in a sense of goading than of providing information for the more slow-witted amongst them who had yet to work it out for themselves. Was it me, or did they, 100 or so yards away behind the opposite goal, immediately look affronted?

I now realise, from the tannoy announcement of the United scorer, that the prat behind the mike is not announcing the scorers of our goals. Trivial point, granted, but it still rankles. Is it just because we scored three times before you even got one, you Yorkshire get? More alarming than this, however, is my conviction that I heard, even in the midst of the celebrations, a worrying crump from the carrier bag I'd placed on the floor at the side of me. This contained not only a sweat shirt that I was going to wear if it got cold (and yes, I've remembered my vest, mum), but a couple of Mars bars I'd bought for us to eat at half time. The noise had not sounded like a sweat shirt being jumped on by an ecstatic football fan as much as a Mars bar or two being jumped on by an ecstatic football fan. Expecting a flattened, cow-pat shaped, glucose, suger and thick, thick chocolate mess, I gingerly open the bag to find that, in fact, my size nines had fortunately missed the confectionary. What they had not missed, however, was a carton of Ribena that I had forgotten I'd bought to wash down the Mars. My sweat shirt and both Mars bars are thus covered in sticky purple goo, as indeed am I a couple of seconds later as the carrier bag splits, but it'd take more than that to dampen my spirits at the moment. We're an amazing 3-1 up, we're in the next round, and Jim Gannon has won me 28 quid. You could have parked an industrial muck-spreader on the six yard box, and squirted liquid shit all over me and I wouldn't have cared (not perhaps strictly true, but you get my gist).

County leave the field to a noisy standing ovation from one end, and I spend a pleasant enough 15 minute break in the bowels of the stand waving my betting slip at anyone I recognise and washing off as much Ribena as I can in the bogs. There is, understandably, an excited buzz amongst the fans. It's hard to believe that the Wrexham game was a mere 14 days ago.

The concern for the second half is not so much that we'll lose (reality having forced its way into my conscious, I know full well that the tie is now won) as that we may sit on our lead and play out a boring 45 minutes. Huh! As if! County continue to pour forward at every opportunity (although it must be easier against a dispirited, beaten side), and after 15 minutes of the second half, Brett Angell gets his third goal in four days when he heads home a left wing cross. 4-1 on the night, 6-2 on aggregate. Sheffield then have a period of pressure which gives them another consolation goal (although they've got a County defensive error to thank), before Alun Armstrong, who has played out of his skin tonight, and is far and away the best player on the field, gets his second, looping a header from another left wing cross over Sheffield's Kelly in the 80th minute. I have to confess to it being a unique experience to hear the chant of "we want six" from a group of travelling County fans. It is the best away performance I can ever remember, and the ovation given to the players is loud and long. To their credit, what remains of the home support joins in.

We dash back to the car in an attempt to beat the traffic and get home to see the goals on ITV. I also want to rush home to share the euphoria with Anna and the kids (despite the fact that they're all in bed, and would hardly appreciate being woken up by a lunatic). The way we came in is blocked off by police so that the coaches can be run out of town, so I take a few back streets in order to get away. A couple of obviously wrong turnings later and I'm heading back into the centre of Sheffield. Thankfully, I manage to catch sight of a sign for Manchester (close enough, that'll do), and manage to achieve escape velocity by whizzing round a couple of roundabouts.

We make it home over the Snake Pass in time for the televised goals and a good laugh at Manchester City, who have lost 1-0 at Maine Road to a Lincoln side we beat 5-0 at Edgeley Park in last year's FA Cup. The York team we beat easily on Saturday have also won, 3-2 against Everton at Bootham Crescent, so we're not only a better team than Man City, we're better than Everton as well. Flicking round the channels, I am amused (well, annoyed, actually) to hear the Sky sports presenter describe our 5-2 massacre as a "comfortable win for Stockport" Comfortable, presumably, in the sense that the Russians' defeat of the Light Brigade was "just about adequate".

I reflect, not for the first time, as I watch York complete their demolition job on Everton, on the feelings I am experiencing now. It is a special kind of euphoria, of a type that is denied to supporters of Premier League clubs: the pride that can only be experienced when you play one of your supposed betters off the park. I want to go out into the street and stop people *"I'm* a County fan" I'd say, before receiving their warm congratulations.

Tonight represents possibly not the most memorable of County games in my

24 years of watching them, but it's easily in the top three or four. Remember how, in the introduction, I described it as pathetic to feel preposterously proud of County? Tonight, I am pathetic.

Saturday September 28th 1996. Gillingham (home).

On Wednesday, County received, as their reward for beating Sheffield United, an away tie in the third round, at Blackburn Rovers. I watched the draw live on Sky, and, by virtue of me ringing them up just beforehand and holding the phone receiver to the telly's speaker, Martin, my dad and my mum were also able to listen to it, by switching their own phone to loudspeaker mode. This was a "Family Football Moment"®, brought to you by News International Corp.

It's a good job Chris Marsden is suspended for today's game, following his sending off against Wrexham, as Gillingham have a reputation for being hard men, and the dressing room attendant (not that I should imagine County employ such a poncey creature) could probably have started the water running for his early bath sometime during the first half. Gillingham won promotion last season with an incredible defensive record, but were also implicated in a mass brawl with Fulham players which led to both teams being fined by the FA

The crowd is boosted, again, by loads of kids, although our recent good form has also led to a few neutrals vacating the woodwork. I yearn, as always, for a good County performance in the hope that a lot of them will return next time. With the team playing as they are at the moment, it's hardly surprising that my hopes seem to be being realised as we get an early goal. After 11 minutes, centre half Mike Flynn launches one of his speciality long throws, which is headed back towards him by a defender. Rather than let it roll out so that he can have another go, however, he beats the full back and whips in a superb cross (the fact that Flynn even considered such a manoeuvre is remarkable enough, let alone that he pulled it off) for Alun Armstrong to deflect a header past the Gillingham keeper.

That is the sum of the first half scoring (a veritable drought, by County's standards at the moment), but County are seeing a lot of the ball (some of it when it's at their own feet), and are only being denied by a strictly enforced Gillingham offside trap. Paul Jones, meanwhile, in the County goal, is performing well when required. The Gills' players are living up to their "hard-man" image by having someone booked every few minutes. The number of times they concede possession through free kicks is astonishing. I can't help but feel that if they didn't commit so many needless, niggly fouls, they would have had far more possession, and possibly, more goals.

Half-time brings the announcement of the ticket prices for the game with

Blackburn at Ewood Park. Sure enough, as I had feared, it is a ridiculous £15 for adults. There will be no problem selling 2,000 or so tickets to County fans, even though Blackburn no longer have Alan Shearer as an attraction. However, the Lancastrians are hardly going to be dragged away from the telly to watch County. I would predict an attendance of only around 10-12,000. If I am right - and I dearly hope I'm not, as I want as many fans as possible to see our victory - it'll be a case of stupid football club management striking again.

The second half starts spectacularly when, in the 48th minute, Paul Jones punts a long, wind-assisted ball downfield. A Gillingham defender attempts, off balance, to head it back to his keeper, but only manages to guide it into the corner of the net. It's the first OG of the season, and reasonably humorous. In case readers might think this comment irrelevant, it should be remembered that own-goals, unlike normal scores, are judged on their laughter content. A sycthed clearance which screws into the corner isn't bad, but give me the attempted back pass any day, past which the keeper kicks fresh air; or the bullet header into the top corner which would probably win goal of the season if it were scored at the other end.

At this point, the chant of *"Oh now you've got to believe us, the County's going up"* makes its first appearance for well over 18 months. It was a regular chant during the Bergara years, but has been conspicuous by its absence since. It may be, of course, that the people chanting it merely mean that we're going up the league a couple of places, but County fans aren't usually quite so literal. The pre-season optimism has returned with a vengeance.

At 2-0, the game should be safe, although Gillingham get even dirtier in an attempt to wrest something from their long journey. In the 88th minute, with six players already booked (to County's two), they do get a goal back, when Onorura lifts a through ball over the diving Jones. We then, understandably enough, play keep-ball, which infuriates the away side so much that Hessenthaler decides to take a wild kick at County substitute Tony Dinning, and is sent off. Dinning is also booked, presumably for not getting out of the way of the kick.

Even that isn't enough for the away team, as mild-mannered centre-forward Alun Armstrong is then at the heart of a free-for-all, which includes members of the Gillingham bench, thus giving a slight clue as to where the team may have been taught their sense of sporting fair play. Armstrong reacted with a push after a scything tackle almost crippled him, and was thus, in the crazy, mixed-up world of the referee, guilty of an offence of the same degree of seriousness as the Gillingham player - both are booked. To add to the brutal nature of the game, Paul Ware goes off with what looks suspiciously like a broken arm. Eventually, the referee's whistle brings an end to the violence, and signals three more points for

County - our fifth win on the trot.

I manage to get home in time to catch the rest of the results on teletext. Sheffield United have beaten Man City 2-0 at Bramhall Lane, so we're definitely better than City. Not sure if that's such a proud boast these days, though. It seems incredible, given our start, that today's is our fifth straight win on the trot. It's been a season of two halves so far - August and September.

OCTOBER

NATIONWIDE LEAGUE DIVISION TWO

	P	W	D	L	F	A	Pts
BRENTFORD	9	6	3	0	19	9	21
MILLWALL	9	5	2	2	17	11	17
CREWE ALEXANDRA	9	5	1	3	13	9	16
WREXHAM	9	4	4	1	12	9	16
SHREWSBURY TOWN	9	4	4	1	10	8	16
WATFORD	9	5	1	3	9	8	16
CHESTERFIELD	9	5	1	3	6	6	16
BURY	9	4	3	2	13	9	15
BRISTOL ROVERS	9	4	2	3	8	7	14
BRISTOL CITY	9	4	1	4	18	15	13
BURNLEY	9	4	1	4	12	12	13
LUTON TOWN	9	4	1	4	8	12	13
BLACKPOOL	9	3	3	3	7	8	12
PETERBOROUGH UNITED	8	2	5	1	16	13	11
PLYMOUTH ARGYLE	9	3	2	4	17	14	11
STOCKPORT COUNTY	**9**	**3**	**2**	**4**	**8**	**9**	**11**
GILLINGHAM	9	3	1	5	10	12	10
PRESTON NORTH END	9	3	1	5	8	10	10
YORK CITY	9	2	3	4	12	14	9
BOURNEMOUTH	9	3	0	6	8	14	9
NOTTS COUNTY	8	2	3	3	6	7	9
WALSALL	9	2	2	5	10	14	8
ROTHERHAM UNITED	9	1	2	6	8	15	5
WYCOMBE WANDERERS	9	0	4	5	8	15	4

Wednesday October 2nd 1996. Millwall (away).

A game like today's is a pain in the backside, literally as well as metaphorically, due to the length of coach journey involved. It necessitates an afternoon off work because the coach leaves at one o'clock, presumably to take account of London traffic. Indeed, such a game, at such a time and on such a day, tends to make you wonder precisely what those people at the Football League who approve the fixtures were trying to achieve. "Well, we can't possibly get away with sending them to Brighton on New Year's Day like last season, so.. er... hang on... Got it! Millwall midweek - first Wednesday in October. They'll have to cross London in the rush hour on the way there, and they won't get home until the early hours. Yes, that'll do. Perfect."

Ideally, I would have got the train, and bugger the expense. I could have probably left work at around 4 o'clock for a 4.30 train, and been home by half midnight or so, but the return journey - crossing from Millwall to Euston at 9.30 - was not one which particularly appealed, because Millwall, as we all know, means hooligans. Now I'm not one who courts trouble, and am therefore sensible enough to realise that there are times when you really shouldn't flaunt your club's colours. In fact, I am fairly proud to say that in my 24 years of watching County - the majority of which coincided with the worst hooligan excesses of the 70s and 80s, I have never once been in any kind of bother. I am a firm believer in the premise that if you want to avoid trouble, you can. That said, I have heard that the atmosphere at Millwall can be downright nasty, and I don't particularly want to have my personal trouble-avoidance theory disproved at such a place.

I have to go to the game straight from work, and have thus arranged to leave my car outside my aunt Lily's house, half a mile or so from Edgeley Park, in the hope that this will render it less likely to be broken into. Had I been travelling on the Fingerpost, I could, of course, have left my car at home, but I'm trying the club coach today not only to see how the two services compare, but also as I figure that the legroom on the club bus couldn't possibly be less than that offered by the Fingerpost for the Bristol trip. In the event, the official club coach is, somewhat surprisingly, far more luxurious, and, yes, the legroom is significantly greater.

The trip starts badly, however, when the guy who is doing the stewarding walks the length of the coach asking whether anyone objects to him putting a Chubby Brown video on. Apparently, they played "Lethal Weapon" the other week, and someone objected to a nude scene, so he's now asking everyone's permission in turn before playing the unfunny Geordie's tape. It's no great surprise that no one objects - they're hardly likely to when they're on a 50 seater coach, and the vast majority have expressed happiness with watching the crap. I've never seen a Chubby Brown video, but have heard enough about them to form a fair judgement of what to expect. Sure enough, the sheer nastiness of his misogyny counteracts any funny jokes he might tell; luckily, my Walkman comes to the rescue again.

We stop for a break at a service station just south of Birmingham, and it feels strange to think that we've only just commenced our trip at a time when the service station is crammed with salesmen and lorry drivers, winding down after a day's work and thinking of home. Despite the fact that I'm neither hungry nor in need of something to read, I go into the newsagents and buy "Private Eye", a packet of wine gums and a bag of Doritos. There's something about coaches that seems to make people want to eat, and something about service stations that makes them want to spend. Back on board, I'm not the only one who scoffs my sandwiches early - I can see others twitching and nervously fingering their butty boxes, wondering how early they can reasonably eat their tea - about half past three, if the evidence is anything to go by.

From this point on, the journey begins to drag, as the rush hour traffic builds. Aylesbury, Warwick, Banbury... the signs roll past with only a second rip-roaring Chubby video to relieve the monotony. This one's a hysterical send-up of the South Bank Show, complete with side-splittingly comic Melvyn Bragg impersonator, and hilarious travelogue of Chubby's home town. God, I hope we win, or at least draw - the journey to the ground is bad enough as it is with this shit; a similar distance home having just been roundly stuffed, would be almost unbearable.

Ardley, Biscester, Oakley. "...she told me it was an Action Man deserter", says Chubby. Roars of laughter from the taped audience, and a few guffaws from the coach. My, Chubby, it must have been, what, 1982 when I first heard that joke. I give up on "Private Eye" and stare blankly out of the window.

Stokenchurch, High Wycombe, Beaconsfield. On and on and on. Sydenham, Uxbridge, Hillingdon. The second Chubby video slimes to a halt. Oh God, no - it's Jim bloody Davidson now! I thought the depths had already been plumbed, but, lo and behold, we find a trench. Davidson's actually been to Edgeley Park, when he was a director of a south coast club - Bournemouth, possibly. My sister Lisa - selling County's lottery tickets at the time - reported seeing him walk out of the players' tunnel well before kick off, long hair and 70s flares flapping in the breeze (and belying the fact that we were by now well into the 80s), to be greeted by a phalanx of Bournemouth fans, lurking at his feet in the paddock that used to be situated in front of the Main Stand, and doing the "nick, nick" bit with their imaginary policemen's helmets. It was, apparently, a fairly bizarre image.

Ealing, Earl's Court, Chelsea, Battersea Power station. Hang on, we're having a tour here. I sit up, suddenly interested. We pass that spectacularly ugly new spy building on the Thames - MI5, or is it 6? Okay, it's uncool, but suddenly I'm an excited tourist. We trundle on, driving right past the Houses of Parliament, and that patch of grass where they interview the MPs. It could well be simply the quickest route, but I somehow didn't expect us to be riding round the landmarks of London at 6 o'clock on the way to a football match.

The place is clogged with homeward-bound commuter traffic, but we make good progress to Tower Bridge police station, where we are obliged to pull in and wait for the escort. It's only ten past six, and there's over an hour and a half to kick off. The coppers are apparently waiting for the Fingerpost coach so that they can save time and effort by escorting us together (and who said coppers were thick? That's a very sensible idea, saving no end of taxpayers' money.) As there's no sign by half six, however, we set off on our own.

The landmarks continue: the Tower of London (*is* that the Tower of London? I expected it to be much bigger); cross the river via Tower Bridge; drive along the Old Kent Road. After a short stop for a quick knees-up with the local Pearlies (*"Gawd bless ver Queen Mavva - wan ver woar for as, she did"*), we finally, at extremely long last, approach the New Den.

The ground is reached by passing under a dank railway arch. Illuminated, shiny and new, the New London Stadium (to give it its official title) presents a stark contrast to its grimy surroundings, and, as there's still almost an hour to kick-off, I take the opportunity for a look round, pausing only to shave my head, quickly scar my face and put on a pork pie hat, so I don't look too much like an away fan. *Do what? Gertcha! Yew slaaag!*

Inside, the ground seems smaller than I expected (I think it's got a capacity of 20,000 or so), and more compact and enclosed. The stands are steep, however, giving us, from the top tier behind the goal, an excellent view which is reminiscent of Bramall Lane. Hopefully, tonight's result will also bear more than a passing resemblance to that remarkable night.

County once again start well, and such is our form at the moment that it's no surprise whatsoever when we take a deserved 24th minute lead; Kieron Durkan gets his first goal for the club, when he half-volleys home a left wing cross from Brett Angell. Millwall equalise five minutes or so later, however, when Anton Rogan (the scoreboard to my left informs me) hits a spectacular 25 yard volley, which is deflected into the corner of the net. Nonetheless, we continue to play well, knocking the ball around confidently, and we reach half time with Millwall lucky to be holding us to 1-1. Such a situation would have been almost unthinkable a few weeks ago; quite apart from our appalling start to the season, we anticipated that this game was always going to be one of the trickier ones.

Nevertheless, we continue to dominate play in the second half, and after an hour Alun Armstrong restores our lead with a brilliant goal. Jeffers and Marsden tie the Millwall defence up in knots on the left wing, and Marsden's superb cross is powerfully headed home. Three minutes later Gannon, incredibly, makes it 3-1, when he wellies home a loose ball following a goalmouth scramble. We're a-leaping and a-hollering in the stand above the celebrating County players now, as that is, surely, game set and match. As if to reinforce County's superiority, Durkan then sends a twenty-five yarder thumping against the crossbar and down onto the goal line, from where Millwall scramble it away. The deafening and dramatic "oooohhh!" from the County fans is probably heard in Stockport.

Millwall fight back, however, and, following a dodgy refereeing decision which goes against them, the home fans go completely mental, which inspires Rogan to get his second with about twenty minutes left. The noise is now clearly lifting the Millwall players, and County look rattled. Sure enough, three or four minutes after their second, they equalise through one of their substitutes. With the home team inspired by the support, County only just about weather the storm, as another of the Millwall subs is inches away from toe-ending a cross in; the foreshortened view from 100 yards away behind the opposite goal gives the impression of a player far closer to the ball than he obviously is, and the relieved noise we make when he fails to connect is thus as loud as that we made for any of County's goals.

Surely, though, we can't possibly concede a last minute winner - it wouldn't be fair after already suffering that fate at Crewe. As if in agreement, County calm the game down, and begin to take control again. A three-three draw away to a team considered pre-season favourites for promotion is an excellent result, and, as the last few seconds of the 90 minutes tick away on the electronic clock to our left, it seems that a draw is indeed the result we have achieved. Then Tom Bennett picks the ball up deep in the Millwall half, and moves forward to the edge of the area. He beats the left back and sends in a hard, low cross, to where Armstrong is waiting, on the edge of the six yard box. Sidefoot. Goal. Four-three. Sheffield mayhem. We've won. We've travelled some 200-odd miles of arse-numbing motorway, taken an unassailable lead which was promptly assailed, and then, right at the death, and following more tension than is probably healthy for grown men and women, we've won.

And we've won, what's more, with a last minute goal. Such a victory - and God knows we've had it done to us more than once in recent years - is probably the most satisfying way of winning a game there is - apart, perhaps, from a five-two away massacre of a team from a higher division. Two of the best away wins you'll ever see, in the space of eight days. Phew!

Tonight's win is not as emotional as the Sheffield game, but it brings a different sense of elation. We have just beaten one of the pre-season favourites for promotion, on their own patch, and we deserved to. This was no flukey 1-0 robbery. We scored four goals, *and we deserved to!* We hit the woodwork twice, dominated the game, and, were it not for the home fans sucking in their third, we'd probably have won comfortably. Once again we're applauding the players off the field at an opponents' ground. It's our sixth straight win, four of which have been league wins, and we're up to tenth in the table (I'd already worked out before the game where a win would place us). From pre-season confidence, to the absolute pits of the Wrexham game, to this. If this is what people mean when they refer to a roller-coaster season, then Alton Towers would do well to consider building the "Stockport County Nationwide League 1996-97" ride. It'd make millions.

Noisy and elated, we reluctantly leave the stadium. The method of departure for those of us who came by coach is now like a precision military operation. We get on board and set off towards one of the dark railway arches, two police outriders ahead. These coppers then instruct the coach to stop and wait just prior to the arch. A hundred yards or so ahead of us, as we lurk with the coach lights now dimmed, we glimpse through the tunnel the main road, with departing home fans marching past and staring down through the gloom at us. It's the closest I have ever come at a football match to experiencing a feeling which could be described as "eerie". As the coppers receive a message through their intercom that the road is clear, they signal to the coach, and we screech away, taking the corner at the top of the road on two wheels and zooming off, the flashing blue lights of the police convoy ahead.

We pass the straggling bunches of fans which make up the remnants of the home support, and some of them live up to their image with vicious gestures; one lad even, via convoluted body language, offering to take on the whole coach, it seems. One or two of the braver souls on board respond with 4-3 finger gestures, and one extremely brave soul with a 2-2 gesture. We reach a roundabout at which the traffic is halted for our safe passage. Sadly for one of the coppers, he is a little bit too cocky with his motorbike manoeuvring at this point, and falls off, raising a great shout of laughter from the adrenaline-high occupants of the coach. Almost immediately, some wag begins a chant of "where's your stabilisers?", in which he is joined by everyone else. Nothing, it seems, can go wrong tonight: a fantastic match, a late winner and now the cabaret.

We head north via Islington and the M1. The coach soon quietens down, and I manage to grab some uncomfortable sleep, dropping off for ten minutes or so in every half hour. At ten past twelve, we pull into a service station so that the drivers can change over. Unfortunately, their schedule - or their bloody-mindedness - means that we also have to have a 30 minute break, so we stagger, bleary-eyed and cursing, into the building. I marvel at the constitutions both of those who immediately head for cafeteria bacon and eggs and those who make, with equal enthusiasm, for the video games.

I force myself to take a slash, even though I don't want one, simply for something to do. Service stations at midnight, miles from home, must be the closest thing to hell on earth there is. I stagger back to the coach, enviously eyeing the long-distance lorries, with their cabs transformed into bedrooms, and occupants deep in the land of nod. Then again, ha! You might be asleep, but you didn't see your team win 4-3 at Millwall with a last minute goal, did you? We eventually set off again, and, following a few more non-relaxing kips, pull into Edgeley at about ten past two. I dash through the silent and echoey streets for the car and zoom home.

When I eventually creep into the bedroom, the clock radio is showing that it's 28 minutes past 2 on Thursday morning. There is an interloper on my side of the bed, but it's only Andrew. Gently easing his tiny body aside, I crawl under the quilt next to him, and will myself to fall asleep quickly. I'll have about five hours in total, and then will be up and helping dress the kids before setting off for eight hours' hard staring at a computer screen. I'll be tired out all day, and probably have a headache for most of it. I'm about thirty quid worse off than I was this morning, and I've lost half a day's holiday I could ill afford to sacrifice.

We won 4-3 with a last minute goal, however, and I wouldn't have missed it for the world.

Saturday October 5th 1996. Burnley (away).

The Fiesta's a bit sluggish today, which, when you think about it, represents a reasonable metaphor for County's season so far: it starts, fitfully, and then chugs along for a bit. You think you've got going and push in the choke, whereupon it gives a great shuddering leap and dies. Starting it again, and taking it easy means that you do eventually get going, and, once the engine's warm, you can cruise nicely. Eventually, with a tail wind, you'll even reach 70.

County are in the slightly unusual position for a football club of not having a natural enemy. Southampton have Portsmouth, Watford have Luton, Newcastle have Sunderland; all those dual-city teams have each other. In fact, the fans of most clubs have a historic rivalry - usually based on geographic proximity - with another club. Not so County. Our rivalries, when we have them, tend to be based on factors such as recent results; a couple of seasons ago, for example, most

County fans' hatred was directed at Stoke, with whom we'd had a number of particularly close and ill-tempered games.

Insofar as County actually have a rival at the moment, however, Burnley are that team. The ill-will seemed to start in the mid-eighties, when, with Burnley struggling alongside County at the bottom of the Fourth Division, the two sides played each other on a number of occasions. The flames of hatred were then fanned by a member of the County supporters club, who wrote a back page column in a local free sheet, and who, on one occasion, related a tale of some pretty inhospitable treatment he had received from certain Turf Moor officials when accompanying County's video crew to a game. This piece was reprinted in a Burnley fanzine, and from then on, it seemed, the two teams were attracted to each other like opposing magnetic poles, playing in various cup competitions as well as regular league encounters, and culminating in the play off final of 1994 at Wembley, when over-officious refereeing from David Elleray - a man renowned for such officiating - meant County had two players sent off in the 2-1 defeat. The atmosphere at County - Burnley games, therefore, is almost always poisonous and hostile, and there are almost always numerous arrests.

I'm accompanied today by my dad and Martin again, as well as one of Martin's friends. We make reasonably good time to Burnley, but, having left a bit late, are forced into parking quite a way from the ground, and thus have to hurry to make kick off. We approach the turnstiles to discover that last year's £8 terrace admission has, due to Turf Moor being all-seater these days, risen to £12; a 50% increase for the dubious privilege of sitting down. Even worse, despite there being a concessions turnstile, it's shut. Martin and his mate are thus faced with the prospect of paying full price, as, indeed, is a man in front of us who has two small girls in tow. He is remonstrating with a steward, "What's going on? I was told there's be kids' prices today". The steward obviously hasn't got a clue: "well, it was open ten minutes ago - I don't know what's happened. Sorry."

A tubby, blazered man appears from one of the official club doorways. Seeing his aura of Turf Moor officialdom, I go over to ask him what's going on. "They'll have to pay full price," he says authoritatively, and is it me, or does he look smug? Full price? Thirty-six quid for this bloke and his two young daughters? "Yep, full price." He turns away with the air of self-righteous officialdom that is so intensely annoying, and, no, it's not me - he *does* look smug. Luckily, a more clued-up steward overhears our problem and informs us that the concessions gate will reopen in a couple of minutes when the turnstile operator has cashed up; this is apparently common practice at Turf Moor. Ridiculous as this procedure is, in our relief we accept it. That fat bastard isn't getting away with it, however. "Oi." I get his attention. "Did you know that the gate opens again when they've cashed up?"

"No."

"So why the bloody hell did you tell us that kids'd have to pay full whack?" He starts to bluster some justification. "You didn't have a fucking clue really, did you, but you thought you'd stick your oar in anyway!" No response. He stares straight ahead, with a blank expression. "Next time, why don't you just keep your fat mouth shut, you stupid bastard?" He turns on his heel, disappears inside, and I chalk a mark next to my name on the "Dave Espley vs Burnley Jobsworth" mental scoreboard. It then occurs to me that he may, in fact, be going to seek reinforcements, so I bugger off into the ground as quickly as I can.

I suppose making such a fuss *is* slightly two-faced, in view of the fact that Martin and his mate are, in fact, both 17, but hey - I was fighting the battle for the bloke and his two daughters.

Inside the ground, from behind the goal where we have been billeted, we get a good view of just what a fantastic transformation has been made of Turf Moor (or "Turd Moor", to give it its colloquial name). The old terrace which used to run from behind the opposite goal round the corner, gaining a roof along the way, has been replaced by two stunning double-tier stands, complete with largely unsold executive boxes, which make the ground look as though it wouldn't be out of place in the Premiership. (It always used to amuse me, incidentally, that the covered part of the old terrace was called the "Longside" - a piece of tautology which made me wonder whether they had considered calling the bits behind the goals the "Shortsides", and the opposite stand the "Sittingdownside"). Sadly, the magnificence of their ground will presumably reinforce the "Big Club" mentality that permeates much of your average Burnley fan's psyche.

The game starts in a manner which hardly does justice to its surroundings, being scrappy and disjointed. County seem unable to recapture their stunning recent form, and Burnley... well, Burnley are just crap. Alun Armstrong, once again, gets more criticism than other players, despite him playing no worse, simply because he is such a far better player normally. "Armstrong you're not a superstar" .shouts a moron behind me, implying that the fact that County aren't winning can be put down to one man acting the prima donna. It never ceases to amaze me that people can be so blinkered.

Despite the fact that neither team deserves the lead, Burnley score first, when an unmarked forward gets his head to a right wing cross after about half an hour. "Where's the marking, you stupid bastards?!" shouts a bloke just in front. Immediately, the bearded man sitting next to me leans forward and upbraids him. "There's no need for that language"

"Yes there is" says the sweary man, and I sense that he only just stopped

72

himself adding "fucking" before "is".

"No there isn't," says the beardy man, "there's kids here."

"They hear worse than that in the school playground every bloody day," says sweary, lapsing a little.

"That's not the point," says beardy.

"It bloody is" says sweary.

"I don't care, there's just no need".

"Ah, mfmgngffmmg off," mumbles sweary, turning back to the game.

It's an amusing little diversion, although hardly one which compensates for the fact that Burnley are ahead. They aren't playing particularly better than County, however; they've just been lucky enough to convert the one chance which they've created.

The break thus approaches with a not insurmountable 1-0 deficit. Burnley, however, have different ideas, and score a second goal which is almost identical to the first - and with a similar lack of marking from the County defence. The cross from the right is from a free kick this time, awarded by a "homer" referee, who seems determined to make a virtue out of incompetence. Almost immediately, he blows for half-time, and leaves the pitch to a chorus of booing from the County fans. In order to sort out bad feeling which has been building this season between managers and referees, there is a clear-the-air conference this weekend. The thought occurs that, with all the good referees presumably at the conference, we've been left with the dross.

Half time is depressing. 1-0 leads can be clawed back; 2-0 means your team has probably lost, and almost certainly won't win. Amazingly, I see Mr Sweary and Mr Hairy chatting. In view of all the kids they are supervising, it seems that they are joint organisers, with a couple of nearby women, of a juniors' trip of some kind. This makes their earlier contretemps all the funnier, and is a fair illustration - albeit on a modest scale - of the way football fans behave differently in the heat of battle than they do when the pressure's off. I have known people whose idea of a fun time of a Saturday is to cruise round Old Trafford or Maine Road looking for opposing fans to fight. Start a footballing conversation with them away from the ground, however, and, no matter which team you support, they will probably be as friendly and as civil as any other non-footballing person.

County need an early second half goal to have any chance, and the players tear out of the traps with a vengeance. The pressure pays off ten minutes into the second half, when Angell heads home a left wing cross. That is the signal for the large County following to make some real noise, and for a minute or two, Burnley look rattled. Only for a minute or two, mind, as after that period has passed, they score another, when one of their strikers is played through a square-looking

County defence, and slides it under Jones in the goal. Arse! We've just had our hopes raised by scoring ourselves when that bloody happens. We're two goals behind again; two minutes ago, we had a good chance of snatching a draw (and, let's be honest, with the illogical optimism so indicative of football fans, we were hoping for a win), and now we're looking at a defeat again. Bugger, arse and fuck.

And shit and crap. With our world rapidly falling apart, Gannon and Todd, normally two of County's most reliable defenders, decide to tackle each other deep in their own half, and yet another goal is scored when a Burnley player, who probably cannot believe his luck, nicks the ball from them and races through to score. Four bloody one.

Following this goal, we get to see some genuinely crap policing. Burnley reserve and youth team players are sitting in an area of the stand right in front of us (a needlessly provocative place to put them with thousands of empty seats elsewhere in the ground), and a few of them turn round and gloat. This so incites some of the more hot-headed of the County fans that they make as if to get the Burnley folk. It's nothing more than posturing really, but the police and stewards wade in, ignore the provocation in front of us, and lay into the County fans. The coppers are from the Stockport force, and the head bobby is a familiar face. From tales I have heard, you'd be hard pressed to find a less sympathetic character - and thus one less suited to handle football crowds.

Back on the pitch, Andy Mutch - a second half substitute for the increasingly ineffective Brett Angell - gets another consolation for County, which is, almost unbelievably, cancelled out two minutes later by yet another Burnley strike. Incredibly, one of the idiots in front of us immediately leaps to his feet, turns round, and directs a big, gloating cheer in our direction. Short of wading into the County fans and actually throwing punches, it's hard to envisage a more provocative act, and, at long last, the police act. All they do, however, is send a single plod in to talk to the guy. No arrest, no ejection, just words. I cannot believe it. As I have stated elsewhere, I am no apologist for hooliganism, but if ever crass and cack-handedly stupid policing were designed to inflame trouble, it is now.

The final whistle ends the agony, and confirms the second 5-2 scoreline involving County in a matter of eleven days. Burnley have probably only had five chances, and have scored the lot; County have had at least as many, and certainly more of the ball, and yet have been tonked. Ooh, football can be so unfair at times. To add insult to injury, we also have to endure a 15 minute lock-in, whilst the local constabulary clear the vicinity of the knuckle-scrapers amongst the home fans. Whilst this is probably a sensible move, it doesn't help that there are one or two Burnley fans (or "Turf Morons", to give them their colloquial name), who have deliberately hung back in the stand to our right, in order to taunt us as they leave. Needless to say, the police and stewards are more concerned with staring blankly at us, imprisoned as we are and unable to move anyway, than clearing away these idiots, whose goading is far more likely to provoke trouble outside than anything else.

We're eventually released, get back to the car and are trundling home, silent and depressed, when Radio Five Live adds to the despondency by informing us that Burnley's Paul Barnes actually got all five goals, having failed to score in any of his previous games since signing from Birmingham for £400,000 a few weeks ago. Crappy Turf crappy Moor's crappy tannoy couldn't be heard from where we were sitting, and so most of us wouldn't have known. Not only, then, have our declared enemies soundly thrashed us, they've done it in a manner which will guarantee headlines in tomorrow's papers. Of all the teams to lose by five goals to, it had to be Burnley, and of all the combinations of possible goalscorers, it had a be a single person getting the lot. What's more, with England playing Poland next Wednesday, there were no Premiership fixtures today, meaning that hacks will be more desperate than usual for football stories. I don't think I'll be buying a Sunday paper tomorrow.

Using my car was indeed an apt metaphor, I reflect, as I pull up later outside my house; just when you think everything's going swimmingly, it's liable to suddenly conk out at the lights. And someone will then crash into your arse-end.

Saturday October 12th 1996. Preston North End (home).

It's a cliché, but what the hell - statements become clichés because of their inherent truth: the weather today, crisp yet sunny, without a breath of wind, is absolutely perfect for football.

Today's game is, of course, the second in succession against one of the so-called "sleeping giants"; those teams who used to be successful and who are now struggling in the lower divisions. Their fans - especially fans of clubs like Burnley, who display their contempt for the surroundings in which they find themselves in the form of arrogant and aggressive behaviour - have never been able to come to terms with the fact that they have slipped from the zenith, preferring instead to view their demise as something of a calumny against football's natural order, made worse by the fact that lowly teams like Wimbledon, Luton and Watford - who, let's face it, *belong* with the crap like Stockport - have all had a consistently better time of it in the last 20 years or so.

Preston, whose success lies further in the distant past than most, seems to attract less of this type of fan than other, similar clubs, but they're still there, glowering under their flat caps and muttering *"Finney... Double... Division One... FA Cup... Fourth Division... Bastards"*. I get the impression, from the numbers milling around Edgeley Park a good half hour before kick-off, that there will be a big crowd today. A hell of a lot of the early millers seem to be Preston fans also, their crap start to the season not seeming a deterrent to a large number making the relatively short trip down the M61.

It's me, my dad and Martin again today, and we sit in the Cheadle End, which seems surprisingly full of the type of freebie kids who normally fill the Vernon Stand. Either this game is proving unusually popular with the youth of Stockport, or County's largesse is spreading such that one stand is not enough for the free ticket holders..

The match kicks off and we experience one of the best feelings for a supporter - an early goal. In the second minute, John Jeffers, on the left wing, gets in a superb cross with two defenders virtually inside his shorts, and Brett Angell powers in a header from about two yards. Yesssss. An early goal can often merely presage a high scoring game, in which your side's eventual victory is in no way guaranteed, but it can also mean that your team settles down and cruises to an easy win. Either way, a goal's a goal, and no one is going to complain about opening the scoring in the second minute.

There is a third possibility, however - that an early goal can in fact be the only goal, and the rest of the game can prove to be pretty nondescript as a result. This seems to be the case today, as Preston, struggling near the foot of the table, don't seem to have the ability to break down a County defence that seem content to hold the ball and wait for the opposition to make the running. Our attack, meanwhile, looks accomplished without ever looking really dangerous, and we reach half time with the score 1-0.

The low-key nature of the game continues in the second half, and is demonstrated by the fact that the second most significant moment of the game, after the goal (and, taking a wider view, arguably the *most* significant), occurs early in the second half, when Alun Armstrong is stretchered off with what seems worryingly like a bad leg injury. I didn't see the incident clearly, although it seemed to me that, in challenging for a high ball, he simply fell awkwardly. Certainly, there is no reaction from the County players, of the type you might expect after a bad foul. The nearest Preston player immediately signals for a stretcher, however, and our best player, face clenched in agony, is carried from the field.

It's a major blow. Despite what some blinkered idiots might think, the team plays better when Armstrong is on song. Indeed, if any player was ever destined for stardom, then Armstrong is he - I have never been so convinced about that with any previous County player. Oh sure, we've had people in my time who have gone on to play in the top division - Dean Emerson at Coventry, Mick Quinn at Newcastle, Jim Willis at Leicester to name but three (and, if I'm honest, the *only* three I can think of off the top of my head). However, even though those players stood out during their time at County, and it was no surprise when they made it to play at the top level, none of them convinced in the way Armstrong does. The fact that he's only 21 - and still standing out in a team of very few mugs - would also seem to indicate a remarkable footballing talent.

The rest of the half meanders its way towards the end. The electronic scoreboard eventually ticks down, and the schoolkids chant along in that intensely irritating way that shows they've little interest in the game itself - which, ironically, livens up as zero approaches. It's been a comfortable game for County, really, but as we head towards the final whistle, Preston begin to press, and there's a real danger that they could now sneak an undeserved draw.

I realise that I sound more than a little neurotic regarding getting away from football grounds (this could be because I *am* neurotic with regard to...), but I leave my seat and head down the aisles to hover by the exit, along with fifty or so others, ready for a dash to the car when the ref finally blows. We are well into the Armstrong-induced injury time, and Preston are on the attack. I cannot actually see County's goal from my corner, as my view is blocked by many other, taller, neck-craning fans, and a couple of stewards, whose realisation of the futility of such appeals doesn't stop them keeping up a constant cry of "can you leave the ground please? No standing in the aisles. *Can you leave the ground please?"*. Although I can't see the ball, there's a scramble in the County area, and then an almighty cheer. Shit, they've scored, is my first reaction, as arms are thrown up all around me, followed by instant realisation that these are County fans of course, and the ball must have been cleared. The amateur whistlers all around me are finally answered by the referee, and the tension ends with another win; the seventh in eight games.

Tuesday October 15th 1996. Luton Town (home).

No doubt the more desperately sad readers will have realised that tonight's game is the clash of the Hatters, both teams being saddled with that particularly quaint nickname. Stockport was once, apparently, the centre of the English hat-making industry (there is still a large hat manufacturers in the centre of town). I'm not sure why Luton share the nickname, however, and, to be frank, I couldn't give a toss.

It's been a clear and sunny day today, which translates into a fairly cold evening - the first really cold evening of the season. It'll get much worse than this, mind, before the season's out. Watching football in person is not for the faint hearted when winter begins to bite, as the temperature at Edgeley Park can approach that of the Arctic wastes in the depths of winter (at least I imagine so - never having been to the Arctic wastes in either the depths of winter or the height of summer. It gets bloody cold, is what I'm trying to say). With a team like County to watch, and warming wins thus never guaranteed, continued attendance in December and January tests all but the hardiest of souls, although one can, of course, resort to the fairly popular option of consuming a bellyfull of ale before the game. This has never been my chosen way of keeping warm, however, as although it does provide a tremendous degree of insulation (I've seen County fans leave the pub and watch the whole game in t-shirts on some of the coldest days of the year), you tend to be too pissed to even be aware there's a match taking place.

My dad and Martin are with me again tonight, although Martin slopes off to meet a couple of girls in the Cheadle End. Not wanting to play gooseberry, we decide to sit in the Vernon Stand, fancying a side-on view, and reasoning that there won't be thousands of freebie kids, it being a schoolday. Wrong. As we pass through the turnstiles, we are greeted by a sight which is how I would have imagined the scene at Rorke's Drift, were the charging Zulus to be replaced by English schoolkids. How irresponsible, I think, as the parent in me indignantly surfaces - bringing them to an evening game on a schoolday. In truth, I don't think it's irresponsible at all - I'm just miffed that I don't have the stand virtually to myself. How dare these kids be here? I've been coming to this ground, man and boy, for nigh on 24 years, and... I realise that I'm beginning to sound like a 60 year old Telegraph letter-writer, and so find a seat and concentrate on the game.

Unsurprisingly, Alun Armstrong isn't playing tonight. There was some talk in the local press about how he fancies his chances of being fit for the Blackburn Coca Cola Cup game next week, but I was talking to someone outside who stated that they'd heard from a club insider (they weren't prepared to say who, which, as the story is hardly one which would result in a sacking if the leaker's identity became known, renders the confidence a little less indubitable) that Armstrong will be out for weeks. However long our deficiency in the blond striker department proves to be, one fact remains - he'll be badly missed. I take some consolation from the fact that his absence, if it does mean that we play worse as a result, might bring it home to the people who criticise him how much he does in fact contribute. Then again, if people are too blinkered to see that anyway, they're hardly likely to be convinced of it when he's not on the field.

It's clear from the early exchanges that Luton are a good team. They look very quick and strong, which is usually a sign of a better team. Whenever we play a Premiership or First Division side in one of the cups, the immediate difference, regardless of the result, between the two teams, is the pace at which our opponents play the game.

Indeed, the question arises in my mind of how could Luton possibly have been the only team keeping us off the bottom of the table early season? As has already been established, we were *really* crap then, yet Luton must have been worse. The fact that they are now above us in the table, and playing us off the park tonight, means that their revival must have been much more stunning than ours; in rather the same way that Lazarus' re-appearance was slightly more impressive than any of Paul Daniel's "oh look, the lovely Debbie wasn't sawn in half after all" routines. Sure enough, after half an hour, they score. A right wing corner is met on the run by a Luton forward, and his header thumps the underside of the bar and bounces down into the goal.

County try hard, but Luton's superiority is clear, and they look the more likely to score another as the first half draws to a close. The kiddies helpfully remind us that half time is approaching, by counting down the electronic scoreboard once again. There is a tangible air of bemusement when they realise that play is continuing despite zero having been reached. Has no one ever explained the concept of injury time to these kids? Dear me, what *do* they teach them at these schools? (*"Dear Sir, I was watching a game of soccer at Edgeley Park the other night..."*)

Half-time does eventually arrive, and Luton are deservedly ahead. The break is the signal for a near riot, as the stewards are now unable to insist that the kids remain in their seats, and the youngsters take full advantage, running up and down the gangways, chasing, playing tag, and generally having the kind of fun they would never, ever have experienced simply sitting down and watching the football match. The rest of us - the older, worldly-wise County fans - sit or stand morosely, muttering glumly to each other until the teams re-emerge. We're losing, and we deserve to be.

County have obviously undergone one of those mystic half time team talks of my youth, however, as we start the second half like a different team. We are playing the ball around, tackling hard, pressing and creating chances. Just before the hour, this play receives the reward it deserves when a corner from the right is headed back by Jim Gannon, and Brett Angell, once again playing like a donkey, but in the right place at the right time, stoops to head the equaliser. I would imagine that there is probably a fair bit of cheering at this point, but such is the noise generated by the kids, increased several decibels when it's pointed out to them by their parents that County have scored, that I am rendered temporarily deaf.

The youngsters remain generally uninterested, sliding down the handrails in the aisles when they can escape the clutches of the stewards, and generally doing everything but watch the game. The high-pitched shrieking is more reminiscent of a swimming baths than a football match. I notice that one of the kids further along our row is drinking a vicious blue drink from a plastic bottle which looks suspiciously like my "Merimate" dandelion and burdock "flavour" drink from York. Is there a manufacturer, I wonder, that exists solely to create the crap that's sold in football grounds? More importantly, would these kids be less raucous if it weren't for the vicious colouring and sodium benzo-whatever that the drinks must be laced with? I seem to remember being pretty high myself after my drink at York, but I put that down to the fact that Brett Angell had just scored twice. I would normally be concerned for the lad who's chucking the artificial flavour and e-number cocktail down his neck, but as he's already left his seat about fifteen times - each journey necessitating me and my dad having to stand up to let the little sod past - I couldn't care less about his welfare. Indeed, it he keeps up his rate of departure from his seat, I'll probably strangle the little bugger myself.

County continue to play as well in the second half as Luton did in the first, and, indeed, have chances to take the lead. However, the final whistle goes with the score at 1-1, and, despite our second half pressure, it's quite a relief to escape from the game with a point. Our record now reads seven wins, one draw and one defeat in our last nine league and cup games. That said, such was our start to the season that we're still only about tenth. It'll take a hell of a run to get automatic promotion from this position; the play offs are a more realistic target. Whatever position we finally achieve, we could do with achieving it before May 3rd; we have to play these buggers in our last away game

Saturday October 19th 1996. Wycombe Wanderers (away).

Today's game is one of those which are the bane of a football fan's existence - ones which cause domestic upheaval.

For the last couple of years, my immediate family (my mum and dad, their five children, four spouses and seven grandchildren) have spent the New Year in a rented cottage in Bollington - a small town, seven or eight miles south of Stockport. As it's my sister Lisa's 30th birthday in a week or so, we also decided to have a weekend there this year to celebrate. Her birthday isn't actually until the 28th, which would have meant Walsall away, and not too much of a problem, but the cottage was booked up for that weekend, and so it's Wycombe away and more than a slight problem.

Give me my due, I did actually volunteer to miss it. Alright, I didn't volunteer very strongly (and I was alone in a locked room at the time I did the volunteering), but I did offer. It must have been the hangdog look and the tears in my eyes (thank God for that onion) that persuaded Anna, but I was eventually given permission. If I wasn't writing this book, I doubt whether my absence would have been tolerated quite so readily, although having said that, if I wasn't writing this book, I doubt whether I'd have even considered going to such a distant game in such circumstances anyway. As I've stated before, I consider myself to be less of an obsessive than a dedicated supporter. A fine distinction, you may feel, but one which means I would not normally go to Wycombe Wanderers on a day when my presence is required elsewhere.

The trip, however, will still necessitate careful planning. It's probably well over 200 miles to High Wycombe, and, although it's motorway all the way, I've got to plan it almost to the minute so that my absence will be kept to a minimum. I'm also on my own, as neither Martin or my dad are at the cottage today. One of my biggest problems, therefore, will probably be staying awake on the way home.

It's the longest drive to a football game I have ever undertaken, with the exception of our first visit to Wembley in 1992 for the final of the Autoglass Trophy against Stoke City. So excited was I at the thought of seeing County in a Wembley final that I decided to drive, taking my dad, Martin, my sister Claire and my cousin John (a County fan who used to take me when I was a kid) along for the ride. So knackered was I after driving back (our losing 1-0 to an offside goal didn't help) that I vowed never to drive that far to a game again. (We beat Burnley in the Northern final, incidentally. See, I told you we were always playing them).

However, needs must, and taking the coach would mean leaving Bollington for Stockport at about 9 o'clock, and getting back to the cottage at around 10. I reckon that driving non-stop, and putting my foot down, I can do the trip in about three hours each way, allowing for a bit of traffic. This would mean leaving at about noon, and getting back at a far more reasonable half seven or so - especially if the scoreline allows me to leave the ground just before the final whistle and thus avoid the traffic (which, I'm told, can be dreadful, as Adams Park is a Legoland-style industrial-estate ground at the dead end of a dead end road).

After all the planning, I eventually set off at about quarter to twelve, Anna having taken the kids into the town. I could have got away even earlier, but forgot to top up the oil and water, and have to spend five or ten minutes doing that. Like an idiot, I also forgot to top up with petrol as well, and so have to delay for a further few more minutes in Congleton.

At least I've blagged the Cavalier, and have thus got a working radio (if I'd contemplated making this trip in the Fiesta, I'd have probably had to set off yesterday). I listen to Five Live, which carries sports news, today dominated by the threatened PFA strike. As a left winger, I'm instinctively supportive of strikes per se, but it seems that in this instance, the PFA have a strong case anyhow. The people who run football these days are, as a breed, so greedy and self-serving that they seem to forget that football doesn't exist merely for the advertisers and the TV companies.

The reports, carry - presumably in the interests of "balance" - irritating vox pop reports from thicko gobshites who say things like "Well, some of these players get £15,000 a week. Why do they need to go on strike?" It strikes me that there's very little difference between idiot in the street and idiot in the Boardroom. What both type of person fails to understand is that most of the PFA's best work is in representing the little guy - the journeyman who's finished at thirty-five, and in many cases has no qualification or experience other than an ability to kick a ball around; precisely the kind of player who has always played for County, in other words. Added to that, and on a purely selfish note, I'm also reasonably supportive of any planned players' strike simply because it won't impinge on County; the only games affected being those that Sky are to show live.

Although the radio's interesting, then, it's still screamingly frustrating trying to get to the motorway. I can't really relax until I'm on the M6, and able, more or less, to drive at my own speed. It wouldn't be so bad if the country roads that take me there were empty - as it is, I'm stuck behind a car driven by Albert One-Gear, the Slowest Drive in the Whole Wide World. For the next five miles or so, I'm constantly sidling wide to attempt to overtake, only to shoot back in when I see the bend in the road, or the juggernaut, which is rapidly approaching.

Eventually, however, there is just enough of a straight clear bit to get past Albert, although, as so often happens, the idiot deliberately speeds up himself as I overtake. I mouth a couple of obscenities, as I zoom past, figuring that deliberately and slowly mouthing them, whilst making no actual sound, will make it easier for him to lip read than if I were to genuinely tell the WANKER to FUCK OFF. I'm not that far off the motorway, sadly, so that the gain in time the overtaking yields is minimal. I hit the motorway at just gone twenty past twelve.

Right, here we go. Twenty past twelve, and, what, 180 miles to go? Two and a half hours, so that's an average speed of... er... well three hours would be 60, so it's going to be higher than that. Hang on, two and a half hours is five half-hours, so 180 divided by five is, five threes are fifteen, leaves 3 so that's 30, five into thirty is six, so it's thirty-six, times two for the full hour - 72 miles an hour. I'm congratulating myself on my mental agility when I spot cars ahead turning on their hazard warning lights. Shit! Sure enough, we hit a massive jam at twenty-five to one, and my average speed is soon 0 mph.

Now this *is* frustrating. I can't really afford any major hold ups or I'll miss the kick off. Despite my screaming, lane weaving, and praying, however, I don't pass the roadworks just north of Stafford that have caused the jam until just before one o clock. Twenty five minutes of crawling, and my necessary average speed has shot up from 72 miles an hour to God knows what.

As I speed up again, I notice that there is a similar backlog on the opposite carriageway, heading north. It doesn't bode well for tonight, but at present all I'm concerned about is that it's gone one o'clock and I'm still north of Birmingham. Still, at least the motorway now seems cle... JESUS CHRIST! The hazard lights are winking at me again in the distance. I know what this is, though - it's not roadworks but sheer volume. A couple of motorways converge here, and traffic always grinds to a crawl. It's quarter past one and I'm once again inching along.

I seriously consider cutting my losses and heading back. The way things are at the moment, I'm almost certain to miss the kick off, and, having experienced before the sheer perversity of the god of football, I wouldn't be surprised to find myself trundling up to the ground at quarter to five and meeting the fans coming out. A completely pointless seven hour drive is not my idea of a fun Saturday at the best of times; combine that with a missed County game, and I would be almost suicidal. I think I might need a slash before long, as well.

Thoughts of giving up are soon rejected, however, when I leave the Brummie clog behind, and am quickly up to cruising speed. If I'm honest, this trip is actually infinitely less wearing than the one to Millwall, firstly because I've not got a Chubby Brown tape playing, and secondly because I now need to keep up a fair old lick, involving a degree of concentration which both keeps me awake and passes the time. It also helps that the radio is now playing Danny Baker's excellent lunchtime football phone-in show. However, I'm definitely going to have to relieve myself ere too long.

The M6 becomes the M42 which in a few miles becomes the M40. I'm on the final leg now; on the assumption that there are no major roadworks on the M40, I've got a clear run to Wycombe. It's still miles away, however - probably over a hundred - so, with less than an hour and a half to go, I am, sadly, going to have to break the law. An average of ninety should just about do it. I might even get to the ground before my bladder gives out.

Forty five minutes or so later and the two o' clock news starts. An hour to go (or, say, an hour and twenty to go; twenty minutes missed wouldn't be so disastrous). I still don't know how far it is to Wycombe, but I've kept up a steady ninety since Brum, so I should have made a fairly big hole in it. My need for a slash is now so acute, though, that I'm faced with a choice between stopping at the next services (Welcome Break 2 miles), trying to pee through the tiny hole into an empty Ribena carton whilst driving at ninety miles an hour, or wetting myself. I stop at the services.

It's busy, of course, so I can't park near the building, but I dash for the toilets like a Hollywood cop chasing the bad guys, scattering people before me, and dive into the gents. (Pointless, I know, when you consider that I'm saving, at most, two or three minutes by rushing like this, but by this point, I'm so caught up in the sense of urgency that rational thought has been left behind in the Staffordshire roadworks). It's ten past two by the time I shake off the drips and hurtle back to the car (I should, perhaps, point out here that it was about nine past two when I entered the toilets. I wouldn't like you to think that it takes me ten minutes to do a wee-wee, or anything). The physical relief is immense (indeed that *was* a Welcome Break), but I still haven't got a clue where I am, or of how far it is to the ground. The motorway still looks clear, however, so if I knew how far I had to go - and thus whether I was likely to make it - I would probably be able to relax. I try and clock the towns which the road signs indicate I'm passing on the opened map lying on the passenger seat, but it's a tricky exercise at the best of times; doing ninety, and occasionally - whoops, dearie me, sorry officer! - a hundred, it's impossible.

All of a sudden, a heavenly choir starts to sing. I look around to see why, and there it is - a sign for "High Wycombe", with a glorious "30" next to it. It's only *(only!)* twenty past two; I'm going to make it. Forty minutes for thirty miles. The sun's out, the radio is happily previewing this afternoon's games, the motorway's virtually empty, and I don't need a slash anymore. I'm going to enjoy this.

As if to enhance my pleasure, the motorway suddenly becomes a theme park. A group of hairy arsed (well, I assume so) bikers zoom past in formation, and, as I haven't slowed down appreciably, they must be doing about 120 at least. Then, passing an aerodrome, a biplane swoops down over the motorway, low enough to see the pilot clearly, before landing to my right. The sun's still out, the radio is burbling away happily to itself, High Wycombe's less than 20 miles away, and I feel that I only need to start singing *"Zippydee doo-dah"* for a gaggle of cartoon animals to appear on the dashboard. Half past two, "High Wycombe 17".

At quarter to three, I eventually leave the motorway. I know from my instructions, painstakingly typed out from the excellent "Supporter's Guide to Football Grounds" and sellotaped to the centre of the steering wheel, that I have about three miles to go. I travel a surprisingly traffic-free distance until I come to the roundabout at which I am to turn left to the ground. It's ten to three, and there is a worrying absence of supporters. It is *Wycombe* today...? I have a sudden thrill of dread as I picture the rest of the County support arriving at Preston, or wherever. Thankfully, it seems that the absence of fans is due to it being fairly late, and the road to the ground being fairly long; as I approach what must be Adams Park, I see reassuring groups of stragglers.

I park up on one of the industrial sites and pay a quid to a bloke standing nearby. I assume he was the attendant; he was certainly directing me into a space. He could simply have been a passer-by, of course, chancing his arm and now a quid richer - probably quite a lucrative scam, with away supporters not knowing any better. I must try that myself at Edgeley Park one day.

I scoot away from the car towards the ground. It's strange that, whilst I would, an hour or so ago, have accepted missing up to half an hour of the game as a reasonable circumstance, I now run like mad in order that I don't miss a single minute. Strange? Pathetic, probably. Either way, I pass through the turnstiles at precisely three minutes to three. I feel a sense of elation, of achievement. I've judged the journey to perfection, and, in doing so, have thus climbed my own personal Everest. Oh yes, and the game's about to kick off.

It's my first ever visit to Adams Park, which has, apparently, improved immensely in the last year. It's looks tidy enough from outside, but has three pitifully small, albeit neat, sides. It also has, however, a massive new two-tier stand built into the side of the hill which overlooks the ground. What I'm not impressed with, though, is the fact that a perfectly serviceable away terrace, which last season apparently cost £7 admission, has had seats bolted onto it, with the result that it now costs £10. This is nothing less than a scam. The club didn't *need* to put seats in there - the requirements of the Taylor Report mean that clubs only have to go all-seater in the Premier and First Divisions (and they get three years after promotion to achieve it anyway). What the club knew - and it was quite a cute move if you've got absolutely no morals whatsoever - was that not one team in the Second Division would bring enough fans to fill the 1,500 or so seats in the away end, so what was the point in providing terracing for 3,000? Why not chuck seats in? At £3 a shout more for each fan, they'll pay for themselves in less than a season, and then start bringing in the spondulicks thereafter. If they draw a big team in one of the cups, well then they've got the new stand to use as an overflow.

I'm starvingly hungry, so buy a burger from the refreshments hut. They're actually offering veggieburgers, so, coward that I am, I forego minced mad cow's testicles and opt for health. I get a nice surprise when, opening the packet once I've found a seat, the burger turns out to be a genuine one, packed full of real vegetables that you can actually see - sweetcorn, peas, carrots, something green, something red, something brown - rather than a soya-bean, imitation beef job. I get an even nicer surprise a minute or two later when Brett Angell runs onto a through ball from Tom Bennett and puts us one up.

Immediately we score, a phalanx of stewards moves forward towards the joyous County fans, aggression personified. They do nothing more than posturing, watch the fans celebrations menacingly for a minute or two, then crawl back to their corner. Which idiot instructed them that this was an effective form of crowd-control? What, precisely, were they trying to achieve? Stopping us storming the pitch and starting a riot at the other end? Preventing detonation of that tactical nuclear warhead we smuggled in? Warning us that enjoying ourselves is simply not an option, not even when we've paid a tenner into their masters' coffers?

Idiot behaviour like this from stewards really pisses me off, especially when their shiny yellow coats are plastered with something like "Acme Crowd Safety Services Ltd". Although I accept that stewarding represents a cost-effective alternative to policing, especially for lower division clubs, I cannot rid myself of the distaste I feel when yet another parasitical organisation dives in for profit on the back of football. Even worse, in the case of exhaustive stewarding, it could be argued that the money is being made on the back of tragedy, as the guidelines which led to greater numbers of stewards being required at football grounds came out of the same Taylor Report which allows clubs to exploit supporters by chucking in unnecessary plastic seats. Tragedy + Capitalism = Profit. It's a sick equation. Although I'm not entirely sure, I think County employ and train their own stewards rather than franchising the job out; their shiny coats aren't plastered with a company name. When you consider that County's stewarding is so successful that, on more occasions than otherwise, there are absolutely no plods inside Edgeley Park on match days, it makes you wonder why other clubs don't do the same, instead of happily lining the pockets of these parasites.

We dominate the ten minutes or so after the goal, but then the home team assume control, and, following a couple of goal line clearances from County defenders, we're extremely lucky to reach the break still ahead. Socialising amongst the 200 or so away fans whilst the teams are off the field, I bump into Louie from the Fingerpost again. Once more, he's got a joke for me, although this one's so obscene, I couldn't possibly repeat it here (the fact that it involves body piercing, of an intimate nature, is probably all you need to know). Needless to say, I laugh like a drain, and am still sniggering when the second half starts.

Again, we dominate the first ten minutes or so, and again Wycombe then assume control. They force corner after corner, and, although we have chances of our own, it seems incredible that we're still ahead. Ten minutes to the final whistle, and the time is approaching when I am going to have to make good my departure. As I had feared when planning this day - and a potential pre-final whistle departure - a 0-1 scoreline, although great in one sense, as it means County are winning, is an uncomfortable one in terms of my planned rapid exit. Andy Mutch didn't help, ten minutes ago, missing a great chance to make it 2-0.

A cross from the right wing evaded the keeper, and Mutch, completely unmarked, had only to nod it into the net, as easily as if he were greeting a slight acquaintance. He was already clearly celebrating the goal, however, before he'd even made contact, which was clearly a contributory factor to him making a complete balls of it and heading wide.

I suppose I'm going to have to risk it. What'll be agonising is if I hear a cheer. Was it us or them? It was a loud cheer, but then again, the away end is the nearest. Hearing on the radio that we've only drawn would be agony. I *could* always stay until the final whistle, and then run like merry hell to the car, but I'm not that close, and what if I do get caught in the traffic? They won't be too chuffed back at home if I don't return until gone nine...

It looks like I'm going to be left to make the agonising decision when Brett Angell puts me out of my misery by scoring his, and County's, second. Following a break down the right, he gleefully heads home a Durkan cross, into the goal right in front of us. Get in!! After a brief mutual celebration between team and supporters, and a further bout of glaring from the stewards, I glance at the electronic scoreboard. "Wanderers 0 Visitors 2 86." That'll do. I hare off through the exit gate (thank God there's not a lock-in) and am away.

There's one problem in County getting a late second - lots of the home fans have also streamed away, but I dodge between them, and am soon at the car, at the expense of being completely knackered. Coughing and wheezing, I unlock the door, clamber in, and, pausing only to re-insert the anti-theft device and flick on the radio for the scores, I'm on the move just after quarter to five.

I take the road indicated by the "M40" sign, and zoom away. After five minutes or so, I'm congratulating myself on my speed of escape (and the fact that the radio has confirmed the game ended 2-0, and Wycombe didn't storm back with three injury time goals) when I realise, with mounting dread, that I don't recognise the road I'm on. The dread turns to horrified realisation as I cross a bridge over the motorway - the bleeding motorway I'm supposed to be on! Arrrrgh! I do a quick three pointer down someone's driveway and head back towards Adams Park, turning the air blue with my cussing. Of all the stupid... Why the fuck didn't you... Oh, for God's sake...!

I travel virtually all the way back to the ground, but such was my early and rapid departure that I'm still, thankfully, in time to beat the majority of the football cars. I turn back onto the road that leads away from the ground, realising my mistake as I recognise the turning I should have taken. I get caught in more motorway-bound traffic than I probably would have done had I taken the correct turning, but it's not too bad, and I'm back on the M40 at just after five. This is where the real pleasure starts, after an away victory, as you listen to the other scores and reports coming in on the radio, and the post-match analysis starts in earnest. By the time David Mellor's "606" show starts, I'm well on the way home, and am serenaded by the dulcet tones of both the moonlighting MP and his callers through the Birmingham junction (no traffic there), and the Staffordshire roadworks (slow down to about 30 through the cones, but in comparison with what I endured on the way down, a veritable grand prix), until, almost before I realise it, I'm turning off the M6 and heading for Congleton.

I eventually arrive back "home" at the cottage at about ten to eight. It's been another hectic day, but, as a result - and because of *our* result - it has absolutely flown by. And we won again. My kids greet me like the Prodigal Son. Aw, that's nice.

Tuesday October 22nd 1996. Blackburn Rovers (away) (Coca Cola Cup R3).

Well, tonight's the big one, as they say ("they", presumably, being people who cannot help but use the most banal of clichés). Or is it? Blackburn at the moment are not a good team. Despite being Premier League champions the season before last, they are currently anchored to the bottom of the table, without a league win so far. Additionally, they have lost the services of Messrs Shearer and Dalglish, and give every impression of a team where confidence is at rock bottom - hardly the state of mind required to play a tricky cup tie against opposition on the crest of a wave, and with 4,500 or so noisy fans expected to cheer them along. If we're not already favourites with the bookies tonight, then we probably should be.

County have got a record of giant killing second to none in this competition, as I have already indicated elsewhere. Away victories against First/Premier Division opposition are nothing new to us, having experienced such delight on no fewer than two previous occasions - Crystal Palace in 1972, and Sunderland in 1980. We also should have won at Old Trafford in 1978, and were only deprived of victory by staggeringly incompetent refereeing that is still talked about in Stockport to this day.

The game was played during the period we were managed by ex-City player Mike Summerbee; a man whose dislike of the red half of the city was thought to be more than apocryphal. Astonishingly, as this was the 70s - a period when County were notable only for being probably the crappiest team in the history of the world - we dominated the whole game, and were unlucky to go in at half time a goal down. We continued in the second half, however, and took the lead when United's hapless keeper Paddy Roche brought down our star striker Stuart Lee, and captain Alan Thompson wellied home the resulting penalty. Delight turned into delirium a few minutes later when Terry Park robbed Greenhoff (not sure which one) on the halfway line and took the ball all the way into the United area before slotting it under Roche. We were 2-1 ahead, playing United off the field at Old Trafford, and there were only ten minutes left. Even in those days, however, United were sporting losers, and Gordon McQueen was sent off for taking a wild kick at County winger Derek Loadwick. Time ticked away; with two minutes left, we were on the verge of the greatest upset in cup history, and Mike Summerbee was kneeling on the ball and theatrically wiping his brow. We were playing Manchester United off the park at Old Trafford, *and our players were taking the piss.*

Referee Peter Willis then broke the hearts of every County supporter in the ground with two amazingly bad decisions. Firstly, he gave an indirect free-kick against County keeper Mike Rogan for time-wasting, which was deflected home. He then awarded a penalty against Alan Thompson, who had just been kicked by Joe Jordan, and who had reacted by kicking him back. United duly scored from the spot, and County were left with a lap of honour, a sense of injustice that has faded over the years not one iota, and an absolute hatred of a slaphead Geordie referee who didn't seem aware of the rules of the game.

I leave straight from work, Anna having taken the kids to her mum's, and pick up my dad, Martin and one of Martin's mates. We leave in good time to make the short trip to Blackburn, along the M63 and M61. We've draped a County scarf out of the car window, as do so many travelling supporters; whether or not it's hanging out again on the way back depends on whether or not we've avoided defeat. The journey passes quickly enough, with no hold-ups, and I'm able to park the car in a side street a few hundred yards from Ewood Park, and - all together now - *facing back the way we came.*

We don't go into the stadium immediately, preferring instead to soak up the atmosphere outside. There seem to be a hell of a lot of County fans about; there must be about forty coaches alone, parked in formation in the newly-flattened car park behind the away end. Milling around and nodding to the odd acquaintance outside the ground, I pause as I hear the teams announced over the tannoy inside. Armstrong's playing! My immediate reaction is excitement, followed almost instantly by worry. Is he fully fit? What if he well and truly knackers his ankle tonight, by rushing back too early, and ends up being out until Christmas? It's a big gamble and, surely, one we don't need to take for a game like this. We're not going to win the Coca Cola Cup, regardless of what we may achieve tonight, so why risk it?

There is a massive queue of County fans waiting to get in, but the Blackburn administration, in their infinite Premiership wisdom, have decreed that three turnstiles should suffice. Needless to say, the queue thus shuffles forward only extremely slowly. Hurry up and get inside, I scream silently at a group of lads in front who seem more inclined to perform for the crowd - laughing, pushing and cracking painfully unfunny jokes at each other - than getting through the turnstiles.

Our tickets are for the top tier of one of the three massive new stands built at Ewood in the last couple of years. We're in the one behind the goal to the right of the main stand, and to get up to our level necessitates climbing more flights of stairs than I have ever climbed before at a football ground. I get my ticket checked by the steward at the bottom of the stairwell and emerge into the stand.

Up here the atmosphere - at least in the away end where we are situated - is electric. There is, even amongst all the noise, a palpable air of excitement, and anticipation. There's no fear, of the type I would normally experience at a Premier club's ground - the fear that we'll lose by five or six goals. All that I feel is confidence and expectation. We find our seats - high up, almost on the back row. It's almost like being at the cinema, as the overhanging stand roof and the tightly-packed County fans offer an almost pitch-black border to the brightly illuminated patch of pitch we can see ahead.

Almost immediately, the taunting of the home fans starts: "Shearer's fucked off home" to the tune of "Football's coming home". I'm sure we're not the first to sing that this season - and I'm absolutely positive we won't be the last - but it's amusing nonetheless. The chanting turns into a deafening roar, however, as the teams emerge. We're wearing a yellow and blue kit tonight - a change which has been forced on us by the fact that our home shirt is blue and our away shirt is white - both colours sharing space on Blackburn's shirts. It reminds me of the kit of a national team - Romania, is it, or Sweden?

As the players line up for the kick off, I suddenly realise - and what a time to realise it - that, having not had any tea, I'm extremely hungry. I decide to risk missing any early goals, and quickly nip down into the bowels of the stand for a pie. The blackboard tells me that a meat and potato specimen will set me back £1.45, which is overpriced, although not unexpected - we are in a football ground, after all. I buy a Mars bar as well, which sets me back an incredible 70p; I've already handed over the £2.15 requested before the mental arithmetic kicks in. Actually, I should be fair and point out that it is a "king size" Mars Bar. It makes me laugh that the catering people presumably think they're giving themselves a watertight excuse for when fans protest at the price *"How* much?! Seventy pee for a bloody Mars Bar!!? They're thirty pee in the shops!!"

"Ah, but it is a king size one."

"Oh, yes, alright, fair enough. Sorry."

I leap back up the stairs to my seat. It's pretty closely packed, and, as there are four empty places in front of us, I step forward and watch the game from there, in relative comfort. The deafening cries of "Davey Jones' blue and white army" ring out all around, and County take inspiration from the noise, starting confidently, and keeping Blackburn's forwards at bay. The home team have a couple of early corners, but they come to nothing, and gradually County begin to take control.

My dad points out from the row behind, however, that Armstrong is limping badly, and sure enough, Andy Mutch is warming up on the touchline. This is ridiculous. I feel only anger towards Dave Jones: what on earth was he thinking, bringing Armstrong back too soon? And in a game that doesn't matter as well! Armstrong himself seems reluctant to leave the action, however, and is soon running without a limp, although it still seems to me that he's not running at full pelt.

It doesn't matter too much, however, as we are giving as good as we get, and the defence is holding firm. We're also looking dangerous from set-pieces, especially the long throws that captain Mike Flynn launches from either wing. He seems to get more distance here than he would at home, because the gap between the stands and pitch at Ewood Park is wide - affording him a longer run up than he would normally get.

In the 20th minute, an attack down the right brings another throw, and Flynn trots across. He launches a huge bomb into the Blackburn area, to where Angell is waiting. He doesn't seem to get a touch, but his presence is enough for Sherwood, in goal, to attempt to punch the ball instead of catching it. I don't see too clearly what happens then, but the ball loops into the air, in slow motion, as though Sherwood's punch only sliced it - or perhaps Angell did get a touch. Whatever caused the ball to deflect, however, has caused it to deflect in an arc, floating back over the keeper's head and into the net. It takes a second or two for us to work out what has happened, and then pandemonium breaks out. We've scored! And who gives a toss how it happened? The County players are trotting back to their marks, with the slightly embarrassed air which goes with not knowing who to congratulate, and the Rovers players are slumped in dejection. One nil to County.

Rovers seek out the equaliser and have a five minute period of pressure that almost brings a goal. Their winger shoots just wide from distance - although I would have thought Paul Jones had it covered - and a blond midfielder I recognise as ex-Man City player Gary Flitcroft (the name "FLITCROFT" across the back of his shirt was a slight clue) brings a superb save out of the keeper.

County weather the storm, however, and almost go further ahead when Jim Gannon just fails to repeat his headed goal from Bramall Lane. Nevertheless, when the half time whistle blows, we're well worthy of our lead. All we need to do is defend it for 45 minutes longer and we're through.

Sadly, however, the County players start the second half as though they haven't read the script. Instead of defending the lead, we storm forward in wave after wave of attacks, and are desperately unlucky not to score again. Tom Bennett has a shot deflected into the arms of Flowers, Lee Todd beats two defenders and hits the bar, and Chris Marsden breaks through and has a shot from the edge of the six yard box blocked by the keeper.

Rovers again attempt to get back into the game, but again they are foiled by County's confident defence. This is epitomised by Lee Todd standing on the penalty spot and coolly chesting a cross from the left wing back into the arms of Paul Jones. Todd is playing outstandingly well, and this piece of skill ranks with anything else seen on the pitch tonight.

I pause amidst our dominance, and wonder whether we are actually playing so well, or is it because I'm biased? It's hard to get an overall picture of a game like this because you're so involved, but on occasions when we've played so well in the past, the following day's newspapers confirm what we thought at the time - oh yeah, that's right, we *did* dominate. All I ever tend to remember from such games is the overwhelming tension.

Despite their best efforts to equalise, Blackburn look a side low on confidence. They seem reluctant to advance the ball into County's area, relying instead on shots from distance, some of which are embarrassingly inaccurate. County, meanwhile, have pressure of their own, but as the final minutes approach - and, amazingly, Armstrong *has* lasted the full game - we seem content to defend the win.

Two minutes before the final whistle, a couple of County fans three rows in front of me stand up and each take a foot long tube out of their jackets. They hold them aloft and each pull a tag on the side. Immediately, we are bathed in blindingly bright light and shrouded by billowing red smoke. The effect from the other stands must be impressive - from three rows behind, it's dazzling, in every sense. I'm not a party-pooper - I think it's a fantastic move, and adds greatly to the celebratory atmosphere - but the fact remains that we're only 1-0 up, and the light is so bright I can't see the pitch, so I'm reduced to shielding my eyes from the glare. The stewards (surprise, surprise) wade in and fight the lads for the flares, thus causing far more of a fire hazard than if they were just allowed to continue holding them under supervision. Coppers wade in as well, and I presume the lads are arrested, although I don't actually see them carted out (I don't see anything much, so bright is the illumination). The stewards attempt to stamp the flares out on the concrete floor, but have no joy, and only succeed in causing even more smoke to issue forth. They really would have been better advised to just let the lads continue holding the flares until they'd burnt themselves out, and then, if they must, have nicked them. As I've indicated before, however, when has common sense ever been part of the job description for football ground steward?

Back on the pitch, County are holding on doggedly. Blackburn are trying desperately to get an equaliser, but their attacks are still limited to inaccurate shots from distance; when they do get into the box, they are tackled by County defenders, or Paul Jones simply catches their crosses with ease. All eyes are fixed to the ref, and the mighty cheer starts as, whilst peering at his wrist, he raises the whistle to his lips. We've won.

We give the players, half a dozen or so of whom have, strangely, stripped to the waist (perhaps wearing the colours of an international team confused them and they were attempting to swap shirts) a tremendous ovation. Even in the midst of this, however, there is a distinct air of it being less of a shock than other games; we were almost expected to win. Possibly because the goal was so mad, there's also a slight lack of euphoria. It seems not so much an incredible win as a job well done.

We finally leave our seats, and trot down the stairs to loud and prolonged chants of "Harford's on the dole" (Shearer's long been forgotten). It seems a touch insensitive, to say the least, to be gloating about the discomfort of the manager of the club you've just beaten, but the wit behind the adaptation of the Shearer chant can't be denied. In any case, as one Blackburn fan outside the stand growls "I bloody hope so", I get the impression that the chant is less of an irritant for the home support than it might otherwise have been.

I jog quickly back to the car ahead of the others, where I learn from Radio Five that it was actually a Sherwood own goal that gave County the win. I hope that doesn't mean that the shine will be taken off, with people thinking that the only goal of the game being freaky means that the win must also have been a fluke. We've missed the match report, so I flick around the dial until I find Radio Flat Cap and Whippet, where Lancashire-born ex-England player Paul Mariner is hosting a phone-in show. We listen to a few callers, but find it strangely unsatisfying, as if we're intruding on private grief. It's not the longest of journeys home, however, and who needs the radio when we're being serenaded by the music of the car horns, from County fans who spot the scarf we again hung out of the window (once we were safely clear of the departing Blackburn fans)?

After I've dropped my dad and Martin off at home, and Martin's mate in Offerton, I try to reflect, rationally, on how good a win tonight's was. If I'm honest, it was less of a noteworthy performance than Sheffield United at Bramall Lane - or even Millwall at the New Den for that matter; Blackburn's confidence is so low. That said, it's difficult to overstate the feat that a Second Division team winning at the ground of Premier League opposition represents, no matter how much deep doo-doo the Premier team are currently in. It's turning into one hell of a season, yet, cup success apart, we seem to have become anchored at tenth place in the league following a successful run - of six wins and a draw in eight league and cup games - which will, knowing County, be bound to end with a mini-run of defeats. We need more league success where we can get it, and that means another win - or at least a draw - in a far more important game against Walsall on Saturday.

Saturday October 26th 1996. Walsall (away).

Wednesday's papers were indeed full of reports of our win over Blackburn, but more because of Ray Harford's increasingly tenuous grasp onto his employment than of any praise for our performance - as I've said, it was hardly viewed as a shock. Sure enough, later in the week, Harford did indeed resign, the humiliation of defeat by Stockport County, of all teams, being the final straw.

The draw for the 4th round was made on Sky on Wednesday night (and, yes, I did perform the phone receiver held up to the telly speaker trick again) and gave us possibly the worst tie we could have received: West Ham away. A slightly less important draw (although arguably more important in the sense that we may actually have a chance of winning the competition) was also made during the week: the first round of the Auto Windscreens Shield will see us travel to Doncaster on December 10th.

As I set off - in the Fiesta, sadly - it strikes me that the season's become incredibly condensed, in the way it does when you go to every game. Today's game is the 20th in the space of 10 weeks, which represents a hell of a commitment; the famous win at Sheffield United seems more like three months ago than one.

Today's journey is probably the longest I've made in this car, so, although I've only got to travel probably about a third of the distance I drove to Wycombe last week, I set off a mere 10 minutes later, at noon. I also need petrol, but the real reason for the early start is that I'm expecting the same motorway hold-ups as last week. Even so, three hours is a ridiculously large amount of time to allow for a seventy-odd mile journey, but what the hell? If I arrive in plenty of time, I'll go for a pint.

Again, I've typed out instructions from the "Supporters' Guide": "M6 Junction 9, blah, blah, blah, left, right, left, left, bingo" (I'm paraphrasing here). The Bescot Stadium is, apparently, one of the easiest grounds in the country to find, lying just at the side of the M6, and within spitting distance of that bizarre, wedge-shaped

RAC building that overlooks the motorway.

Forgetting which car I'm in, I hit 75 soon after joining the motorway, but the noise of the engine is enough to persuade me that 60-65 is a speed more conducive to mental wellbeing. I don't mind, though - it's a fine sunny day, and I've got ages to make Walsall. I might as well relax and enjoy - insofar as you can enjoy a motorway drive in a tin can like this - the journey

On the M56 which joins the Stockport M63 with the southbound M6, I pass what used to be my old school, St Augustine's Boys Grammar (I say "used to", as it's now a housing estate). I was never more than an adequate schoolboy footballer myself (and "adequate"'s probably pitching it a bit high if I'm honest), although one or two lads in my class I remember as being pretty good. One of them in particular, Johnny Maher, was a decent player, who, I believe, was even offered trials with a First Division club. Somewhat strangely, he decided not to pursue every schoolboy's dream of becoming a footballer, preferring instead to change his surname to Marr and becoming an international rock star, along with another classmate, Andy Rourke, and a bloke called Morrissey. There's nowt so queer as folk, as they say up here.

I can't quite remember when it was I first realised I was no good at football - around the age of 7 or 8, I should imagine. I was a regular for St Bernadette's Primary School, although filling in at the less than glamorous position of left-back was probably more due to there being not many more than eleven boys who could even kick a ball, rather than any skill I might have possessed. My brief footballing career ended when I left school, and I don't think I've kicked a ball in anger since I was about 18.

Just after passing my old school site, I overtake a fully-laden taxi on the way to Manchester Airport, and thence presumably to sunnier climes (or at least hotter - today's bright sun would make for an extremely pleasant journey if it wasn't so noisy). On the face of it, they're lucky swine, zooming off on holiday whilst all I've got to look forward to on Monday is work, but they aren't going to see County play Walsall, are they? The weather's pleasant, and I'm on my way to the football - who cares if I'm in a tinny old shed, and am being overtaken by more cars than I manage to pass myself? The cassette player seems to have decided to work again, so I've even got my "driving music tape" - the Lightning Seeds and REM - to enhance the pleasure.

I pass through Lymm at twenty five to one, and am soon on the M6, heading south. A touch of rain clears to bright sun, and a godawful smell of cow shit blasts in through the air vents. This evaporates (or whatever it is bad smells do) soon enough, however, and I seem set fair for Walsall.

Around one o'clock, I pass yet another of my educational establishments,

Saturday Night and Thursday Morning

Keele University (or at least Keele services, which amounts to very much the same thing). Ironically, at a time when most fans, if anything, might normally be expected to attend fewer games than otherwise, my attendance increased for the two years (season 1982-83 and 1983-84) I was there before they found me out. I still went to all the home games, but student railcards meant that all of a sudden, away games were a cheap option. In case there are any students reading this in their McDonald's tea-break (or if Burger King's a bit slack and they've had to clock off), and scorning the ridiculous concept of a student with disposable income, can I just reassure them that these were greatly different times. Grants, whilst not over generous, were not frozen; railcards offered a genuine half-price, on all journeys; admission to football matches was usually less than two quid; and unicorns gambolled and frolicked in sun-dappled fields all over the land.

After failing at Keele, I eventually picked up and glued back together the shattered pieces of my higher education by completing a part-time degree at Manchester University, over the years 1986-1992 - a period which spanned County's recent renaissance as the current Chairman took over from the previous regime following a brief power-struggle. I was at the University when one of the darkest episodes of the discredited previous County administration occurred - a Coca Cola Cup tie with Sheffield Wednesday which stills stands as a breathtaking monument to boardroom incompetence.

County had made the worst start to a season in living memory (and that's saying something, when you're talking about a Stockport County side of the 80s), yet had managed to get through to the League Cup second round, and had drawn Sheffield Wednesday. The first leg at Hillsborough ended in a 3-0 defeat, yet the idiotic County hierarchy decided, in their infinitely small wisdom, that the travelling hoards from over t'Pennines would not be able to be accommodated within the confines of Edgeley Park, and switched the second leg to Manchester City's cavernous Maine Road. To add insult to injury, the equally idiotic police decreed that County fans should be given the away end - an open, rainswept corner between the Kippax and the Platt Lane stand - and kept behind after the final whistle had blown on a 7-0 victory for Wednesday. Me? I was on a bus to the University when the rest of the fans were heading for Maine Road, joining the County fans' boycott that kept the final attendance down to a measly 2,089 It wasn't the only time that a football club had displayed arrogance, lack of foresight, bloody-mindedness, and downright stupidity, but it was probably the worst example we've ever had at County. For a Board to display all those characteristics at once was simply breathtaking. It was the only time I, and I suspect many others, have ever joined in a boycott of a game I would otherwise have attended.

I hit the Staffordshire roadworks crawl just after one o'clock, but am expecting it, so feel mellow enough. I do still have two hours to get to the Bescot Stadium. Nevertheless, out of sheer force of habit as much as anything else, I lane hop, trying to gain a yard or two's advantage. It soon becomes clear, however, that the lane I leave is destined to always then become the quickest moving, so I shuffle out wide and stay in the overtaking (overtaking - ha!) lane, from where I log the first County scarf car at ten past one. In doing do, however, I lose concentration and almost ram the car in front.

After half an hour or so of crawling, I see a sign for roadworks ahead - 2 miles. It's clearly going to be a much longer delay than last week, but what really gets me is that I know from the trip to Wycombe that the roadworks are only in one lane. There isn't even a contraflow: it's merely a question of three lanes merging into two, so why the bloody hell do we keep coming to a dead halt? I'm getting more and more anxious the longer we're stuck.

I look at my watch. Just gone quarter to two. I've been stuck now for 40 minutes - quarter of an hour longer than last week, and I sense that I'm nowhere near the end of the jam. As if in confirmation, a sign then crawls into view: "Delays Possible"! You Don't Fucking Say!! The next sign is slightly more encouraging - "Roadworks 1 Mile". I guess that I must have already crawled about ten miles, so I should only be stuck for another five minutes or so.

Sure enough, after a final delay of 45 minutes, I'm underway again. It's ten to two, and I still should make kick off fairly easily. I relax and start to enjoy the journey again. I used to dream about this kind of freedom as a kid - being able to drive where I wanted, when I wanted, across the country to follow County. My parents never had a car when I was young, so outings - and later County matches - were always on public transport, with timetables, routes and departure points fixed and immovable. It's strange, but now I actually have the freedom and resources to be able to do exactly what I once dreamt of doing, I don't appreciate it one little bit.

Freedom, my arse. I grind to another halt at two o'clock. Presumably, this is the Birmingham clog, which is worrying to say the least, as I'm still two junctions away from where I'm supposed to leave the motorway. I come to a distressingly dead stop at five past two. At ten past two, I'm crawling again, and I've gone right round my tape. I re-commence the lane hopping, like a madman, trying to gain an extra few yards each time. The time is now twenty past two, and it seems as if that ridiculously early departure might turn out to have been cutting it a bit fine.

At twenty-five to three, we've edged towards the junction before the one which I know is the best one for the ground. As this one is actually signed "Walsall", however, I wonder whether I should get off here and head for the ground from the town. We move another hundred yards in the next five minutes.

Saturday Night and Thursday Morning

Yes. I leave the motorway, and head for Walsall. It turns out to have been the correct move, as, after fannying around the town centre for a bit, I head back out in what I hope is the right direction. Yippee! I see first of all a sign for "Bescot Stadium", followed by the RAC building itself half a mile or so away. I let out a great cathartic scream of joy.

The football traffic is clearly being directed, so I join what looks like the correct queue, and eventually find myself approaching the ground, which is in the middle of a fussy retail park. It costs a ridiculous £2 to park the car, but with time running out, I don't really have much choice. I pull into a space, walk to the away end and clock the time as I arrive at the turnstiles as ten to three. It's taken me almost as long to get to Walsall as it did to get to bloody Wycombe. It's funny, though - because I'm here, and on time, I find it hard to get worked up. All my road rage of half an hour ago has simply evaporated like so much steam through my ears. I pay my £10 (Walsall are as cute as Wycombe when it comes to ripping off away supporters), and go inside.

The teams are announced, and Alun Armstrong is out. This makes me almost as angry as the hold ups on the motorway. What the hell was the point in risking him for the Blackburn game, if it meant he could well not make the following Saturday? We constantly hear football manager-speak which informs us that the league is more important than the cup, the cup is a bonus, at the end of the day all credit to our opponents concentrate on the league Brian, yet here's Dave Jones playing a guy in a meaningless (in the long-term) game, which has cost us his services for at least the following league game, and possibly more.

The game starts to the echoey noise of the players' shouts, emphasised by the sparse crowd and the enclosed ground. County have chances, but Walsall are dominating. Just before half time, they get the goal their play deserves, but in a highly controversial manner. The referee - alone in the ground, it seems - decides that Brett Angell, back "helping" the defence, has climbed all over a Walsall attacker, and gives the home team a penalty, which they duly despatch. Soon afterwards, the ref blows for half-time, and leaves the field surrounded by protesting County players.

The referee's decision is bad enough, but it is then pointed out to me by someone with a programme that he is none other than ex-player Steve Baines - a guy who received a fair bit of media attention a couple of years ago, by obtaining accelerated promotion up the referee's greasy pole, in an attempt to inspire other ex-pros to take up officiating. All very laudable, I'm sure, but the amazing thing is that, as the programme states, he used to play for Walsall! No one amongst the travelling support is suggesting that he's biased (like hell they're not); it seems highly strange, however, that the authorities won't let you referee a game within

30 miles of your home town, yet you can take charge of a game involving one of your ex-clubs.

My indignation is diluted a little by hearing over the tannoy a message which, come May, will have been announced at every ground in the Second Division bar Edgeley Park. A group of fans have decided to write to all the away grounds asking for a dedication for one of their mates, Peter Collins; the twist being that they started with his age being in the late seveties, and add a year on at each successive ground. The tannoy announcers get cheesier and cheesier the "older" he gets.

I also hear at half time that not only will we have to pay £18 to see County at Upton Park, but that a club official at a supporters' meeting in the week said that should we get a replay (not beyond the realms of possibility, given our current form), County will be charging the same for the Edgeley Park game. This would normally be dismissed as a ridiculous rumour, but such is County's current enthusiasm for ripping fans off wherever possible, it has the ring of truth

The second half starts, and County, fuelled, no doubt, by indignation at the referee, charge out of their blocks in search of the equaliser. Walsall, however, playing in a manner which belies their lowly league position, continue to look dangerous on the break. Thus continues the rest of the match, with the result that County look as though they're going to have to settle for a referee-effected defeat.

As the match moves beyond ninety minutes, however, County's attacks assume an air of desperation, and Walsall are forced to defend deep. It doesn't seem to do us any good, though, as the injury time minutes tick by. It must be in the third or fourth minute of this added time that County launch another attack down the left. The ball finds Chris Marsden, who hits a curling left-foot cross into the box. It evades everyone, including the keeper, until it reaches the far post where Kieron Durkan is charging in to bundle it home. **"Yeeeeeeaaaaarrrrrrrgggggghhhhhh!"** I shout (or words to that effect). Would you believe it, we've done it again. The bloke behind me doesn't believe it. "Get in! Get in! Get in!" he shouts, over and over again. It is in, mate, it is in. We've done it again.

The whistle goes and I hurry to the car, still hardly able to believe that we've pinched another last minute goal. Disbelief doesn't prevent me being elated however. As I edge my car into the departing traffic, I'm not even fazed by a bloke at my side steadfastly refusing to let me enter the flow, staring ahead, grim faced. Must be a Walsall fan. Hahahahaa, mate - go ahead. Have your 13 foot advantage. One-all, pal! Hahahahaaaa!! Yet another crucial last minute-er! You could almost feel embarrassed about this... Naahhh. We had lots of pressure in the second half, which deserved a goal anyway, and this bloke's being petty and small-minded about not letting me in. Last minute goal, you tosser. Ha ha haaa!

I'm on the motorway again just after five. I realise we're getting dangerously close to "Reliant Robin owners flashing their lights at each other in recognition" territory here, but I perform a pretty dangerous, wobbly, put- scarf- in- window- with- left- hand- whilst- driving- with- right manoeuvre, which I probably wouldn't have bothered with had we lost. But we didn't - we drew! Ha ha haaa. The scarf makes an alarming whacking noise on roof of the Fiesta that I didn't notice in the Cavalier on Tuesday. It's only a garish piece of blue white and red acrylic, but it sounds as though it's going to punch a hole through the tinny roof of my tinny car at any moment. I don't care, though. I'm getting hoots of recognition from other elated County fans as they speed past me, and we scored an equaliser in injury time. Ha ha haaa!

By the time I reach the roadworks, I've calmed down a touch, and the traffic flies through with no need for any outside lane jiggery-pokery. I arrive home at three minutes before half six. The journey there took almost three hours; the journey back just over an hour and a half. I get home to find out from Teletext the outcome of the third cup draw of the week - the FA Cup - which was made at ten past five, and which I couldn't hear because the radio in the Fiesta is knackered. Amazingly, we've drawn Doncaster again, although this time we're at home. It's not a bad draw - at the same stage last season, we won 5-0 against a Lincoln team who were in roughly the same position in the league that Donny are now. With our current form, that should be a passage to round two, especially if we enter the last minute on level terms. Ha ha haaaa!

Tuesday October 29th 1996. Chesterfield (home).

Last night's weather forecast was for gales, but any wind there might have been seems to have died down, which means, sadly, that there will be no repeat of a renowned game in County folklore - against Cambridge, I think - which took place in the early eighties.

On that particular night, there was a gale blowing which I still find hard to believe wasn't strong enough to cause the game to be postponed. Edgeley Park, before the new Cheadle stand was built, had two open ends, and as the ground lay roughly in an east-west direction, the prevailing wind tended to be funnelled between the two large stand roofs. This not only made the ground one of the coldest in the country, but meant that there was, at times, a distinct advantage in attacking the Railway End.

County, presumably, won the toss (I cannot envisage anyone winning the toss and being stupid enough to choose to play against the wind in the second half), and twenty one players spent most of the first half in the County penalty area. Cambridge managed to scramble two goals in, but there was a sense that they hadn't cashed in quite enough; I certainly have never been so convinced in my life that we could overturn a 2-0 half time deficit. My optimism was well-founded, as three second half strikes from Sword (pen), Brown and Hodgkinson gave us a 3-2 win, with all the game's five goals, unsurprisingly, being scored at one end. The writing was on the wall for Cambridge from the point when, early in the second half, their keeper took a goal kick which attained a reasonable height before curving back, in the teeth of the wind, and flying back over his head for a corner: an incident which I had never before seen on a football pitch, and will be extremely surprised if I ever see again.

I meet up with Tom again outside the ground, and conversation turns, after beginning with our mutual loathing of the Yank import that is "Trick or Treat" to general, non-Halloween pranks we played when we were kids. "Knock and Run" was one such, and Tom reduces me to tears with his description of the variation they used to play in his part of Manchester when he was a kid. Apparently, the trick was to tie one end of a piece of string loosely to the door-knocker of the first in a row of terraced houses, and the other end to the knocker next door. They then tied that string to the next knocker, and so on down the line. Rattling the first door thus meant, when the occupant answered, that they caused the next door knocker to operate, and so on until the giggling kids observed a whole street of puzzled occupants: "did you knock on my door?" "No, did you ..?" "I definitely heard a knock" "well, who...?" When I've stopped laughing, I retaliate with a prank I've heard of, but never seen performed, which may mean that it is purely apocryphal. I bloody hope so: carefully stick the pointy bit of a drawing pin in a dog turd (plentiful enough on the pavements), and stick it, point outwards, to a doorbell, using blue tack. Hours of fun for all the family can then be had by observing the consequences of a caller to the house pricking their finger on a dog turd stained pin as they try to ring the bell, and then, automatically, sucking their painful digit...

Tom's just back from a week's holiday in Spain. Before he went, he was full of the fact that he'd booked it, without reference to the fixture list, only to discover with glee that he'd managed to avoid missing any home games at all. All he would miss would be the League Cup third round, which County wouldn't be in anyway. Oh dear. He then tells me of the problems he had finding out the score from Ewood Park, traipsing from bar to bar before he found out we'd won. He found out eventually from one barman, stayed for a drink (it seemed only polite), before insult was added to the injury of him missing the game when he moved on to his regular haunt to be informed that the County goal had just been shown on the satellite telly two minutes before he got there. I laugh like a drain; you don't get sympathy from a fellow-fan if you're daft enough to book holidays in the football season, as I know from experience.

Just before we go in, I break my usual habit and buy the second programme of the season, not for any great desire to read it, but because it'll have ticket details for the West Ham game. Sure enough, the price is confirmed as a ridiculous £18, but, in a gesture born out of sheer altruism and not by any means because they want as many fans there as possible to boost their share of the gate money, County have kept the coach price "as low as possible". Yes, instead of the £13 which they charged for Millwall, they are only charging - wait for it - £12 for the coach to Upton Park. Well, pardon me if I don't faint with gratitude, won't you?

We're sitting in the Cheadle End tonight, me and Martin, in the white seats that make up the top stroke of the "F" in "SCFC". From here, we see the first half develop into an exciting game, albeit one in which County, understandably in view of the fact that we are at home, show more imagination and endeavour than the visitors. There are chances at both ends, however, and both teams come close to scoring on more than one occasion. That said, we seem destined to reach the half time break without a goal. Then a County move down the right reaches John Jeffers, who dodges around for a second or two, as is his wont, before attempting to cross. The ball shoots across at groin height, travels into the box, and then smacks against the hands of a Chesterfield defender, who seems to be doing no more than trying to protect his crown jewels. The linesman pauses for a second or two, presumably fighting back laughter, before flagging for an infringement and a penalty to County that is at least as unfair as any we have conceded this season.

The Chesterfield protests are loud and long, aimed at both linesman and referee. In view of the fact that there must have been many hundreds of thousands of penalty decisions which have been awarded in professional football over the years, none of which, to the best of my knowledge, have ever been rescinded after protest to the officials, it's no surprise when the decision is allowed to stand. Nonetheless, the defenders' anger is transformed to mere righteous indignation a minute or two later, when Bennett hits a weak penalty that the Chesterfield goalkeeper saves fairly easily.

Half time is therefore reached without a goal being scored, but it is far from being a dull match. I slope off under the stand with my shiny new Dictaphone, in order to speak some notes about the game; I am thus caught lurking by another friend, Richard Singleton, who sees me start guiltily and put the machine back into my inside pocket. God, I hope he doesn't think I've got a mobile phone.

The second half continues in the same vein as the first, although Chesterfield's game plan seems to have been that if they didn't manage to score in the first half, they'll throw men back and play for a point in the second. Although this tactic thus invites County pressure, our attack is relatively toothless without Armstrong (missing *again* , for God's sake), and we look no more likely to score than we did before the break, despite good chances falling to strikers Angell and Mutch.

Then, with the game petering out into stalemate, and the scoreboard showing 88 minutes gone, County get a corner on the right. Chris Marsden floats the ball into the box, Kieron Durkan flicks it on, and Tony Dinning - filling in at centre half in place of the injured Jim Gannon - arrives like a train to head home.

This is unbelievable, I think - yea, even amidst the jubilation - another bloody last minute goal! It'll be the winner, of course - these days, County can defend a lead for a minute and a half with the best of them - but it seems so... well, so cheeky. I genuinely feel like giggling, as though I'm a schoolboy again, and someone has just farted in assembly.

Chris Beaumont immediately gets sacrificed as Chesterfield sling men up front in a last desperate throw of the dice. He walks off to an amazing ovation from the County fans: "There's only one Chrissy Beaumont" rings out across the ground. Whilst Beaumont was a fairly popular - and long-serving - player at Edgeley Park, it is, to say the least, highly debatable whether he'd have received such acclamation had we not just scored. I'm not sure Beaumont appreciates it either, as he makes no sign of acknowledgement. He either thinks it won't be appreciated by the fans of his new club if he's seen waving to the fans of his old one just after going a goal down, or he's muttering "sarcastic bastards" under his breath; I'm sitting too far away to see. Whether the applause was adrenaline fuelled or not, however, it's nice to hear a counterpoint to the vitriol which has been directed against Beaumont from a bloke behind me for most of the match. Whilst the ovation was probably exaggerated, there was no need to treat him like a pariah.

The whistle goes a minute or two after Beaumont departs, and County have extended their run to one defeat, two draws and ten wins in the last 13 league and cup games. October began and ended with last minute winners, and saw some extraordinary games in between, some of them verging on the fantastic. Roll on our first game in November (four days from now, in fact).

NOVEMBER

NATIONWIDE LEAGUE DIVISION TWO

	P	W	D	L	F	A	Pts
BRENTFORD	16	9	5	2	28	17	32
MILLWALL	16	9	4	3	28	19	31
BURY	16	8	5	3	21	14	29
CREWE ALEXANDRA	16	9	1	6	20	15	28
BRISTOL CITY	16	8	3	5	31	18	27
LUTON TOWN	15	8	3	4	21	15	27
WATFORD	16	7	6	3	18	15	27
CHESTERFIELD	16	8	3	5	13	11	27
WREXHAM	15	6	8	12	11	5	26
STOCKPORT COUNTY	16	7	4	5	20	19	25
BURNLEY	16	7	3	6	23	20	24
BRISTOL ROVERS	16	6	6	4	16	13	24
PLYMOUTH ARGYLE	16	5	5	6	18	20	20
YORK CITY	16	5	4	7	20	23	19
GILLINGHAM	16	5	3	8	17	25	18
BLACKPOOL	16	4	6	6	16	18	18
SHREWSBURY TOWN	16	4	5	7	16	22	17
NOTTS COUNTY	16	4	5	7	12	16	17
PETERBOROUGH UNITED	16	3	7	6	25	30	16
WALSALL	16	4	4	8	15	22	16
BOURNEMOUTH	16	5	1	10	12	20	16
PRESTON NORTH END	16	4	3	9	15	20	15
ROTHERHAM UNITED	16	3	3	10	16	26	12
WYCOMBE WANDERERS	16	2	5	9	16	26	12

November 2nd 1996. Bristol City (home).

Like Tuesday's, the game today represents a reasonable test of how good we really are at the moment, as we're again playing a team above us in the table. It's fairly surprising that there still *are* so many teams above us, in fact; we're still only tenth, which was where we moved to after the Millwall game a month ago. Considering that of the six league games since that date, we've won three, drawn two and only lost one, it seems a trifle unfair, to say the least.

Julia's decided to come today. I tried to talk her out of it, reasoning that she'd be more likely to see some goals and a good win when we play our next home game - Doncaster in the FA Cup first round, but she's decided that she'll simply go to that game as well (and, having tempted fate like that, it'll probably be a 0-0 draw).

It's an amazingly warm day - almost balmy, and certainly warm enough for shirt sleeve order, which seems to have had the effect of getting people out for pre-Christmas shopping, because the traffic's terrible. Me, my dad and Martin have gone on ahead - my mum is giving Julia a treat by taking her into Stockport on the bus, from where they'll come up to meet us at Edgeley Park just before kick-off. It also means that I can have a pre-match pint without an eight year old secreted in my coat pocket (I must stop eating those damn mushrooms).

The weather is so nice that there are people drinking in the streets outside the Edgeley pubs. It's hard to believe that it's November. Halcyon days, indeed, given our current form. At quarter to three, we take our partners for the "time-to-sup-up-and-head-for-ground" quickstep and leave the pub. I separate from Martin and my dad and head for the meeting point.

They aren't there. Okay. Right. Think. Not to worry, don't panic, they'll be here in a minute. They aren't. Five minutes? No. Six? No. Seven? No. It's gone five to three now, and a roar from behind me tells me that the teams have emerged. Where are they? Er, remember that traffic...?

This is terrible. I can't possibly go in and leave them: I'm not that bad a father. However, what if they're not here until half time? Or full-time? Or half-time in the Doncaster game next week? Don't be ridiculous. Look, here's a bus - they'll be on that.

No they won't.

Behind me, I can hear noises which indicate that the game has kicked off. Where. *Are.* **They??** I know full well where they are, of course - stuck in the bloody traffic. If my Dictaphone was indeed a mobile phone, I could have rung them at home and warned them to set off earlier. Never mind mobile bloody phones; I could also have rung them from the pub - the fact is that it didn't occur to me to warn them to set off earlier until I emerged from the boozer at quarter to three, by which time it was far too late.

They eventually get off the fifth bus to arrive, at nearly ten past three. I grab Julia's hand and we run to the turnstiles (I swear her feet leave the ground and she takes off behind me at one point). We get inside, and the lack of celebratory cheering I heard from outside is backed up by the electronic scoreboard at the back of the Railway End, which confirms it's 0-0. We've missed nowt of importance. We climb the stairs to the back of the lower tier, to find that our seats are at the extreme left hand side of the stand. The stand is hardly full, and I can see plenty of free seats in a more central position, but realise that Julia can see much better where we are, with no one in the two rows in front to block her view, so I decide to stay put. Ah, the joys of parenthood - I miss the first ten minutes and then have a crap view.

I glance around the field. Having already established the score, I'm now checking for a young, bottle-blond striker. Nope, Armstrong's still out, so the stupid decision to play him at Blackburn has now cost us his presence in three league games. And counting.

Martin, who, like most fans, has seen all the game so far, tells me that County are playing well. Sure enough, a measure of our domination is shown when full back Sean Connelly - who *never* scores - runs onto a great through ball from Marsden and sends a fierce shot against the foot of the post. For some reason, the scoreboard decides to display an image of a tank firing a football into the back of a goal, the netting of which promptly bursts under the power (well, it would, wouldn't it?). Presumably, this bizarre image is to keep people's attention on the scoreboard, and thus the many advertisers who have paid good money to have their adverts scrolling across. I know from experience that the scoreboard has another hilarious graphic in its repertoire - a referee ticking off a player, from whose eyes tears are seen to emerge (the fact that the cartoon referee in the graphic who's doing the finger-wagging has a baseball cap on belies the machine's Yank origins). Naturally, the operator uses this image when a player's being booked, which I'm sure, it could be argued, virtually amounts to club-approved taunting. I'd love to see such a player lose his rag, chin the ref, and then claim at the disciplinary hearing that he was provoked by the scoreboard.

I have often wondered, in fact, what's the point of a scoreboard anyway? Other than notifying the score to idiots like me, who can't arrive on time, is there ever a game at which the score at any given point is ever in doubt? Okay, yes, I know there have been high scoring games (I remember a 6-6 draw between Tranmere and Newcastle a few years ago) where this may have been the case, but, even then, I'm sure most fans would be able to keep a mental tally of the goals.

As the half develops, City come more into the game, although it's still an undeserved lead which they take a minute before the break, when Clayton Blackmore, a Manchester United reject seemingly scrabbling for his crust round Division Two these days, manages to get some part of his anatomy on the end of a left wing cross, and bundles the ball home.

Half time thus arrives with us 1-0 down, although it's hardly comparable to the last time we were in this situation, against Luton a couple of weeks ago. On that occasion, we deserved to be behind, and it was difficult to see how we would get back into the game. Now, however, we most certainly don't deserve to be losing. That said, against Luton we were then transformed in the second half and managed a deserved draw. By the same logic, today we'll probably be transformed into a bunch of gibbering buffoons, and lose about three-nil.

As if to disprove another of my Bizarre Footballing Theories, however, the team continue as they did in the first half, and are unlucky not to equalise. Bristol, however, also play better, and, as Paul Jones pulls off a couple of great saves to keep the deficit down to a single goal, the game develops into a cracker.

Time is running out, however, and it seems, with 83 minutes showing on that ever-so-useful scoreboard, that we'll have to resort to another of our patented late goals. With that in mind, Mike Flynn launches a long throw in from the left wing, Brett Angell shows surprising skill in controlling it and hooking it back over his head, and Tom Bennett (I discover from the tannoy) bundles it home from two yards.

This all takes place at the far end of the ground, and at first it's not clear exactly what has happened. Although the equaliser is a well-deserved, and vital, score, the celebration is thus more along the lines of "is that in? Well, I can't go wild in case it isn't and I look foolish. It *is* in, I think. Yes the players are celebrating. Yes! Wa-hay!!" rather than the explosive "YEEEEAAAARRRGGHHHSSSS!" that it deserved. Nonetheless, it proves to be the final significant moment of the match, and we've gained the draw our play at the very least deserved.

Later on in the evening, I learn from the weather report after the late news that it was Manchester's warmest November day for fifty years. And Stockport had the worst traffic jams since the invention of the wheel.

November 9th 1996. Brentford (away).

Blackburn beat Liverpool 3-0 last Sunday, at Ewood Park, so we're better than Li... oh yes, you know how it works, don't you?

Well, that *was* pleasant: a week off - no Tuesday or Wednesday game for only the second time since the start of the season. It's only November, and yet today's is already the 23rd game I've attended - over 40% of the season completed already, I've been pathetic enough to work out, assuming we don't get to all three cup finals.

It's the train again today; I've become a junkie. Yes, even though the coach is once more £12 cheaper, I so enjoyed the luxury of rail travel when I went to Watford that bugger the expense, I say (you'll notice that I've even, shamefully, stopped using the "more time with my kids" excuse). I've even gone to the trouble of getting ticket prices quoted for forthcoming trips to Peterborough and Bournemouth (£35 and £45 respectively, so I don't think I'll be abandoning the delights of coach travel just yet). The expense has a silver lining, however - it's preparing me for what it must be like to follow a Premiership team, ready for when we get promoted into that division in a year or two (I'm being ironic, in case you hadn't guessed).

I leave my car in the municipal car parks of Edgeley (50p for the whole day as opposed to £3 in the BR station lot), and walk the few hundred yards to the station. The train arrives on time, I get on, and, as it's fairly full, I seek out the reserved seat that an APEX ticket guarantees. It's a table seat, of which two other places are occupied, but at least it's facing forwards, and next to the window. The problem is that the other two occupants are, sadly, a couple of ignorant bastards - a lad and a girl - who have been on since Manchester. They are sitting with their legs jutting forward, and make no attempt to move them when I arrive, so that I am forced to sit with *my* legs scrunched up under my seat. I direct a series of mental hate waves at them, which makes me feel a bit better.

The train is once again teeming with fun-packed metropolitan life. This time, however, I'm joining them in the Smoke, instead of getting off with the bumpkins at Watford. Isn't it exciting!? I wonder whether I'll become so intoxicated with the Bohemian lifestyle that I reject my northern suburban existence? I wonder if I'll take a dingy basement flat somewhere in Hampstead, from where I'll turn out unpublished novels about the human condition on a battered old typewriter? Then I'll grow a beard and move to Paris, where I'll live in a top floor apartment on the Left Bank, getting up at noon, smoking Gauloises, painting masterpieces in oils, and having a passionate, yet ultimately doomed, affair with Simone Signoret.

Or maybe I'll just go to Griffin Park and watch County.

Sitting opposite people like this on a train reminds me of one of my most embarrassing moments, one which can still literally make my toes curl up inside my shoes when I think about it (there they go now, look). It was during the period when I was doing my part-time degree at Manchester University, and used to go there straight from work. Following the evening's lecture, I was, by the time I'd walked the couple of miles down to Oxford Road station, fairly hungry, having not eaten since dinner (middle of the day dinner, that is - I'm from oop north, remember?). As there was usually twenty minutes or so before the Stockport train arrived, I was in the habit of getting a cup of tea and something to eat from the station buffet. This particular night, I'd had a packet of crisps and a jam-filled doughnut (not the most healthy of main meals, granted, but then there wasn't much choice in a station buffet at nine o'clock), and was soon on the train home.

Two young girls then got on at Piccadilly station and sat opposite, and I could soon sense a slight disturbance from their direction. As I casually put down my paper and coolly stared out of the window, I could clearly see, from the reflection, that they were giggling, and it was equally clear that it was at me.

You've still got it, Dave, I thought to myself. I was wearing a new light brown leather jacket that night, and was feeling particularly good as a result. The lecture had gone well, and whilst the girls were only kids of about seventeen - and I was seven or eight years older, and married with a child on the way - it did no harm to my self-esteem to be the object of their attention like this. The briefcase and economics textbook probably helped as well, and I could almost sense the slow enlarging of my head as I sat there.

The girls didn't stop, however, and things soon began to get a touch wearing, as being laughed at tends to, especially when the giggling turned to outright snickering. I glanced across at them and caught the eye of the one on the left. I gave her what I imagined to be a cool, aloof look. Her response was to stifle back a laugh with a great snort, which then set off her mate. I couldn't believe this. Attracting the attentions of pretty young girls is one thing - being the object of their amusement for no other reason than that they'd probably been knocking back the cider under the arches of Oxford Road rail bridge was quite another

I decided I wasn't going to take any more, and as the train pulled into Heaton Chapel station - the last halt before Stockport - I stood up with a final disdainful glare, got out with as much dignity as I could muster, trotted down the platform, and re-entered in the next carriage along. Now I can relax, I thought, as I slumped into the new seat, catching sight, as I did so, of the six inch long glob of fresh doughnut jam that had been slowly slithering down the front of my new leather jacket ever since Oxford Road.

The lad opposite goes to fill up his nosebag at the buffet car, and I take the opportunity to uncurl my aching legs. You've slipped up there, mate. Possession is nine tenths of the law, and I'm buggered if you're going to be able to stretch your legs back onto my territory again, even if it means a frantic game of footsie when you get back.

Macclesfield, Stoke, Milton Keynes Central, Euston. We're there, it's ten past one, and I've got nearly two hours to get to Griffin Park. I know from the

"Supporters' Guide" that the tube station I want is Sarf Ealin', and I know from the tube map in Anna's borrowed diary that I pathetically consult on the Euston forecourt, trying desperately not to look like a provincial pleb, that I need to change at Leicester Square for the Piccadilly Line. Joining the queue for tickets behind a group of Rochdale fans on the way to their game at Barnet, I buy a Zone Three and descend into the murky depths.

Crossing London via tube on a November Saturday, it hardly feels as if I'm going to a football match. The train is packed with early Christmas shoppers, heading for Knightsbridge and Leicester Square (see? I know where the shops are. Call me a provincial pleb would you?). It may, of course, be packed because of all the County fans heading for Brentford, but I doubt it.

Sure enough, by the time, I ascend onto Ealing High Street, half an hour or so later, the train has virtually emptied. I thus make the pleasant enough mile and a half walk alone, and I get to the away end at about twenty past two. It's been one of the least eventful trips I can remember - no delays, no roadworks (tricky to experience, admittedly, when travelling by train), and no getting lost. I'm not complaining, mind. My hair is still just about black, even after the trips to Wycombe and Walsall; pleasant journeys like today's can only help keep the grey at bay. The fact that Stockport County are the team I'm following, of course, is an entirely different kettle of fish.

Not being one of those types who like to get into a virtually empty ground as soon as they possibly can, I hang around the turnstiles until just before kick off, socialising as the County fans trickle in. I see Louie from the Fingerpost approach. As is his wont, he doesn't bother with conventional greetings, his first words to me being "so there's this bloke goes to the doctor, right. And he says, 'Doctor, me arm's started talking to me.' So the Doctor says 'Let me examine it,' and feels it" *(here, Louie grabs his arm near the wrist)* "and the arm says" *(he adopts a squeaky voice)* "'lend us a quid.' And the Doctor feels here" *(Louie demonstrates a bit further up)* "and the arm says, 'lend us a fiver.' And the Doctor feels here" *(even further up)* "and the arm says, 'lend us a tenner'. And the Doctor says, 'I know what's wrong with it. It's broke.'"

I knew the day had been going too well.

Five minutes before kick off, I pay my eight quid and enter the tiny away terrace. The terrace occupies the area left behind when a new stand was built on stilts behind one of the goals. It's shallow, narrow - only about 10 rows - and has a pretty poor view. It's covered, though, by the new stand above, and thus a few spectators can generate quite a noise. County fans are not renowned for being particularly quiet anyway, so the atmosphere is pretty good. It helps that the majority of the home support are in the newly seated stand to our left, with those most intent on winding up the opposition fans sitting towards our end. This makes for some terrific mutual antagonism, which continues throughout the game.

The teams are announced. Incredibly, Armstrong is *still* out, so Mutch and Angell once again lead the line, with attacking options in the shape of Luis Cavaco and the seemingly out-of-favour Richard Landon on the bench.

The game kicks off with County attacking our end in the first half. Almost immediately, however, Brentford surge forward in a five minute period of early pressure, which encourages their fans. *"You're the shit of Manchester"* This geographical ignorance is given the prolonged *"ahhhhhh!"* it deserves. Back on the field, Mike Flynn is forced to head over from under his own bar when Paul Jones is beaten by a lob. *"Manchester, wank, wank, wank, Manchester, wank, wank, wank..."* Couldn't agree more. *"We don't come from Manchester. Chesh-i-yure, Chesh-i-yure, Chesh-i-yure.."*

After ten minutes or so, County build down the right. Brett Angell beats the keeper to the ball and squares to Mutch, standing near the penalty spot. He takes a wild swing at the ball, visibly salivating at the sight of the unguarded net, but misses completely. Look out for that one on the next Danny Baker video. His miss causes much anguished head-holding in the County end, and brings the home fans to their feet again *"Northern bastards, Northern bastards, hello, hello."* County respond with a classic move, adopting the Pet Shop Boys' ubiquitous "Go West": *"Stand uuup if you beat Blackburn"* (Brentford lost to Blackburn Rovers in the same round of the Coca Cola Cup that we beat Sheffield United), which shuts up the home fans almost immediately, although one or two of them attempt to mime an indignant "huh, yeah, well, what do *we* care?". From a sitting position, mind.

The game is now being played from end-to-end. Brentford, frustrated by County's pressure, respond with the threatening *"will you sing your songs outside?"*, complete with "angry man offering out other man" gestures, but County hit back almost immediately: *"You're the shit of West London"*

"Ahhhhhh!"

Half time arrives with the score at 3-3. No one has managed to break the deadlock on the pitch, however.

The second half starts, and County immediately go onto the attack with their second original song of the game: the esoteric *"Fooled by a whistle, you're only fooled by a whistle."* This refers to Brentford's last away game, covered fairly extensively in the media, at Bristol Rovers. The match was level when their keeper heard a whistle which he didn't realise had come from the crowd, and placed the ball down, expecting a free kick. A Bristol Rovers forward, unable to believe his luck, then booted the ball into the net for the winning goal. It's a touch of genius to resurrect this incident in order to taunt, and once again, the home fans are reduced to the silence of the seething.

Back on the pitch, County's performance is heartening. We're matching the side that were running away with the league a few weeks ago - and at their own ground as well. It cannot last, however, and sure enough Brentford score, following a mixup in the County defence. Tom Bennett, under pressure, attempts to play the ball back to Paul Jones, but underhits it, allowing a Brentford forward to shoot. His effort is well saved by Jones, but another forward follows up and hits the ball into the unguarded net.

"You're not singing, you're not singing, you're not singing anymore. You're not singing anymore."

"Sing when you're winning - you only sing when you're winning."

"We are top of the league, I said we are top of the league"

It all gets worse with about fifteen minutes left, when, despite County still continuing to look dangerous on the break, Brentford score a second. County keeper Jones is responsible, diving over a speculative but weak 25-yarder from the Brentford centre-forward. That's it now - the game's over. The Simone Signoret option begins to look ever more attractive.

"... You're not singing anymooorre. Yoooou'rrrrrre not si-i-ing-ing annn-yyyy-moooorrrre."

"Oh, fuck off" (an individual effort that represents my own sole contribution to the afternoon's banter).

Four minutes after the goal, however, we are thrown a lifeline when Brett Angell heads in from a Chris Marsden corner. At least I think it's Angell who scores - it's hard to see from my vantage point, and the Brentford announcer is another of those screaming lunatics who only announces the home scorers. The Brentford fans continue to support their side, but you can tell that an air of desperation has crept in, whereas we're right behind the team now, sniffing an equaliser on the back of our recent late-goals record. We lose the choir for a few minutes, as the support takes the form of roaring. There is an opportunity to return to the banter five minutes later, however, when Cavaco - brought on for Mutch after Brentford's second - cuts in from the right wing, seems to beat at least three Brentford defenders and curls a beauty inside the keeper's right hand post. From our end we see the shot travel goalwards, but have no idea how accurate it is until the side netting bulges. YEEEARRRRGGGHHHFFFUCCCKKKKKOOFFFFF! we say, in unison, to the home fans. There's a moment or two of mayhem before it's our turn. *"You're not singing, you're not singing, you're not singing anymore. YOU'RE not singing anymore"*

There isn't enough time for very many more chances, and as time runs out, the Brentford fans resort to the standards: *"And it's Bre-ent-entford. Bre-ent-*

entford FC. We're by FAR the greatest team, the world has ever seen". County fans immediately hijack the refrain, making the obvious change to the name of the greatest team the world has ever seen. It's always made me laugh, that one - if either of these two are genuinely the greatest team the world has ever seen, then it sure as hell is a goddam crazy, mixed-up world. Surely only the fans of the 1970 Brazil World Cup winning squad can legitimately sing this song? It's fitting, however, that the final whistle thus goes with supporters of both teams singing in unison. An honourable draw. And so was the match.

On the way out, I confirm the scorers with a friend, Ken Riley. He tells me that I was right about Angell and Cavaco (although we could both have made exactly the same mistake, I suppose). I bid farewell to the coach-travellers and start off back to the Underground, a journey which offers a highly enjoyable contrast with a similar journey at Watford: the accents are the same, the discussions aren't. This time, it's pleasant to be walking back amongst them.

"Frew it away. Bladdy frew it away!"

"Yeah. They want their bladdy awses kickin'.'"

"Not a bad team, Stockpowt, though."

It's ten to five. My train back leaves at twenty past six, so I've got an hour and a half to get back to Euston. Despite an incredibly crowded train, made worse by platforms six deep at Knightsbridge (Christmas shoppers, presumably) and Piccadilly Circus (there must have been a matinée, although I can't see the attraction myself - I never did like circuses), I make it back with twenty minutes to spare.

The train home is only about a quarter full, so I'm able to blag a table foursome and relax with my legs splayed, and shoes off (see? Unlike some ignorant sods, I at least wait until there's no one sitting opposite). After two hours, we pull into the familiar surroundings of Crewe station, from where I used to get trains home regularly when I was at Keele. Only about twenty minutes to go from here, and I should be home for about nine. Oh no I won't. The guard comes on the tannoy to announce that *"some lawless little gits have cobbed stones from a bleedin' embankment and cracked the front window of the driver's cab"* (I'm paraphrasing again), so we'll have a half hour wait until they can get us a replacement engine.

We get underway again at ten past nine, and by the time we pull into Stockport, it's well after half past. Not to worry. If we'd lost, I might have been a bit more upset, but having gained a point - and in such circumstances - at second placed Brentford, I'm still happy. Ironically, walking back to the car on Edgeley, I see what must have been the club coach drawing away: I didn't save any time at all by taking the train.

Saturday Night and Thursday Morning

Back at home, I work out that we've now scored in the last fifteen league and cup games. We've also still only lost one game in that run. Teams that get promoted only lose around ten or eleven games in a whole season. Our horrendous start left us with four defeats by the second week in September. We'll have only lost five, though, by November 19th, by which time we'll have played nineteen league games. By the time we play Peterborough on December 14th, we'll have played half the season. If we can avoid defeat, then, in our next four league games, we're on course for Division One.

Stuff like this keeps me sane, honestly.

November 16th 1996. Doncaster Rovers (home) (FA Cup Sponsored by Littlewoods Pools R1).

Julia makes her third appearance of the season today, which is appropriate in many ways, as both she and Doncaster Rovers played an integral part in the second occasion - following the sin of being on holiday during the football season - on which I transgressed the unwritten law of County watching - the birth of my first child.

The game - a routine Division Four clash with Donny - was at Edgeley Park on Saturday 1st October 1988, and, whilst Julia was actually born at around 5pm on the Friday, there was no way I was going to be able to wangle two hours away from my visiting duties. Actually, I have to confess that as the County butterfly of success was only just emerging, blinking in the sunlight, from the larvae of failure which was the 70s and 80s (other bizarre similes available on request), the anguish of missing the game while I played with our new baby was not really as strong as it might otherwise have been. The details of the match, out of interest, are that County won 2-0, with goals from John Cooke and Rodger Wylde, in front of a pitiful crowd of 1,959, which we'd be ashamed to get at an Autoglass game these days. And it could so easily have been 1,960.

Three and a half years later, in April 1992, the birth of Christopher saw me only just avoid becoming a repeat offender, as he made his entrance (or, rather, exit, I suppose) at 3am, the night we beat West Brom 3-0 (now that *was* a night to remember...). By the time Andrew was born, 16 months or so ago, our kids were beginning to understand, presumably instinctively, the importance of County in their dad's life, and he duly appeared on a Thursday, just about the only day of the week that domestic football isn't played.

It's a grey, drizzly, misty day; one which, of course, according to southern prejudice, would be ideally suited to a game of football between Doncaster Rovers and Stockport County. Outside the ground, however, the garish colours sported by one or two away fans give the lie to this idea - that flat caps, whippets and grim and grimy football is the order of the day. The away fans seem to have entered into the spirit of things, many of them wearing hats and rosettes and all the other pathetic paraphernalia that the excitement of the first round of the Cup engenders. Note that's "Cup", not "cup". *The* Cup, the one which merits Capital Letters, not just any old cup.

Inside the ground, it's clear from the crowded Railway End that quite a few Doncaster fans have made the trip, and equally clear that many County fans haven't; the attendance will be around 4,000 or so, I would guess. Thankfully, Alun Armstrong makes his long-awaited return. Playing him against Blackburn cost us his services in four games, and I'm sure his presence would have helped us turn at least one of the drawn matches into a victory.

Doncaster start brightly, and it's soon obvious that today is not going to be a walkover of last season's Lincolnian proportions. Indeed, the visitors have slightly the better of things in the first half, and we can count ourselves lucky to reach the break with no score. Julia's bored, but I tell her that if she keeps coming, she'll be bound to see an exciting game, quite possibly even before she starts secondary school.

The second half opens with a bang - literally, for the referee, who, standing on the goal line to the left of the goal, gets his face in the way of a header from a County player which was going wide. Smack. Dazed referee with just enough awareness to blow his whistle collapses to sympathetic noises from the County fans behind the goal: *"You soft bastard. You soft bastard."* As is the way of things in these circumstances, the senior linesman trots over to offer whatever help he can. I know from a friend, however, who works with a league linesman, that, for all his *"are you all right?"*'s and *"do you want the physio?"*'s, he's actually thinking *"stay down you bastard - stay down and get carried off so I can take over,"* as indeed is the fourth official in the stand, who's flag-waving arm is beginning to twitch.

The ref sits up, however, and after a quick rub-down from the County physio, is able to continue, and, presumably, to admire Doncaster's opening goal a few minutes later. Their right-winger is released and manages to skip a couple of tackles before slotting the ball under the diving Paul Jones for a superb goal. Now this is awkward. County are playing badly enough for this to be the winner, and whilst I know we'll take our leave of the FA Cup before very long, I don't want it to be in the first round, at home to a lower division club.

Thankfully, the goal galvanises County, and we equalise five minutes later with the simplest of goals, Mike Flynn heading home a Chris Marsden corner. Even better, a couple of minutes after that, a sweeping cross-field move sees

Kieron Durkan make good progress down the right wing before laying on a cross into the six yard box that not even Andy Mutch, with his recent embarrassing record, can miss.

Immediately, almost as though the job of stamping down the upstart Rovers is seen as complete, County relapse into lethargy, and the Yorkshiremen come close to equalising again. The final whistle goes with no more additions to the scoreline, however, and we've well and truly buggered up Doncaster's day out. Sorry folks, but there you go. That's life; that's football.

We rush back to my mum's, having heard on the radio that the draw is taking place at quarter past five. I assume it's on Sky, which my parents don't have, so am pleased when I discover that it's actually live on "Grandstand." Less pleasing is the order in which the balls emerge - Mansfield beat us to it, so it's a trip to Field Mill inked in for December 7th. It could be worse, however - Mansfield's not too far away, and it's another new ground for me.

November 19th 1996. Blackpool (home).

It's arrived fairly early on in the season, but today is one of those legendary cold days that test the resolve of all but the most hardy (or foolish) of football fans.

The first inkling comes with Julia and Christopher's delighted yells as, looking out of the bedroom window, they realise that a good two inches of snow have fallen overnight, followed closely by Andrew's happy grunts, as he in turn realises that something exciting is happening, although he's buggered if he can work out quite what.

Although I can recognise the kids' excitement, and recall similar feelings from when I was their age, I look upon the winter wonderland with less feelings of delight than they do. It's not just that at my age I no longer look forward to the thrill of snowmen and snowballing - indeed, I'm as sentimental as the next fully grown adult at the magical silent whiteness. No, it's just that snow and frost mean games get called off, and fixture backlogs cause teams to slip up towards the end of the season.

Luckily, a thaw sets in during the day and come five o' clock, most of the snow has melted. A couple of calls to the club establish that the game's on, unlike a number of other fixtures which have succumbed. This is handy - it gives us the chance to steal a march on some of our rivals who aren't playing. We'll have then played a game more, but, as they say who enjoy mixing their metaphors, points in the bag are better than games in hand.

Julia's appearing in a kiddies' fashion show at school tonight, which means that I've agreed to delay my departure until Anna's twin sister Maria arrives to babysit. I set off for the ground in reasonable time, however, with about fifteen layers of clothing on - the night is so bitterly cold that on the way to the ground, I pass a couple of brass monkeys donning lagging. It seems barely credible that for the Bristol City game on November 2nd - just over two weeks ago - people were drinking outside the pubs of Edgeley in shirt sleeves.

Inside Edgeley Park, there's not a trace of snow anywhere to be seen, although frost might be a problem later on. The freezing conditions mean that the crowd is as small as Saturday's - the fact that minimum admission at Edgeley Park these days is £9 also doesn't help. £18 in four days represents a hefty wedge to anyone for whom money's a bit tight, and as County seem not yet to have moved into the middle-income arena from where teams in the Premier League appear to attract a growing number of their supporters, home games on a Tuesday immediately following an Edgeley Park game on the previous Saturday are usually extremely poorly attended.

Out trot the teams - County in royal blue, and Blackpool in tangerine. It's actually orange, of course, but Blackpool have pretensions, in much the same way that Burnley refer to the colour of their shirts as "claret" (it's purple) and Wolves claim "old gold" (yellow). There seems to be a simmering undercurrent of bad feeling between these two sides, both on and off the pitch; each time we play, it's a physical game, with bookings and sendings-off aplenty, and occasionally crowd trouble as well. Sure enough, once the game starts the opening exchanges promise a lively evening, with fierce tackles flying in, and the fairly reasonable away support roaring on their team. Entering into the spirit of things, the County fans attempt to keep themselves warm by chanting, and a lively atmosphere is generated. Blackpool are playing in a manner which belies their lowly position in the league, and are playing so well it seems they have more men on the pitch. Hang on - nine, ten, eleven, twelve, thirteen, fourteen... they *have* got more men on the field! Oh sorry - my mistake, I've counted the stewards at the far end.

It really is an exciting game, albeit not a comfortable one for County fans; Blackpool are much the better team. The game is end-to-end, and reaches a crescendo in a two minute spell just before half time. Down at the far end, Blackpool score. Following a goalmouth scramble, their winger crosses to the far post where an unmarked forward heads home. In that precise moment, our hearts sink; such is the way the game's going, a Blackpool goal, even now, could be decisive. However, spirits immediately soar when the goal's disallowed; County take the opportunity to break immediately and go close at our end - so quick was our break that the Blackpool "goalscorer" is only able to run across and frantically berate the linesman a good two or three minutes after his effort was chalked off.

119

The referee takes a dim view of this belated chastisement, and, with the away support going wild, promptly books the poor sap. Ha ha ha. *"The Blackpool beach is full of shit, shit, and more shit!"* is the response to the away fans' anger. An EU hygiene observer at the end of our row nods his head sagely.

Half time arrives with, despite the many chances, no goals. The thought occurs that the game could well be a nil-niller. It wouldn't be the first time a game like this had not managed to produce a goal. As if to augment such fears, ten minutes into the second half, Blackpool have another goal disallowed for a push on Jones. Their fierce protests are stopped, however, by another quick County break. The game is proving really exciting; either team could pinch it, yet it still might end nil-nil. *"You can stick your fucking tower up your arse - sideways!"* comes the chant from behind me in direct response to the away fans' anguish at the disallowed goal, an adaptable song which is also, of course, employed against Chesterfield *("fucking spire")*.

People behind me are slagging Armstrong again. I'll accept that he's not been as effective as before his injury, but it's only his second game back, for crying out loud. Why are they having a go anyway? It seems to me that there's a certain type of English football fan that cannot cope with skill, seeing it as something poofy and foreign. They want rough, tough, get-stuck-in merchants - the type of typically English player, in other words, that has seen us fall further and further behind the rest of the world in the game we invented.

With about twenty minutes left, the breakthrough finally arrives, and it's County who score. Tom Bennett picks the ball up from a left wing throw-in, displays superb skill in lifting the ball over the head of the last defender and sends a left footed volley across the keeper into the corner.

Following the goal celebration, I sit down, conscious of my freezing cold applause muscles screaming with indignity at this unwarranted attack. I wonder whether I'll suffer in the morning - when County scored a late winner in the 1993 play off semi-final against York City, I leaped around so frantically that I wrenched a neck muscle badly enough for me to be forced to walk around for the next week with the top half of my body contorted in pain, my head held on one side and a face like a grimacing village idiot.

Following the goal, there's trouble in the Blackpool end - they're either fighting amongst themselves, or - more likely - with the stewards. As I said earlier, County's policy these days is to have no coppers at games when they can possibly help it, preferring to save money by just employing stewards. Sure enough, it's left to the tangerinecoats to wade into the fighting and drag out the offenders.

With fifteen minutes left, the shivers set in. No amount of extra clothing can prevent the arrival of this point in any cold game, as predictably as marathon runners hitting the "wall": when the final traces of warmth depart your body, and you're left to rattle in your seat like the first coin in a collecting tin. I have reached a level of coldness now which lies beyond freezing - approaching Absolute Zero, seemingly; I wouldn't be surprised at this point to be informed that William Thomson, first Baron Kelvin conducted most of his early research at Edgeley Park. What's needed is some event on the pitch to take my mind off the cold. The referee obliges by sending off Blackpool's Mickey Mellon - for what reason nobody seems quite sure, although it could well be for having a daft name. The Cheadle End offer their sympathies: *"Cheerio, cheerio, cheerio..."* We're in the final few minutes by this stage; following the Preston game, we're once again holding on to a 1-0 lead against a Lancashire "sleeping giant". When the final whistle does blow, however, we've extended our unbeaten run to ten games, extended our "only one defeat in" run to 17 games, and scored in them all. Guess where we are in the league, though? Yup, tenth.

November 23 1996. Shrewsbury Town (away).

It snowed once again last night, although, like Tuesday's game with Blackpool, it was that poncey, slushy snow that's of neither use nor ornament. That said, our journey south - avoiding the motorway and the Staffordshire roadworks - is through the minor roads of the Cheshire/Shropshire countryside, so I wouldn't bank on us avoiding some of the thicker stuff a bit later on. I'm making the trip with John Taylor, a fellow County-sufferer, who was stuck for a lift. Sadly, I can't offer him the luxury of the Cavalier, as Anna is taking the kids out, and I wouldn't inflict my crappy little tin can on them with snow still on the ground. The journey therefore takes a lot longer than it should, as the winding country roads of Cheshire, whilst picturesque, do not facilitate rapid traversing in a 950cc Fiesta.

We eventually park up in Shrewsbury at about twenty to three - after a journey that has taken almost two hours - and enter the small yet charming Gay Meadow (aka, in school playgrounds throughout England, Homosexual Fields). As usual, the crowd have tended to congregate near the turnstile through which they entered, which gives the impression of the terrace being fairly tightly packed, although I know from experience that were we to move away from the turnstiles, we'd have far more room. John seems unwilling to vacate the leaning-post he's managed to nab however - part of the roof support - and as it would be rude to leave him and go off on my own, I stay put.

The trouble is, I find myself next to one of those extraordinarily irritating types who chew gum with an open mouth. Schlop, schlop, schlop goes his gob, and I soon realise that if I don't move away soon, I'm going to have to thump it. As the teams line up to kick off, I content myself with stepping back onto the step above, from where, behind his head, I can't hear his disgusting slurping.

The game is a cracker. Brett Angell celebrates his new contract by putting us ahead after seven minutes, and that's the way it stays until half time, despite numerous chances to both teams. Fifteen minutes or so into the second half, however, Shrewsbury equalise. A cross from the left is deflected to the far post, where one of their strikers is completely unmarked. He takes great delight in leathering it home and it's 1-1. A couple of minutes later, and with County still pouring forward at every opportunity, disaster strikes when Paul Jones lets a fairly weak header slip in at the near post. This is not, however, as calamitous as it might have been; County are playing well enough for thoughts of an equaliser to be strong beliefs rather than faint hopes. In fact, as there are still a good twenty minutes left to play, and such is the dominance of our play, that, notwithstanding the scoreline, I'm still hoping for a winner.

Sure enough, we continue to pour forward. Luis Cavaco, a substitute for Kieron Durkan, is playing superbly well down the right wing, and the Shrewsbury defence is showing signs of panic. With about ten minutes left, Cavaco again beats the full back, and squares the ball past the three panicking defenders that have been pulled across to him for the unmarked Chris Marsden to sidefoot home.

Now we *can* get a winner. But so can Shrewsbury. And they do. With five minutes left, one of their attackers is fed the ball out on the left wing. With a couple of County defenders marking him tightly, and no one in support, he launches the ball towards the County goal, over the head of Paul Jones, and into the far corner. It's an amazing goal - no fluke - and is comparable to a famous one Dean Saunders scored for Aston Villa a couple of seasons ago (famous because it was such a spectacular goal that John Motson rashly proclaimed it, in his commentary, as the "Goal of the Nineties". "Oh no it isn't," said Alan Hansen and Trevor Brooking, rather taking the wind out of Motty's sails by placing it no higher than third in that month's "Goal of the Month" competition.)

Following this, there is still time for County to launch two further attacks, either of which could have led to another equaliser, but it seems the game is destined to be won by a wonder goal. Sure enough, the whistle goes, and we troop back to the car reflecting on only our second defeat in 18 games. I bet we're still tenth, mind.

In the torrential rain which accompanies us homewards, the Fiesta drives like a dog. With each misfire, and juddering pull-away from traffic lights, I keep thinking we won't make it home. Thankfully, however, we do, and as I drop John off at his house I notice that the bonnet isn't properly shut. The engine has probably been taking in water like the Titanic - it was no surprise that we struggled home. I could probably come up with some bitingly witty metaphor at this point regarding the opened bonnet, the bumpy journey, the damp leads and their relationship to our trip to Shrewsbury.

But I can't be arsed, quite frankly.

Wednesday November 27th 1996. West Ham (away) (Coca Cola Cup R4).

Well, this is the big one, except that it isn't really, of course, as I hope I've made clear in the past. The next "big one" is on Saturday when we're at home to Walsall. Tonight's game is merely a night out; an expensive one at that. We may achieve more cup glory in which to wallow for a while. We may get stuffed. We may get a draw and ripped-off by our own club in the replay. It doesn't matter. We're not going to win the thing, so the game with Walsall - and who knows, if we win, we may even rise to tenth! - is far more important.

I'm travelling down today with Andy Cairns, John Taylor and Martin. The ticket price being what it is, I decided to try and minimise the overall cost if possible, by cadging a lift off someone who was driving, rather than going on the coach or the train.

Now I know this is going to make me seem even more desperately sad than I do already, but I have a modem attached to my computer, and I'm member of a County e-mail list. Don't let the technical intricacies bother you too much - all it means is that I can participate in a discussion group on matters County with like-minded people all over the world (although, unsurprisingly, most are in the environs of Stockport). It also means that on occasions like this, I can post a request for a lift to West Ham, and sit back and wait for the offers to come flooding in. Andy Cairns was the one fellow-anorak who extended the cyber-hand of electronic friendship, and so it is in his car, for a share of the petrol, that I am making today's trip.

On the way there, we discuss the ridiculous ticket price, and whether we think it will affect the size of the County portion of the crowd. One of the main complaints I often hear posited about the price of football is that it offers a poor comparison with the other forms of entertainment which compete for people's disposable income. For eighteen quid, Anna and me could take Julia and Chris to the cinema, buy sweets and drinks, a full fish supper, a tram home and still have change from a tanner. Oops, sorry, lapsed into satire there. But the point is a valid one: compared with the cinema, football can offer, at times, all the value for money of a £37.99 poke in the eye.

Then again, as any true football fan will tell you, the cinema can never, ever, hope to give the buzz a football game does. Have you ever leapt to your feet to shout "OOOOOOH!", or "YESSSS!" or "FUCK OFF REFEREE, HE NEVER TOUCHED HIM!!" in the cinema? No? Well, I do that at preliminary round AutoWindscreens Shield games.

That said, it can't be denied that football is massively overpriced. The point is that although I, and many others, will pay daft money because of a type of brand loyalty that Marks and Spencer would die for, a significant number won't, preferring the warm glow of a feel-good movie to the ecstasy (well, sometimes) of a County win. Unless they're educated otherwise, and encouraged to try football by means of attractive prices, they'll continue to be resistant to the charms of Edgeley Park and the like.

The result is that these days, much smaller crowds generally than there were when I started watching County, pay ever-increasing amounts of money to watch their teams. It doesn't matter to the money men, however. As long as the overall revenue is kept up, who gives a toss that the ground isn't full? Take tonight. I would guess that there'll be a good few thousand empty spaces. But to fill them, the price would probably have to be reduced to a level where overall revenue was less, even though the stadium was full. Maximising revenue at all costs, therefore, even if it means a half-empty stadium, is thus seen as the ultimate goal by the people who run football these days. I find that tremendously depressing.

Andy tunes his radio into various local stations on the way down - all of them seemingly staffed by the kind of crappy, smarmy, cheesy DJs who would probably be kicked off hospital radio for making the patients sicker than they were anyway. Incredibly, one of them actually trails the *news*, using the death of Michael Bentine as a taster: *"And in the news today, a Goon has died. Find out who at three o'clock."* Unbelievable. I find myself dreaming up further examples: *"A senior Royal has died. We're lining up the solemn music, but in the meantime, the first caller to ring in with the correct stiff wins a t-shirt"*, or *"We're just getting reports that China has launched a pre-emptive nuclear strike against the West. We'll have more right after the latest single from the Spice Girls"*

Thankfully, the Staffordshire roadworks have finished, although we slow the car down to fifty or so in homage. We thus make good progress, and have already hit the M25 when darkness falls. There's a bit of a clog coming off the North Circular road (the radio announces that a Pearly King has shed his load on the westbound carriageway), but we've pulled up and parked just after five o'clock.

Goodie, goodie, time for a pint or three. The Stockport coaches haven't yet arrived, so the Boleyn Tavern - the closest pub to the ground - is virtually empty. It's obviously a football pub, as in a fairly large room there are no tables and

124

chairs whatsoever. It's equally clear, when the coaches arrive half an hour later, and the pub fills almost to bursting with thirsty County fans standing shoulder to shoulder, that the Taylor Report doesn't apply to football pubs.

Time passes quickly, as is its wont when you're boozing, and it's soon time to head for the ground. "Where the hell's Stockpowt? I only know it exists because we're ploiying vem in va cap" says - or rather shouts - a pissed-up Hammer to his cronies as we walk to the turnstiles. Still be saying that at half past nine, will you, I ask him - but only in my head.

Our entry into the ground is delayed by an army of stewards carrying out a mammoth searching operation. Tickets are checked, bags are thoroughly rummaged, and bodies are equally thoroughly frisked. This is, as always, irritating in the extreme - when was the last time anyone found anything, I am tempted to ask. That said, I can, just about, accept the argument that the fact they don't have incidents these days in football grounds is precisely because of such procedures. Eternal frisking is the price of liberty, although it seems a bit rich to be considering the concept of "liberty" having just experienced such a gross violation of same.

Inside, I've got a pretty crap view for my £18 - in the 4th row. I sneak a look at my neighbour's programme over her shoulder. The West Ham squad list is enormous, and contains more foreign names than the guest list for the UN Christmas party. The last time I saw so many foreigners on the pitch was when we once played a Yugoslav team ourselves - Zeljeznicar Sarajevo - in a mid-season friendly in the late 70s.

The game was memorable not so much for the football itself, as for the pre-match warm-up. The Yugoslavs came out about half an hour early to loosen their muscles with a few token shots at their keeper. They got such a rousing reception from the County fans in the Railway End, however, that they started to play to the crowd, blasting spectacular shots in from all angles, with the keeper diving equally spectacularly all over the place to stop them. This was entertaining enough, but was topped when a ball which had whizzed over the bar from a particularly ferocious shot headed towards a couple of blokes standing a few feet in front of me, halfway up the terrace.

The ball was clearly going to pass between the men, but, with a reflex action over which he presumably had no control, the guy on the left pushed out his right arm to deflect the ball away. Unfortunately, he deflected it straight into the face of the second bloke, standing less than two feet from him. The ball impacted with a loud fleshy smack, and such was the force of the shot that it then flew fifteen feet or so into the air, as the bloke who had been hit let out a loud "ooof!"

As a typical teenager, this little drama was, understandably, a godsend. I was helpless with laughter as the injured party's high pitched tones rang round the terraces. "What did you do that for?! You didn't have to touch it, you silly get!"

"Well, I didn't know..."

"It was missing you! Right in my bloody face, you silly get!"

"Oh shut it" With no justification for his action, the first man resorted to annoyance of his own.

"It was nowhere near you! You didn't have to bloody touch it!"

"Oh fuck off"

"You silly get!"

"I said fuck off"

"You silly get!"

Perhaps surprisingly, the two didn't come two blows, as the man who'd deflected the ball sidled away, to a final high-pitched volley of "you silly get!"s. Even more amazingly, County went on to win the game 4-2, which left me immensely proud a couple of years later when I saw the name of Zeljeznicar Sarajevo in the UEFA cup, and beating a good team - Bayern Munich, it could have been. *We* beat them! We beat them 4-2, and now they're in Europe, beating Bayern Munich! In the same way that our successive September victories over York City and Sheffield United meant we were better than Man City and Everton respectively, this result meant County were better than Bayern Munich!

The level of County support has been predicted in today's local paper as around 1,300. I'm torn between feeling proud that so many of us are willing to spend big money and take time off work, and affronted that so many have come out just for the big game. Where were you when we played Millwall, eh, I ask, with the self-righteousness that comes from attending every game, and thus being a Real Fan.

The game starts, and County are immediately forced onto the back foot, as Dowie goes close in the first minute. West Ham, heartened by this, force the pace, causing their fans in the seats to our right - who stand up en masse whenever West Ham attack - to direct some serious taunting in our direction.

County rally from the early mauling, however, and it is thus slightly against run of play when West Ham take a 10th minute lead. It's one of their foreign players who scores, although the tannoy announcement is unclear. It could be that it's *extremely* unclear, and the announcer was saying "Dicks" or "Dowie", but I don't think so. Not that I could care less who's given them the lead - all I'm concerned about it that I don't want us to be on the receiving end of the drubbing that is now on the cards..

That dread prospect doesn't seem to worry the fat bloke who's sitting next to me, and who continues to feed his face. The person who should be between us hasn't turned up, so Fat Bloke is actually sitting on two seats, one for each buttock. At least, I assume the person who should be between us hasn't turned up - it could be, of course, that Fat Bloke has simply bought two seats for his own personal comfort. £36: the cost of having a fat arse.

County continue to play poorly, with terrible distribution, and it seems as though our excellent cup run will end tonight. West Ham look fast and skilful, and their approach work is deadly. It's only our excellent defence that keeps the score down to one, and half time arrives with relief the overriding emotion in the County end.

I'm slightly disappointed to discover at this juncture that West Ham haven't bothered turning on the two massive TV screens they've got in each corner - I wouldn't have minded seeing what's happened in "Coronation Street." Presumably a game against little Stockport didn't justify half time highlights, although the game is being shown on the TV monitors under the stand. If the balance of play continues in the second half, they'll have missed out on showing a lot of Hammers goals.

County make a half time substitution, with Cavaco again coming on, this time for the ineffective John Jeffers. West Ham also make a change, with their sub being announced as Lazirides. *"Who? Lazarus? He looks like death warmed up"* is the response from behind me. It's the County sub who is by far the more effective, however, and County begin to assume control, inspired by the little Portuguese.

We're attacking the far end goal in the second half, which at least means we don't have to bob up and down every two minutes in order to see County's attacks. We thus all get a clear view of our equaliser, and, inevitably, it's Cavaco who scores. Dicks is poncing around (although I wouldn't say that to his face) with the ball about forty yards out, when Cavaco robs him. The little man then bears down on goal, takes it wide of the last two defenders, and sidefoots it into the corner. Oh, nice.

Following the goal, I can sense West Ham getting flustered; now *their* passes are going astray. We almost grab a second five minutes later when a shot from Cavaco - again - is deflected high into the air, and almost drops in. The home fans to our right are silent now, worried that the delightful vision of an expected bagful of goals against a lower division team has mutated, horribly for them, into the spectre of a mere draw.

In the last fifteen minutes or so, West Ham again assume control, although they, like Blackburn before them, are thwarted by the County defence. When they do break through, their forwards are stopped by some excellently timed tackles, and their shots from distance are dealt with easily by Paul Jones. The final whistle goes, and County have earned the most creditable of draws.

We salute the players, and rush back to the car. We're trying to get started on the long journey home as soon as possible, but we're stymied by the police holding up the traffic in order that the numerous County coaches can steal a march. We're thus reduced to sitting impotently, listening to the radio, although that in itself is pleasant enough, as Radio Five Live carries the news that there has only been one other draw in the fourth round, meaning that County, possibly for the first time ever, are in the last ten of a major cup competition. Even better, the draw for the quarter finals is made, and County - should they manage to win the replay - are drawn at home to the winners of the other replay, Southampton or Oxford.

It's the first time I've ever heard a quarter final draw with County's name in it. Well, that's not strictly true. In 1979, thick snow lay on the ground for so long that the FA Cup quarter final draw was actually made with many third round ties - including County's at Wrexham - still unplayed. As we lost that game 6-2, after about seventeen postponements, though, we can hardly claim to have almost been in the quarter finals.

Andy's car is a comfortable one; so much so that, just south of Coventry, I find myself dozing nicely. I assume it'll be a case of ten minutes here and there, so it's actually the nicest surprise of the night when I next open my eyes to find that I've slept for a good hour and a half, and we're off the motorway in Lymm. Andy drops us off near my mum's house - where I left my car - at half past one. I scrape the thick ice off the windscreen, and head for home. I'm once again putting the front door key in the lock in the early hours of a Thursday morning, and once again, I've lost half a day's holiday, travelled about four hundred miles, been on the road a total of fourteen hours, and seen a great County performance. Mad? Moi?

November 30th 1996. Walsall (home).

First things first: ticket prices for the replay have been announced, and they are £12 in all areas of the ground, not £18; and Sky TV have chosen the game for live coverage.

The ticket price thing is really cute. It wasn't a fevered rumour, either; I heard from more than one person that County's Finance Director, no less, had said that the replay, if needed, would be priced at eighteen quid. Of course, when they then announce the prices as twelve, it's with a sense of relief that people accept it, despite the fact that £12 represents a 33% increase on normal prices for the cheapest seats anyway.

Sky coverage is more exciting. County have actually been on live TV three times in recent years (two Autoglass Trophy finals at Wembley, and one semi final at Edgeley Park), but none of the games have been as significant - or as likely to attract a large TV audience - as this one.

Christmas trees (both domestic and council) have started sprouting, I notice on the way to the ground. It's hard to feel festive, mind, when we're not even out of November. In any case, there are more important things to occupy my mind today: County are to issue a priority voucher, for tickets for the West Ham game. This will have the effect of increasing the crowd slightly, as part-time glory hunters come along to guarantee West Ham tickets, but lending an air of unreality to proceedings, as many of the crowd won't be in the slightest bit interested in the game with Walsall at all.

I'm interested, though, especially when the game turns out to be one of the most one-sided I can remember at County; such is our dominance that it seems impossible that this is the same team that were outplaying us for large periods of the game at the Bescot stadium a mere five weeks ago. Can home advantage really count for so much? Whatever, we reach the break a goal ahead, following a surprising display of skill from Brett Angell, who coolly places the ball under the advancing keeper after being put through from midfield.

Half-time sees the parading of our new signing, "Kiko". He is another Portuguese player, joining his compatriot, Luis Cavaco, on County's books. By all accounts, he is supposed to be even better than Cavaco - "shit hot" is one phrase I heard used to describe his performances during his two game trial for the reserves at the end of last season. The cost of a potentially "shit-hot" player is, theoretically, nothing, although the fact that the two Portuguese agents who facilitated the arrival of both Kiko and Cavaco are also paraded on the pitch might suggest to a cynic that a fee, of some description, could well be payable by County for the player's signature.

As the second half progresses, and we double our lead through another goal from Angell, this time a header at the Railway End, the pitch begins to cut up badly - a worrying sign, considering the re-laying a mere 18 months ago. County play controlled, passing football of a style beloved by football purists throughout the land; it's hard to remain as true to your principles when playing on a mud-bath, however, and with the worst of the winter still to come, we could do with the pitch holding up as well as possible.

At the final whistle, our dominance has seen us win by a mere two goals, albeit with a number of shots against the woodwork. I get home, turn on the teletext and find that the latest win in our current tremendous run has seen us rise to... tenth! It's not really disappointing, however, that we're still anchored there;

Saturday Night and Thursday Morning

it simply wouldn't seem right, somehow, for us to be anywhere else, as we bid a
fond farewell to the month of November.

DECEMBER

NATIONWIDE LEAGUE DIVISION TWO

	P	W	D	L	F	A	Pts
MILLWALL	21	11	7	3	32	23	40
BRENTFORD	21	10	7	4	33	25	37
BURY	20	10	6	4	30	20	36
WREXHAM	19	9	8	2	27	20	35
WATFORD	20	9	8	3	23	17	35
CREWE ALEXANDRA	20	11	1	8	28	19	34
LUTON TOWN	20	10	4	6	32	25	34
BURNLEY	21	10	4	7	28	22	34
CHESTERFIELD	20	10	4	6	20	15	34
STOCKPORT COUNTY	**21**	**9**	**6**	**6**	**28**	**25**	**33**
BRISTOL CITY	20	9	5	6	35	22	32
BRISTOL ROVERS	21	7	7	7	22	22	28
YORK CITY	20	7	5	8	23	27	26
SHREWSBURY TOWN	21	7	5	9	25	32	26
PRESTON NORTH END	21	7	4	10	21	24	25
BLACKPOOL	21	5	9	7	20	22	24
BOURNEMOUTH	21	7	3	11	19	26	24
WALSALL	20	6	4	10	20	19	22
GILLINGHAM	21	6	4	11	19	26	22
PLYMOUTH ARGYLE	21	5	7	9	22	29	22
NOTTS COUNTY	20	5	5	10	15	21	20
PETERBOROUGH UNITED	21	4	8	9	31	39	20
ROTHERHAM UNITED	20	3	6	11	18	32	15
WYCOMBE WANDERERS	21	3	5	13	16	33	14

December 3rd 1996. Rotherham United (away).

I've spent much of the last few days poncing around trying to get tickets for the West Ham replay. This season is the first for a few years in which, being a bit skint over the summer, I didn't buy a season ticket - and thus a guaranteed big match ticket. It's strange how you tend to find out who your friends are at times like these; a group of five lads with a season ticket each - and thus fifteen guaranteed West Ham tickets (the club allow three per season ticket) between five people - couldn't promise that they could get me one. Well, thanks *very* much, boys. One or two other people did offer, thankfully, and I eventually got my greedy mits on a ticket at ten past seven last night (yes, the phone call was logged that precisely), courtesy of a season ticket-holding friend - the good and saintly Jack Oldham. (I accept, by the way, that it's probably a bit silly to be worried like this: I've never known a County match yet where tickets haven't eventually ended up on open sale - even those games which have eventually sold out. Look, I'm neurotic, okay? Get off my case).

Tonight's game is, on the face of it, routine, albeit one which we should be fairly confident of winning; Rotherham are currently anchored to the bottom of the Second Division. However, there are a number of reasons why I'm looking forward to the match with more than the usual relish, foremost of which is the fact that tonight sees us play a team managed by Danny Bergara for the first time since he was sacked by County

You will not be able to find a County fan with a bad word to say about Danny Bergara; indeed, were the town to start a fund to erect a statue of the little man outside the Town Hall, people would probably be knocked down in the rush to contribute. I'd certainly be at the front of the queue.

Consider the facts. When the little Uruguayan was appointed in April 1989, County were an awful team. We'd been in the basement division for 19 consecutive seasons, with not so much as a sniff of promotion - our highest finish had been 11th. We'd also had more managers since the war than any other English League club at that point. When he left us, he was one of the longest-serving in the league.

We were, however, safe from relegation in that particular season, leaving Bergara with the option - which he took - of experimenting with his squad, weeding out the dead wood, and judging the scale of his task. Of the 12 games between him taking over and the end of the season, not one was won, with the first seven games all being drawn. Such a good job did he do in those dozen games, however, that the following season, we finished an unbelievable fourth - only slipping away from automatic promotion in the last few games, and losing to Chesterfield in the play-off semis.

Saturday Night and Thursday Morning

The following season - 1990-91 - we were promoted, in second place, ensuring the elevation with a 5-0 home win over Scunthorpe on the last day of the season, and only being denied the championship by Rochdale's failure to take a point from Darlington. The following season was expected to be one of consolidation; the Third Division was particularly tough, with high-expectation clubs such as West Brom, Stoke, Birmingham and Huddersfield in there. No one had read Bergara the script, however, as we stormed through the season playing the same cavalier football that had been so successful the previous year, and finally finished fifth. We then qualified for the playoff final by beating Stoke over two legs. Oh yes, and we won through to the Autoglass final as well, where we again played Stoke.

We lost both Wembley games, but were back there the following season, again in the Autoglass Trophy, against Stoke's neighbours, Port Vale, against whom we lost a few days earlier in yet another play-off semi final (I know this is getting complicated, but stick with it).

The following season we were, incredibly, at Wembley *again*, having reached the playoff final once more. Thanks to David Elleray, we again lost, however - to Burnley, in the bad tempered final referred to elsewhere. The incredible run of success, almost inevitably, had to end, however, and, with the team in mid-table, Bergara was sacked in April of the following season - although not because of the team's disappointing performances.

Danny - County fans feel as though they are first name terms with the man, and minor details like never having met him change that feeling not a jot - was sacked following a dust-up with the Chairman at a sponsors' function at a local hotel. Details of what happened only emerged in court during Bergara's unfair dismissal hearing (which he eventually won with 75% liability awarded against the club, leaving County with a large compensation bill to pay). Following what seemed to have been resentment which built up over a number of months, Bergara and club Chairman Brendan Elwood came to blows at a posh suits and arse-licking do at a local hotel. Despite the way the fracas was reported in some areas of the media at the time ("Boss Thumps Chairman Shocker!"), it was Bergara who called the police and accused Elwood of the fisticuffs; Danny was never accused of starting the thumping (he was accused of being pissed, but that's another matter). There are some who say the knives had been out for him for a while, however, over expenses spent on booze, and the fact that he wouldn't move to Stockport, but I wouldn't know. All I would say is that if he came back to manage us tomorrow, I'd be ecstatic.

Okay, four Wembley losses, no pots, and only one actual promotion to show for his years in charge. But for a team as crap as County were previously...? At the end of the day (which seems a curiously apposite phrase), Bergara's

134

stewardship of County was magnificent, and the sordid manner of his departure left a bad taste.

I need petrol, so I end up buying a packet of wine gums and some crisps from the garage where I fill up - away games really are the curse of the junk food junkie. The crisp manufacturers are running a competition with incredibly tacky prize of 2 million Daily Mirror/Daily Record newspapers "to be won". *("Yes! YES! I've won, I'VE WON!" "Ohh myyyy Goddd, what?* **What have you won?!?"** *"Er, a newspaper.")* I'm actually quite chuffed that I *don't* "win" a Daily Mirror, not only because I wouldn't want to read the trashy rag following the jingoistic crap it printed during Euro '96, but also because it's probably harder to lose such a competition than otherwise

At the risk of sounding like one of those roads bores you try and avoid at parties, I've got a choice of three routes from Stockport ower t'Pennines toneet. I can either take the conventional Snake Pass (so-called because of its shape, rather than any reptilian proliferation), head north and take the Woodhead Pass and the M1, or south for the complicated Edale/Peak District route I travelled back in September for the Sheffield United game. As the other two routes involve going through Sheffield, I decide on the Woodhead option. And did I ever tell you about the time I went on the good old A30 through Okehampton? Mmm, what tasty vol-au-vents. Now that *was* a journey...

It may be the hopeless romantic in me, but I like Yorkshire. My sister Carole and her husband Kevin (Sheffield Wednesday) live in Brighouse, and so I'm over there relatively (hur hur, geddit?) often. I think the Yorkshire countryside is some of the most beautiful in England, and, even at night, there's a certain something about breasting the Pennines and seeing, as tonight, the lights of Barnsley spread out in front of me.

Here on the top, I can also feel the car being buffeted by the strong wind which has been picking up all day, wind which hardly drops as I descend into Rotherham. Luckily, I've wangled the Cavalier again; had I been in the Fiesta, I would probably have been able to admire those lights of Barnsley from a unique vantage point, as I was blown off the Pennines to land smack on top of them. However, I survive the pounding, and arrive at the ground at about twenty to seven, leaving me ample time to park up and have a pint. As I open the car door, it's caught by a gust and almost ripped out of my hand. It really is quite incredibly windy.

I buy my first away programme, because it's Danny's club and I not only want to read what he's got to say about us, but I also want to experience again his superb managerial notes. I'm not one of those people - sadly all too prevalent today - who think wogs begin at Calais; and I think you *can* laugh at a foreigner's uncertain grasp of the English language without being a bigot, just as I wouldn't mind if a Frenchman were to crease himself at my own schoolboy efforts (I failed French "O" level, largely, I still feel, because during the oral examination, if I couldn't quite remember the correct French word, I reverted to a rather silly habit I'd developed, of saying the English one backwards). Danny didn't used to mix metaphors as much as stick them in the blender and purée them, on one memorable occasion attempting to draw a comparison between the club's development and housing. We had apparently been a small terrace when he took over, and were now a semi. We were aiming to become a detached, with a double garage.

I enter Millmoor, and take a leak in the bog from hell - one of those "conveniences" unique to football grounds, where, in order to gain access, it's necessary to actually step over a trough of piss. It's a close call between here and Chesterfield for the title of "worst bogs in football", but I think, on balance, that I'll award that particular honour to Millmoor. It's a rattly, atmospheric old ground, of the type that would normally bring a tear to the eye of the football ground anorak. Tonight, however, with the wind buffeting the stand roofs and whipping through exposed corners, it's merely a dilapidated, freezing old dump. The crowd is small, Rotherham's poor recent form reducing the home support, and the weather affecting the County following as well. It's thus one of those games where the players' shouts are audible off the pitch (we used to have these all the time at County; I remember one particular game in the early 80s with a paltry crowd of 1,500 or so. One of the players yelled something and a bloke standing behind me on the Railway End shouted "can you be quiet on the pitch, please, there's people trying to talk back here!" I swear the whole ground - spectators, all 22 players, both linesman and the ref - laughed). The attendance contrasts markedly with my previous visit last season. Rotherham had just won the Autoglass Trophy at Wembley, and were parading the trophy for the first time in front of a full house of glory-seekers.

The teams emerge, and the ovation we give Danny Bergara brings a tear to the eye. If only there were more County fans here. I wouldn't like him to think that the manner of his leaving the club coloured our view of him. I'm sure he doesn't, but if he's in any doubt, I can guarantee he'll get a "stander" when he brings his new team to Edgeley Park in March.

The game starts, County score early, and the overwhelming feeling is that we've won already. Rotherham are a genuinely poor team, and County seem to be treating the game, once they've got the goal, as a kind of extended training session, with absolutely no danger whatsoever of conceding the lead; you get the impression that if Rotherham were presumptuous enough to score, County would immediately rush down the other end and restore their lead with the minimum of fuss.

The goal is a Kieron Durkan free kick which takes a massive deflection. I'm right behind in line to see the ball balloon off the wall and into the opposite corner of the net to that which the keeper was guarding. I think that's what's known in the trade as a "wicked" deflection. You really do have to feel sorry for Rotherham: it never rains but it pours, which is another particularly apposite phrase in the circumstances, as it now starts to rain, precipitation which the gale causes to "fall" horizontally. The majority of the brave (stupid?) Rotherham souls who had been standing on the open terrace at the far end scuttle under cover, leaving a mere handful (definitely stupid) who stick it out (fancy sticking it out in this weather - it'll drop off). I can only thank God that we're in a ground which provides cover for visiting supporters, unlike Edgeley Park. The weather is so wild now that the shadows on the pitch are wobbling as the floodlight pylons shake, and the rain is now sleet. If it turns to snow, the route back home might be a bit dodgy - or even closed.

Half time arrives with County in complete control, and the appearance of what I hear described at my side as an "absolutely fucking crap mascot." I can only concur, as "Dusty the Miller", battles to keep his floppy inflatable head on in the wind. Now, listen - I know these people probably do it for nothing, and we have to attract kids back to football, but come on. I mean, *come on!* If a six year old kid had made this thing in a primary school art class, they'd probably call in the educational psychologists; if a kid had made it in a secondary school, they'd have been chucked out of the class for being ridiculous.

The second half is as uneventful as the first, although County keeper Paul Jones almost scores with a wind-assisted end-to-end kick. We once had a keeper who actually did this - Brian Lloyd, whose spell at the club contained little of note otherwise. It was in a game at Bradford in the 70s, and Lloyd scored the opening goal of the game. The Bradford keeper was apparently laughing all over his face as he picked the ball out of his net, presumably safe in the knowledge that Lloyd's abilities would not prevent the Bradford forwards scoring six in reply, which they duly did.

The only other action of note before the end is an incredible miss by Brett Angell after Armstrong had not only laid it on a plate for him, he'd provided cutlery, cruet, finger bowl, glass of wine and a tasty side salad; Angell still contrives to sidefoot delicately over the bar from about six inches out. Not to worry, though: we're in control, and the final whistle blows on another away win.

On the way out, I only just avoid standing in one of two great steaming piles of police horse shit, right in the line of the County fans' departure. When the final whistle does go, and a couple of hundred people try to funnel through a six foot wide gap at once, it's going to be impossible to even see the crap, far less avoid stepping in it. I consider for a moment staying to watch the fun, but decide on balance that a quick getaway is preferable.

I'm soon away and on the motorway, listening to Newcastle's latest European game on the radio; one of the nicest feelings in the world is slowly warming up after having been absolutely bone marrow cold, at an away game your team won. However, no matter how warm and comfortable I might be, the weather is still brutal, expressing itself now by means of driving snow. I see a worrying road sign, which indicates I've still got 24 miles to go. Thankfully, the blizzard eases off, however, as I let the car in front slip away so that I can put the full beam on. After a journey perhaps more nerve-wracking than it should have been, I arrive safely back home just after half past ten. I limp inside, as I seem to have pulled a left buttock muscle, presumably running to the car after the game whilst freezing cold. It's one of those injuries, like "ricked celebratory neck," "questioning referee's parentage strain" and "disallowed goal protest hernia" that are peculiar to football fans.

December 7th 1996. Mansfield Town (away) (FA Cup Sponsored by Littlewoods Pools R2).

Today, following the midweek jaunt over t'Pennines in a blizzard, is another mad weather day. (Interestingly, local radio revealed that the Woodhead Pass was indeed closed by Wednesday morning, so that's my own personal "How I Cheated Death" story sorted. Remind me to ring the Reader's Digest, will you?). The "mad weather" in this case means dense fog, which closes in on the outskirts of Mansfield. I'm giving John Taylor a lift again, and our main topic of conversation as we also close in on Mansfield, and the fog gets thicker and thicker, centres around whether the game will survive.

Arriving early enough for a pint or two, we ask a couple of coppers the way to the nearest pub. After establishing that we are away fans, they direct us to a large pub packed to the gills with County fans. It's sad that segregation is even deemed necessary in pre-match drinking dens these days. Needless to say, the pub is heaving with County fans. After a single pint, I leave early, as I've had no northern middle-of-the-day dinner, and am starvingly hungry. Luckily, there's a chippy opposite, and a portion of greasy chips and a soggy cornish pastie fills the physical hole, if not the gastronomic one.

I approach the away turnstiles, but am reluctant to enter just yet. The fog is so thick that I wouldn't be at all surprised if the match were to be abandoned sometime before quarter to five. In such cases, the less cynical amongst you will perhaps be surprised to hear, clubs don't offer refunds, or even free admission to the rearranged game. On one infamous occasion a couple of years ago, Torquay, of all places, called off a half past seven evening kick off at just gone twenty past, with most County fans already inside the ground; it apparently took them until then to realise that the torrential rain which had been falling all day had made the pitch unplayable. I figure that if I wait outside, socialising, until *just* before kick-off, I increase my chances of not falling foul of just such a rip-off. Knowing my luck, of course, it'll probably be called off at five past three.

John returns from the pub full of a story about winding up some Mansfield fans he got talking to; the pub obviously wasn't exclusively for the away support. He apparently told them - to the accompaniment of a massed lighting-up of home supporters' eyes - that we've got loads of players out injured and suspended - all complete lies, of course. If we turn them over this afternoon, there'll be at least one small group of Mansfield fans with the idea that the County squad is hellishly strong.

Inside the ground, John disappears, and I amble away to a quiet corner of the away terrace. Squinting with all my might, I can just about make out the players on the halfway line. Someone said outside that the criterion for abandoning a game is when the referee can't see both goals from the halfway line. Well, that's all fine and dandy for the referee, but what about us fans behind the goals? What I assume is the goal County are attacking (unless Mansfield have a very peculiarly shaped pitch) is completely invisible, engulfed in a soggy, white blanket.

Not to worry, though - we have our own entertainment, as some braindead Mansfield throwbacks have grouped in the County end, and start their taunts soon after kick off. It's funny, but I don't really associate Mansfield with hooliganism (that said, I'm not sure what exactly you *do* associate it with - Centre Parcs? Robin Hood?). Sure enough, it kicks off in the crowd as well, and a couple of scrappers are ejected. Of course, the police cannot believe their luck, and indulge themselves in a bout of fussing and manoeuvring, eventually standing in front of us, achieving nothing more than obscuring our view,

Incredibly, despite the fact that the trouble was started by a group of Mansfield fans who were simply out for bother - actually paying to get in the away end such was their feeble-minded desperation for a scrap - they're not ejected en masse; they're escorted back to the home end. I know I'm sounding like Disgusted Telegraph-Reader of Surrey again, but come on! A bunch of slack-jawed, dribbling fuckwits like this, easily identifiable to all and sundry, deliberately (it's their ground, for Christ's sake, so they can't claim mistaken turnstile identity) come looking for trouble, and, instead of being chucked out, they're patted on the head like naughty boys, and escorted like returning heroes to their own territory. Meanwhile, the brave boys in blue, of course, line up in front of us, blocking our view, and glaring at us for being so stupid as to not realise that entering the ground through the "away fans only" turnstiles was simply asking for it.

You may have detected a strain of anti-police sentiment running through this tome. I'm not really such an anarchist, however; it's simply that this book is about attending football matches, and virtually all my experience of crassly bad policing has been at football matches. That cannot be coincidence. Better social commentators than me have pointed out elsewhere that there's a certain type of bobby - perhaps in the majority, perhaps not; I don't know - that likes policing football purely for the chance it gives them to bash a few heads. I find that intensely objectionable.

The fog hasn't cleared any - if anything, every so often, it gets thicker. I can't see the other goal clearly, still less make out the action in the area; at times the whole far end disappears from view. I presume that when the players disappear, we must be attacking; every so often, however, Mansfield players appear, bearing down on the County goal. None of their attacks come to anything however.

It's during one of the invisible player periods that we score. The rest of the County fans have occasionally been letting out loud "ooohs!" - they've either got better eyes than me, or they're liars. I'm glancing distractedly across at them, when a celebratory cheer starts, and ripples through the crowd, gathering flailing arms in its wake, so we must have scored.

It could be, of course, that the fans aren't in fact cheering a goal. Maybe a Mansfield player has been sent off, or the referee's got the ball in his face, or a female streaker... Nope, that's a goal all right - the players are lining up again to kick off (unless they've actually had half time, and I didn't notice). I permit myself the lowest-key County goal celebration I've ever indulged in - an enthusiastic clap - figuring that I'd look rather stupid if I suddenly started leaping around like a pillock twenty seconds after everybody else. I ask a couple of people who scored, and they don't know. One takes a guess at Armstrong, although it's clear he's got no more clue than anyone else. I'm quite relived at this, as it means that they were indeed lying with their "ooohs!" earlier, and my eyes aren't that bad.

Half time arrives about a minute after the goal, and even more fog arrives just after that. Peter Collins is congratulated on his 77th birthday, but if this fog gets any thicker, it's a good bet that he could well be 78 in a week or two - at the rearrangement.

Thankfully, the game is much more exciting in the second half - the far goal is still completely invisible, but County are attacking our end. Every so often, we're all peering into the gloom, when suddenly County players appear, running towards us with the ball, and the excitement builds, far more quickly than in a conventional game. It's during one of this moments that we increase our lead. The ball is lofted out of the gloom towards Armstrong, who plays an absolutely superb first time pass into the path of Kieron Durkan. He charges through the defence and slots it into the corner of the net. Whoo-hooo!! I saw that one! Yeeearrrghh!

The 0-2 deficit is the signal for the home fans to drop a subtle hint to the referee: *"we can't see a fucking thing."* When that doesn't work, and play continues, they change tack: *"The referee's a wanker!"* *"Just because you're losing,"* reply the County fans, which seems fair comment.

Meanwhile, the soup is just as thick. I find myself, for example, watching vague shapes on the wing, thinking "he'll cross it soon", when suddenly there's a loud "ooooh!" from the home fans - it's already been crossed and near-missed. It's just after 4.15 now, and the fog's ridiculously thick. We don't seem in any danger of losing the game, but real danger of suffering an abandonment.

Now that County are attacking our end, I can see that Luis Cavaco's got gloves on - a foreign players' affectation that I never thought I'd see from someone in a County shirt. The Mansfield defence seem to view him as a bit of a pansy as a result, and hack him down relentlessly. From the free kick which results from one of these fouls, County score a third, Durkan curling a superb left footer into the top corner. We're in round three. Thankfully, the referee agrees, and allows the game to continue to a finish.

I dive out at the final whistle and hare back to the car. John's not as neurotic as me (doesn't he realise the importance of that five minutes we'll save, hey, hey?), and doesn't appear until I've got the car started, moved to the end of the road we were parked on and and am impatiently revving the engine. Nonetheless, we get underway reasonable quickly and set off home. Annoyingly (I'm sure entirely *why* it's annoying, but it just bloody is), the fog proves to have been incredibly localised, and lifts almost as soon as we leave the town. The radio confirms not only that there has been no fog anywhere else in the country (or if there was, they didn't mention it) but also that County's first goal was yet another OG. And I wasn't even able to laugh at it.

December 10 1996. Doncaster Rovers (away) (AutoWindscreens Shield R1).
The FA Cup 3rd round draw was made last night. County got Stoke away, which isn't the worst tie that could have emerged; it's fairly close, and with our current form, there's a good chance of getting a result (that's football-speak, by the way. Losing 5-0 would, of course, technically be a "result", but you know what I mean). However, the very fact that we were in the draw meant that the match

scheduled for 3rd round day has obviously had to be postponed. And what was that unfortunate game? An Edgeley Park-er? Or a local away trip - Bury, perhaps, or Blackpool? Nope, the longest journey of the season, all the way to Plymouth, will now be rearranged for midweek, and yet another return home in the early hours of Thursday morning.

Never mind; that's in the future. It's time now to concentrate on tonight's little exercise. Two hour journey; Woodhead Pass, M1, M18. New ground for me, and my first ever experience of a crowd of less than a thousand - understandably, as it's a poxy little tournament which only awakens interest from around the quarter final stage onwards. Mimicking the FA Cup tie, Donny take a first half lead through a penalty; County then score two in two minutes to win 2-1. No traffic problems in either direction; I'm home by half ten.

I'm tempted to leave it at that - it is only the first round of the AutoWindscreens Shield after all. However, tonight saw quite possibly a significant and momentous game in the history of Stockport County FC. When the story of football in the late 1990s comes to be written, it may well be that tonight's game has a rather greater significance than many of us realised at the time. For tonight, less than one thousand people see the English debut of Kiko Charana, the "paradee" from half-time in the Walsall game. Yes, gentle reader, mark this well: the first appearance in English football of the "Kiko" who has gained international footballing stardom in the short time since this book was published was for Stockport County against Doncaster in the AutoWindscreens Shield, on 10th December 1996.

Now, I realise that unless events come to my rescue, I could well look a total prat for writing these words. But I'm not so sure. It is a matter of some little pride to me that I spotted the potential of Alun Armstrong in a pre-season friendly at Cheadle Town, a game we won 11-0. His control and touch on a bumpy pitch marked him out as an instant star - at least in my mind - and if he hasn't quite realised his full potential, it can only be a matter of time.

Charana has a similar impact. In fact, he is a revelation, with his close control and dribbling leaving the Doncaster defenders in knots. He scores County's equaliser - albeit with the help of a big deflection - and has a hand in the winner. He also should have had a penalty; dribbling past a handful of defenders, he is upended in the area, and only his theatrical dive prevents him getting the decision (you can almost read the referee's mind at this point: *"we don't do that kind of thing here, lad. It's a man's game. You'd have got the penalty if you hadn't behaved like such a pansy. And take those bloody gloves off"*). He also performs a good half dozen more of those "mazy" run thingies, beating a number of Donny defenders each time.

142

All this, and he only came on as sub with half an hour to go. Mark my words - a star is born.

December 14th 1996. Peterborough United (home).

Big family news of the week is that Martin has landed a part-time job at a local sports superstore. Whilst the chance of earning regular pocket money is a godsend to an impecunious seventeen year old, the hours - Saturday afternoons and Tuesday evenings being the most shocking - mean that he'll now miss out on most County games. I can't help but think that his dedication to the County cause is less than mine.

In 1981, aged 17, and after God knows how many applications (and one memorable monosyllabic grunted interview at Marks and Spencer following which I wasn't surprised to be turned down; in retrospect, if it'd've been me conducting the interview, I'd probably have slapped me across the face), I was eventually offered a Saturday job at British Home Stores. However, in the period between applying for the job and being offered it, I had joined a local cricket club, Bredbury St Marks (off-spin and lower order right hand bat, thanks for asking), and thus, of course, had to refuse the position. (I say "of course" with a confidence I didn't possess at the time; I didn't tell my mum that I'd turned down a job for cricket until years afterwards). Come to think of it, I didn't even turn it down for *County* (who in any case, tended to play most home games on Friday nights in those days). Dearie me, what is the youth of today coming to?

At the ground, the word is that the West Ham game might not be a sell out - I feel this is hardly surprising in view of the live television, the fact that it's only a week before Christmas, and the County Board's decision to rip people off, but for there to be spare seats at such a game is disappointing, to say the least.

And that's about it. We do play a game, after a fashion, but are prevented from scoring for the first time in 24 games by a Peterborough side who themselves show little in the way of attacking ideas. No, really, that's it. 0-0.

Wednesday December 18th 1996. West Ham United (home) (Coca Cola Cup R4 replay).

Ooh, by heck, I'm excited. The tension has been building all day, with virtually every other person at work making the usual "ah here comes the token County fan" comments *("So, are you going tonight, then?" "Nah - I've been to every game this season, home and away, but I thought I'd give the biggest cup tie for 25 years a miss")* They mean well, of course, but I wish they wouldn't bother, even if it is the only topic of conversation for some of them - I'm nervous enough as it is. It's not only the build up for tonight at work that's getting intense, either - interest in the local media has been incredible; fuelled, I suspect, by the game being covered by live TV.

It's been raining all day; drizzly at first, but as kick-off approaches, it turns into a downpour. If the state of my front lawn is anything to go by, the pitch is going to be virtually waterlogged. I wonder whether it will prevent us playing our passing game which has been so productive of late? Normally, weather like this would benefit a lower division club, but we play football. As indeed we always did under Danny Bergara's stewardship, despite the fact that many people claimed we were simply a long-ball team. Bergara's philosophy - and it's a good one, which I wouldn't be upset about if we still played - was to get the ball to the halfway line as quickly as possible, and *then* start playing the football in your opponents' half. It's a subtlety sadly lost on boss-eyed idiots who could only ever see that we had the six foot seven Kevin Francis up front; ker-ching! - the words "long" and "ball" then appeared in their eyes, like a cartoon cash register. Consolation came from the realisation that the most vehement protesters about our supposed playing style were usually connected, curiously enough, with sides we'd just roundly beaten.

Outside the ground, I hear that a player called Moody of Oxford (Ron?) was earlier being interviewed on Radio Five Live, and apparently the reporter made comments of the "you've got a tie with West Ham waiting if you get through" variety. To his immense credit, he responded along the lines of "I wouldn't be so sure; they've got to get past Stockport first". There's been a lot more "West Ham are going to win" media bollocks nationally, I've noticed myself - It'll be all the more satisfying if we do win. The same radio ham also tells me that Howard Wilkinson - expert summariser for Radio Five Live - has opined that he'll be surprised if the game goes ahead, as there are puddles of water visible on the pitch.

Once I get in, however, it's clear that he was being unduly pessimistic (strange, that, for a Yorkshireman); whilst it's far from ideal, and will certainly need taking care on, the playing surface is actually not as bad as I was expecting. There's no actual surface water; the usual indicator of the game being in danger.

Despite the worries expressed about not selling out the County ends, there don't seem to be many spare seats in the Barlow Stand, where I'm sitting tonight. There are a couple, but the Cheadle End and Main Stands look pretty full also. The only area which looks at all sparsely populated is the Railway End, where the poor, drenched West Ham fans are standing. I feel embarrassed, truly embarrassed, that we've charged them twelve quid for this. Never mind that they're used to paying more at Upton Park, it's a bloody rip off, pure and simple, and the people who decided the prices should be ashamed of themselves. As, of course, I'm sure they are.

I've not got a bad seat, considering, although as Jack Oldham got me the ticket and Martin and my dad got their own, I'm doing a Billy No-Mates impression. I'm fairly central, however, and all around me is the evidence of the televisual paraphernalia necessary for live broadcasting. The commentators and main cameras are perched up in a small, meccano-style "gantry" that a local scaffolder threw up as a favour to County five or so years ago. There are a couple of pitchside cameras protected by straw bales, and also, suspended from the roof, the two remote controlled "offside" cameras. A couple of seats behind me, on the back row, and sitting next to a friend, Richard Harnwell, whom I spot, is a guy with headphones and one of those peculiar lip-mikes, looking at what seems at first glance to be a computer monitor, placed on a makeshift table which has spread over five or six seats in front of him. He looks to me like the commentator, John Helm, although I thought he worked for ITV. Presumably he's freelancing for Sky; I guess he's identifying the players, perhaps for the TV captions. Strange that he should have to spread across so many seats in one of the stands, though. It's hard to avoid the overriding feeling of unreality that this game I'm watching is simultaneously being watched in tens of thousands of living rooms nationwide, including my own, where Anna and Julia have promised they'll be glued to the screen; indeed, Julia has been allowed to stay up late to see the whole match.

West Ham start well, and dominate early proceedings, as you might expect. The greasy surface isn't causing too many problems, although one or two players end up on their arse when they try and be too cocky. County settle, however, and start to play the ball around nicely, and, more importantly, to get stuck in hard whenever West Ham are in possession. We know we're no match for the talent on display in normal circumstances, and if we played West Ham ten consecutive times, we'd probably win about twice. But if we are going to have a chance tonight, we've got to let them know they've been in a game, and not let them settle.

That said, after twenty minutes, West Ham go and score. Bollocks. A shot from one of their forwards is deflected over by a desperate Mike Flynn and, as the resulting corner is swung in, Julian Dicks thunders in like a train, with superb timing (so, perhaps, not *too* like a train, then), and sends a header thumping into the net at the Cheadle End. Ah well, we got to the fourth round for only the second time in our history.

Amazingly, however, we equalise what must literally only be about a minute later. Mike Flynn launches a long throw in from the right, and when it's cleared back out to him, heads it back towards goal. Alun Armstrong seems to get a good touch on it, and then it's headed back into the net from someone on the far side, but seemingly without a County player anywhere near it. We all rise as one as the side netting bulges, but no one seems to be taking the credit. Another own goal? Maybe, but who gives a toss? We're level.

And five minutes later we're ahead. We've started playing the ball around beautifully on the slippery surface, and it's a passing move which started with the ball in Paul Jones' hands that leads to our goal. The ball is worked up the left wing to Tom Bennett. He sizes up his options before lofting what seems to be a hopeful ball into the area, in the general direction of Brett Angell. Angell steals a yard on his marker and heads it towards goal, where it loops into the top corner of the net, just under the bar. Miklosko, the West Ham keeper, doesn't move a muscle.

We all leap again in unison with a great noisy yaaarrrrgh. For my part, I adopt the posture of Ian Botham during his five-for-one spell at Edgbaston back in '81, an image that's frozen in my mind as the embodiment of joyous celebration: chest out, arms back - Yusss!! Almost my first thought is of Anna and the kids, watching this at home. Two of them - the females - will be leaping around almost as madly as we are at the ground at this moment, whilst Chris and Andrew will probably be looking on bemusedly and wondering why Julia and their mummy have just gone mental, and can they have Fireman Sam on?

West Ham bounce back and again dominate for a short period, which ends with Bishop - one of the recognisable players, with his long hair plastered down by the rain - shooting against the top of the bar. Just afterwards, Paul Jones, dives to his left and makes a great one handed save before diving on the loose ball in front of the onrushing Dowie. It's not going to be Dowie's night, it seems, as a couple of minutes later, he hobbles off following a Jim Gannon tackle.

Half time thus arrives with us perhaps slightly fortunate to be still ahead. I wander back to talk to Richard Harnwell, and discover that what I thought was a computer monitor is in fact a TV monitor, what I thought was John Helm is in fact John Helm, and what I thought was John Helm's employment is in fact him sitting on the back row of the Vernon Stand because Sky have got the gantry, commentating for Carlton, the London TV station who will be showing highlights of this game after News at Ten. Needless to say, with a TV monitor showing highlights of the first half, a sizeable crowd builds up behind him, and we get to see that our equaliser was one of the funniest own goals you'll ever see. Iain Dowie - and God only knows what he was attempting, twists and arches to send Armstrong's flick-on bulleting past his own keeper. It would have been a fantastic goal at the right end; it *definitely* wasn't Dowie's night.

Following the replays, and presumably whilst people at home are either watching a studio discussion or ignoring the adverts, the Sky techies get a bit of practice in with the penalties graphic, presumably not realising that with the score at 2-1, there cannot possibly be penalties, as, if West Ham equalise, they'll have scored more away goals.

However, County play even better in the second half, and West Ham struggle to break through, although not for lack of trying. Long shots from distance, though, don't trouble Paul Jones, who is having a fantastic game in goal. The clearest-cut chances fall to County; after about an hour, Alun Armstrong breaks clear, rides a tackle and bears down on goal. His shot is straight at Miklosko, however, who parries the ball away. Brett Angell retrieves it and then chips it back across goal, where Armstrong is just not tall enough to direct the ball into the net.

County take heart from this miss, and Armstrong creates another great opening. He chases the ball to the touchline with a Hammers defender, lifts it skilfully over his tackle (as it were) and bears down on goal again. The angle is a bit tighter this time, however, and Armstrong unselfishly tries to square the ball to Angell, from where it is scrambled away for a corner.

West Ham come again, but the best they can manage is a penalty claim when Lee Todd clearly fouls their right winger. It's outside the box, mind, so it shouldn't have been a penalty, but the referee enrages the Hammers fans and players by awarding a corner. This comes to nothing, and as the clock ticks down to zero, and Paul Jones makes another couple of good saves, I realise that we're going to win.

Dave Jones makes a timewasting substitution amidst a screech of frantic whistling from the County fans. The noise gets louder as Dicks is booked on the far side for dissent. County are playing keep-ball, and the atmosphere has begun to sound like a jet engine just prior to take off when the referee blows the final whistle. I've moved down to pitch level at this point, and, face upturned to the floodlit deluge, I let out a final, Botham-postured roar of delight.

A good portion of the crowd pour onto the pitch, in the traditional giant-killing way, and after watching them for a few minutes, I leave to join the excited, noisy babble outside - muffled as usual in these circumstances by temporary deafness caused by the crowd noise. I grab someone to ask who won the other replay - something which I wasn't in the slightest concerned with before the game. It's Southampton, apparently, who we'll be playing in the quarter-final.

I dash back to the car, huddled like everyone else against the deluge *(après victoire, le deluge)*. Bugger, sod and arse! It's the Fiesta - I couldn't really justify the Cavalier for a home game - and there's no radio. No glorying in the post-match analysis from Five Live, GMR and the Stockport-based Signal, then, all of whom will have had commentators at the game.

My dad arrives a couple of minutes later, but it's a while after that when Martin and his mate amble slowly back to the car. Irrational old me is stupidly hopping around, wanting to get off; wanting to get home to glory with my family in the result they shared thanks to telly. Myself, I'm probably no more excited than Blackburn, Millwall or Sheffield United, at this point, but I was only frustrated on those occasions when I got back; there was no one to share the excitement. This time, they've watched it on telly.

I drop off the others, then home I zip. Anna and me exchange big cheesy grins, and "well then, eh?"s, and "hee-heee"s (neither of us are the most demonstrative of people), then I dash upstairs for a slash. I nip into Julia's room afterwards to sort out the bed-puddings that all the kids seem to enjoy mixing during the night, and she wakes from her bog-eyed grunting as soon as she realises it's me. Wide-awake, she tells me excitedly about it: "Dad - County won! They were on telly! Brett Angell scored!" I don't bother reminding her I was there, as, frankly, I'm enjoying being told, and not just because it's cute.

Like any child, Julia can turn off the excitement as though with a switch, and as I say "night-night" she's virtually asleep again. Back downstairs, Anna regales me with stories of the reaction at home. I was doing Christopher and Andrew a disservice; both of them were cheering the goals, albeit in Andrew's case slightly bewilderedly, and probably only because everyone else was jumping up and down, and he wanted to join in. That, or his nappy needed changing.

At eleven o' clock or so, with everyone else in bed, I put on the tape of the Sky coverage, and fast forward, creating my own personalised set of edited highlights. As I sit in front of the telly, glorying in the events of a couple of hours ago, I guess that all over Stockport now, there are people (those with dishes on the walls or cables under their gardens), doing exactly the same as me. It's half an hour into Thursday morning when the recorded post-match analysis starts; I eventually finish watching and crawl upstairs ten minutes later, feeling far more tired than I did after getting to bed much later following the Millwall and first West Ham games. Not to worry, though; I've got three full days to recover before Bury on Saturday.

As I lie there, buzzing brain meaning sleep will be a while yet, I remember with a smile the pissed-up Hammers fan outside Upton Park three weeks ago: *"Where the hell's Stockpowt? I only know it exists because we're ploiying vem in va cap"* Presumably, he knows where it is now.

December 21st 1996. Bury (away).

The prices for the Southampton game have been announced, and County, true to their past record, have raised them yet again, to a minimum £14. They really are grasping sods. Trouble is, with the game being after Christmas, I can see more people willing to pay it, and, therefore, there's a good chance it'll sell out - which the Board will see, of course, as justification. I suppose, from a purely financial point of view, if it does sell out, it *will* have been justified. Silly me, thinking that a football club has any moral obligations to its less well off supporters.

My sister Claire has today returned from the States for Christmas, with her American husband Jason, whom she met over here and moved out and married a couple of years ago - a kind of War Bride without the War (and he was a student, and not a G.I.). They've inconsiderately got a flight which arrived too late for today's game, however, so I make the short trip to Bury alone.

It's a bitterly cold day, and I have a confession to make. The other day, I bought a bright blue and white woolly hat, as I've finally been persuaded both of the fact that most body heat loss is through the head, and that it doesn't matter if you look a complete prat at a football match as there will be so many other people looking complete prats that you won't stand out.

It's a short trip to Bury - indeed, I would guess they're our nearest rivals this season, so this game could arguably be described as a "derby". It's an easy route via the M63 and M66, the sun's shining, and the car's running like a peach, thanks to some work I had to done on it on Tuesday. Okay, since I'm in the mood for shamefaced confession, the "work" I had done on it comprised changing the plugs and points. Yes, and I paid a garage to do it. I know what you're thinking - he'll be wearing gloves next, the ponce. Look, they tuned the engine as well, okay?

It was worth the money, though; I'm actually able to drive in the outside lane, which is almost unheard of in this car. I suddenly realise that my speed's up to 80 - it must be the wind behind me, as I'm heading due west on the M63, and the weather men have said it's an easterly, blowing piercingly cold weather in from Siberia (cue Frankie Howerd-style ooh missus joke about wind whipping round your Urals).

I park up on Gigg Lane itself, and have a stroke of massive luck whilst hanging round outside the turnstiles. A bloke approaches and asks if I've got a ticket yet. Misunderstanding him, and assuming he wants to sell me one, I say that it's not an all-ticket game. He realises that, but says that he knows Bury's centre forward; he and his two mates have thus got "player's lounge" passes. Thing is, they've been given four, and as there are only three of them, and they're County fans, they'd like to give the spare to a fellow County fan, and do I want it?

Er, let me think. Do I want to freeze my nuts off, having paid a tenner to sit on a cold plastic seat behind the goal, or do I want a side-on view, and free entry to the cosy, warm world that is corporate hospitality? Handing the bloke his arm back, which I seem to have clumsily snatched off, I say yes, and am handed a beige piece of cardboard marked "Bury FC," and with the words "PLAYER'S GUEST."

I wait outside until just before kick off, giving the finger to, and waving the golden ticket at those of my friends whom I recognise on their way in to Proles Corner. When I have exhausted my gloating, I turn tail and head away from the turnstiles and towards the altogether more civilised "Reception Door 2", as indicated on the pass. It's locked.

Huh! We Player's Guests don't let a little thing like a locked door stop us - we're Player's Guests! I rap sharply on the door with the end of the gold-topped cane which seems to have appeared under my arm. I check my splendid pocket watch - it's almost three - and twiddle my mutton-chop whiskers as someone inside fumbles with the lock.

"Good day," I say to the man who opens the door, waving my ticket imperiously, "I'm a Player's Guest." I realise that this makes me sound more like a wartime cigarette than someone requesting entry to the inner sanctum of a football club *(twenty Player's Guests please mate)*, but the face of the rotund doorman, initially scowling at having to open a door locked presumably because they don't expect freeloaders to arrive this late, changes to a beatific smile as I brandish the pass. "Gawd bless yer, guv'nor" he grovels, as I tip him a florin.

Inside, all is opulence, and the cane, fob watch and top hat melt silently away to be replaced by my standard winter match apparel of jeans, trainers, four sweatshirts, and t-shirt tucked into my underpants to keep out draughts. The doorman offers me a freshly printed team sheet, and points me upstairs to the seats. Huh! You don't get rid of me that easily "Can you tell me where the toilet is?"

He directs me through a door, and I walk down a plushly carpeted hallway. Just before the entrance to the gents, on my left, I see what is presumably the Directors Lounge, in the middle of which is a table groaning under the weight of a splendid buffet, all ready for their snuffling snouts at half-time.

I pause. I am on the verge of walking in and helping myself to a butty. It's one of those situations you can use to impress your mates in the pub with later *("and so I just walked in and helped myself. Bet they were wondering at half time who'd messed up their neat sandwich arrangement, ha ha ha")*. However, my bottle goes, and the story will have to remain untold (or, that is, it could well in fact be told, but, like 99% of similar stories, it'll be a lie).

I make my way back up through the stand into the seats. It is freezing cold here, although as I'm sitting with the home fans, I decide it would be prudent to remove the Stockport County woolly hat. It would also be prudent not to respond to events on the pitch, I realise, either cheering County's goals, or gloating at Bury's misses. This renders my afternoon's entertainment as amongst the most bizarre I've ever experienced; I have to fight not to react to County attacks. It's equally strange to hear the chanting from the County fans, from the point of view of the opposition for once. "We" don't half make a lot of noise at away grounds - you suspect this is the case when you're in amongst it; it's nice to have it confirmed.

The first half is fairly even, with no goals, although it wouldn't have been an unfair lead which Bury almost take after half an hour. Paul Jones makes an ill-advised charge out of his area, and a forward lobs just wide of the empty goal. As the ball's travelling through the air, the fans around me stand up with arms aloft - "yeeeeeeaaaa... oooooooh!" is their reaction. I, meanwhile, would have loved to have stood up and shouted "oh shhhhhhhhhiiiiiiiiiitttttttt... ha-haaaaahhhhhh!!!" But I don't.

I also have to keep quiet when Lee Todd, who has done it before, and has obviously been reading the rules, knees a ball back to Jones, who picks it up, causing the Bury fans around me to leap up en masse: *"backpass!"* The referee, of course, waves play on, as the rule is that it's only classed as a backpass to the keeper if it's played with the leg *below* the knee, a subtle distinction I must admit I wasn't initially aware of. That said, I realised instantly that it must be a legal manoeuvre the first time I saw Todd do it - he was making such a deliberate job of kneeing it, and surely no keeper would be so stupid as to pick it up if he thought it was an illegal pass. Nonetheless, the Bury fans are apoplectic: "bloody blatant, that was!" screams one bloke, presumably genuinely believing that the referee didn't see it, or did, and thought it had been headed back. I'm absolutely *dying* to shout something like "learn the bloody rules, man - you're *allowed* to knee it back" with the self-righteousness of one who has only learned that fact recently. I would have too, if I was sitting with the County fans. Strange, that: if I *was* with the County fans, no one would hear me, yet I still feel frustrated at being denied the chance to shout it.

County dominate the second half, which is gratifying, of course, but merely adds to the frustration, as I have to continue to pretend to be upset at "our" defence as County go close time after time. As the half develops, however, I worry more and more that our pressure will leave gaps at the back which Bury might exploit for a last-minute winner. Any goal would be hard to take sitting amongst hundreds of home fans; a late winner would be a disaster, ironic as such a goal might be in view of our record this season.

Saturday Night and Thursday Morning

I needn't have worried, however; our pressure doesn't pay off, and the final whistle blows on one of those moral victory 0-0 draw thingies. I'm not too disappointed, though. Apart from the fact that Bury have been in the top three virtually all season, and have an unbeaten home record, for a couple of fleeting hours, I was, by the standards of the quasi-feudal hierarchy of a professional football club, a Somebody; I was a Player's Guest. I'll probably never come as close again to experiencing the opulence and grandeur of the way the other half watch football.

Thank Christ.

December 26th 1996. Wrexham (away).

Barrrrrrp! That's better. Excuse me.

Nice game for a Boxing Day, this one - if we can't be at Edgeley Park, an away game within an hour's drive is the next best option, and that is precisely what we have today. Wrexham are, of course, one of three teams - Swansea and Cardiff being the other offenders - whose hatred of all things English doesn't prevent them plying their trade in the English professional leagues. I hate xenophobia myself, but such an attitude rankles a bit, as I know it does with many other English fans. I relieve my feelings not with mindless bigotry, however, but, rather, a delight whenever we beat the buggers.

Jason has decided to come with us today (me and my dad, that is - Martin's working). It's not the act of a bemused Yank wondering why the hell these Limeys don't use their goddam hands, however; he's actually quite knowledgeable about, ahem, "soccer" - wisdom gleaned from his years as a student in Liverpool (if you spend more than a couple of years in Liverpool and at the end still don't possess at least a passing interest in football, then I suppose there's really no hope for you).

I'm expecting a fairly large number of fans today, it being the traditionally well-supported post-Christmas fixture, and, sure enough, even though we are early, and well before the coaches, the Turf Hotel - the pub which is not only closest to the ground but which I believe actually *owns* the ground - is probably the most crowded drinking den I've ever been in. My dad elbows his way to the bar, and eventually gets served, and luckily, we can then edge over to a spot near the toilets where the human density is just about low enough to allow us to raise our pints (two bitters and one cider, which you apparently can't get in the States) to our lips, albeit necessarily in formation. There's absolutely no chance of getting served again at a bar now ten or so deep before kick off, so we barge our way out of a handy nearby fire door, and head for the ground.

There's the option of standing for £8 or sitting for £11 (which, I suppose, does put County's £9 Cheadle End price into perspective). On a decent sized terrace, I'd normally stand, but the away terrace at the Racecourse ground is pathetic - shallow, narrow and fenced, giving a completely crap view, so we pay the extra and sit.

If you can avoid the seats with views obscured by the two roof supports, the view from the stand is almost as good as the terrace view is crap - steep and high. It also affords a fine view over the top of the fence which runs the length of the pitch to our right; a structure erected to obscure the complete eyesore which is the Mold Road side of the Racecourse Ground.

This area is a dark, ramshackle heap, with the remains of a small, gloomy wooden stand about fifty yards from the pitch, and, in front, a terrace that, even when open, must have been ridiculously shallow. In short, it's a complete mess, and you wonder whether it was the Taylor Report, or simple aesthetics that caused them to throw the fence up in front and forget all about it. Over the years it's become neglected and overgrown, and I've heard rumours that there are at least twenty indigenous species (including Welshmen) living in there, and David Bellamy can often be seen poking around.

The game starts badly for County. Wrexham are unbeaten at home this season, and have been amongst the pacesetters for the last couple of months. They start as brightly as you would expect with such a record, and take the lead after eight minutes; a Steve Watkin shot takes a deflection almost as big as the one we benefitted from at Rotherham, and gives Paul Jones no chance as it bounces in off the post. Even worse, after quarter of an hour, they double their lead. Ex-County man Peter Ward takes a right wing corner which finds the head of another ex-County man, Martyn Chalk. Presumably as a courtesy to an old mate, none of the County defenders are marking him, and he is thus able to head back across goal where one of his mates scrambles the ball home. Crap. Chalk gives a great taunting salute to the County fans behind the goal - the get - and, after fifteen minutes, we've lost.

Two minutes later, however, we haven't, as the ball is fired in from an acute angle at the far end. Cavaco makes good progress down the right wing, and I first of all assume that it's he who has scored, but the better-sighted County fans around and in front of me start to chant "there's only one Alun Armstrong," and it's clear that he's finally ended his goal drought. His last goal was the winner at Millwall, an amazing 21 games ago, and even though he missed 6 of those games through injury, I would imagine it'll still be a relief for him to find the net again.

Half time thus arrives with us only 2-1 down; still a hell of a disadvantage, as we could really do with a win, and to claw back two goals might just be beyond us. A draw is certainly within our sights, however.

The first fifteen minutes or so of the second half are pretty even, but following a right wing corner, Jim Gannon comes steaming in at the far post to slam home an equaliser. This goal is still being celebrated when, a minute later, Luis Cavaco twists and turns the Wrexham left back just inside the area, and is brought down. The home players protest vehemently (has a referee ever said "oh all right then - goal kick" in such circumstances?), but it was as clear a foul as you'll probably ever see. Presumably, they were appealing to the ref's potential distaste for effeminate players - Cavaco's got the gloves on again.

I'm not sure who our penalty-taker is supposed to be. Tom Bennett has taken (and missed) them in the past, and is suspended for today's game in any case. Of the likely candidates, I wouldn't trust Brett Angell, having seen him hit a penalty out of the ground - literally - before now, and Alun Armstrong's confidence is probably too fragile to risk him missing. In the event, we're all slightly surprised to see Tony Dinning step forward and strike the ball low into the right corner, as easily as if he does it every day. All of a sudden, two minutes after battling desperately for an equaliser, we're protecting our lead.

Now that *was* cheeky. Wrexham indignantly press forward, and almost score themselves, through one of those terrific comedy goalmouth scrambles. It's down at the far end, however, so we don't get as good a view of it as the home fans - and they probably don't appreciate it anyway, as the ball is finally booted behind for a corner, rather than into the net.

Wrexham's pressure leaves gaps at the back, and we have a couple of chances to score a fourth, but it's clear that the god of football - a mischievous imp at the best of times - is going to take this one down to the wire. The final five minutes or so are agonising, as Wrexham press for an equaliser with the desperation of men with an unbeaten home record to protect. They're probably fairly surprised, if not actually affronted, that we're winning in any case; we're the team, remember, against whom they gained what must have been their easiest victory of the season - possibly their easiest ever - back in the dark days of September; the last game before our current amazing run. Despite their huffing and puffing, there's no third goal for the boyos, however, and the referee blows the final whistle to a massive, festive-fuelled cheer from behind the goal.

May God bless us, one and all! It's Christmas, we've beaten the Taffys - fellow promotion contenders - on their own ground, it's Christmas, we came from two goals down, it's Christmas, and we're on our way back to my mum's for a festive tea, with mince pies, figgy pudding, crackers, carols, wassailing, and...

Er, ahem. Sorry. It's actually back to the Glitter Jewellery Maker, Game of Life, Thomas the Tank Engine Train Set, Cuddly Postman Pat and Rosie and Jim videos. And the kids got some nice presents, too.

JANUARY

NATIONWIDE LEAGUE DIVISION TWO

	P	W	D	L	F	A	Pts
BRENTFORD	25	13	8	4	41	25	47
LUTON TOWN	24	14	4	6	43	26	46
BURY	24	11	9	4	36	23	42
MILLWALL	25	11	8	6	33	26	41
STOCKPORT COUNTY	**25**	**11**	**8**	**6**	**32**	**27**	**41**
BRISTOL CITY	25	11	7	7	43	28	40
BURNLEY	25	12	4	9	38	28	40
CREWE ALEXANDRA	24	13	1	10	34	27	40
WATFORD	24	9	12	3	25	19	39
WREXHAM	23	10	8	5	31	27	38
CHESTERFIELD	23	11	5	7	23	18	38
SHREWSBURY TOWN	26	8	8	10	34	40	32
WALSALL	24	8	6	10	26	28	30
BOURNEMOUTH	26	8	6	12	23	31	30
BRISTOL ROVERS	25	7	8	10	26	29	29
PRESTON NORTH END	25	8	5	12	24	29	29
YORK CITY	24	8	5	11	24	34	29
BLACKPOOL	24	6	10	8	25	27	28
PETERBOROUGH UNITED	25	6	9	10	37	43	27
PLYMOUTH ARGYLE	25	6	9	10	29	38	27
GILLINGHAM	26	7	6	13	25	36	27
WYCOMBE WANDERERS	25	6	5	14	22	38	23
NOTTS COUNTY	24	5	7	12	15	26	22
ROTHERHAM UNITED	24	3	8	13	20	36	17

January 15th 1997. Stoke City (away) (FA Cup Sponsored by Littlewoods Pools R3).

Oh, hello - not seen you for a while. Been away?

Yes indeed, the "why don't we have a mid-winter break" merchants have been out in force during the last few weeks, as a cold snap which started with a heavy fall of snow during the weekend after Christmas has played havoc with the fixtures, causing County to lose no fewer than eight games: Watford (H), York City (H) and Gillingham (A) in the league, to add to the Plymouth game which was postponed because both teams were still in the FA Cup. In addition, the Stoke FA Cup game was postponed until tonight, and the game at Burnley in the AutoWindscreens Shield, scheduled for Jan 7th, was called off because of the Coca Cola Cup quarter final with Southampton - which itself failed to beat the frost. The slight silver lining peeping tentatively round the cloud of postponements, however, is the fact that because neither of the two other Coca Cola Cup quarter finals which were actually played needed a replay, we're going to appear live on Sky again, the TV company figuring that Ipswich and Leicester (the other postponed quarter final) together offered less of an attraction than us and Saints.

I suppose, if I was a bit of a prat, I would be writing something here along the lines of "this break gives me an opportunity to assess the season so far..." Well, I'm not, and I won't. In the same way that I refuse to break my life down into 365-day chunks, and start each January 1st by considering whether the previous calendar year was "good" or "bad", I don't view the season in halves; I do not, in fact, split it up into fragments larger than individual games, following each of which any conjecture, speculation and general navel-gazing takes place. For example, I seriously start wondering about whether we're doing quite enough to achieve promotion immediately after the first game in August, and I'm thinking about it in precisely the same terms in April, albeit perhaps with slightly more tension.

One feature of the postponements was the fact that, for the first time since mid-August, I was at home on a Saturday afternoon. This was a strange feeling, indeed - I was left kicking my heels, not feeling right, not knowing what to do. It was also hard to fight the ridiculous notion that I was wrong, I had been misinformed, and the game hadn't been called off after all. Okay, add paranoia to the ever-lengthening list of my psychological deficiencies, but well might you laugh: when I first hear a game's off, I'm satisfied that I don't have to make the trip only when I've received the information from at least three different media, usually teletext, local radio and the "premium rate" 0891 County... Clubcall... Line... with... all... the... very... la... test... news... from... Edg... e... ley... Park (I

159

write that in the assumption that this is the correct way to express the name of the service; it's certainly the way the guy on the other end of the line does it).

Anyway, what else has been happening? Well, three cup draws were made, giving us potential ties at Bury (if we beat Burnley in the AWS), Birmingham (if we beat Stoke tonight) and - most mind-bogglingly - a two legged Coca Cola Cup semi final (yes, *"semi final"!*) against Middlesborough - Juninho, Emerson, Ravanelli et al (yes, *"Juninho, Emerson, Ravanelli et al"!*) - if we beat Southampton. Oh yes: last Monday I was 33, and - following the Christmas period - Martin's been laid off, so he's able to come with me tonight.

All clear? Good.

On the way down - reminders of when I used to regularly make this journey in the early 80s leaping out at me on all sides - I realise, amidst the normal pre-match excitement, that I like Stoke's Victoria Ground a lot. Not only did I go there on three occasions whilst I was at Keele (I would probably have gone more, but I wasn't actually at Keele long enough), but it's also a tremendously atmospheric, old-fashioned place. Covered on all sides, with a kop behind one goal, and paddocks in front of stands on the three other sides, it epitomises what your average fan would probably design were it not for the requirement to go all-seater - a requirement which will see Stoke leave in the summer for a new ground being built a mile or so away.

Actually, I suppose I must qualify that. Although I called it a tremendous old ground, that particular judgement is based more on vague feelings of atmosphere and what is "right" about a football arena than a level-headed view of the place's suitability as a venue for watching a game. I know from standing there when they played Manchester United in 1983 that the view from the Boothen End kop is okay, as, I imagine, is the view from any of the seated areas. However, the paddocks - into which the away fans are shoehorned - seem to have been fashioned by the kind of idiot architect who was presumably unable, early in the century, to gain employment designing normal buildings, but had discovered a nice little earner devising plans for football grounds that made it as inconvenient as possible to actually see the game. The paddocks descend to about six feet below pitch level, so that, at the front, your eyes - if you are tall - are level with the players' ankles. Even at the summit of the dizzy heights of the back of the paddock, six rows or so up, your feet are still below pitch level. For this reason - and for this reason alone, as I wouldn't like you to think I've started wearing gloves or anything - I have bought a ticket for the seats, rather than the terrace.

We arrive, and are early enough to park up in the side-streets. The ground looms over the surrounding terraced houses, just as I remember it from when I first came. I realise with a shock that it was over fourteen years ago - it seems a hell of a long time, yet it was *after* I'd left sixth form college. I suddenly feel melancholy, and realise I'd better get inside the ground quickly before I get out a guitar and start singing. There is, however, a worrying amount of freezing cold fog billowing around. A steward informs us that there is to be a pitch inspection at quarter to seven; the ground is apparently perfectly playable, but the fog might put the game in jeopardy. For that reason, presumably, the turnstiles are closed, and only open following a deafening tannoy announcement just before seven that the game will go ahead. This is actually a very nice touch by Stoke - I can think of a number of clubs (and, sadly, try as I might, I find it difficult to exclude County from the list) who would have thrown the turnstiles open regardless, without any thought of whether fans already inside the ground would be entitled to a refund if the game succumbed.

The benevolence of the announcer, however, is in marked contrast to my experience of Stoke fans in general, who can be as bad tempered and nasty as they come. In the 1992 playoff semi final, we beat them 1-0 in an acrimonious game at Edgeley Park. This was thought by most people to be too narrow a margin of victory, however, and it was widely expected - not least by their own fans - that Stoke would win it in the second leg. However, a Chris Beaumont goal in the first minute planted rather large seeds - bulbs, in fact - of doubt, and, despite a late reply from Mark Stein, County hung on to win on aggregate. Sporting and good-natured in defeat, the home fans poured onto the field from the Boothen End, and attempted to attack both the celebrating County players, and the County fans, penned in behind the opposite goal; it took a mounted police charge to clear the pitch. It was with little surprise, therefore, that I read of identical scenes in last year's play offs, when Stoke again lost a second leg, at home, which they were expected to win. It's a great shame when a fairly well supported club like this attracts a larger than average moron element, because there are, amongst its followers, as many decent and well-behaved fans as any other club. I remember having a hilarious discussion with such a group when we first played them five or six years ago - early in the season of the infamous play off game - when Stoke had first dropped into the Third Division, and before any bad feeling between the clubs had developed. We'd met them in the pub before the league game at the Victoria Ground, and I'd questioned why they were wearing beer towels sewn across their shirts. The reply was that the club had changed their sponsor to a brewery during the close season, and had used the change as the opportunity to promote a "new" shirt - virtually identical to the previous one in all respects except the sponsor's name. Unwilling to be ripped off in this way, the more enterprising of the Stoke fans had simply gone into the pubs owned by the brewery concerned, and pinched the towels from off the bar when the bar staff weren't looking. These items, sewn over the old sponsor's name, effectively updated the shirts without costing the fans a penny.

We wander in and find our seats, noting the huge mound of snow in the paddock in front of us - presumably that which has been cleared off the pitch, and dumped there because there wasn't a big enough carpet nearby to sweep it under. The tickets are "unreserved" (ie, sit anywhere) so, as there seem to be a few gaps in the corner of the ground to my right, I head towards them, only to find my way blocked by a steward who was obviously off sick when they ran the "Dealing With The Customer" course at Stewarding School. "Where are *you* going?" he asks rudely.

"Getting a seat" I reply, genuinely perplexed and showing him my ticket.

"That's for this area," he says, indicating the seats I have passed to my left, and backing up his surly attitude with a sneer as he tells me so. So what am I supposed to be - psychic? There are no signs to indicate that the area to which I was attempting to gain access was out of bounds for my ticket, and I'm afraid, gentle reader, that I was just a touch rude to the steward. Okay, fair enough, I was attempting to sit in a place where my ticket wasn't valid, but was there any reason to be so bloody aggressive about telling me so? I don't set out to be deliberately hostile towards stewards, and had he been polite - or even merely civil - whilst telling me I couldn't sit where I was heading, fine. I would probably have even come over all English and apologised. Treating me like some kind of yobbish low-life, however, makes my blood boil. Seething, once again, about officious little twats in orange coats, and only slightly mollified by having given this particular one a mouthful, I retrace my steps, and we manage to find a couple of seats together. It's not a bad position we end up with, as it happens: level with the penalty area, and reasonably high up - right in front of the executive boxes, in fact.

The game starts slowly, and the only noteworthy event of the first quarter hour is the barracking of County's central defender Jim Gannon. Last time we played Stoke City here - a 2-1 defeat in 1993 - Gannon was thumped by Mark Stein as the players left the pitch in what was euphemistically described in the local press as "a heated atmosphere". Gannon sued for assault, and won his case, but his victory was overshadowed by claims made in court by Stein that Gannon had racially abused him - claims which understandably grabbed the headlines. The net result was that Gannon emerged as the villain of the piece, despite Stein being found guilty. The crux of Gannon's case was that any remarks he made were in the heat of the moment - and publicly regretted - and as a response to Stein jumping around in front of him at the end of the game, and goading him about the result.

It's a tricky one for a liberal, this. I absolutely abhor racism - quite apart from being horrified and repelled by the notion that people can possibly be considered inferior simply because of the colour of their skin, I see it as the same form of depressing stupidity and fear of the unknown that afflicts so many of the Little Englanders who are currently so prevalent.

Equally, it never fails to disturb me that what seems to be a large proportion - the majority, even, God help us - of football fans hold such narrowly bigoted views; earlier this season, at Watford, someone behind me responded to a home player's injury with "he's only a nigger," a declaration made even more dispiriting by the fact that so many of his slack-jawed cronies laughed like drains.

That said, I found myself, at the time of Gannon's court case - and still do now, if I'm honest - taking his side against Stein's. Racial prejudice is a blight on our society, and it frustrates me immensely that it so often finds an outlet for expression at football grounds (oh-oh, he's winding up for a "but"), but how many liberals like me can honestly say, in a situation such as the one that particular night, we wouldn't have acted similarly? Following defeat in a vital, and extremely tense, match, with the noise of 15,000 home supporters booming all around, a history of bad feeling between your side and your opponents, and a member of that opposition team jumping up and down in front of you, gloating about the result, how many of us can say with confidence that we wouldn't inadvertently slip in a "black" somewhere amongst the "fuck", the "off", the "you", the "ugly", the "little", and the "bastard"? Doesn't make it right, I know, but it makes it far more understandable. The irony is, of course, that as an immigrant Irishman himself, you can bet your life that Gannon has experienced more than his share of bigotry over the years.

Whatever was in the past, however, the home fans' goading seemingly has the effect of making Gannon play out of his skin - he looks as comfortable on the ball as I have ever seen him, and he and Mike Flynn are controlling the defence to such an extent that Stoke seem hardly likely to score.

Mind you, neither do we. Not, that is, until the 25th minute, when we do - right in front of the Boothen End. Luis Cavaco - minus his gloves, which Tom Bennett seems to have bagged - makes a tremendous run down the right wing and crosses the ball into the box. It goes behind the onrushing Alun Armstrong, but Kieron Durkan, unmarked on the left, swivels and hits a superb first time shot into the opposite corner.

With our defence in such fine form, we can almost feel confident about defending such a slender lead for over an hour, and, sure enough, half time - a period spent hopping around in the gangway in front of the executive boxes, trying to keep warm under the patronising gaze of their occupants - arrives with the score unchanged, and Stoke's attack looking unlikely to do anything about it.

You might have thought that following a tongue lashing at half time, Stoke would have dominated the second half - they're playing at their own ground, after all, in front of thousands of their own supporters, baying for victory. Not so. County's defence, with full backs Lee Todd and Sean Connelly complementing Gannon and Flynn in the middle, are so comfortable on the ball, and our midfield so commanding, that the second half simply mirrors the first. Stoke have slightly more possession - as you might expect being the home team - but cannot get close enough to threaten County's goal. We, meanwhile, look composed, skilful and dangerous on the break.

Stoke become more desperate, throwing on as many substitutes as the rules allow, but to no avail. As the final minutes tick away, the whistling from the County fans reaches a crescendo - and I've moved to the end of the row for a quick getaway - when Andy Mutch, one of two time-wasting substitutes used by Dave Jones, is released down the right wing. With virtually his first touch - which makes it all the more admirable - he beats the full back and whips in a low hard cross, of the type - curling away from the keeper, midway into the penalty area - that defences hate, and attackers like Alun Armstrong, sliding in to score at the far post, absolutely love. Get in! There's a great joyous explosion from the County fans, directed variously at the pitch, the executive boxes and the Stoke fans to our left.

We've won now, obviously, but I'm still shouting at the ref to blow, albeit for quite different reasons than normal: I want to be able to gloat at as many home supporters, streaming away on all sides of the ground, as I can, before they all disappear. The final whistle does eventually get blown, after two or three mystifying minutes of injury time (neither trainer has been on the field) and we've won our tenth cup tie of the season (the other being the draw at Upton Park). After a quick Botham bellow, I whip round and catch the reluctant eye of one of the suits. I helpfully remind him of the score - thinking as I do so how fortunate it is that we scored two - and blow a huge kiss before ducking out under the boxes and back to the car as quickly as I can.

It's childish, petty, and not something to feel particularly proud of, but a gloat like that doesn't half make you feel good. At times, in fact, I feel you *need* a big gloat against a team you hate; I wonder if you could get it on prescription? And to think, almost fifteen years ago, I used to come to this place to cheer on Stoke.

January 18th 1997. Millwall (home).

Today is scheduled to be - amazingly on the face of it - our only league game in January, thanks to postponements and cup success. It could hardly be a more important one, however.

Since our momentous win at their place back in October, Millwall have bounced back, and, with the odd minor hiccup, they're now, after being placed top on more than one occasion, handily positioned in third place. We're three places and three points behind, although we could actually go ahead of them today - if we beat them and score five. A more realistic prospect would be simply to win and thus continue our amazing run - currently standing at a mere two defeats in the last 28 league and cup games.

It's another one of those "ideal for football" days again - fresh and cold (but not freezing cold, thank God), and with a pale sun smiling wanly down. I set off for the ground feeling ridiculously optimistic. The way we have been playing for most of this season (we'll draw a veil over the first month and a half), it's hard to see us losing at the moment. Obviously, we *will* lose - and have, of course, at Burnley and Shrewsbury - but the point is that my perception before virtually every game now is that we'll win, and such a perception breeds extreme confidence. It seems to me that the players must also be thinking the same way currently, and confidence, as any fule kno, counts for about 90% of what constitutes a successful team.

It may be the optimism generated by the sunny weather and the anticipation of this afternoon's game, but for whatever reason I find myself singing the jaunty "Postman Pat" theme tune on the way to the ground. It may, of course, be simply that it was playing on the video as I left (and being studiously ignored by Andrew, for whose benefit it was ostensibly being played - but just you try switching it off for "Football Focus"). *Early in the morning, just as day is dawning...* Frustratingly, as I'm in the Fiesta, and the radio's bust, there's no alternative to drown it out of my head - I'm lumbered with it.

Mayyy-beee - you can never be sure - there'll be knocks, rings, letters through your door. I pick up my dad and Martin, and off we head. I'm able to park up fairly close to the ground; although I'm expecting a big crowd, it being a top of the table real six-pointer and all, we've arrived nice and early.

Everybody knows his bright red van. Following a quick pint, I see Tom outside the ground, and remind him that today, of course, represents our first chance of a "double" this season (double, for most teams other than Manchester United, referring to two victories, home and away, against the same team, and having nothing to do with winning two particular trophies in the same season). We both laugh off the notion, with the surface pessimism that's an essential part of supporting a club like County, but inside my confidence is barely shaken. I actually *do* think we'll win, as this team seem to be able to raise their game

165

against tough opposition. In addition, Millwall were no great shakes back at their place, and we thoroughly deserved that memorable victory.

Inside the ground, it's clear that there is indeed a fairly big crowd, notwithstanding the fact that Millwall don't seem to have brought that many. There seem less away fans than we took to their place, or certainly not many more. On that subject, I feel self-righteously smug about today's crowd - how many of you went down to Sarf Lahndan on October 2nd, eh, eh? Well, *I* did.

The match starts and County tear into Millwall, as though their absence from league action since Boxing Day has made them ravenous. Wave after wave of attacks come pouring in, and Millwall hardly venture out of their penalty area for the first 10 minutes. It's therefore a deserved lead which we take when Andy Mutch powers in to head home at the Cheadle End, after a Mike Flynn long throw is flicked on. The frantic start to the game, the significance of the opposition, and the large, noisy crowd make it one of the best goal celebrations of the season so far; leaping up from my seat, my feet leave the ground by a good six inches. Following the onslaught, that is surely not going to be the only County goal this half.

We continue the pressure, but the visitors gradually fight back, occasionally managing to penetrate our half. It's still undoubtedly against the run of play when they equalise, however. A cross into the box is headed goalwards, and Lee Todd just manages to head it away off the line. Oh no you didn't, say the officials, and award Millwall a goal. Todd's furious protests lead to him being booked, and Millwall are level.

They might be level, but there's no way they're back in the game. Sure enough, a minute or two after their "goal", we restore our lead, following another goalbound header from Mutch, which is stopped on the line by a Millwall defender. Sadly for him, however, he has stopped it with his hand (he virtually catches it and throws it away, in fact), and therefore condemned himself to an early bath. With Tony Dinning out of the side, Alun Armstrong grabs the ball and confidently sidefoots home the penalty.

A couple of minutes later, we're 3-1 up. Ray Wilkins - recently signed by Millwall and thus running the gauntlet of the "you bald bastard" chants - was the most vociferous of the Millwall protesters when the referee sent off the defender, and takes out his frustrations now with a two-footed lunge from behind, at Armstrong. Despite the fact that FIFA were supposed to have instructed referees to send off such miscreants, Wilkins is merely booked (as, in fairness, would any player have been under the liberal interpretation of FIFA's edict currently applied by English referees), but suffers appropriate punishment from the resulting free kick. Chris Marsden - who is playing superbly well in midfield - sends in the cross, and, as the defence advance en masse in an attempt to play offside, Mike Flynn runs in to thump a header joyously past the keeper.

We have further chances to score as we dominate the rest of the half, but the midway point arrives with no further goals, and the crowd pausing for breath almost as much as the players. I realise that the goals have gone in in exactly the same way as they did at Millwall: we went 1-0 up, Millwall equalised and we then scored two more. I can't somehow see today's game ending 4-3 however. We're dominating even more than we did down there, and surely Millwall can't force their way back into a game from 3-1 down *again*?

If such thoughts were concerning anyone else during the break, they are dispelled mere seconds after the restart. Straight from the kick-off, County break downfield and work their way into the Millwall penalty area. Some good work from Armstrong keeps the ball in, and Kieron Durkan sends a cross to the far post, where Luis Cavaco outjumps the fullback to head home. What a pisser that must be for the sparse crowd gathered on the Railway End - any faint hopes of battling back for a draw they might have had extinguished, a matter of seconds after fifteen minutes' worth of building them up. Ahhh, shame. Even better, it seemed to me that a County player definitely handled the ball in the build-up, on the blind side of the referee and linesman, but not of the Millwall players and fans. Our joy at the goal is thus heightened by a couple of minutes of fierce protests.

Five minutes later and it's five. The Millwall keeper makes a rash charge out of his area to the feet of Andy Mutch. Mutch rounds him, and the ball breaks for Cavaco to sidefoot his second into the empty net. Five-one after five minutes of the second half. Well, you can't say it wasn't deserved.

Such a lead with well over forty minutes to go is, let's face it, a reasonably comfortable position to be in. In fact, the "Shit on the Millwall, shit on the Millwall today" song gives way to "Let's all laugh at Millwall, Let's all laugh at Millwall...", and thence to "Wilkins Wilkins what's the score?" when Wilkins, supporting a rare Millwall attack, comes within thirty yards of the Cheadle End. To his credit, he acknowledges the chants with a upraised hand, and five fingers spread. I bet he wishes it was 2-2, mind.

The rest of the half is mildly disappointing, as the game goes off the boil. Millwall seem resigned to their fate, and County disinclined to inflict further damage. A number of the away fans start to leave with about fifteen minutes left (I actually noticed one or two leaving after the fifth goal, with forty minutes still to go), prompting cries of "cheerio, cheerio, cheerio," and "We can see you sneaking out." They don't miss anything, however, as the final whistle goes with no further addition to the score. Despite easing off, the team deserve - and get - a marvellous ovation. Darting for the car, my route takes me past the Railway

End, disgorging its pissed-off occupants. I find myself once again in front of London-accented fans walking away from a game, and, despite my hurry, feel compelled to slow down and earwig. With the blind optimism and deliberate ignorance of the football fan they have already, mere minutes after its conclusion, put today's game behind them and are clutching at straws of consolation, albeit ones with which to beat their team around the head. *"Wewll, if we down't git samfink from next wik'end, we moight as wewll bladdy give ap on vis season".* Walking away from Watford, Brentford and Edgeley Park after beating Millwall. Compare and contrast.

Later on that evening, with the elation of the day's performance once again seeping into everything I do, I see the first Stalinist rewrite of the day's performance on local teletext (actually, I say "local" - there's a clear bias towards Millwall, leading me to suspect that it was actually a southern stringer responsible). The report tries to claim that the sending off "changed the course of the game". Like bloody arse it did. If ever a match report had *"written back in the studio by someone watching the wires from Associated Press"* stamped all over it, it is this. That's the trouble with being a small, insignificant club, of course. If a corresponding result had happened in the Premiership - Chelsea or Villa beating Arsenal by a similar margin, say - it would have made headline news, and, more importantly, our domination, both before and after the sending off, would have been made clear. Still, who gives a toss? Well, me actually, but not to worry - we've taken another great step towards getting promotion this season, and even my few quid on County for the title looks less ridiculous than it did a couple of months ago.

In summary, then, *Pat feels he's a really happy man.* And so do I. Can we play Millwall every week?

Wednesday January 22nd 1997. Southampton (home) (Coca Cola Cup Quarter Final).

Last night we moved, albeit by default, into the last five of a major competition, thanks to Leicester beating Ipswich 1-0 in the only other quarter-final still to be played (look, if I could say we were in the quarter final draw after the game at West Ham finished level, I can say we're now in the last five of the Coca Cola Cup, okay?).

Actually, despite what I wrote against Stoke, I *will* pause for reflection here. Tonight is our 12th cup tie of the season. So far, we've won ten and drawn one. Of those victories, no fewer than four (five if you count Sheffield United twice) have been against teams from a higher division - two from the Premiership, and two challenging for promotion to the Premiership. We've scored twenty-four cup goals and conceded nine. And that's not counting our current league record of only two defeats in twenty games. Blimey. Whichever way you look at it, that's one hell of a record. And if you think I'm fickle, following what I was writing after our dreadful start, well, I'm a football fan. What do you expect - consistency?

Er, ahem. Excuse me, but every now and then I have to metaphorically pinch myself in this way in order to prove it's not a dream. It's also useful to stand back and view the season from outside, as it were, to see what a fantastic run this actually is; I've perhaps tended not to appreciate this when writing about the games as they happen. I made a conscious decision to go to every game, home and away, back in June, when I was reasonably optimistic that the year could prove to be memorable. What's transpired, in fact, is that there's a good chance it'll be the most memorable in my 25 years of following County, and an outside chance it'll be County's most memorable ever.

It's weird, but despite today's being the most important game in County's history (or so the media keep telling me), I've not exactly been full of the old butterflies for days beforehand, as you might expect. (I would disagree about it being the *most* important, incidentally; the game which secured promotion from the Lancashire Combination back in 1905 was far more significant, leading, as it did, to our highest ever finish - 10th in the old Second Division in 1905-06). The lack of tension might be due to the opponents being "only" Southampton, or the fact that with so many games having been postponed, I'm not quite yet back into full County mode. Whatever the reason, the adrenaline rush did start at work, and, come kick off time, I am as nervous, uneasy, afraid, agitated, overwrought and tense as I usually am for such a big game - really looking forward to it, in fact.

Yesterday and Monday were both quite frosty, which gave brief cause for concern, and meant worried attention paid to last night's weather forecast. In the event, it's an overcast, dull, damp sort of evening - ideal for football you might say. It's funny how so many differing types of weather are regarded as "ideal for football" - as it seems to be virtually all types except the extremes, it would probably be easier to point out which types of weather *aren't* suitable.

As with the West Ham game, there's an atmosphere of subdued excitement outside the ground, with thousands milling around, and long queues forming at the turnstiles; people seem eager to get inside and soak up the atmosphere. I go in myself and make my way up to the seat that Jack Oldham has managed to get for me on his season ticket. It's an aisle seat, which is a bonus, legroom being at a premium in the Cheadle End stand.

The game kicks off to an atmosphere which is one of the best I can remember at Edgeley Park. Again, with the game live on Sky, my initial thoughts are for Anna and the kids watching at home: Julia excited, but tending to boredom if there isn't a goal every five minutes; Christopher wishing he could have Thomas The Tank Engine on rather than this football stuff; and Andrew taking time out from biting pieces out of a bath sponge to wonder why the funny box in the corner seems to be so interesting tonight.

I'm soon able to concentrate on the game, however, as LeTissier's first touch causes some moronic booing - no less depressing because I expected it - to spew forth from the mean little mouths of a sadly large number of tiny-brained pricks. It really is incredible - to boo a guy purely and simply because he's a talented player. I could understand it if he had a reputation for being a nasty sod, or had done something like... I don't know, jumped into the crowd and kung-fued a fan, say, but for God's sake! Of course, it's a backhanded compliment that they're paying him - he's obviously the best player on the pitch and Southampton's major threat, but there are surely better ways of expressing fear that he might inspire his team to a win? Well, yes, there are in fact - a loud chorus of "you'll never play for England" rings out. Now this is amusing - and a legitimate verbal weapon, in my opinion, because it at least has its foundation in humour. Simply booing the guy for no other reason than that he's talented, is shameful.

Almost as disgusting is the fact that the bloke sitting across from me has decided to treat the aisle as his own personal spittoon. Hollow-cheeked and goatee bearded, with his woollen hat, and pulling on his own roll-up joint, he leans out and spurts a stream through his teeth and into the aisle every few seconds.

I try to avoid looking at the rapidly widening pool of sputum to concentrate on the game, which is easy enough; County start confidently, dominate the early exchanges, and go close a couple of times. This is not unexpected, however - the underdogs playing at home are almost expected to start like a train. What is more significant is if they can turn their frantic early superiority into a goal. There is, in fact, a score after fifteen minutes, but it's Southampton who go ahead. Mike Flynn goes upfield to launch another long throw on the right wing, and Lee Todd moves across from left back to provide cover in the centre. The ball is cleared to Todd, and whether it is the unfamiliar position he finds himself in - central, with Saint attackers bearing down - or the fact that the pitch is in such a state, that causes him to panic, he makes a complete balls of his clearance, belting the ball high into the air. Southampton's Nordic looking striker Ostenstad bears down on goal, easily outstrips the covering Jim Gannon, and slots the ball confidently under the diving body of Paul Jones.

There is a loud, sad, "ahhhh" of disappointment from all around me, followed by a delayed reaction to the goal at the far end, as, a second or so after the ball hits the net, the away fans realise they're ahead. The bloke beside me lets out a quiet "shit." Er, I think perhaps I'd better qualify that - it was a verbal emission, okay? Personally, I'm more concerned that the goal was taken so confidently. They had been heavily under the cosh, yet broke away and, with seemingly the minimum of fuss, scored. That's the mark of a superior team; you think you've got them, but all your pressure is shown up as so much bluster when they score, clinically, as though they could have done so at any moment, had they so chosen.

Following the goal, the County fans immediately attempt to lift the players, but I find myself wondering whether the bubble finally bursts here. I won't be too upset if it does. In a normal season, we won't beat anybody from a higher division (indeed, County's record over the years shows that we'll often be beaten by a team from a lower division); in a good season, we'll beat a team from the division above, perhaps even a Premiership team at home; in an outstanding season, we'll beat a Premiership team away. I'm therefore running out of superlatives to describe this current one, but whichever way you look at it, if we lose tonight, the season has still been more than outstanding...

How could I ever have doubted County, this season of all seasons? Ten minutes after Southampton's goal, and with my mental damage limitation exercise still buzzing around inside my head, a ball gets played into the Saints area from a free kick on the left. Brett Angell seems to control it on his chest, and manages to find Alun Armstrong. He steadies himself - his body language indicating that he's got an incredible amount of room inside the area - and places a deliberate shot inside the far post, past the diving Beasant's left hand. We're level.

The crowd around me erupts. As against West Ham, we've conceded a goal and promptly (okay, ten minutes later) stormed back to equalise. Even better, we didn't have to rely for our leveller on a ridiculous own goal this time, preferring instead to imbue our response with a touch of class. The crowd are immediately lifted, noisy and excited. Less than a minute after this cause for celebration, however, comes an even greater one.

Following the restart, County gain possession, and immediately move forward, attacking on a wave of confidence. The ball finds its way out to the left wing, where Chris Marsden is waiting in space. He quickly moves the ball onto his left foot and sends in an early cross. Cavaco is unmarked in the area, and glances the header goalwards. The ball hits the right hand post, and I'm at first not sure what's happened to it - has Beasant picked it up? No - he makes a despairing "oh fuck where was the marking it's in the net now bugger" sort of shrugging, pointing gesture, and it's clear he's not even attempting to get hold of the ball; it's in the net, and less than a minute after we equalised, we're ahead.

You thought what I described at Sheffield represented mayhem? The last minute goal at Millwall? The winner at Blackburn? Equaliser at West Ham? Tea parties, the lot of them - *this* is mayhem. I am surrounded by a cacophony of shrieking, roaring, bellowing, yelling, clapping, screaming, embracing, cheering humanity. Heat and noise everywhere. For my part, I'm leaping up and down, clapping over my head, attempting to see the pitch to reassure myself that it was indeed a goal, and releasing strange animal noises. I'm suddenly aware that in the excitement I'm actually starting to black out, which is momentarily frightening, it never having happened to me before at a football match (we used to make each other black out at school, but in another set of circumstances entirely - for "fun"). Fazed, I lower my arms to clap at waist height and take deep lungfuls of air, which seems to do the trick.

Absolutely unbelievable. As the teams kick off, there's an instantaneous telepathic agreement between most of the crowd, and "you're not singing anymore" rings out, louder than I've ever heard before. Somewhere in a remote farm halfway up the Pennines, a farmer looks across at his wife. "We waasn't blaady singing anyways - what's they on about?"

Is this really true? Have we really come from a goal down to lead, in an even shorter period of time than we did against West Ham, *against another Premiership team?* If this is a dream, can I have one every night? *"Are you watching Manchester?"* shout the County fans, the mixture of geographical proximity, live TV coverage and the fact that we are the only north west team still left in this competition combining to inspire the taunt.

The gobbing of the bloke opposite seems to have increased in frequency with his excitement; the aisle is now awash. Does his excitement express itself similarly in other areas, I wonder? Watching the final round in Family Fortunes, does he hawk repeatedly against his living room walls? On Christmas morning, did he express his joy at his new de-luxe cannabis cultivation set by flobbing a loogy at his wife? On the job, does he...? No, no, the thought of him on the job is simply too horrible to contemplate, and I turn my attention back to the game.

Half time arrives with us still in the lead, and with one foot in the semi-finals. Southampton haven't really threatened, and whilst neither have we, at least we've got the lead. My friend across the aisle has disappeared, possibly to shoot up in the bogs, so I idly watch the pool of gob being trampled underfoot and wait for the restart.

County are slightly less assured in the second half than they were in the first, and Southampton quickly assume control. For all their possession, however, they fail to create many clear chances, and, as the electronic clock behind the Saints fans in the Railway End ticks inexorably down, the realisation slowly dawns that we can win it. We can actually win it, put out a third Premiership team, and advance to the semi finals. As the game moves into the last ten minutes, Southampton press with increasing urgency, but even when they breach County's resolute defence, Paul Jones performs heroics in the goal.

So you can probably understand how much of a pisser it is when they score.

They're attacking on the right wing when the ball gets played into the area, towards one of their front men, who has a ridiculous amount of space. He is quickly closed down, but the balls squirts away from him, there's a brief commotion, and suddenly the Railway End is teeming, the referee wheels away pointing to the centre spot, and it's 2-2. Shit.

All around I sense the deflated resignation of long-suffering football fans who had dared believe the impossible (with the exception of Mr Sputum, who gobs disgustedly). A bloody replay two hundred and fifty bloody miles away when, according to the bloody clock we were only eight bloody minutes from bloody winning it. There is a collective slumping back into seats. On the Railway End, however, things are different, as the away fans sense their team can pinch it. And so do the players.

But for all their expectation, the clock ticks past 90 minutes with no more goals, and a replay it is. Except that Le Tissier has different ideas. As he's loafing about on the right wing, smoking a fag and reading the Daily Mirror, the County defence decides that he represents no great threat, and leave him completely unmarked. Sure enough, the ball gets played out to him, and as he closes in on goal and lifts a shot over the diving Paul Jones, we're out. In that instant, as the ball travels the ten yards or so towards the empty net, 9,000 hearts sink, and a similar number of mouths shape an expletive. But cometh the hour, cometh the Mike Flynn. From nowhere, he dives across the goal to head the ball behind to safety, what must be a matter of inches from the goal line. He ends up in the back of the net, and I leap to my feet with a great yell, celebrating a headed clearance as loudly and as fiercely as I did either of our goals. It's nothing less than magnificent - a save any keeper would have been proud to make with his hands, and caps another superb display from Flynn.

There is no more action of note - that really would have been the winning goal - and the final whistle blows on a draw. It's our fourth game against Premiership opposition, our seventh against a team from a higher division, and we've yet to lose any of them. The team receive a prolonged and deserved ovation, following which I splash my way gingerly through the flood of spittle in the aisle and head home.

Back home, the difference between tonight and the West Ham game is marked. Instead of exchanging "way-hays," with Anna, we exchange "what a bummer"s. Instead of rewinding the Sky tape in glorious, gloating appraisal, I crash in front of the Granada highlights, cursing our luck as Saints equalise, and then realising that the luck wasn't all one way as I see more closely Flynn's headed clearance. Even so, we were eight lousy minutes from a victory that would have seen us in the semi final of a major competition for the first time in our history. Arrrrrgggh! It's an incredibly mixed bag of emotions: pride and excitement that we've achieved another magnificent result, allied to annoyance that we couldn't just hold on, combined with relief that Le Tissier didn't pinch it, mingled with irritation that the replay means another midweek game, miles away.

Anna tells me that Julia was crying with emotion at the goals, especially when her hero, Alun, scored the first. She also, apparently, wanted to hug me when she was told that the result would mean a midweek replay on the South coast. I feel like crying myself.

January 25th 1997 Birmingham City (away) (FA Cup Sponsored by Littlewoods Pools R4).

I don't like Birmingham City. In fact, for various reasons, I can't bloody stand them.

Members of the jury - I ask you to consider the evidence. Firstly, their fans have a disgraceful reputation; as well as having been implicated in numerous incidents of violence both at St Andrew's and elsewhere in the country, they ran riot on both occasions they played at Edgeley Park in the last few years, causing trouble both inside and outside the ground.

Secondly, ticket prices for today's game are £13. This is bad enough, although hardly surprising. What is inexcusable is the fact that there are no concessions for away fans - another example of the shameless rip-off justified under the heading "market forces." It's interesting to note that Birmingham were successfully prosecuted recently - by their own fans bringing a case to the attention of the Trading Standards Office - over a scam they were running regarding the selling of away match tickets. For all the bleating of the club when the case made court, it was a splendid day when fans at last were able, with the might of the law behind them, to state that enough is enough, and they had been exploited just once too often.

Thirdly, following our 4-0 demolition of them in the pre-season friendly which filled us all with so much optimism before the start of the season, their manager Trevor Francis bleated to the press that the grass on the Edgeley Park pitch was too long - they might as well have had a training session instead of a game, he moaned. Whilst they obviously wouldn't have lost a training session 4-0, these remarks smacked of a manager getting his excuses in early, for the benefit of an expectant Chairman not known for his patience in regard to extending his managers' employment. Francis, pre-judging us as a "long-ball" team - despite clear evidence to the contrary - who would obviously not be hindered by long grass, also conveniently ignored the fact that the grass was uniformly long - to the detriment of *both* sides - and that only one team scored four goals, to the other side's zilch. It really was a clear example of excuse-making at its most pathetic.

Fourthly, they pinched Kevin Francis off us. The second highest goalscorer in our history - and without doubt the greatest folk-hero ever, rejoined his home town club in 1995. Once he had heard of their interest, there was really no way he was going to stay at Edgeley Park. Fair enough. But a player who had scored over a hundred goals in just over three seasons was a valuable asset, and warranted a large transfer fee. The version of the tale County made public is that Birmingham initially agreed, and offered over a million, following which County gave them permission to discuss personal terms with the player. These agreed, Birmingham then apparently - again according to the furious County account told to the local press - faxed us, saying that their offer was now £800,000, take it or leave it. Having got access to Francis under false pretences, they'd now reduced their offer, knowing that County wouldn't want an unsettled player on their books - one now desperate to get away, moreover - and would probably reluctantly accept the lower price. Which we did.

Fifthly - and I agree that my reasons are getting a little feeble at this point - the club is bailed out on the back of profits made from porn, with David Sullivan and the Gold brothers holding the controlling interest. Whilst I'm far from being a prude, it does tend to add to the impression of a seedy, dirty, vulgar club. And that's the way I like to think of them. Seedy, dirty and vulgar.

Well, the Coca Cola Cup semi final draw was made in the week, and Middlesborough await the winners of our game with Saints next Wednesday. It's academic, of course, as I'm convinced we won't go through now. You might well beat one Premiership side on their own ground in a given season; you might even, the same year, get a draw at another. But to *beat* a second? No, it's hard to disagree with the pundits who are now saying that we've blown our chance by not winning at Edgeley.

I arrive in Brum in good time, accompanied by Martin, and am able to park up on a fairly close street, facing back to the motorway. As we plod up the hill towards St Andrews, I realise that whatever my feelings about Birmingham City as a club, it can't be denied that they've got a tremendous ground. Or, at least, half a good ground. On two sides, they've rebuilt the stands in the style of Old Trafford - a sweeping cantilevered roof curving round from behind the goal and along one side. The other two sides, however, contain the old stands - wooden benches, restricted views and all. There are no prizes for guessing which part of the ground the County fans' kids will be occupying for their £13. Incredibly, the ramshackle old stand we're in actually has a fence in front of the seats - as though it's the nasty visitors who always cause the trouble. Thankfully, our tickets today are for the top tier, so we don't get our view restricted by the metal.

The whistle blows, and we're off. County start in a lively enough manner, and seem, distressingly, to be keen on winning. Indeed, Alun Armstrong almost caps our domination with a header against the bar. As the half develops, however, the home team move up a gear and snatch a thus only slightly undeserved lead after half an hour, when one of their forwards turns in a shot from close range. Such are my feelings about today's game, however, that I couldn't really give a toss. The only thing that does bother me is the sound of the celebrating home fans; their time-delayed roar is louder than usual because there are thousands more of them than we usually get at Second Division grounds, and the acoustics of the new stand seem to channel the noise towards us.

As half time approaches, Kevin Francis comes out to warm up, and gets a big cheer from the County fans; he replies with an equally big grin. It's a mark of the impact he made in the short time he was at County that he is afforded such an honour - not many players will have been cheered by fans of the opposing team this season, I'll wager. Just before the break, to avoid the queues, I go and get a coffee and a couple of Mars Bars (I decide to give the cardboard cup of fizzy cola a miss at £1.05 - bloody Birmingham again!). I return to the seats, where Martin gratefully accepts a Mars Bar. He's sitting at the side of me, eating and minding his own business, when, for some reason, I suddenly give a great Jack Douglas twitch which spills coffee over him. I don't quite go as far as to shout "Whoa! Wah-hay! Give over!" and jerk my legs around, but it's still a mystifying incident. It's happened to me occasionally before, and whilst a psychologist would probably say that it was caused by thinking that my cup was slipping whilst my mind was elsewhere, and then massively and suddenly overcompensating, I prefer the altogether more romantic notion that the current tremendous season is affecting my subconscious in more ways that I would have expected.

Just after half time, however, our current tremendous season is suddenly slightly less tremendous, when Birmingham score again. They win a corner on the left, and before they can take it, County make a substitution - something I always thought was covered in chapter one of *"How to be a Manager"*, under the heading "Dos and Don'ts - **Don't**" Sure enough, Birmingham score when the ball comes across, and the tie is effectively over.

There are about twenty minutes left - and Francis has made his appearance to more applause from the away fans than the home - when the effects of the coffee begin to manifest themselves, and I decide to pay a visit rather than have to stop on the way home. I'm standing alone in the ancient bog, doing the necessary, when I hear a goal-celebrating cheer. Was it us or them? Are we back in the game, or is it well and truly over? The tannoy kicks into life, giving me a couple of seconds of delicious anticipation, before... *"Birmingham's"* Crap! *"third goal scored by... Kevvv-innn Fraaaancissss!!"* Would you bloody believe it?! *"Bollocks"* comes an echoey voice from one of the traps; I wasn't alone after all.

I slope back up to my seat, to see County finally, and to add insult to injury, begin to play. With ten minutes left, Brett Angell deflects an Alun Armstrong shot into the net. Thus inspired, we take complete control, and shots begin to rain in from all angles, many of them fizzing just wide. Angell is put through on the keeper, who just manages to turn his lob over the bar; Todd hits a fierce shot just wide. It's an amazing late blitz, but comes far too late to have any effect on the result. The final whistle blows, and we've lost our first cup tie of the season, at the 13th attempt.

I wouldn't be distorting the truth if I said that my overwhelming feeling is one of relief, and that's not just me being disingenuous because I'm disappointed. It's true - I'm relieved. A club like County is never going to win the FA Cup, and, it could be argued, the only reason for us entering such competitions is for the brief moments of glory, with commensurate financial rewards, that occur from time to time. Well, as we've already had the glory and rewards in the other cup competitions, the only result of our continued presence in the FA Cup would be fixture backlog, potential injuries and financial hardship for fans. Genuinely, then, who gives a toss that we're out? Pity it had to be to such an obnoxious set of buggers, but you can't have everything.

Birmingham hasn't finished with me, however. Just to wind me up even further, whilst we were inside the ground, some get went round shifting all the houses, and laying new roads and unfamiliar alleyways, with the result that it takes us a good twenty minutes wandering around, getting ever more frantic, before we eventually happen upon the road on which I've parked.

Ah, cobblers to it. We may be out of the cup, but who gives a toss? Who won the friendly, 4-0, eh? Eh?!

Wednesday January 29th 1997. Southampton (away) (Coca Cola Cup Quarter Final replay).

Well, whatever the team manage tonight, at least *I've* had a result.

Although following County with the intensity I do represents a virtual full-time commitment, it doesn't actually pay me a wage. I occupy my days, therefore, with computer programming (I've taken until now to tell you this in case the very notion of my being such a nerd mentioned earlier on made you throw the book to the floor with a disgusted snort. Had I mentioned that my employer is the Civil Service, you'd have probably thrown it at the wall). With one of those all too rare strokes of luck, such as winning the lottery, or having your toast fall butter side up, I have been working on a piece of software for a place in Portsmouth. Yup, Portsmouth - Southampton's closest, and most deadly, rivals. Well, as I remarked casually to my boss, the morning after the first game had finished level, it'd be silly if I'm going down there anyway not to call in and deliver the software to our customers in person. Good PR, and all that...

It was finally agreed on Monday, therefore, that I will drive myself down to Southampton, get put up in a nice hotel, travel back at my leisure the next day, lose not one minute of flexitime nor a single day of my holidays, and, with Civil Service petrol rates at 24.4p a mile, and reasonable meal allowances (I'll probably buy myself a couple of portions of chips), make around a hundred and twenty quid on the deal. Approval for my trip wasn't expressed in *quite* those terms, but, as I said, result.

I'm less sanguine about the game, however, than I am about swinging such a jolly. To win once on a Premiership ground might be considered good fortune; to win twice would be preposterous. The general view in the media is that we missed our chance last week, and it's one with which I cannot disagree. It's not even as if we'll have great support cheering us on; although a remarkable 700-odd tickets have apparently been sold to County fans (this is a club, remember, who just over ten years ago had a *home* attendance of 1,039), not everyone can swing a trip like mine, and with the game once more live on Sky, it's understandable that most County folk have decided to stay home and watch it down the pub.

I've got company for the trip. Martin, on my suggestion - I knew how much I'd have appreciated such a gesture at his age - is coming with me. The plan is that he'll sneak into my room, crash out on the floor (or on the bed if we drop lucky and they give me a twin room rather than a single, as has happened in the past when I've stayed on business trips in hotels out of season), and sneak out again the following morning. Basically, he'll then get to see the game for six quid, all in (he's pretended to be a child again, and got one of the generous concessionary tickets Southampton offered to the first 100 applicants).

We set off, then, around eight o'clock in the morning, in a state of nervous anticipation (now there's a surprise). We're in the Cavalier - naturally (if I'd taken the Fiesta, I'd have probably had to set out sometime on Monday) - so I'm banking on the journey taking about four hours, which will mean that after checking into the hotel, I'll have the full afternoon to do my stuff with the floppy disks. Our anticipation is heightened by the local Signal Radio station talking up County's chances. The motorway traffic is light, the sun's out, and with the lightness of spirit generated by the circumstances of my trip, I'm about as happy as it's possible to be. Even if we suffer the expected loss, I won't have the arse-ache - literally - of an early-hours coach journey home; I'll be tucked up in a nice warm hotel bed by eleven, dreaming of my leisurely journey back the next day.

We make excellent progress, and are soon listening to the South coast radio stations talking up Saints' chances with slightly more conviction than the Stockport station did County's. I perform my usual getting lost trick in Southampton itself, but finally, after only about twenty minutes' delay, we turn into the impressive gravel-lined drive of... now, here's a problem. I'm not in any way conceited enough to think that the readership of this book will be wide enough to encompass very many members of the hotel trade. Nonetheless, you never know, and I would hate there to be any repercussions concerning my disgraceful flouting of any national hotel rules concerning number of guests normally permitted per single room, should Martin's sneaking in become common knowledge. To serve the purpose of identification, then, as well as attempting to convey some of the nature of the place, I'll simply refer to our billet as the Hotel Posh. It's not too far wide of the mark.

Leaving Martin alone with the tea and coffee making facilities and satellite telly, I nip back out to the car, and spend a frantic afternoon driving to the two establishments in Portsmouth to which I have to deliver the software. Although I'm fairly confident that the programs I am demonstrating actually work, and manage to give the presentations coherently enough, I still feel that the afternoon is an irritating distraction from the true business of the trip - despite the opposite actually being the case. There is some doubt as to whether I'll finish in time, and thus have to return in the morning - which would be disastrous for my feelings of this being the perfect away trip - but, thankfully, I'm back on the M27 to Southampton before five o' clock. I get back to the Hotel Posh at around half past five, quickly employ the tea and coffee making facilities, and we set off for the Dell at around six.

As so often happens, however, in a strange city where the football ground isn't immediately visible (yeah, like my navigational skills are otherwise superb), I am soon lost - and you wondered why I left the hotel so early for a 7.45 kick off? Stopping in the town centre, I ask a bloke where the ground is. He pauses for a moment. "Well, if you go up the road to Asda, then... actually, I'm going to Asda myself - if you give me a lift, I'll show you." Bloody hell - we must be miles away from the ground, I think, as he gets in the back seat, but thankfully, it turns out he's just a lazy get, and Asda appears in a couple of hundred yards. After an increasingly panicky twenty minutes spent driving around the ground trying to find a parking space, I manage to spot a gap on a road about half a mile away, and, with about an hour to kick off, we can relax.

Outside the ground, I see Louie from the Fingerpost again. His latest offering: there's two blokes meet up to go to the pub, and one of them's got his dog with him - a poodle. The first bloke says "you can't take that in - the landlord doesn't allow dogs". The second bloke says, "it'll be alright - you'll see." Anyway, they get to the pub and sure enough the landlord says "sorry mate - no dogs." The bloke (here Louie stares into the distance) says "it's me guide dog". The landlord replies, "guide dog? Guide dogs are bloody labradors or spaniels - not them little things!" So the bloke (here Louie makes as if to feel a tiny imaginary dog) says "why? What the fucking hell've they given me?!?"

I'd heard tales of Southampton's cramped ground, but the entrance to the away stand still causes eyebrows to be raised. A tiny group of turnstiles, set into the perimeter wall a couple of feet from the road give access to a gloomy passageway. Once in the seats, however, alongside the touchline, the view is pretty good - even if it's only probably because, in my case, I've not got any of the roof supports in the way. It's a steep little stand, with bugger all legroom, but almost seems to overhang the pitch, and my particular seat thus has a great view. I wonder if there's anyone nearby called Jack, so I can tell him I'm alright?

The game starts to a tremendous roar from the County fans. We may be about to lose, but it seems that, with God knows how much effort and expense incurred in getting down here for the match (for most people, anyway), the majority are absolutely determined to enjoy themselves. That determination is stretched to the limit, however, after ten minutes, when Le Tissier scores a masterful goal.

The ball is played into the area from the left, and, in one sweeping movement, he controls the ball on his chest, shielding it from the challenging Lee Todd, before swivelling and crashing it home with his left foot. It's a complete bummer, of course, coming so early, and will probably now herald a comprehensive stuffing, but I can't help thinking that it's a form of poetic justice - one in the eye for the idiots who booed him back at Edgeley. Interestingly, there's been none of the booing tonight - as though the true fans, those who'll follow the team to the south coast for a midweek match, realise that such behaviour is the stuff of morons. Ironically, even the chants of *"you'll never play for England"* are tonight countered with *"he'll never play for Stockport"* from the home fans - a riposte no less witty for the fact that it is clearly employed at virtually every Southampton home game, with only the team name altered. Knowing of LeTissier's apparent anti-wanderlust, it could well also be true on every occasion.

I might have been concerned that we're now going to lose heavily, but it becomes clear that, once again, no one has read County the script. We bounce back from the early blow, and if Southampton have chances to increase their lead,

180

they are more than matched by the pressure we put their goal under. Armstrong in particular goes close, although as it's at the other end of the pitch, it's unclear exactly what happens - the anguished head-holding from the County players serves as our guide. Nonetheless, half time arrives with no more scoring, and the gradual realisation that, say, extra time might not even be beyond us.

The second half starts with County now attacking our end, and the noise level rises appreciably. County continue to press, and Armstrong has a scrambled effort cleared off the line by, of all people, LeTissier. He's playing out of his skin - daunting when you realise that LeTissier playing well inside his skin is too good for most teams. Sure enough, he takes aim with a thirty yard free kick, and is finding the top left hand corner until Paul Jones dives across and makes a magnificent save - tipping the ball around the post at full stretch.

We refuse to buckle, however, and the game develops into what cliché-mongers call "a real cup tie" (as though there were artificial cup ties, ones you could buy from market stalls). It's clear now, however, that Brett Angell - doubtful before the game due to illness - is tiring, and people around me are calling for him to be substituted. They aren't to know, of course, that he is about to equalise.

We're in the Southampton half, over on the left, when Cavaco loses the ball. It's won back by one of our midfield, however, and as it pinballs back to Armstrong, standing just outside the area, he senses Angell moving up alongside. He attempts a backheel into Angell's path, and whether or not he gets a touch is irrelevant - the action itself is enough to throw the home defence. The ball falls perfectly into the path of Angell, running clear on goal, and, after taking what seems to me to be almost a week to steady himself, he slots it confidently under the diving body of Beasant. The net bulges in a way that is almost exquisite, and we're level.

Once again the chant of "You're not singing anymore" is being sung with gusto by County fans in a cup game - once the absolute mayhem of celebration has died down a bit. It's a fair enough taunt, but "we're going to Wemberlee," which follows on fairly soon afterwards, is probably a bit cheeky. Then again, a place in the semi-final is anybody's now, and the tension is almost unbelievable. What doesn't bear thinking about is the fact that we've got another half hour of this unless someone scores in the next ten minutes. And then, unless we score again, we're out, as I believe that away goals count extra in the Coca Cola Cup, but only after a period of extra time has been played - almost as though someone at the Football League HQ recognises that they have a good system for settling drawn games in Europe, but is too much of a Little Englander to incorporate it into our competition lock, stock and barrel. It looks like there'll be no need for any system of settling level games, however, as Southampton surge forward again.

Thankfully, their attack breaks down when the ball goes out of play, and County make a substitution. Angell finally leaves the field, to be replaced by Andy Mutch - manager Jones obviously having learnt his lesson from the first leg that tired players can be a liability.

The game restarts, and Southampton press. Tony Dinning, with no pretence at playing good football at this stage, boots a massive clearance out under pressure. Anywhere will do. The ball falls into clear space, however, where Alun Armstrong chases it, pursued by a bear-like Saints defender. Amazingly, Armstrong steals a march on him, and, summoning up reserves of energy from God knows where, outpaces the bugger. Suddenly, he's through on goal. Come on! The County fans leap to their feet en masse as he heads for the area - this is a genuine chance. Beasant comes out to narrow the angle. The defender seems to have made up the ground, but if Armstrong manages to shoot... He enters the area at top speed, and does shoot, just before the defender gets in a tackle. Beasant half blocks the shot, but it's not enough. The ball carries on and it's going in. In that instant, that split-second - literally - the realisation dawns that we're going to win. The ball's on its way in, there are only minutes left, and, once again, after being a goal down, and, in truth, having had no expectation whatsoever that we'd do anything tonight, we're going to achieve probably the finest victory in over 100 years of our history, and qualify for the semi-finals of a major competition for the first time ever. It's Armstrong's goal, but Andy Mutch, substitute of less than a minute ago, is following up, and hammers the ball home from about six inches. It was going in anyway - we could see that from where we're sitting, but apart from the fact that Mutch - misser of more than one absolute sitter this year - might not have known that, who gives a toss who finally propelled it over the line? It could have gone in off Beasant's arse as far as I'm concerned - the fact is that it's in, we're ahead, and we've won.

The goal celebrations just get better and better, as the goals themselves get more and more important. Crammed together in a hot, noisy, old wooden stand, the fans leap up, in a single surging mass of humanity: screaming, yelling, crying and clapping. The players themselves celebrate, probably as unable as us to believe what is happening. Armstrong, over on our side, salutes us briefly before being swamped by his team mates. Mutch, wheeling away on the other side of the pitch, is similarly mobbed.

Gradually, order is restored amongst the County fans, some two minutes after the game has restarted. Southampton are now desperate for the equaliser, but despite their pressure, we break away and actually manage to hold the ball in their half for significant periods. With about three minutes left, they get a break on the edge of the area, and one of their players hits a shot that looks as though it's going in, but curls away at the last minute to miss the post by inches. See - we're going to win.

It's desperation stations now for the home team, as the game moves towards injury time. They get a corner, and as the whistling around me begins to sound like a jet engine's pre-take off surge, Beasant comes up, leaving his goal empty. Thankfully, there is an infringement, and County have possession again. We almost break away, with Beasant out of his goal, but rather than try and score a spectacular third, we sensibly retain possession. It's still not over, however, as this time Southampton get a free kick, deep in their own half. Beasant launches it forward and as it's headed clear by the County defence, back to the halfway line, the final whistle goes. We've won.

As the crowd again rise in acclamation, I give a great, arms spread bellow to the heavens, and prepare to spend the next ten minutes clapping. The team wander over to join in. There is the usual (the *usual!*) self-conscious pitch-posing for the press and TV, and the usual tired smiling and clapping from knackered players who have just achieved something unforgettable. I can make out more red smoke billowing out from the lower tier, as someone has again brought a Blackburn-style flare. I look around me to see tears in almost every set of eyes. It really doesn't get much better than this. There is shouting, cheering, swearing, embracing, and every single fan has a smile as wide as a particularly chipper Cheshire cat.

Amazingly, the home supporters have stayed behind in their thousands - many no doubt, simply stunned, and too unable to believe what they've witnessed to do anything as complicated as walking away. It's clear, however, from the superb ovation the County players get - gratefully acknowledged by the players - that most of them have stayed behind simply to applaud their conquerors. This, I find amazing. Southampton's whole season, with now only a relegation battle to occupy them between tonight and the end of the season, effectively ended five minutes ago. Yet their fans have stayed behind, not to boo or to call for the heads of either their manager or Board, but simply to applaud the victors. Amazing. I'm ashamed to admit that there is no way I could ever be so magnanimous.

We finally snake away from our seats as the players disappear into the dressing room in the opposite corner of the ground. In the gloomy wooden corridors under the stand, all is noise and excitement, which continues outside. Wanting to get back to the car quickly to listen to the radio and back to the hotel in time for the highlights, we rush away, past the depressed knots of home fans, whom I cannot now bring myself to mentally gloat at, due to their amazing generosity at the final whistle. We make the car, flick on the radio, and after a mere ten minute detour, manage to find the route out to the hotel.

I stride into reception, asking for my key with the air of a lower division

Saturday Night and Thursday Morning

football fan who has just seen his team win at the Premiership side in whose town the hotel is situated, whilst outside, Martin slopes up the fire exit to the veranda. I let him in through the French windows, and we make the sleeping arrangements. Generous to a fault - although I could never bring myself to applaud an opponent's win - I offer to sleep on the mattress on the floor, if Martin crashes on the bed frame itself. We make the furniture arrangements, and after a shower, a cup of tea, and half an hour of Danny Baker's Radio Five phone in, it's highlights of the game on ITV, complete with sorrowful south coast presenters. After the glory of seeing the goals again, complete with camera angles and excited commentary, and as Martin, keeping twilight teenage hours, plugs in my CD player for a couple of hours midnight listening, I turn off the telly, and settle down on the mattress to sleep.

Had we lost, I reflect, it would have still been a memorable trip - what with the money being made, and the two buckshee days away from the office for the sake of an afternoon's work. The fact that we won, however, makes it, without doubt, the most memorable ever. I drift off to sleep to thoughts of the full English breakfast awaiting me in the morning.

FEBRUARY

NATIONWIDE LEAGUE DIVISION TWO

	P	W	D	L	F	A	Pts
BRENTFORD	28	14	10	4	45	27	52
LUTON TOWN	25	14	5	6	43	26	47
CREWE ALEXANDRA	27	15	1	11	40	30	46
BRISTOL CITY	28	12	8	8	45	30	44
STOCKPORT COUNTY	**26**	**12**	**8**	**6**	**37**	**28**	**44**
MILLWALL	28	12	8	8	37	36	44
BURNLEY	28	13	4	11	43	33	43
BURY	25	11	9	5	37	26	42
CHESTERFIELD	25	12	5	8	24	20	41
WREXHAM	25	10	10	5	34	30	40
WATFORD	25	9	13	3	26	20	40
SHREWSBURY TOWN	29	9	9	11	39	45	36
WALSALL	26	10	10	11	31	30	36
BLACKPOOL	27	8	9	10	32	30	34
BOURNEMOUTH	29	9	9	13	36	34	34
PRESTON NORTH END	28	9	9	13	39	34	33
PLYMOUTH ARGYLE	28	7	7	11	31	42	31
GILLINGHAM	28	8	10	13	30	38	31
BRISTOL ROVERS	28	7	12	11	27	31	31
YORK CITY	27	8	8	13	28	42	30
PETERBOROUGH UNITED	27	6	8	10	39	45	29
WYCOMBE WANDERERS	27	7	9	15	26	41	26
NOTTS COUNTY	27	5	7	13	20	33	24
ROTHERHAM UNITED	27	4	8	14	24	42	21

February 1st 1997. Brentford (home).

Today is yet another bitterly cold day, in this winter of bitterly cold days. It's quite incongruous, then, to see people standing on the street corners selling t-shirts. Ah yes, but these are no ordinary t-shirts. The bootleggers who have produced them - and you have to admire their chutzpah if nothing else - have made accurate copies of the County home shirt, complete with "Adidas" and "Robinsons' Best Bitter" logos, and "Angell" with a big number 9 on the back. They are probably, if you include street trading rules, flouting about three separate laws at once, and are, of course, doing a roaring trade. It's slightly disappointing, then, to see County officials come marching out and ensure that the police arrest the t-shirt sellers. If the "genuine" replica shirts sold in the club shop weren't so massively overpriced at about forty quid a throw, people might be less inclined to buy the unofficial, maybe shoddy, but undoubtedly cheaper, alternative.

To the game itself, then, and this is a genuinely big one - without argument, bigger than Wednesday, for all County's heroics that night. That said, I fall into a conversation with a bloke outside - a nodding acquaintance - in which he states that he thinks the cup is more important at this stage. In his words, "I'd love to see County in Europe." It's an interesting conundrum, although I have no doubt whatsoever that it'll remain a merely hypothetical question - there's no way we're going to win the Coca Cola Cup. Whilst it would be quite a spectacle - indeed, a bleedin' miracle - to see County up against the likes of Inter Milan and Barcelona, for the sake of a year's delay in promotion (assuming it would be only a year), I still think success in the league remains more important at this stage.

It looks like a virtually full house inside, at least in the County areas; a bloke comes into the Cheadle End and sits behind us with tales of "no tickets left - I got the last one". The crowd is undoubtedly boosted by the fact that we're playing the league leaders, but also because, with tickets for the Middlesbrough semi final due to go on sale imminently, a lot of people will be expecting County, as they have done in the past, to hand out a voucher at the turnstile. Amusingly enough, however, there is no voucher today, which will doubtless piss off a number of fair-weather supporters who have vacated the woodwork for that very reason. Snigger.

County start the game the better, and are unlucky not to go ahead early on. Brentford, however, a physically big team, with few frills but plenty of balls, come back into it, and we're probably slightly lucky to go in at half time level, with no goals having been scored. As well as being a big, strong team, Brentford look quick, as indeed they did down at Griffin Park. Although we coped with them there, however, coming back from two down for a memorable draw, today it seems as though the cup hangover has taken its toll.

Half time is probably the most eventful of the season so far. Firstly, the ticket prices for the semi final are announced - a whopping £18 full price and £12 concessions. This compares with the usual prices of £9 and £4, and is gratifyingly greeted with loud and prolonged booing. County have increased the prices ever since the West Ham game, with bigger and bigger hikes on each occasion - the god of market forces once again being invoked to justify the shittiest of shitty rip offs.

The other half-time event is the parading of yet another Portuguese signing, along with the ubiquitous two agents who have facilitated the move. This guy, called "Nelson" apparently, is a full back. Considering our relative strength in that department, and the fact that he's apparently only 18, he does well to acknowledge the applause that rings out as though we've just signed Alan Shearer; it might be a while before he hears it again.

The pitch is finally purged of assorted mascots, groundstaff and Portuguese agents, and the game restarts. Brentford are soon wishing it hadn't, however, as we take the lead through Luis Cavaco, who at first seems to have lost possession before he leathers the ball into the roof of the net with a force that belies his slight frame. The goal is greeted with something approaching indifference by a worryingly high number of the home "supporters," reinforcing my belief that we have a lot of big game merchants in the ground today. It amazes me, this; how can they be so impassive at such a game - a promotion challenging County against the league leaders - yet, presumably, be willing to shell out £18 quid to cheer the same team on against Middlesbrough in a week or so? Well, I actually know why, of course - they're glory seekers, who have less interest in seeing County than they do in seeing Juninho, Emerson, Ravanelli, et al. When I sit and think about it, I wish these people would fuck off, I really do. I'd rather there were only four or five thousand in the ground for the semi-final rather than a similar number of these buggers.

I'm jolted from such poisonous thoughts by Brentford's equaliser. A corner on the left is flicked on, and in, by one of their tall forwards. Simple as that. Corner - bang - goal. Bugger. They are immediately inspired by their equaliser, and press forward in numbers. As we are forced to defend rather more desperately than is comfortable, I realise that a draw will be a good result today. Indeed, with about 15 minutes left, as I'm bloody freezing, and beginning to rattle again, I find myself wishing the referee would blow full time, and sod the last quarter of an hour; I'd definitely settle for 1-1. Brentford are such a quick, fast, confident team, that a point would probably be as much as we could expect. We're fated not to get even that, though, as Brentford score again, when a forward flicks a great volley into the corner.

Sure enough, it proves to be the winner, as our last few minutes' huffing and puffing amount to the square root of bugger all. The final whistle thus blows on our first home defeat since the horror show that was the game with Wrexham on September 10th. It's a real downer, coming just three days after the ecstasy of the game at the Dell, and is made more painful by the fact that I'm still clinging to hopes of winning the title, and picking up at least half of my bet from Mr W Hill (Newcastle have let me down well and truly). Despite the fact that we're still playing well enough away from home, however, I can't see us overhauling Brentford at the top, especially when, today, we added an effective six points to the gap between us.

February 4th 1997. Burnley (away) (AutoWindscreens Shield R2).

Hey-ho, cup tie number 15 (postponed, because of weather, cup success and cup replays, from January 15th, January 22nd and January 29th).

My God, have the last couple of days been stressful. Following Saturday's announcement that Middlesbrough tickets were to go on sale on Sunday, Monday and Tuesday to season ticket holders, with the rest on open sale from Wednesday morning, my idiot mind moved into overdrive. What if I couldn't get one for myself, let alone the three extra I want for my dad, Martin and Anna? Jack Oldham can't offer me more than a single ticket, and, as Anna wants to go to the game, it'd be pointless taking him up on the offer, as I'd then be unable to sit next to her.

By Monday lunchtime, I had eventually succumbed to the paranoia, nipped down to Edgeley Park, and bought a pro-rata season ticket for the last ten league games, at £75, and the three Middlesbrough cup tickets it thus guaranteed me. Even allowing for the fact that I'll get £18 of it back from my dad, that means I've shelled out a cool £111 for, effectively, the guarantee of seeing one particular game. A small price to pay, I reflected as I drove back to work, for the intoxicating feelings of light-headedness I experienced, three semi-final tickets tucked inside a new season ticket wallet - as though an enormous weight had been lifted off my shoulders. Pathetic, eh?

The ticket situation is merely a staggering indication of how County's success has, once again, gripped the imagination of many people who wouldn't normally give our results a second glance. The whole town seems to be alive, with all the usual paraphernalia a small side's cup success brings - special editions of the local paper, novelty decorations in shop windows, and the like. The home leg will be live on ITV, too. It's the fourth time in this glorious run that'll we'll be live on telly, but this time it's proper telly - the one that everyone's got, without needing a dish on their wall. It'll mean, I would guess, the biggest audience ever to watch a County game - measured in the millions. That's also reason to marvel: people in Cornwall, Norfolk, London, Aberdeen, Cardiff and Belfast - all watching County (and most of them cheering us on, probably).

And to tonight's little diversion, and the simple fact is that I want out of the AutoWindscreens Shield. Not that I've got anything against such a prestigious competition, of course, nor that I don't want a cheap day out at the splendidly up to date and reasonably priced Wembley stadium. No, the only reason that I want County to take their leave of this competition is that we're now facing a severe fixture pile-up. Add to that the fact that we've an outside chance of appearing at Wembley in the Coca Cola Cup final anyway, which, with European entry for the winners, carries slightly more prestige than a competition such as this, manufactured solely for... well, I'm not quite sure, actually. It's well nigh impossible to find anyone who can give a convincing answer to the question: AutoWindscreens Shield - why? At its inception in 1983, it was, through novelty value, presumably, taken fairly seriously even in the early rounds. Now, however, it's only really at the northern or southern final stage - with a Wembley final a mere two legs away - that any given club will attract an attendance higher than their league average. In the early rounds - shown by the sub-1,000 attendance at Doncaster - no one but the idiots, such as me, gives a toss about the competition. In County's position, absolutely nothing can be gained from winning tonight except fixture congestion, tiredness and injuries, and the very real possibility that success in this poxy thing could well be at the expense of promotion.

Having said all that, of course, it *is* Burnley we are playing, and whilst wanting County to lose goes against my every football-supporting instinct, wanting County to lose against Burnley actually proves to be physically impossible. I eventually settle on a compromise - I'll want us to beat Burnley and lose to Bury in the next round. That's better - once decided, I actually feel quite relieved that I can cheer County on tonight.

Inside Turf Moor, the contrast between the atmosphere tonight, and that on the awful day of October 5th couldn't be more marked. The ground seems deserted, even with an admission price of a fiver (and much as it grates to admit it, well done to Burnley for that). It's like a reserve game; or, at least, how I imagine a reserve game to be, never having experienced such a beast. Indeed, with the reduced admission, the crowd seems so small that, after paying all the various expenses occasioned by staging a midweek floodlit match, Burnley could well end up losing money on the night. I do hope so.

No one in the ground - players, officials, fans from either side - seem to be interested tonight, except, perhaps, the referee, who ponces around as though it's his first big game since graduating from Referees' School. Dave Jones has, sensibly, decided to play a virtual reserve team; only Gannon, Todd and Dinning survive from the Brentford defeat. It's a smart move; lose and it was "only our reserves"; win and Burnley can't even beat our reserves (I'm sure Jones' reasons for doing so are more concerned with giving squad members a game, and allowing first teamers to rest rather then the potential gloat factor we fans will enjoy, but his team selection does mean that we've got nothing to lose tonight).

As a result of the sparse crowd - although due to the gloomy purple and blue colours Burnley have used for their seats, it's fairly hard to see just how empty it is - the large ground is really echoey, and the players' shouts are clearly audible. Many of them are directed at County's Adie Mike, who is having a nightmare up front. One or two of the crowd join in with the barracking, although his surname doesn't really lend itself to angry abuse: "Come on Mike, you fucking idiot!" sounds a touch odd, to say the least; it feels wrong to be hurling abuse at someone and using what sounds like their first name.

Still, there is the fact that it is Burnley that we are playing to maintain the interest. An indication of the high regard in which we hold our opponents can be gleaned from the fact that reserve keeper Neil Edwards, in trying to punch clear a cross midway through the first half, inadvertently connects with a Burnley attacker's head, and lays him out cold. Edwards gets the loudest cheer of the night, followed by his name being chanted ecstatically by the away support.

That's about the most exciting thing that happens in the first half, with the exception of County scoring. Martin Nash, a Canadian international signed recently, meets a right wing cross on the volley and hammers it past the home keeper. Huff and puff as they might, Burnley cannot get back into the game, until they are gifted a penalty with about fifteen minutes left. Damon Searle is adjudged to have handled on the line, and, despite fierce protests that seem more than token, leading us to think that he may have a point, is sent off. The Burnley player who takes the kick, however, leathers it straight at Edwards, who saves easily. There is no more action of note, and County's reserves have indeed beaten Burnley's first team, for our 15th cup win of the season. It hardly compensates for a 5-2 thrashing in the league, but, in advance of the league game at Edgeley Park in April, it'll do for now.

February 7th 1997. Bristol City (away).

Bristol City - inspiration for virtually all 1970s British cinematic humour. Bristol City. Titty. Yukyukyukyukyuk! Ooooh, Matron! Look at that loverly pair of Bristols! Yukyukyukyukyuk! Strange how the "Carry On" films are viewed these days as being somehow part of a fine tradition of British humour - willies, bums, farts, the lot - whilst in reality, it seems to me, they simply weren't funny. If the tradition of British humour is supposedly represented by one or two basic jokes, repeated ad infinitum through thirty years of lengthy feature films, then where does The Goon Show, Monty Python, Fawlty Towers and Vic Reeves fit in? Yours sincerely, Disgusted, Tunbridge Wells.

I had considered the luxury of the train again for today's game, but decided against it on the grounds of being skint, and the fact that Bristol have moved the match to a Friday night, for reasons unknown. I've not got many days' holiday left, either, which means that I'm going to finish work only slightly early rather than take a half-day (thank heavens for flexitime), and drive down. I figure if I leave just after the kids come home from school (about quarter to four), I'll just about do it.

Stuck in traffic on Hall Street, about a mile from my house, and five minutes from the motorway at just before five to four, however, I begin to wonder. It's all very well being a soft dad, and wanting to see your kids before setting off, but that's not going to help you get through the Birmingham snarl-up, is it now? I crawl onto the M63 out of Stockport at just before four - I've got three and three quarter hours to get to Bristol's ground. It's Wycombe all over again.

I make reasonable time onto the M6, however, and am soon driving through the big sweep of countryside just before Keele: one of my favourite motorway places, if having favourite bits of motorways doesn't make me sound too pathetic. It cuts through a picturesque piece of land, which is always beautiful, but seems different every time, in whatever weather. Today, at dusk, it's golden browns and reds, and a hint of dark green - it makes you wonder with a jolt, of course, how nice it was before they stuck a bleedin' great motorway through it.

The rest of the journey down is fairly uneventful, with a satisfyingly small clog around Birmingham, and the mother and father of all sunsets as I coast down the M5. There is a deep orange glow over the hills to my right, which I presume is the last vestiges of the sun going down, although it it looks like nothing so much as one of those nuclear holocaust films which were popular ten or so years ago, in which the explosion always conveniently takes place on the other side of a hill, thus saving no end of money from the effects budget.

It's soon dark, and I start, as is my wont, picturing myself driving on a massive map. The motorway is unlit at this point, and the car's headlights illuminate ahead of me in a way that makes it seem as though I'm driving along the tunnel that is the M5 into the south west As well as the idea of driving along a map, it's hard to dismiss the feeling that "south" is downhill (when I was a kid, I was convinced that charity Land's End to John o'Groaters would never make the journey from south to north: they'd enough of a job to do without having to go uphill as well). On that subject, I still find it hard to believe that West Brom's ground, the Hawthorns, is the highest above sea-level, as it apparently is. What about all those that are further uphill - Newcastle, Sunderland and Carlisle, for example?

I'm soon at the exit which the route I've typed out from the Supporter's Guide and stuck to the steering wheel indicates is the correct one for the ground. As the time is only just gone seven o'clock, I'm going to be well in time for the kick off. Third exit, off to the right. I'm a bit concerned, however, that the roundabout I'm supposed to hit after half a mile is nowhere to be seen, and when the route starts going on about traffic lights and non-existent pubs, I start to worry. I pass a signpost which welcomes me to a farty little village called Portishead, and realise I'm going to have to retrace my route. Bollocks and arse! I zoom back to the motorway as quickly as I can. It only takes three circuits of the roundabout for me to establish that I should have taken the first exit not the third, and that the directions I had were for traffic coming from the opposite carriageway of the M5.

I shoot off in the right direction, swearing fiercely, and am soon dropping into Bristol from above, with the town lights spread out in front of me. I spot the floodlights, thankfully, and, as cars seem to be parking on the road I am coming in on, I essay a quick turn down a side street and park up myself, facing back to the M5.

The next bloke along seems to have a friendly enough face, so I ask him for directions. Better than that, he says he'll take me there himself. We get to chatting about our relative teams; he telling me about previous trips he's made to County and me shamefacedly admitting I've never been here before (well, except to Bristol Rovers earlier in the season, but I figure it's better not mentioning that to a City fan). We're soon at a subway on the other side of which is the ground. He points me in the right direction, and with a final last friendly word and a handshake, he's off to join the home fans. Such an example of instant friendship between football-supporting strangers is by no means a rare occurrence. I can guarantee that you could start a conversation with a home fan at any ground in the country and so long as you don't act aggressive, or antagonise, you'll get on well enough, no matter how important the game is to your respective sides; I've done it often enough myself. I watch the bloke descend into the subway, then run after him and kick his fucking head in. Only kidding.

There aren't many County fans here tonight, understandably, so I am able to nod to Peter Collins on the other side of the turnstiles. He looks remarkably sprightly for his 86 years. I move into the away end, behind the goal; Ashton Gate is a cavernous ground, big and impressively rebuilt with nice new stands on three sides. The away end, however, has been fitted out with the most ridiculous seats imaginable, bolted on to the old terrace. From a distance, they look like conventional red plastic ones, but once I arrive at my chosen spot, I realise that they are actually *backless* tip up jobs - just about the most uncomfortable combination imaginable. I'd like to bet that such seats aren't to be found in the home end, but as we all know, away fans, once you've taken their money, are for dumping on, aren't they?

It seems like a big crowd inside, justifying City's decision to change the game to a Friday night. Fifteen minutes after the start, home fans are still coming in, reinforcing what the bloke I was talking to outside said: City fans are notorious for arriving late. Don't they score early goals, or something?

Big crowd, big disappointment (I could write slogans for the Labour Party, me); County take the lead after ten minutes. A scramble in the home area seems to have ended with a home defender hoofing the ball away. Sadly for him, however, it smacks straight into the referee's arse, and rebound into the path of an unmarked Alun Armstrong, who reacts superbly well, and slots it home confidently. I don't know whether to laugh or celebrate, so I settle for a mixture of both.

There's no more scoring in the first half, although County ride their luck. Our lead even survives an amazing miss by Bristol, when one of their attackers manages to hit the bar from six yards out, with the keeper miles away to the right. *Let's all laugh at Bristol* is the away fans' response.

Despite it being slightly against the run of play, therefore, we reach the break with a 1-0 lead. I fall into conversation with Martin Frost and Jeff Lawrenson, who are sitting just in front. Rather than me baffling them with another of my Bizarre Football Theories, we talk about County's latest ticketing débâcle. As if charging £18 wasn't bad enough, the way they have actually decided to allocate tickets is absolutely despicable. Out of a home capacity of around 9,000, they claim to have 2,000 season ticket holders, who are being allowed a ridiculous three tickets each. What is worse, however, is that of the 3,000 tickets left, an incredible 2,000 are being allocated to arse-lickees (aka sponsors) and other assorted freeloaders, leaving just 1,000 on open sale. When you consider that County's average home attendance (excluding freebie kids) is around 4,000, it's clear that that when season ticket holders are excluded, there will be 2,000 regularly-attending fans fighting for 1,000 tickets. Sure enough, between the three of us we come up with numerous examples of lifelong supporters, unable to fork out for season tickets but who go to every home game, missing out on arguably County's biggest home game ever. County may be sponsored by the local brewery, but I'd bet my mortgage that they're never invited to run a piss-up there.

The people who run County seem, at times, to be the biggest bunch of incompetent amateurs in town, which, when you consider exactly what it is they are attempting to administer - a football club - is just about the most damning indictment I can level at them. I hope the person or persons who took the decision to sell tickets in this way can sleep at night; I know I couldn't. To add insult to injury, God knows how many of the extra people will actually *be* County fans - they'll most likely simply be clients of those various sponsors, being buttered up at a big sporting occasion, and depriving regular County fans of the opportunity of being there. If, when the teams run out for the semi, I hear someone behind me say "which one's County then?" I will be seriously tempted to stand up, turn round, and thump them. (Incidentally, I realise that I could be open to charges of hypocrisy, as Anna, who hasn't been at all this season, is coming to the game. Not guilty. She came regularly with me before we had kids - the main reason for her not coming these days, in fact - and, as a regular during the dark days of the eighties, was actually in County's lowest crowd ever: the 1,039 who saw the famous game with Southend in 1985. She's as much right to be at the game as anyone).

Towards the end of half-time, I go to get sustenance so that I don't faint through malnutrition on the way home (it *could* happen). It's thus on the way back to my seat, armed with pastie, coffee and Mars Bar, therefore, that I see Bristol's equaliser, a matter of thirty seconds or so after the restart. A winger flies down the flank in front of me and sends over a perfect cross which Goater heads powerfully back into the opposite corner.

Bugger. I had thought that the somewhat charmed life our goal led in the first half might mean we'd sneak a spawny win tonight, but obviously not. A defeat is on the cards, but, luckily, we find our rhythm, and manage to stifle most of what Bristol produce for the rest of the game. Indeed, we almost nick it ourselves late on, when Alun Armstrong manages to round the keeper, but he rushes his shot under pressure, and screws the ball wide.

Amazingly, as the game meanders to its climax, I see quite a few people leaving early from the stand to our right. By the law of averages, there must be some of those who arrived late doing so; these people have paid a fairly high ticket price yet have thus only seen an hour of the game. Still never mind, eh - at least you'll beat the traffic (said with the smug superiority of one who's got traffic-beating down to a fine art).

The game ends at 1-1 - probably a better point for us than for them. Although they're ahead of us in the table, I think our games in hand make us better poised to finish ahead of them at the death. Outside, this view is reinforced by sounds of the locals' disappointment. "Oi thorrt they was the betterrr soide" says one, following a diatribe from his mate about their team's shortcomings.

Saturday Night and Thursday Morning

I amble back to the car, knowing I'm on a fairly direct route out of town, and with the motorway not far away. I pick up the pace, however, when I realise that my new friend might be there. Whilst it was pleasant enough to converse with him on the way into the ground, I don't want to analyse the game in depth standing next to the cars, desperate to be away, and a final handshake would be simply too cheesy for words.

I find the car, and discover I was actually parked very near the Clifton suspension bridge - I hadn't noticed it earlier because it wasn't illuminated as it is now. I'm tempted to hang around and see if there are any suicides, but, in what I imagine might well be the final words of quite a few of the jumpers themselves, I'd better be off. I've got a long drive home, and that bloke might be back any minute. For some reason, a bizarre image of a big American-style manly hug springs unannounced into my mind, and I dive into the car with a shudder.

I know that there weren't many County fans at the game, and that most of them would have been in the coaches I've left behind anyway, but the motorway still seems remarkably empty. Am I going the right way? It's eerie being the only car on an unlit motorway at night; I cannot rid my mind of the ridiculous notion that I've made a mistake, and I'm careering the wrong way, or I half expect to see another car's lights coming directly towards me, like in "Planes Trains and Automobiles." It doesn't help that there are a worrying number of signs saying "end," but no indication of what precisely they are indicating the end of. Thankfully, one or two cars do eventually pass, which makes me relax - *they'll* crash into the oncoming juggernaut instead of me.

I stop for a slash at quarter to twelve; the service station is amazingly busy, with, for some reason, loads of Americans kids loafing around. Am I missing something here? I get back underway, to find that the motorway is also extremely busy, with loads of big wagons thundering past. What, are the Yank kids all driving wagons or something? It's late, and the sooner I get home the better.

I finally leave the M6 at half past midnight, and head for home through the Cheshire opulence that is Mere. I'd like to live in Mere; quite apart from being home now, I'd be dead rich. To keep myself awake on the non-motorway roads, I flick around the radio channels. Some bloke on Talk Radio is going on about a girl he once knew that had three nipples. I don't hang about. I eventually get home at ten to one, satisfied at a point gained, but once again absolutely knackered following an arduous away trip. I'm going to be lethargic *again* at work tomorr.. no! It's Saturday! Get in, as it were! I go to bed with a light heart.

February 11th 1997. Bury (away) (AutoWindscreens Shield R3).

There's more mad weather tonight for the latest cup tie in this marathon season. Unlike our last game at Gigg Lane, when it was freezing cold, today is absolutely lashing it down, with the result that there's quite a lot of traffic on the way to Bury. Nevertheless, it's a nice short journey that Martin and I make, and we're once again there in good enough time to park in a side road off Gigg Lane itself, ready for the quick getaway.

Sadly, I don't bump into my friends the Players' Guests again (despite hanging around the away turnstiles from about four o' clock), so I have to pay £10 to sit behind the goal. It's a stupid price to charge for a game like tonight's; as a result, I would guess there's only about 2,000 in the ground - and a lot of them from Stockport, most of whom wouldn't have known the price until they got here. If they had, I guess the away section would also be about half as full as it is. At least they've had the sense to charge only a fiver if, like Martin, you're a kid. Or, strictly, if, like Martin, you're not a kid, but able to pretend you are.

There seem to be a depressingly large number of clubs at this level charging a tenner and upwards for seats - I fully expect County to do the same next year, despite the fact that the leap from seven quid to nine this year was a hell of a jump. I can't believe that a Board as eager to grasp the main chance as ours won't have copped the seat prices being charged on their travels, and thought they could get away with the same trick at our place. Easy decision to make, really, when you get in to grounds for nowt, and can snuffle and slurp at the trough of hospitality before, during and after the game

Such negative thoughts are particularly appropriate, I feel, as I take my seat, as I really want the team lose, for quite probably the first time ever. The "reward" for the winner tonight is a trip to Crewe, in the northern semi-final, no less. Big deal. Another game, more expense, and progression in a pointless competition. Nope, a defeat will do me very nicely tonight, thank you.

Trust County not to heed my desires, however. We take the lead after about ten minutes, when the referee awards a penalty, that no one, least of all the players, was expecting. Whilst the ground is still in a state of mild shock, Tony Dinning grabs the ball, puts it on the spot, and puts us ahead with the minimum of fuss.

Thankfully, the home team come to my rescue ten minutes or so later, when, following a scramble in the County box, one of their strikers leathers it home from two yards. Following this goal, neither team looks like scoring again, and the prospect of County's first ever Golden Goal extra time period looms. This particular competition was the pioneer of this way of settling deadlocks - indeed, Birmingham won the trophy a couple of years ago with such a goal in the final.

Saturday Night and Thursday Morning

It's hard to think of a less suitable venue for a concept called "golden" goal, however, than Bury v Stockport on a pissing wet February Tuesday.

Nonetheless, following a fairly tense last ten minutes, in which a goal would probably have effectively been pretty shiny anyway - and I noted a good number of complete idiots actually leaving the ground early - the ref blows for time, and sudden death it is. Once again, as at Burnley, I'm now presented with a dilemma. I still want County to go out of the competition, but not in this manner. A normal time defeat would be acceptable, but either a sudden death goal or a defeat on penalties would not. I'm therefore reluctantly obliged to start supporting the team again.

The players stand in a huddle, steaming quietly, and Martin and I, anticipating a goal for either team, move over to a couple of seats near the exit. We manage to grab an aisle seat, and it's with a strong sense of déjà vu that I find myself next to my friend from the Southampton home game, the hollow-cheeked Mr Sputum. Sure enough, the aisle is once again awash.

I don't have too long to endure the repulsive spectacle, however. After five minutes or so of extra time, Brett Angell is put through at the far end, and slots the ball confidently under the advancing keeper. I cheer the goal, of course, perfunctorily, before dashing for the car. We're through to the next round! Bugger.

February 15th 1997. Shrewsbury Town (home).

Quite a momentous game in prospect today, in many ways, as, for the first time since the Middlesbrough tickets went on sale, I can sit in my new pro-rata season ticket seat. I'm also confident that we'll beat Shrewsbury, so a good afternoon is in prospect all round.

My mellow feelings are enhanced when I find my new seat - the view is brilliant. It's just below the central gangway in the Cheadle End, and dead centre - right behind the goal. Sadly, however, as the game gets underway, I realise that a lot of my fellow spectators - many of whom are presumably also season ticket holders, this being such an excellent position - seem to be founder members of the Angry Club, particularly one woman sitting right next to me, who seems to be as fond of tutting as the hollow-cheeked junkie was of gobbing. Fairly early on in the proceedings, I decide that, on balance, I preferred the gobbing.

County are playing crap - that much is obvious - but they don't deserve the reception they're getting from the miserable sods surrounding me. I get the impression that many of the crowd have their minds more on the forthcoming semi-final than the everyday grind of the league, and the players seems also to be preoccupied. I suppose they won't consciously play at less than 100%, but they

198

must surely be aware that an injury now would make it likely that they will miss the big game.

Alun Armstrong, however, not as wordly-wise, perhaps, as some of his older team-mates, is still giving it his all. After about ten minutes, he receives a great ball in his stride, and takes it round the keeper. His shot is blocked, but he is the quickest to react, retrieves it brilliantly and crosses, only for keeper to catch well. Great football. "Pathetic!" snorts the tutting woman as the keeper catches. Jesus! I've heard of having high expectations, but give it a rest, woman.

As least she's not gobbing, although I suppose she could start at any minute, as she's obviously not enjoying the game much. Or is she? Perhaps people like this - and there seem to be a hell of a lot of them around me - are only truly happy when they're angry. Perhaps they only come to games to let off steam. Certainly, people behave differently at a football game than they would virtually anywhere else; I've made that clear enough myself when describing my own behaviour. If that's the case, and people like this woman come and pay their nine quid in order simply to moan and groan, and huff and puff, then they can do it away from me. I resolve to sit elsewhere in the second half.

Nothing of note happens in the first half, other than the hilarious sight of the slight figure of Luis Cavaco squaring up to an opponent who towers a good foot over him, after a bad tackle by the latter. "Come and Cavaco if you think you're hard enough" shouts a bloke behind me, who gets a laugh for his pains. Finally, to a last torrent of tuts, sounding like a geiger counter at Sellafield, the whistle blows. In some ways, it's a shame - the woman was tutting so frequently, she seemed to be reaching a crescendo - as though she might have exploded at any minute. Now that I would've liked to have seen.

I know roughly where Tom sits, so wander over to him for the second half, giving a great exaggerated yawn when the announcer chooses to read out the result of the latest England chase-the-egg game. We're football fans, pal, at a football ground - why do we need the rugby scores? Why stop there - why not read out the results of the Boat Race, or the Badminton Horse Trials, or the National Tiddlywinks Championships?

There's an empty seat next to Tom, and I drop into it, explaining about my dilemma with the moaning old biddy. The trouble is, that's my season ticket seat, and it's a great view as well. One of the arguments often used against the imposition of all-seater stadia was the fact that you're stuck in a single position, and can't move from any obnoxious person you might find yourself near. I'm pretty sure they didn't cite a tutting woman as an example, though. Tom puts my moaning into perspective, however, when he mentions a bloke at the engineering plant where he's employed, who, because of shift work, was unable to get down and join the ticket office scrum for the open-sale Boro tickets. It'll be the only game he'll miss all season.

Sympathy for Tom's mate, and poisonous thoughts about people who pay good money simply to moan unjustifiably about the team are banished after fifteen minutes of the second half, however, when Shrewsbury take the lead, with a goal almost identical to the one Millwall scored against us a few weeks ago. The ball is flicked on from a corner, and headed goalwards where once again Todd heads it away - and once again a myopic linesman flags that he didn't. Todd's protests are more vehement than ever - understandably, as I remain convinced that a player standing on the line who gets enough purchase on the ball to clear it could not possibly do so if the ball had completely - *completely* being the operative word here, linesman - crossed the line. I'd like to continue the debate with the officials, but of more immediate concern is the fact that Shrewsbury are now ahead. When you consider the nature of Shrewsbury's lucky win against us at their place, it seems that they could be on for a fortunate double that could cost County dear.

With fifteen minutes left, then, things are looking a bit desperate, and I'm half considering going back to my season-ticket seat for a spot of tutting, when Brett Angell equalises. Another Mike Flynn long throw is flicked on and Angell hammers a header past the keeper. Relief at the equaliser, but it's still not enough. To maintain our challenge we need a win, and a minute later, as if it were preordained, Brett gets his nut on another cross, this time from Kieron Durkan, to flick a header into the far corner. County are on fire, but back storm Shrewsbury, and for the last ten minutes, we've got a game. It's a pity it took eighty minutes for it to happen, but at least County seem to hold the upper hand. That is confirmed in the dying minutes when Armstrong again shows his quality in reacting quickest to a loose ball and hitting a shot across the keeper and in.

For the 11th time this season, we've come from behind to win. What's more, other results went our way, placing us in the top ten, with games in hand on everyone else. Tut at that, you small-minded old cow.

February 22nd 1997. Blackpool (away).

The weather teased us unmercifully on Wednesday, as the first leg of the Coca Cola Cup semi final with Middlesbrough (my God, it feels good typing that) was postponed, due to rain making County's crappy pitch unplayable. It's so bad at the moment, you almost feel that too much gobbing by the players in any given game might also make abandonment a possibility. The way the heavens opened on Wednesday, it was understandable that the game couldn't go ahead, although that didn't stop me getting togged up, and driving down to my mum's, where the dreadful news was revealed to us all via teletext.

There was still time for a little chest-puffing, though, as ITV, before showing the film they'd had ready to slot into place for just such an eventuality, went over to Edgeley Park for a little five minute slot with Bob Wilson, who relayed the sad news to the masses and interviewed Dave Jones from a little box that, by the look of it, had been specially erected in the no-mans-land between the main stand and the exit. Fancy! Little us, warranting a slot on peaktime telly before the watching millions, and not even for a proper game, either!

It was a bad cup football week for County fans in any case; our cup thunder this season has been well and truly stolen, by either Chesterfield or Wrexham, both of whom won through to the FA Cup quarter-finals last Saturday, and one of whom, by virtue of them being drawn against each other, will match our achievement in reaching the semis. They'll actually receive more kudos than us, of course, as the FA Cup is a far more noteworthy competition than the Coca Cola Cup.

Ah, so what - promotion's the thing, as I keep telling myself with a frequency that probably hints at my true feelings with a major cup semi-final a mere four days away. Still, today's game is always one that is eagerly anticipated, often for reasons other than the football. Blackpool away is one of the best games for the boozers, for example, with God knows how many drinking dens along, or in the streets just behind, the seafront. To make a day of it, most fans usually want Blackpool away in either April or May, so that, with the sun quite possibly shining, they can kid themselves they're on holiday as they cruise the Golden Mile in their shirt-sleeves. Me, I like Blackpool out of season. It's far more atmospheric, and even if it is a bit of a dump in February, atmosphere is everything, I feel.

I'm about to leave the house at just before twelve when John Taylor rings me up for a lift. He was leaving it a bit late, but was lucky. I arrange to pick him up by the M63 in the town centre, and, pausing only to collect my dad and Martin, proceed to the rendezvous. Once John's aboard, we make surprisingly good time, and, despite me not exactly putting my foot down, are in the depressing hole that is a winter Blackpool after just over three quarters of an hour. We're so early that I am able to park just about as close to the away turnstiles as I have ever parked at a football ground, in one of the vast car-parks that surround Bloomfield Road.

After a quick slash to justify actually going in to the Manchester Arms - a pub on the sea front that is playing music so loud I almost hanker for the kid-ridden Barlow Stand at Edgeley Park - and a rapid retreat to another pub in which we can have a pint without having our eardrums perforated, we head back to the ground.

Bloomfield Road, for all its history, is a complete and utter dump these days.

Saturday Night and Thursday Morning

There are three fairly small and rickety old stands and the one huge kop, behind which we're parked. Over half this terrace is closed off, and what remains is given over to away fans, with an overflow along the side of the pitch. From the top of the kop, where we stand today, you get a panoramic view of the rest of the ground, and extremely grotty it is too. Blackpool are constantly threatening to move to a new ground, the plans for which get more ambitious every week or so. I believe that currently, the new place will have a retractable pitch, a sliding roof and a massive hotel and entertainment complex attached. I've always thought, strange as such grandiose plans seem on the face of it, that Blackpool is just about the only place in the country outside London that could make such a scheme work. The fact that they've been threatening it for God knows how long might make a cynic question whether they'll ever leave Bloomfield Road, however; having your Chairman jailed earlier this season for rape probably doesn't help matters. All in all, Bloomfield Road remains a pimple on the arse of the Golden Mile. And that's saying something.

The first half is absolutely crap, and neither team comes even close to scoring. The half time whistle brings blessed relief, and I head towards the back of the terrace for a wander. Right at the top, I look out over the top of the fence, past the absolutely pointless razor wire (what is there worth nicking inside this place? I suppose it could be there to stop people escaping *from* the terrace, which today is probably a distinct possibility). Peering out over the wall, I see the old exits, similar to the ones that caused the disaster at Ibrox - crumbling old steps leading down from the heights, evocative of the days when thousands would surge down these steps, having seen Matthews and Mortenson conjure up another First Division victory. You get the impression now, however, that if you kicked a stanchion hard enough, the whole ground might collapse: a fairly apt metaphor for Blackpool themselves, languishing with the dead men after their glory days of the 50s and 60s. It must have been one hell of a kick they got, sometime around 1978.

Resting my chin on the wall, I spot the car and am transported back twenty five years. I came to Blackpool for a day trip once as a kid, and the coach parked more or less where I've parked the car today. It was the first football ground I'd ever seen that wasn't Edgeley Park, and I remember being incredibly impressed; it was huge and imposing, and the painted signs over the turnstiles saying "Spion Kop" impressed me no end. How times change: Edgeley Park is now a much better place (that's not to say it wasn't falling to pieces itself in the eighties), and with a far bigger capacity.

This part of the town, lying, glowering, just behind the glister of the seafront, is grimy and bleak. It's not that much better at the height of summer; now, on a grey and cold winter's afternoon, it's absolutely horrible. To think how excited I used to be at the thought of a visit to this town, and how childishly impressed I was by what's become a complete dump of a ground. I suppose it could be the effects of the half-game I've just seen, but if I'm not careful I could catch a severe case of melancholia. At least Blackpool are providing less of a threat than us. We should also have what's become a very strong, albeit swirling, wind in the second half, so I may yet see County avoid defeat at Bloomfield Road.

I meander back to my place for the second half, which begins with County playing as badly as they did in the first. The difference is that Blackpool are not playing as badly as they did earlier, and take a deserved lead after ten minutes or so, when defensive ineptitude by County leads to a Blackpool forward, completely unmarked on the far post, hammering home. Even worse, fifteen minutes later they go two up, and all of a sudden, after holding out wind-assisted hopes for the second half, we've lost. "Sheepshaggers, sheepshaggers, sheepshaggers" shout the home fans in celebration, although I concede that they may be shouting "Seasiders"

County seem to accept that the game's over, and as the match peters out, it's clear that we're never going to score. Ironic, then, that as I troop disgustedly for the exits, and join hundreds of other County fans taking their early leave of the place, I hear on local radio inside the car that Andy Mutch has headed an injury time consolation. The local commentator is frantically cursing the excessive injury time added on by the referee, and I am half -considering getting out of the car and running back inside, when he excitedly announces the end of the game, echoed by a distant cheer from the Blackpool fans. It's a defeat that I really didn't expect, and one that is hammered home by the absolute necessity of at least a point today to maintain our position towards the top of the league. It's a quiet and melancholy drive home.

Wednesday February 26th 1997. Middlesbrough (home) (Coca Cola Cup Semi Final First Leg).

Tonight is arguably County's biggest game ever - and if you pause, and think about what that actually means, you realise just how staggering a statement it is. The whole town is once again up for the game: the local paper has produced a 32-page supplement, the ubiquitous bakers' shops have all baked "up for the cup" blue and white cakes for their windows, as bakers' shops are wont to do on these occasions, and even the town centre Asda has a "Good Luck County" sign hanging from the ceiling. At the risk of seeming churlish, however, I just wonder whether any of these organisations will do the same again should there come a game, a couple of month's hence, at which promotion can be secured?

Saturday Night and Thursday Morning

Once again, virtually everybody I meet at work makes reference to the match - more so than for previous cup ties, as tonight's game is live on ITV, directly after Coronation Street, thus guaranteeing an audience of many millions, at least for the first few minutes, before they all realise it's not Man Utd and switch over to "How Do They Do That" (*search me - at the end of August, I thought they were going down*). I still find it scarcely credible that we're going to be live on national TV. It will, presumably, be the highest audience ever to watch County - I don't think Sky games even attract a million unless it's United, or another big Premiership club playing. I also find it wondrous that not only will Julia, Chris and Andrew be watching the game - and as Sky veterans, they'll be blasé about it anyway, not that they know what blasé means - but my mum at home, Carole and Kevin in Yorkshire, Lisa and Pete in Lymm, and various other relatives, workmates and ex-schoolmates all over the country - many of whose only recollection of me would be "oh yes, he was the one who supported County, wasn't he?" - will all be watching Stockport County, from Edgeley Park. Live and Exclusive on ITV. Amazing.

All the build-up has left me nervous and twitchy, feelings which start to build to a frenzy from about half past three, when I finished work. When I get home my right leg's aching like mad - probably through tiredness, but also possibly because of the tension. It hasn't helped that I've felt the need, every ten minutes or so throughout the day, to check that I've still got my ticket, which I've secreted inside my shiny new season ticket holder.

I pick up Martin and my dad - no Ceefax disappointment this week - and arrive at the ground well before Anna, who is waiting for her mum to arrive and babysit. Once again, the curse of the Coca Cola Cup has struck, and it's pissing down. Today's referee, David Elleray - a man who seems to court controversy as much as one of his infamous predecessors Clive Thomas - is obviously inside, and lapping up the attention for all he's worth, as he keeps us hanging on before declaring the pitch fit. To their credit, County haven't opened the turnstiles whilst there's still a chance of the game being called off, but Elleray delays his decision so long that there's a serious danger of crowd congestion outside, so the gates are opened, and in go the punters. I'm not so daft, however - you won't catch me going through those turnstiles until I know for definite the game's on, so I hang outside and wait for Anna. In the time before she arrives, I spot no fewer than six touts all selling tickets - they must have thought it was Christmas when County cocked up the distribution like they did. *Open sale, as many as you like, form an orderly queue gents, please* - Jesus!

We go inside, and Anna mentions how much the ground's changed. I had forgotten that she hasn't been inside since the Cheadle End was built - I think her last game was a playoff with York City three years ago. It must be quiet an awesome sight to see what is, for us, a monster of a stand behind one goal where previously you remembered a pathetic four shallow terrace steps. Awesome - not a word I've often heard used to describe Edgeley Park.

The game starts, and it's clear from the very earliest exchanges that the pitch is going to prevent a classic. The absence of Juninho, away on international duty, might have helped matters in that regard, but you won't hear any home fans moaning. The first fifteen minutes are all County, but I would guess we need to score. Then again, other games against Premiership sides have gone like this - we've actually conceded an early goal in four out of the five prior to tonight, and gone on to either win or draw them all.

The crowd in the Cheadle End are certainly up for it tonight, with the noisy partiality you would expect; an early injury to a Boro player brings a rather frenzied shout of "let him die," which seems a bit excessive. Far better the classic I once heard at Edgeley Park years ago, in conditions which were, if anything, even muddier, as an opposition player writhed in agony: "tread him in."

The game settles down, and I find myself wondering how the rest of my family are reacting to the game, especially Carole and Lisa, who used to come here themselves in the old days. In view of the fact that we're not really playing that well - although, as we're more than matching another Premiership side in the semi final of a major competition, it shows the high standards we're currently judging County by - I find myself wishing that this game had been on Sky, and one of the others on ITV. Imagine how fantastic the win at the Dell would have been if viewed by millions, rather than the few hundred thousand who actually saw it.

I also clock the crappy merchandise which has been given out - and, even worse, willingly displayed by the fans. Coca Cola have provided megaphones, the Manchester Evening News have provided plastic blue and white hats, and the cable TV company Nynex have provided what can only be described as "things", resembling nothing so much as oversized table-tennis bats, with their logo printed on them. Outside, I also noticed one or two away fans with those ridiculous blow-up sausages that are currently trendy in the Premiership. All examples of attempts at manufacturing atmosphere - something that plainly isn't needed at football games, especially games as important as this one.

The half time whistle goes with no score, although Ravanelli came close with one little chip that just trickled wide, and I find myself glancing involuntarily at the illuminated ITV box, which is, indeed, a portakabin on scaffolding. I wonder how their experts'll read it. As ever, I'm far too involved to do so, but realise that our chances will be being replayed, and commented on, at this very moment: *"And here was that shot from Armstrong..."* During the game, all I'm thinking is "Go on, Alun, go on... OOOOHHHH!" Overall, I rather fear that their analysis will be along the lines of small side huffing and puffing, Premiership side controlling game. Yes, but we outplayed West Ham, Blackburn and Southampton, the latter two on their own grounds! Why the hell can't millions be aware of those games? We're good! We are. Don't judge us on this...

The second half continues in the same vein as the first, and I begin to think that we might end up travelling to Middlesbrough level. With twenty minutes left, however, Boro score, and, in that instant, I feel, finish us off. A Boro midfielder chips the ball through to one of their front men, who looks yards offside from where I am, behind the goal, and he slots it through Paul Jones' legs, in the same way that the Saints player did back in January. The goal prompts a mini pitch invasion, from the away end initially, and then followed up by a handful of slack-jawed fuckwits from our stand. Although most of the latter are County fans, there are clearly Boro fans sitting in with us, and it almost turns nasty for a few moments, illustrating once again the idiocy of the County ticket allocation strategy.

Another couple of names find their way into the referee's notebook after the goal, as County become desperate; I can recall about seven yellow cards in a game that isn't the slightest bit dirty, despite the conditions. Elleray and his ilk ruin the game, they really do. Granted, one or two of the players have been a bit snappy at times perhaps, especially now when we're chasing the game, but you'd expect that in a cup semi-final. A tactful referee would have had a few quiet words and have probably ended up booking two or three players. "Tact," however, isn't in David Elleray's dictionary - it's been ripped out and thrown on the fire along with "caution," "prudence," "subtlety," "common" and "sense."

Five minutes after their first goal, Boro get a second, when a defensive cock-up by County lets them break down the right. The ball is scrambled across to Ravanelli, and despite a great block on the line by Mike Flynn from his first shot, he's able to slide home the rebound. As he runs away, for some strange reason pulling his shirt up over his head, and looking rather foolish as a result, I think most of us know that the game's up. At 1-0 down, quite apart from the prospect of equalising on the night, we'd travel up to Boro with an outside chance - after all, this is the team that beat Southampton on their own ground, on another occasion when the Premiership team thought they'd done the hard work. However at 2-0, we're out. Shame it had to end in this way, I think, as we file out of the Cheadle End following the final whistle, shielding our eyes from the glare off John Barnes' jacket in the portakabin, but then again, at the risk of sounding tediously repetitive, the league's the thing.

We pass close by the TV shed, inside which can be seen, as well as Barnes, Ron Atkinson, stretching and yawning ready for a hard post-match session of analysis. Also there is the cup itself, highly polished and gleaming under the floodlights in the portakabin window. It's the only time it'll be inside Edgeley Park this year.

Outside the ground, all is subdued - probably because the fans who care passionately about County are greatly diluted by the big-game merchants (and, on this occasion, sponsors' clients). What really pisses me off now is the way all these gobshites will probably be saying things like "ah well, the superior class told in the end." Like screaming great fat hairy bloody arse it did. What told in the end was our tiredness (it was our 47th game of the season - more than Boro will play in total, probably, and it's still only February), which was exploited by Premiership players' speed on the breakaway; speed which led to both goals. County matched them man for man over the game (certainly in the first half and had we had a couple of breaks inside the box, might have gone ahead. And then what?).

It's funny how you can't stand the away fans after a result like that, especially when I hear comments outside along the lines of "well, I'm glad we don't have to play this Second Division shit every week.". Before the game, you can be as friendly as you like, but afterwards, you hate them. I'm sure feelings like this are what initiate hooliganism; I personally can control myself, and confine my frustration to muttering and glaring, but others can't. I find myself thinking "ah well, you're going to get hammered at Wembley" In this case, that could well be probably true, with the potential opposition being Wimbledon or Leicester, both of whom have enjoyed a far better league season than Middlesbrough. I also find myself hoping they go down, and judging by the noisy chants of "Boro's going down," I'm not alone. Mind you, winning the Coca Cola Cup would be a consolation to them if they did get relegated; they've had at least one season in the Premiership. I still feel *losing* a cup semi-final wouldn't be a consolation to us, if we missed out on promotion.

And so our biggest-ever game ended with something of a whimper. It's easy to lose sight of just what we did to enable this game, though. Yes, we've gone out (or rather, we're going to go out) in the semi-finals, but - the semi-finals! We've never previously reached even the quarter finals of any major cup competition in the club's history, and this year we made the semi-finals. There's also no little consolation to be gained from the fact that we've stuck it right up Premier-fixated ITV, who must have been sooo pissed-off when they paid all that money to share live coverage with Sky, only to discover that having second choice of game meant they had to come to Stockport. And also the part-timers. It's somehow satisfying that they've been ripped-off to the tune of eighteen quid for their only appearance at Edgeley Park this season, and they've seen a crappy game, without even an upset to hold their interest. Ha. Come back against Rotherham on Saturday, why don't you?

MARCH

NATIONWIDE LEAGUE DIVISION TWO

	P	W	D	L	F	A	Pts
BRENTFORD	31	16	11	4	49	29	59
LUTON TOWN	30	16	7	7	54	33	55
BURY	30	14	10	6	43	29	52
BRISTOL CITY	32	14	9	9	52	34	51
MILLWALL	33	14	9	10	42	41	51
BURNLEY	34	14	8	12	50	39	50
CREWE ALEXANDRA	31	16	2	13	42	36	50
WATFORD	30	11	16	3	31	21	49
STOCKPORT COUNTY	30	13	9	8	43	34	48
WREXHAM	30	11	14	5	36	31	47
CHESTERFIELD	30	13	8	9	27	23	47
WALSALL	31	13	7	11	37	33	46
BLACKPOOL	32	10	12	10	41	36	42
BOURNEMOUTH	35	11	9	15	31	37	42
GILLINGHAM	32	11	8	13	37	42	41
BRISTOL ROVERS	33	10	11	12	36	37	41
SHREWSBURY TOWN	34	10	10	14	43	54	40
PLYMOUTH ARGYLE	33	9	12	12	37	47	39
PRESTON NORTH END	34	11	6	17	34	46	39
YORK CITY	33	10	7	16	36	52	37
WYCOMBE WANDERERS	32	9	7	16	31	43	34
PETERBOROUGH UNITED	33	7	11	15	44	57	32
NOTTS COUNTY	33	5	10	18	23	43	25
ROTHERHAM UNITED	32	4	11	17	25	48	23

March 1st 1997. Rotherham United (H).

As so often happens, today's game is loaded with far more significance than merely that of a team pushing for promotion hoping to stick a few past a struggler. Today, County versus Rotherham means Danny Bergara's first visit back to Edgeley Park.

County's fanzine, *The Tea Party*, has asked fans to give him a standing ovation as he walks to the dug-out, and I'm confident that that will happen (the official programme seems to have declared him a non-person). What is probably of more concern to him is how he'll be treated behind the scenes - I'm dead sure he won't be allowed into the Boardroom, for example.

It's a strange situation, and one I would expect doesn't happen much in life. I know that people who win successful unfair dismissal cases are often awarded their jobs back as well as compensation, but I bet not many actually go back to work there when the reason for their claim in the first place was the boss allegedly thumping them. I would imagine today will be more of an ordeal for Danny than merely the footballing ordeal we're all fervently hoping he undergoes.

In the event, the County fans warm the heart with a tremendous ovation as he takes the field. After two years, it's a chance to say thanks - one we were denied by the ignoble way he was dismissed. He was apparently ordered to clear his desk, and had to beg the groundsman to let him store his gear in a shed until he could arrange for it to be collected.

The game starts, and early on, the signs look good - it's an open, flowing game, although, worryingly, Rotherham are playing as well as us. Despite that, I still get the impression that if County score one, they'll get loads. Why is it that whenever I do get that impression, County don't score any? Probably something to do with the fact that the way Jones has them playing, although successful, hardly produces avalanches of goals. One-nil wins, yes - for which I am immensely grateful, don't misunderstand me - but not many goals, with the result that when a team arrives, realises after an early flurry that they're not going to score themselves, and shuts up shop, we can quite often be immensely frustrated.

Half time is slightly more entertaining than the game, as Tom takes over Louie's mantle as official joke teller. There's this bookie at the Grand National who walking the course before the race and he comes across a bloke fishing in Becher's Brook. "What the hell are you doing there" says the bookie

"Fishing"

"Fishing!? You'll never catch anything there - it's a bleedin' horse jump."

"I bet I do catch something"

"I'll give you 100-1 you don't"

"You're on." So the bloke gives him a quid, and the bookie departs. After the race, he remembers the bloke and so goes back to Becher's. Incredibly, the bloke is sitting there with a smile on his face, holding a big flat fish. "Amazing," says the bookie, "here you go." and hands him £25. "Hey," says the bookie, "you offered me 100-1!"

"I know," says the bookie, "but you only get a quarter the odds for a plaice."

The final whistle blows (yes, the second half was that exciting) and, after Peterborough and Notts County, we've drawn yet another game 0-0 against a team who will probably be relegated. The unpalatable truth is that teams that get promoted simply don't do that kind of thing.

March 4th 1997. Crewe Alexandra (A) (AutoWindscreens Shield Northern Semi final).

You could become slightly blasé about cup semi-finals, if you were a County fan this season. That said, tonight's is arguably slightly less important than last Wednesday's.

As both teams have a reputation for "playing football" - as opposed to netball, or hockey, or whatever game it is that teams managed by Dave Bassett and John Beck play - a game of what I have heard described as "fanny football" is anticipated: lots of passing across the field, intricate movements, none of that up-and-at-'em hoofing it forward nonsense; in other words, potentially as boring as hell. Never mind, at least there are the magnificent surroundings of Crewe's majestic Gresty Road stadium to admire if the football isn't up to much.

It's another pleasant drive tonight, through the green Cheshire countryside in the Cavalier. The traffic's fairly light as well, and soon enough, I'm approaching Gresty Road, at which point I get into the right hand lane, ready to perform my roundabout trick again. This time, however, I don't need to drive all the way around - I see a dozy old dear hasn't reacted quickly enough to the moving traffic and has left a slight gap, which I dive into, adopting a Spike Milligan high pitched quaver as I do so; "ooh, you naughty boy" I shout (it's often occurred to me in the past that if anyone were able to travel incognito in the back seat whilst I was driving (not easy in a Fiesta, I grant you), they would have reasonable grounds for having me Sectioned).

I manage to park in my usual side street and head for the away end. Once again, I want County to lose, it being the AutoWindscreens Shield, and resolve to myself that there's no way I'm going to be cheering tonight, no matter who scores. I even considered, for a fleeting moment, standing with the Crewe fans, but decided against it, partly out of an innate sense of loyalty, but mainly because I might get recognised going through the enemy turnstiles; Gresty Road isn't large enough for them to be far enough away from the County fans' entrance.

Inside, I find a seat and settle down, resolute in my determination not to enjoy myself. Trouble is, there's a thin line between not enjoying yourself and actively disliking what you're doing, and my immediate neighbours have pushed me across it. I seem to be surrounded by complete and utter demics: there's a tramp in front of me, who has decided to sit with his arm hanging over the back of the seat, and seems disinclined to let the presence of my legs deter him. Another bloke arrives late, stinking, and barges into me, before plonking his fat arse down at the side. There's yet another dickhead sitting in front who's pissed out of his head, and keeps turning round to make what he no doubt imagines to be humorous remarks to all and sundry, and on my left is a bloke who's making disgusting hawking noises for all he's worth. Finally, there are a group of laughing old biddies behind me, whose every screech grinds a piece of chalk down the blackboard of my soul.

Yes folks, tonight's edition of "Hell on Earth" is brought to you from the away end at Gresty Road. I've got to move. Luckily, I spy Andy Gosling about ten seats away, with plenty of empty seats around him, so I make my excuses and leave Loonies Corner.

We've started off playing worryingly well, which might cause more problems should we therefore win. Andy informs me that we actually run out of weeks if we win tonight - as things stand, we've got a single spare week until the end of the season; and a victory here will mean a two-legged northern final (i.e., one that's played with flat caps and a tin bath afterwards in front o't'fire), and therefore one week where we have to play three games. Thankfully the Boro result means that we won't have to fit in yet another game to replace the one that the Coca Cola Cup would shove aside, but were we to reach Wembley in the AutoWindscreens...

Come on Crewe.

Thankfully, they heed my cry, and score after twenty-odd minutes. One of their nancy-boy strikers swivels on the edge of the box and fires home. It's a good goal, which makes his deliberately low-key celebrations all the more irritating. The arrogant sod simply shrugs, raises a hand and says "aw shucks, I do that every day. It's only Stockport"

The goal inspires the band that inhabit Crewe's Popular Stand to my left. There are drummers, trumpeters, and what sound like some rather pathetic types playing tissue-paper-and-comb. The band keeps up a constant din throughout the game, inspiring and accompanying an eclectic repertoire of songs. Or at least that's the way I look at it. "It's a fucking male voice choir" shouts a clearly-frustrated bloke behind me. "Put a goal past them and shut the fuckers up" adds someone else, and, lo and behold, Chris Marsden obliges just before half time, with a shot from the edge of the area that crawls in through a forest of legs. Bugger. I stay seated, sulkily clapping for appearances' sake, as the fans around me rise.

Half time shuts the band up, but brings a narcissistic display from Crewe's mascot, a weird looking beast which could be a lion, but could equally well be a duck-billed platypus. Once again I find myself wondering at the wannabee Disneyland Mickey Mousers, with their annoyingly exaggerated gestures of surprise, or laughter, or constipation, compensating for the fact that they can't speak. I used to wonder, even as a kid, why, at Disneyland, Mickey Mouse is struck dumb - as though they ripped out his voice box when he moved there, and he had to compensate by overdoing it with the gestures. Football club mascots take this affectation to its extreme.

The second half produces an even noisier cacophony from the band, but no more goals, despite my wanting one for the home team. Indeed, given our record this season, and the fact that I want us to lose, I wouldn't really object to the irony of a last-minute goal against us at this point. However, it is not to be, and once again we enter a period of sudden death extra time. This is really tricky. Although the potential build-up of fixtures means that my resolve won't weaken, as at Bury, and I start wanting County to win, I really would rather not lose by either a golden goal or on penalties.

At least the game is by now a really exciting one, so there's some small consolation to be gained from the evening. Unlike Euro '96, where the prospect of "next goal wins it" made, by and large, for a particularly sterile period of extra time, tonight both teams are going at it hammer and tongs.

I spend this extra period standing at the back, lurking for a quick getaway should somebody score, in the same way I did against Bury a few weeks ago. This is different from that night, however; Crewe are a different prospect from Bury. Even at this level, sudden death is genuinely tense, and even though I don't want us to win, and it's a poxy tournament anyway, I can't help getting involved. The band is going frantic, playing what sounds like either The Flight of the Bumble Bee, or Benny Hill's chase music.

The referee blows for the end of the first period; there is an immediate rush for the bogs, by people whose bladders cannot cope with the nervous tension. I'm not surprised. After a generally competent but uninspiring ninety minutes, both teams have served up fifteen minutes of extra time that rank with the most exciting football I've seen this season. The band don't seem to agree, however, sending out a chant that I'm sure goes "Da-da, da-da-da, da-da-da-da... Bollocks!" It's only by listening closely that I realise the last word is "Alex."

The second period of extra-time is, if anything, even better than the first. We attack, and then the play breaks towards our end. There's a scramble in our goalmouth, which leads to a massive "YES!" from the home fans, followed by a loud "NO!" from me, despite myself. The trumpets sound the charge, and we respond by surging towards Crewe's goal, and almost nicking a last-minute winner ourselves. It's to no avail, however, as all too soon the referee blows the final whistle.

For only the second time in my years following County, therefore, I'm going to see a penalty shoot-out. I could do with a repeat of the last occasion, actually. That was also against Crewe, in a previous incarnation of this competition back in 1984; a game which I actually returned from Keele with Andy for the evening to watch. We fought back from being twice down to force a 2-2 draw. Great was the excitement, therefore, as the penalties commenced. It must have got to the players, as all the three penalties that County took were blasted over the bar, whilst Crewe despatched theirs with the minimum of fuss. What added insult to injury was the fact that we had an on-loan player at the time, one Stuart Parker, who was apparently giving the three sken-eyed spot-kickers some grief in the dressing room after the game. The following Friday night, inevitably, County were awarded another penalty, at the same end. Up stepped Parker, and... I don't really need to finish this, do I? Yep, he scored. Only kidding - he blasted it over the bar, of course, in *precisely* the same manner the three stooges had in the cup game. I'd've liked to have been a fly on the dressing-room wall on that particular night.

Tonight's ref has decreed that the penalties will be taken at the end with the County fans, following which decision, all the police and stewards immediately move to take up positions behind the goal. Of course, they are only doing their job (and a difficult one it is too, let no one tell you otherwise), not to merely block people's view, or to get the best view of the excitement for themselves.

Andy Mutch scores the first County penalty. The first Crewe player then blobs the ball over the bar, in homage to that great game thirteen years ago. Luis Cavaco scores for County. The Crewe nancy boy with the hairdo scores, and makes a defiant gesture to the County fans. Tony Dinning scores. The next Crewe player scores. Tom Bennett scores. A Crewe player scores. Paul Jones - County's goalkeeper - steps up to take the piss. He leathers the ball in, and puts us through to the northern final. Now, come on - I've got to cheer that, haven't I? Well, not cheer, exactly. My resolve holds, although I run back to the car laughing my head off.

And, for the first time tonight, the band shuts the fuck up.

March 8th 1997. Bury (home).

Although this season has seen its fair share of downpours, we've also had one or two ridiculously warm days too, and today is one of them. It's almost a shame to go into the ground and the shade of the Cheadle End. The weather seems to have flushed out the part-timers, as the ground seems pretty full, including the Railway End, where a healthy number of Bury fans have come to witness possibly the most important game ever between these two teams. Judging from the relatively few gaps, I'd guess there'd be 8,000 or so here today.

It's not the first time we've had bizarre weather between these teams. Back in 1981, a game took place, which, thanks to the ridiculous English climate, has entered the annals of County folklore. On April (remember April, it's significant) 25th, County were due to play Bury at Gigg Lane. In those days, such was the ramshackle organisation of the club that players were allowed to make their way to local games such as this under their own steam, arranging car-shares and lifts as appropriate. In a further demonstration of the ineptitude of the club at the time, star player Terry Park was absent, not through injury, but because he was getting married. On the assumption that the game was going to take place on the Friday night, he had arranged his nuptials for the following day. Okay, but we could still raise eleven players, yeah? Well yes and no. Thanks to a freak (told you April was significant) downfall of snow, manager Jimmy McGuigan and centre-forward Les Bradd were held up in Chesterfield and Nottingham respectively. Even worse, David Sunley and Chris Galvin, two other first-teamers, rang Gigg Lane just before kick-off to report that they were stuck behind a snow-plough on the M62. The unsympathetic referee (really? An unsympathetic referee? Now there's a thing) decreed that the game must start, and so County kicked off with only nine men on the field. Winger Tony Coyle had instructions to hover around the halfway line and hold the ball as much as possible to waste time, whilst the other eight men camped out deep inside their own half. Amazingly (in their previous game Bury had beaten Scunthorpe 6-1), we got to half time level, at which point Sunley and Galvin arrived (Galvin had actually been named as sub, so had to start with a number 12 on his back). The pay-off? You've already guessed it, haven't you? Yup, a second half goal from Martin Fowler gave us a 1-0 win, thus securing safety from having to apply for re-election that year. Bury, meanwhile, lost their seventeen game unbeaten run.

As I don't fancy sitting in my season ticket seat today, Martin and me sidle into a free row to the extreme left of the stand. Ominously, however, after kick off there are still people pouring into the ground, and sure enough, a couple of girls head towards us with that "you're in my seat" look in their eye. We stand up to move and immediately a steward's radar homes in on us. "Where are your tickets for?" he asks, possibly in order to help, but probably also because he thinks he's got a couple of troublemakers on his hands. "Season ticket" I grunt, and make to move away without feeling the need to prove it. Not to be outdone in his quest to justify his existence, he spots the cans of Coke we're both drinking, and the first instinct of stewarding leaps to the front of his conscious. "You can't drink cans in here." Arse! Bloody arse! Bloody fat hairy arse! I've nothing against this guy personally, but when was the last time - *when was the last bloody time?* - that a can was thrown at a football match anywhere, let alone County? As with frisking, I know that confiscating of drinks cans removes the opportunity for people to actually chuck the things, but such knowledge doesn't decrease my sense of frustration at mindless bloody pettiness. I hold out my can, still a third full. "Here."

"No," he says magnanimously, "you can finish it if you want."

"No, have it," I insist, at which he takes it with a look of disgust and realisation that he's got a disposal problem that he wouldn't have with an empty one. I don't stay to see what he does with it preferring to stomp away to my rightful seat, feeling only slightly mollified at having inconvenienced him so.

Thankfully, the tutter doesn't seem to be around today - perhaps *she* was in the wrong seat last week as well. That said, even she probably wouldn't have been able to moan today - County start like a train, and for the first half hour, play some of the best football I've seen all season, against a team which, for all that they're in the top three, where they've been all season, looks as inept as any I've seen all year.

The period of pressure is triggered off by a goal just after I've finally found my seat. A long throw on the left from Mike Flynn is met by Andy Mutch, and his header loops over the keeper into the net. Straight from the restart John Jeffers has two efforts saved by the Bury keeper, and then three separate shots rain in from various forwards as County make Bury look like complete saps. Despite the pressure, however, we suffer from the same frustration we did at Gigg Lane in the league game, and can't find the net again. Frustratingly, then, half time arrives with Bury still in the game when they shouldn't have a prayer.

Perhaps with this in mind, County attempt to relax us all with a second goal just after half time, and what a brilliant one it is too. Literally seconds after the restart (I know that an 89th minute goal is, technically, seconds after the restart, but you know what I mean), a great move down the right involving Sean Connelly, Andy Mutch and Alun Armstrong ends with Armstrong sending over a low cross which is hammered home by John Jeffers, diving in feet first from the edge of the six yard box.

2-0 should be enough, but with half an hour to go, Bury score, and the reaction from the County end almost makes my ears bleed. There is a great number of schools in freebie attendance today (the announcer read out the names of about fifteen), and all the kids do a peculiar double thumbs-down salute, like a melodramatic Roman emperor signalling the despatch of a gladiator. It beats flicking the Vs, I suppose, which is what I would have done at their age. Mind you, if they come often enough, they'll learn.

Bury come more into the game after the goal, and start to look threatening. Never mind - County can defend one goal leads. Er, well, yes, they can, but today is different. Bury sense that they can claw something back from this game, and even better, do it against one of their promotion rivals. As a result, the last half hour resembles a cup-tie, albeit a slightly one-sided cup tie, with Bury on top. County are denied what looks like a certain penalty, only for Bury to break down the other end and draw a fine save from Paul Jones. He then releases Marsden, who finds Todd, whose cross is clutched by the Bury keeper. What do they think this is - the second half of extra time against Crewe?

County finally decided to shut up shop in the way they have tended to do this year, rather than that "attacking when you're leading" nonsense, a strategy which invites Bury to press forward. Although in the context of the game as a whole, Bury don't deserve anything, they are unlucky not to score in the last quarter of an hour. Still, when has luck ever won you points, eh? There's time for a final superb one-handed save from Paul Jones, and with, yet again, hearts pounding, amateur whistlers shrieking and the bloody referee being cursed left right and fucking centre, you bastard, we've hung on for another win.

Wednesday March 12th 1997. Middlesbrough (away) (Coca Cola Cup Semi Final Second Leg).

Even though we're going to go out tonight, we made the last three, as last night Leicester beat Wimbledon.

Tonight's game illustrated yet another example of County's disgusting greed, confirmed to me by a journalist friend who, in the course of his research, spoke to a reliable source in the Middlesbrough ticket office. Apparently, some high-up joker at County - presumably the brains behind the £18 charge at Edgeley Park - was a bit disappointed that Boro were "only" charging County fans £12.50 at the Riverside Stadium, so, incredibly, actually phoned them up to ask them to charge us £18, knowing that County would get half the extra money. To their eternal credit, Middlesbrough told him to get stuffed (in as many words, hopefully). Not satisfied that away fans get such a raw deal anyway, here we are with our own club officials trying to organise yet another rip-off. Whose side are you on, pal? As if this weren't bad enough, they've also ensured some of their fans have missed out yet again. We were allocated 2,500 tickets for the game, with an option for a further 2,500. The first lot were sold well before the first leg, following which people arriving at the ticket office were being told to come back after the first game, as there would then be the second allocation available. As soon as we lost the game, however, County sent that allocation back for Boro to sell, figuring that we wouldn't sell all 2,500, Boro would, and it'd thus be a few grand more to add to the million and a half we've made from the cup runs this year. The fans without tickets? Oh, sod *them*.

The game isn't live tonight, at least nationally. ITV had the option to cover it, but figured, probably sensibly, that it would be a non-event after the score in the first game. Two regions are showing it, however - Granada (us) and Tyne Tees (Boro), with the rest of the ITV network reduced to broadcasting highlights after News at Ten. Live coverage in those two regions pushes a special Dunblane anniversary film back 24 hours - the rest of the country is watching it tonight.

I have to confess I won't be, tomorrow. As a parent myself, I simply cannot cope with trying to imagine the horror of what happened in that school. At the time it happened, I didn't read a newspaper, or watch the television news, for a week. I've mentioned before how my kids cheer me up, and help me get things into perspective when a County defeat threatens to gets me down. People do Bill Shankly a great disservice when they use that quote about football being not a matter of life and death, but much more important. From what I've read about Shankly, he knew precisely where people's priorities should lie (he was a socialist after all) and when he said that phrase, he was after a laugh - something the idiots who quote him incessantly would do well to bear in mind. If ever anything placed a simple game into its true perspective, it's Dunblane.

I'm on the club coach again today, with Martin. The buses are scheduled to leave the ground at three, so I arrange to meet him there. My mum is also there, prior to going to her sister Lily's in Edgeley, and she's made butties for our tea, bless her. That's what mums are for, after all.

We're soon enough underway, the second in a massive convoy of coaches. For some reason there's more excited babble on this particular coach than any I've been on before. I put this down to the fact that it's full of fans who don't normally go to away games; coaches to Millwall on a Wednesday night tend to be full of the cynics who have seen it all before. The excitement leads to some ridiculous optimism, of the "if we get an early goal" variety. I've been saying to people at work all week that, in response to that particular line, if we get an early goal, Middlesbrough will get seven. Logically, I think it's true, but there is an element of damage limitation too, as, with the muddle-headed optimism of all football fans, I keep telling myself at the back of my mind, that if we get *two* early goals... or *three*...

After a two hour journey, made slightly disappointing by the North York moors - which I expected to be much more bleak, quite frankly - we spot the impressive white tangle of tubular metal that is Boro's Riverside stadium. As we approach, the classical CD I'm listening to through the headphones is playing Handel's "Arrival of the Queen of Sheba," which sounds as though it should be appropriate, but in fact provides a bizarre aural counterpoint to the grimy industrial landscape. I should be looking out at New England in the fall, at one of those American colleges, where everyone is going to be a writer, no matter what they're majoring in.

As we circuit the stadium on the approach roads, dropping off right outside, I can see that there's an absolutely massive ship next to the stadium, which is almost half as big again as the stand roof. Is it that prison ship that's been in the news, I wonder? Whatever it's purpose, it's so tall that I would guess you'd get a fair view of the game from the top deck. Both the ship and the stadium are illuminated, and look equally impressive in the gathering twilight.

The County fans who are already here seem to have been making the most of the beer that is served under the stands; an absolutely deafening chorus of "Two-nil down and we don't give a fuck, we are Stockport County" (to the tune of The Camptown Races) echoes across the wasteland. We pass through the turnstiles and up to the concourse, which is absolutely swimming in spilt beer, with the odd island of a broken plastic pot disturbing the surface. There seems to be a virtual army of cleaners employed to sweep up the empties, whilst the bar itself is packed with desperate punters. It's bedlam. Standing guard across the entrance to the seats are stewards, because there is of course, that eminently sensible rule about not being able to consume alcohol in view of the pitch. As if it makes any difference - you're either going to get pissed or you aren't; beer is no less potent drunk underneath a stand. The most ridiculous aspect of all concerning our football stadium licensing laws is that you can be refused admission - or even arrested - for simply smelling of booze at the turnstiles. And don't scoff - I've heard of it happening. Theoretically, you can go through the turnstiles stone cold sober, drink five or six pints in half an hour - out of view of the pitch, of course, because that increases the alcohol content of each mouthful, you know - become rolling drunk, and you're somehow committing less of an offence than the bloke who has a quiet half in the local boozer, and gets refused admission because it can be smelt on his breath. Amazing really, when you think that for years Britain has been renowned for its sensible licensing laws.

We head past the stewards and up to our seats. Normally, I would take in the view when I emerge from under the stand, but today someone has draped a massive County flag over the stairwell, and so, after ducking under this, I have my back to the pitch as I climb the stairs. I find my row, then my seat, bend to pick up a balloon to bat cheerily away, and then turn to take in the magnificent vista. Now that is what I call breathtaking. Having the view hit you, like that, is probably the best way of first seeing the inside of such a magnificent stadium, and for a few moments I look around, open-mouthed. From our seats, we can also see the ship peeping over the top of the stand, looking for all the world like a block of flats, of the type that towered similarly over the stands at Southampton and West Ham.

The atmosphere is fantastic; if anything, it's better than Blackburn - the previous best so far - which is amazing, as this is a completely meaningless game. The second ticketing fiasco at least made it known that there are precisely 2,500 County fans here tonight, and they seem to be making far more noise than the 4,000 that were apparently at Blackburn. Then again, it could be all the booze that was drunk earlier that is responsible, of course.

The game starts, and a Juninho-inspired Boro tear out of the blocks. It's clear how much they missed him for the first leg, as a move he inspires ends with one of them hitting the post after a couple of minutes. It doesn't matter, though, does it? We're going to lose the tie no matter what happens tonight, an attitude that helps me relax; I'll be equally mellow even if they score.

What ruffles my feathers somewhat is when *we* score, however. A high ball down the right wing is flicked on by Armstrong and somebody - I can't tell who at this distance, although I think it may be Cavaco - hits a superb first time shot across the keeper, and the side netting bulges.

All round me is pandemonium. I don't care what noises people were making before the game, no one, not even the most optimistic and blinkered of County fans, genuinely expected the early goal that, it was argued, would put us in with a chance. Certainly, I'm convinced that the frenzy of the reaction of the people around me must be partially a result of the unexpected - the unbelievable, in fact - suddenly becoming just possible. That said, I'm still not convinced, and, after the stresses of the excitement which has been a regular feature of this incredible season, I'm buggered if I'm going to become overwrought tonight, not when there are still league games to come which will potentially generate the greatest excitement of all. Not until we get a second, anyway.

The most likely scorers seem to be Boro, however, for whom Juninho is outstanding; he seems quick and amazingly fast. To be honest, most of Middlesbrough's players look better than us as well, but our team spirit seems to be pulling us through. Sure enough, despite a looping header from a home forward just before half time, we reach the break ahead.

Most of the County crowd seem to head below for liquid refreshment, and it's from there that the word floats back up that the scorer was Sean Connelly. To add to the air of unreality that is the second leg of a major cup semi with County still in it, Connelly, County's left back, has never before scored for the club, in any competition. What a game to choose (as if players can choose such things: *"yeah, I think I'll score at Boro tonight - why not"*)

The re-emergence of the players, with Boro's singularly-named players (do they charge by the letter at Brazilian christenings, or what?) looking more eager than their home-grown counterparts, is the signal for the boozers to return to their seats, one in particular breathing an extremely noxious beer and vomit pot-pourri over me as he pushes past. I notice a hell of a lot of photographers are behind this goal for the second half. I can't see many down behind the home goal - do they suspect something we hope for?

They seem to have it wrong, however, as Boro continue to dominate, but again, we hold them at bay. They do come close once or twice - most particularly when a County defensive cock-up allows Juninho to lob just over, but the thing is, it's still not really that tense, because we're only one up. I came to this ground expecting nothing, so I'm not going to let myself get disappointed when we get nothing - although a win on the night would be nice. In any case, the joy of winning through to the final would have to be tempered by the cost of getting there, an even greater probability that we'd lose on the day, and another game having to be shifted to make room, making our end of season promotion push all the more difficult.

All the mental justification and forced mellowness in the world, however, is shown up as so much bollocks, when, with about twenty minutes to go, I'm up out of my seat, screaming, literally, with anguish. Lee Todd makes a strong run forward towards the Boro penalty area. He's blocked by a defender, but there's a scramble and all of a sudden, Luis Cavaco's inside the area, and running in on goal. The County fans, already on their feet because of Todd's attack, hold their collective breath. If Cavaco can score here, it's on. In the fraction of a second before he shoots, we know - and we don't have to think about it, it's instinctive - what this goal will mean. He's *just* over-stretching, however, and in going for a shot rather than a little chip - and I'm not criticising here, because if I suddenly found myself in the same position I'd have probably wet myself and burst into tears on the penalty spot - he allows the keeper to make the save. That was it - that was our chance.

After that, everybody in the stadium, including all 22 players, knows that it's going to finish in a 1-0 win. Towards the end, I sense that Boro aren't really trying too hard to score themselves. They know they've done enough, and we *just* haven't. Ravanelli, however, still has time for a spot of cheating. There's a bit of argy-bargy down in the corner flag to our left, and a home defender finally gets the ball and moves upfield. As Dinning and Ravanelli run after him, Dinning responds to some shirt-tugging by the Italian with a little kick against his ankle. It's seen by the linesman, and is probably a bookable offence, but the modestly-named Fabulous throws himself to the floor as though he's been shot, and stays there, writhing in agony for the two or three minutes it takes for play to stop, the referee to consult his linesman, the idiots to identify the correct player (between them, they at first try to send Flynn off), and the ref to brandish the red card at Dinning. As soon as this happens, Ravanelli gets back to his feet.

Now I'm not going to get all bigoted and jingoistic, with such crap as "an English player would never do that," because as anyone with half a brain knows, English players can be as bad as anyone else when it comes to bending the rules. That, however, was disgusting. In those few minutes, my resolve against Middlesbrough - and the Silver Arsehole in particular - hardens. I now know for certain I want them not only to lose the final, but get relegated as well. He'll have long buggered off by then, of course, but I want to play this team again - and do them - in the league. Unfair, I know, to develop a hatred against a team because of the antics of one particular player, but that's the way it is in the world of football-following, I'm afraid.

The final whistle goes, and the whole stadium rises - ourselves to salute yet another fabrizio performance from County, and the home fans to acclaim their team's first major final in 121 years. Following the handshakes, the tannoy announces a lap of honour by Boro, if the home fans will be patient. Yup, a lap of honour. We've only lost 1-0 at home to a ten man Stockport County - that deserves a lap of honour at the very least. I don't stay to watch.

As the coach doesn't have a toilet, I decide to force myself to go before I leave the stadium. Inside, there is another salutary example of the folly of selling as much beer as fans want to drink in football stadiums: a bloke, completely and utterly out of it, standing with his flies open in the middle of the room, pissing merrily onto the floor. He is absolutely pie-eyed, yet presumably, somewhere in his sozzled conscious, he is merely standing before one of the troughs, making use of Middlesbrough's splendid facilities, rather than causing dozens of fans to dance frantically around his home made fountain. If those nice people under the stand are going to sell him as much booze as he can drink, how can anyone moan when his urinary aim is somewhat awry?

The coach is full of "we were cheated out of it"s, referring to Dinning's sending-off. Well, no, that's not actually true, and it wouldn't have changed the game one iota. "We played them off the park", say a couple of old biddies sitting behind the driver, once the "we wuz robbed"s have finished. Again, not exactly true - *they* played *us* off the park. Let's be happy with what we've got - another

Premiership scalp. None of us was really expecting to win the tie tonight.

I put my headphones back on, and play the classical CD again. One track in particular seems to sum up the mood - Khachaturian's "Adagio from 'Spartacus'," the opening bars of which seem wholly appropriate for the mood. Go out and get a copy yourself if you don't believe me - you'll find it on a disc called "20 Cheesy Classics For Plebs Who Want to Appear Cultured", only £1.99 from the Woolworth's bargain bin. Damn! And I nearly had you fooled into thinking I was a sophisticate.

The journey back is a bit bizarre, what with almost breaking down near Brighouse on the M62 (the coach slows to about 30mph for quarter of an hour, with the driver frantically pumping the pedals, before picking up speed again for no apparent reason), and the snappy coach driver almost leaving people behind at the services following a reluctant stop, but it's difficult to feel angry, amused, or anything really. It's in keeping with the mad nature of this evening as a whole: we've won at the Riverside, but gone out.

I drop Martin off just before ten to two, and fifteen minutes later, I'm home. As a fan with a lisp might say, our cup runneth over - but there's still a tremendous sense of pride tonight. We beat yet another Premiership team - the third time we've done it on their ground - and only lost the Coca Cola Cup semi final - *the Coca Cola Cup semi final!* - by one measly goal. That's worth being proud of. It's soft, I know, as I head upstairs, but the thought of the kids cheers me up after a night like tonight as well - all three of them are laid in bed, tucked up and warm, not giving a toss either way about football (except possibly Julia, and even she doesn't let it get her down). They've got their own little thoughts and concerns to worry them, such as who they're going to play with tomorrow, and whether Thomas the Tank Engine will be on telly. I always feel kids help you to keep things in perspective, and whilst it may be incredibly cheesey to say so, it's true.

In any case, ten years ago Anna and I used to watch County in front of 1,500 people in a ramshackle ground, wondering whether this would be the year we'd finish in the top half of the Fourth Division. Can I really be disappointed that we've lost a cup semi-final?

March 15th 1997. Peterborough United (away).

Another day, another Boro. The games are condensing ridiculously now - today's is the 17th in 8½ weeks.

I had considered the train again, figuring that as Peterborough's far closer than London, it'd be cheaper, especially if I could get an Apex ticket. Silly me. The

prices. £1.10 for a pie, and 30p for a Mars Bar. Proper shop prices! Value for money at a football ground! Wow! The catering seems to be an amateur operation run by the supporters' club, and the service is therefore as good as the prices. It just shows what you can achieve when you *don't* franchise your catering out to "Supa Catering" or "FootySnax". I can hardly get over the fact that the tea and coffee are properly brewed, from an urn, with real milk poured on. And that announcer, too - suddenly, I *like* Peterborough.

I don't like the first half, though. There's hardly a chance, with County seemingly still having half their mind on Wednesday, and Peterborough... well, Peterborough are shit this season, I'm afraid. The break thus arrives with the score 0-0: can no one score between these two teams, or what?

I only rarely waste my money on programmes, so half time, especially at an away ground, usually represents the most boring fifteen minute period of the day. Today, however, in a moment of National Lottery induced hysteria, I succumbed to the scratch card sellers outside, and "invested" as they say in the bookies, 50p, secreting the card guiltily in an inside pocket, ready for when I could be alone.

Football scratchcards are stuck in a timewarp; a twee throwback to a different era. Not for them the post-80s, go-getting, "I want it now" single game of the National Lottery Instants. No, the *"Posh Lottery - win £1,000 instantly"* scratchcard is an example of a product similar to Wagon Wheels, and hot liquid Bovril - those items you will only ever find at football grounds. This particular lottery ticket is a classic of the genre, comprising no fewer than 6 separate games.

"Cash Match" eases me gently into the scrapeathon, with its ready familiarity. I scrape off 8 little footballs, and look eagerly to see if I've got three similar amounts. Nope, so it's on to "Scratch 21," a game based, as you might have guessed, on Pontoon: three cards, totals over 16 win amounts ranging from 25p to £25. My total of 15 wins me an amount of nowt, although the cheeky scamp of a designer got the adrenaline flowing with those first two cards - a king and a four, by God!

Well into the swing of things now, I turn to the sweetly-simple "Dice." Yup, three dice to scratch, and totals to add up (a derivative game, granted, but how easy is it to add variety to a scratchcard, for heaven's sake?). Esoteric sums of 7, 15 and 18 would have won, but I don't trouble the scorer. Next I try a frame of "Snooker" where a number of balls are scratched (insert your own joke here), and three of the same colour pays from 25p to £50. My skill at scratchcard snooker mirrors my skill at the genuine game, and try as I might, I cannot pot three balls of the same colour, not even reds.

Not to worry, here's "Three In A Line" to test me. There are no fewer than nine panels to reveal. Three identical numbers in a line wins the amount revealed at the end of the line. Ah, but here's the rub! By using horizontals, verticals *and* diagonals, they've cleverly managed to cram a magnificent seven winning pots onto the card! None of them winners today, mind, but it's the thought that counts.

Finally, with my wrist threatening imminent RSI, I move to "Photo Finish," which requires me to reveal four horses' names. If any of them appears under the "winners" panel, I would win the amount under the "winning post". Sadly, despite their pedigree, Red Rum, Arkle, Mr Crisp and Shergar cannot quite prevent Laughing Boy from crossing the line first, so I miss out on fifty quid. Damn! A final check that I haven't revealed any pots of goal anywhere on the card (three would have won me a grand) and my session's over. Blimey! No one can say you don't get value for money from the *"Posh Lottery - win £1,000 instantly"*. I give the card a practised flick over the heads of my fellow-supporters and applaud the teams back onto the field.

I'm still flexing my aching wrists a few minutes into the half when County take the lead. A Mike Flynn long throw is headed back out to John Jeffers over on the left. His cross is deep, and makes its way to Cavaco whose shot somehow manages to creep into the corner.

Boro come back into the game, and Paul Jones has to make his usual couple of good saves, but in reality County are comfortable. They even lazily decide to get a second with about five minutes left - just to make sure, you understand; another deep cross from the left by Jeffers is headed into the near bottom corner by Chris Marsden.

I had thought that as Peter Collins' birthdays are by now ridiculously unfeasible, the announcer had deduced it was a wind-up and wasn't going to bother - we certainly didn't hear anything at half-time. Oh no. This is Peterborough - a nice club, remember? The announcer actually comes on-line (or whatever the adjective is to describe tannoy-announcing) during a break in play towards the end of the game to announce that Peter Collins is 90 today. That's the best result yet, although I suspect that the only reason it was read is that the announcer recognises a kindred spirit - he sounds about 90 himself. I shouldn't take the mickey out of him, though, as he's the kindly old soul who thanked us for our cup exploits.

The final whistle goes, and after the traditional clapping of the players (in which I can fully indulge when I'm on the coach, and not neurotically running for the car), I wander across the car park in the warm early evening sunshine. All is well with the world. We've won, Brentford lost and Luton drew with Crewe, which puts us 7th, a bloke on the coach with a radio has worked out, and there's a pleasant ride home in prospect. I'll come here again.

On the way back, we pass the Fingerpost coach, who, amusingly, are watching the same tape of the Middlesbrough game that we were on the way here; I can clearly see the recorded winning lottery numbers scroll across the bottom of the screen. It's funny how you can see another coach's video like this, zooming along the motorway at 60 mph. I bet it wasn't as funny, though, as the time Alan, the Leeds fan I work with, came back from a European game on a coach which was showing a hard-core porn film. I bet there were a few near misses on the motorway that day.

March 18th 1997. Carlisle United (away) (AutoWindscreens Shield Northern Final First Leg).

I've decided to drive today; I'm quite looking forward to the scenery, in fact. What I didn't expect, however, was to be absolutely knackered due to spending yesterday evening in casualty with Chris, who broke his collarbone at a schoolmate's party. He fell over playing football, in which he's starting to show a gratifying interest. It could have been worse, I suppose: he could have broken it doing something stupid. Nonetheless, three hours sitting cringing on a vinyl seat in A&E, pretending that the kid who's throwing himself madly around in the play area isn't with me - and even if he is, he's genuinely hurt, honest - isn't the best way to prepare for a 300 mile drive the following day. Cruel as it might sound, it was with a certain sense of relief that the x-ray showed he had genuinely broken the bone, and I could parade him and his slinged arm through the waiting room: *see, I told you.*

I'm expecting today's journey to take me only a couple of hours, even though it is, of course, uphill all the way. The traffic's surprisingly light for tea-time, and, once I get past the turning for Preston, gets even lighter, as though there's nothing much people want to drive to beyond there except the Lake District, and at this time of night, of course, that's shut. "Hicksville 30 miles" says a sign, whilst tumbleweeds blow down the opposite carriageway. It's quite a momentous trip to be making, I realise as I pass the signs for Windermere: until now that's the furthest north I've ever been. Ever. On the planet.

Needless to say, tonight I *really* want to lose, no matter whether it's on penalties, golden goal or "scissors, stone and paper." I discovered in the week that the final would be on Anna's birthday. I'd have to go, of course, and Anna's not the type to make a fuss anyway, but even so. Missing one family member's birthday for a football match - as I have done already this season - is bad enough; missing two would be unforgivable.

As I head further north, the countryside becomes rugged and bleak; I seem to have climbed above the tree-line. Carlisle 44. An enormous black object looms mightily to my right - is that what's known as a fell? Is that a bragg on top of it?

228

A phalanx of hunterdavies take off to my right, with a screech. The countryside is another example of what must have been a beautiful area before they slapped a motorway through it. The drizzle, which has been, well, drizzling since I set out gets heavier, adding its own atmosphere to the beauty of the landscape, now rain-lashed and misty, with hints of mountains looming in the distance. I drive along the side of an absolutely spectacular valley - the other carriageway is probably about seventy or eighty feet below. Breathtaking, indeed.

As I approach the outskirts of Carlisle, I flick round the radio channels, trying to find a local station which might mention the match. I manage to find Radio Cumbria, but the signal seems weak. Just as they're getting to the sports news at the end of the six o'clock bulletin, and a promised preview of "tonight's big game," the bloody thing fades out, to be replaced by, of all things, a crystal clear Radio Cymru. Needless to say, they don't have County's team news. Finally, after a journey far less arduous than I was expecting thanks to the sights, I leave the M6 and drive the mile or so to the ground, where I am early enough to park on the main road facing back to the motorway.

Signs indicate that the away end is at the far side of the ground, so I wander behind the old main stand, where contrast is provided by a posh-looking new restaurant called "Foxes". Just outside this are what are clearly the Carlisle bigwigs' vehicles, although there is a sign on the perimeter fence against which the cars are parked, which states, by one particular space, "Chairman - Do Not Park." Although I have no affection whatsoever for football club chairmen as a species, I feel this is a bit mean to say the least - of all people you think they'd let the chairman park his car. Then again, Carlisle's chairman is Michael Knighton, who, reportedly, has claimed to have been in contact with aliens on the M62, so maybe the club have got a point.

I continue towards the away terrace, which is situated behind the far goal from the main road. Placing the ground on my mind-map I realise, with a sharp thrill of excitement, that not only is Carlisle the furthest north I have ever been, but the position of the ground - roughly north-south, evidenced by a giant new stand they've recently built, which is signposted as the "East Stand" - means that the actual point which marks the furthest north I have ever been on the face of this planet will lie somewhere behind the away goal. The pitted surface is so full of pot-holes, themselves full of water, that I would have probably dodged into this immensely significant position without realising it. This cannot, of course, be appropriate, so I ceremoniously and deliberately walk about fifty yards beyond the away turnstile. I stand solemnly in a field for a few moments, before walking slowly back to the ground, feeling somewhat moved. And extremely muddy.

Inside, I peruse the menu before deciding on my evening meal. There is in fact a surprisingly large choice from the small hut at the back of the terrace, albeit mainly on a theme of pie, and I am torn between a pastie and a "scotch pie". Now I've got vague childhood memories of small pies, spicy and full of flavour, which went under the name "scotch pies," and so I plump for one of those. Mistake. A "scotch pie" at Brunton Park is simply an English one that's been thrown into the deep fat fryer for just long enough to render the crust impenetrable. I wander down the terrace, wondering exactly what I'm going to do with this culinary marvel - stand on it? Hurl it at a policeman's helmet? Putt it? - when I see Andy Gosling. He's obviously more astute than me, as he points out a simple truth: never buy a midweek pie from Brunton Park when Carlisle have been at home to Hereford the previous Saturday. Determined not to let the beast beat me, and buggered if I'm going to shell out for another one (I presume they wouldn't offer refunds, not even on the basis of mistaken identity). I manage to force it down, at the cost of a couple of fillings, finishing just as the teams emerge.

I wander down to take up a viewing position halfway up the terrace, greeting a friend, Sandy McGregor, as I do so. He's Scottish (oh, you guessed) and so presumably there's no way he would miss this game, being the closest he'll get to his homeland following County. I think the kilt and woad's overdoing it a bit, though.

The miserable weather has kept the County following down to a couple of hundred, although the players don't seem to be affected by it. Amazingly, a Carlisle player's got gloves on, but Luis hasn't. He must be toughening up. He's probably taking more time getting used to the English thud and blunder though - of which tonight's game, helped in no small part by the strong wind, is a prime example. It's awful, and the only highlight of the first half is when a bad foul by a County player leaves an opponent writhing in agony, and as he's getting treatment, the classic shout of "leave him there - he'll tread in" makes a reappearance. Someone was obviously thinking the same way as me at the Middlesbrough game.

At half time, being a sucker for football architecture, I take a good look at the new stand to my left. For some reason, like the one behind the goal at Turf Moor, it's been built askew -although this one markedly so, about twenty feet out of kilter. I presume they're going to move the pitch at some point, when other new developments kick in, but it could just be that the architect was pissed.

The second half gets underway, and is about as bad as the first, at least for about ten minutes, until Carlisle score. A mistake by Lee Todd allows them to break down the right, and their winger's superb cross is met by a striker in the middle, who hits it back across Jones and into the corner.

The goal is greeted by one of the most amazing things I can remember after a goal at an away ground. The screaming announcer isn't that unusual *"Carlisle's goal scored by number 9...... Owen Archdeacon!!"*, but as he reaches a crescendo with the player's name, he fades in a deafening, mad, snatch of the Can-Can, at which the home fans start to jump around dementedly. It's an absolutely brilliant touch. As the home fans dance around to the manic music, the faces of the County fans around me register an astonished mixture of anger and bemusement, which leaves me in absolute hysterics. I'd like to think that this was a genuine reaction on my part, and not one enhanced by the fact that I want us to lose. I'm sure it is, especially as I find myself willing another home score, not just for the obvious reasons, but so I can hear that mad bloody noise again.

The goal is the signal for some barely credible barracking, especially of Cavaco, who is having an admittedly poor game. This season, of all seasons, we go one down at Carlisle and to listen to the reaction of some of the fans, you'd think we're were fighting a losing battle against relegation. Amazing. I suppose some short tempers aren't helped by some little kids in the stand to our right gloatingly shouting "Ravanelli, Ravanelli!" "Shut up, you little shite" growls one of our number, viciously, before adding "Hereford, Hereford, Hereford" (despite their fans not finishing the pies off, I presume they must have won here last Saturday). "He's letting the kids get to him" says one of the bloke's group. "Yes, I am" he seethes.

It doesn't seem as though Carlisle are going to score again, however, and with five minutes left, County seem to be on the way to a not insurmountable 1-0 deficit. By now it's extremely cold, still pouring down, and my coat, trousers, socks and shoes are all soaked. I overhear Sandy's mate telling him that he's going to drive home without his trousers on. It's dark, he's on his own in the car, and his strides are soaking, he reasons, so why not? Talk of driving home makes my mind up for me, and I decide that my quick getaway will best be served by leaving now.

I hurry back to the car. I assume that I'll be able to pick up Radio Carlisle in the town which bears the station's name, and sure enough, I can. As I get in the car, start up, move away and switch on, there seems to be some kind of a commotion. Shit, we haven't scored have we...? No, it's a sending-off, and what's more it's a County sending off. Chris Marsden, County's resident snapper, has committed some misdemeanour which neither commentator managed to see, and has been shown the red card by the same fussy little baldy referee who sent him off against Wrexham early in the season. I listen to a game getting more exciting the further I drive away from it, as, from the free-kick, Carlisle go onto the attack, and, a minute or so after losing Marsden, Lee Todd brings down a home forward in the area, and it's a penalty to Carlisle. Come on, come on... Yes! The spot kick is duly despatched, and the home team are two up. The final whistle goes a couple of minutes later, and I flick in a cassette. Wanting County to lose and feeling satisfied is one thing; I don't have to listen to the gloating aftermath of home commentators in order to complete the betrayal.

I feel quite happy and light-hearted at this outcome, especially as I missed seeing the goal go in, and similarly didn't witness the sending off. In many ways, it was the best outcome of all. Get out of this competition and we really do have a chance in the league. The general election was called on Monday, for May 1st - the Thursday before the last game of the season. Will that week provide a double celebration for me?

March 22nd 1997. Notts County (away).

My only other visit to Nottingham (apart from almost ending up there by accident when we couldn't find Center Parcs a couple of years ago) was a visit to the University, to which I had applied to study Philosophy after my A levels. Careers advice: I wouldn't recommend the fact that you consider it to be a good pose ("oh yah, I'm studying philosophy, actually") as reason enough to choose a subject to study to degree level, frankly, as it can lead to no end of grief later on. I suppose I should have recognised the warning signs when, after a quick tour of the campus, the particular lecturer who was hosting the visit had us into his room and started to ask bloody questions. About Philosophy! And the Nature of Understanding, for Christ's sake! I wasn't expecting this and shrunk back into a shell from which it took me four or five years to emerge.

On the face of it, today's game should be an easy victory, as Notts went bottom last Saturday. Then again, we only got a 0-0 against Rotherham the other week, and Notts got a similar result at Edgeley Park at the start of the season. Then again, everyone was getting decent results against County at the start of the season, and what happened when we played at Rotherham, eh?

Let's face it, I haven't a clue what's going to happen today.

It's another really nice sunny day as I set off in the Fiesta. I've decided to go via Chesterfield onto the M1, although my best-laid plans went somewhat awry when I had to delay my departure due to having to sort out the bog, which some child had put too much paper down. Slightly put-out by that delay, my mood lifts markedly as I get out into the Peaks once again. This is just about the perfect weather for a drive like this, and so what if my car struggles up the hills again? It just gives me more time to admire the views.

And what views. This is probably the most beautiful part of the countryside I've seen on my travels this season, and the teams we have played have meant I've seen it more often than I might have expected. On a day like today, with the sun shining down - albeit only a feeble March sun - the countryside looks absolutely fantastic, with hazy mountains in the distance lit up by shafts of sunlight. Cows loaf around, chewing the cud and not realising how lucky they are to live in this place, with its trees, hills, dry stone walls, and remote farmhouses dotted around. I climb a hill, and glance behind me as I take a sharp right-hander; the scenery is unbelievably spectacular. I'm almost tempted to stop and feast on the view, but I'm slightly behind schedule, so I won't. Flicking off the blower, which is filling the car's interior with the powerful aroma of cowshit, enhanced by the heat, I pass a local church hall, which is offering "An Evening With Mendelsshon." That'll be interesting, if a touch smelly

I'm reassured by the car behind me having a scarf trailing out of the window, but then again, just after Sparrowpit, I passed a car going in the opposite direction at speed, also with a blue and white scarf hanging out of his window. I hope he wasn't a County fan, although he was going so fast, he might just be going back having forgotten something vital.

After Sparrowpit, the Peak District displays again its propensity for bizarre village names, as I spot signs pointing to, in order, Perryfoot, Smalldale, Wormhill, Chuffpiles and Knobwaggle. Okay, I made the last two up, but you have to do something on a long journey in a Fiesta with no radio. Perrymuckletonthorpe. Scrapedale. Jimdale. Fun for all the family.

I remember coming through this area years ago when going to my aunt in Norfolk for a family holiday; I also remember never appreciating it, because I was too bored with the journey, and being wedged in the back seat with three sisters. I now like this countryside so much, I'm tempted to bring my kids up this way for a picnic this summer, but I know for a fact they'll be the same as I was all those years ago - moping around, kicking, biting and scratching each other, bored stiff with the bloody view, and are we there yet? (Julia holds the record for this question, asking it, on the aforementioned trip to Center Parcs, just past Disley, about five minutes after leaving home).

Another blue and white scarfed car comes the opposite way. I do hope Chesterfield are playing someone on our side of the Peaks - Crewe maybe? I have a sudden thrill of fear that they could be County fans coming back the other way because the road's shut.

On I go, passing the most touristy of Derbyshire tourist spots. Eyam, for example, the plague village, and Chatsworth, in which town lies the stately home of the Duke of, wait for it, *Devonshire*. I wonder if there was some cock-up during the ennobling ceremony centuries ago, when the Sovereign of the time misheard "Derbyshire", and no one had the balls to correct the error, for fear of having their extremities scorched with a red hot branding-iron.

Although it's got no radio, the car's held up pretty well; I did have a recurring nightmare about it breaking down and me missing the game. As I join the M1, though, I'm quite relaxed because if it were to break down here, I'm close enough to walk, and leave the bloody thing on the hard shoulder, to be worried about later. It's a question of priorities, d'you see?

I pass a brown heritage sign, for the "American Adventure Theme Park." Odd that that's considered our "heritage" - drive-by shootings, 24-hour Pornoramas and the like (nothing like some good ole' fashioned prejudice, eh?). The sign actually has one of those old-fashioned up and down roundabouts to illustrate, if nothing else, what kind of rides there sure as hell *won't* be there.

I leave the motorway shortly after airing my bigotry, and follow the route recommended by the Supporter's Guide, which circuits the city so widely I think we actually leave Nottinghamshire for a time. Never mind, I'm soon enough crossing the Trent, past Trent Bridge, the City Ground and over the river to Meadow Lane.

Although it suffers in comparison with the two neighbouring international sporting venues, Meadow Lane is still pretty darned impressive by the standards we're used to in Division Two. A few seasons ago, they chucked up three brand new stands in the space of about 17 weeks one summer. This has led to the ground being called MFI-land by Forest fans, but it's still a fairly striking place, and more than adequate for their immediate needs, doomed as they are to almost certain relegation this season. A fourth stand was added a couple of years later, by which time stand constructors had woken up to the money to be made, with the result that the final stand apparently cost more than the other three put together.

Although I sit in the away end, I'm actually joined by a Notts fan, Ivan Bainbridge, who is also a friend. Having given up on his own team this season, and having a soft spot for the proper County anyway, he has decided to sit for the first time in the away end. Out of deference to his true affiliations, I decide we'll sit towards the side of the stand, where we're away from the more partisan of the away support.

For this reason also, I essay a fairly low-key goal celebration when we take the lead after half an hour. We've had slightly the better of the game until then, although Notts are playing well enough to make a neutral wonder at their lowly status. We get a corner on the left wing, and when Durkan's cross comes over, it's bundled into the net. No one seems quite sure who's scored, but the announcer eventually credits it to Mike Flynn.

Following this setback, Notts come more into things, playing a long ball game that's quite effective with a large striker in the shape of Devon White. They also play it pretty physically, and, although there are a few County players more than capable of looking after themselves, it's a couple of home players who are shown yellow cards before half time.

The second half initially sees our County gain the upper hand, with Armstrong once more running his socks off for the cause, but it's Notts who get the next goal after an hour or so. A cross from the right finds a striker totally unmarked in the middle, and his header across Jones is so precise that it hits the far post, and bounces back into the opposite side netting.

This is a blow; County seem once again to be struggling to overcome sides for whom this season will surely eventually be viewed as a disaster. The completely knackered Armstrong is replaced by Andy Mutch with about ten minutes to go, but to no avail. We press hard, but there are no clear cut chances, and with a couple of minutes left, I decide, as Anna is going out tonight and I could do with being home early, to make a quick getaway.

I say my goodbyes to Ivan, and head for where I've left the car. As I'm going behind the stand which was to our left, I hear what I think might have been a cheer, but which, if so, didn't seem loud enough for a goal - or was it the County fans cheering? Home fans start to come out of the stand; perhaps it was the final whistle? I don't think so, however, as it's definitely not a "final whistle" exodus. So why did so many decide to leave at once? *Have* we scored? With a football fan's sixth sense, I begin to realise that, logically, we must have. I'm not going to get excited, though, until I hear it confirmed. By now, I'm at the exit gate of the stand behind the opposite goal, so I wander up and casually ask a steward the score, making out I'm just someone with a passing interest. Thank God the Stockport accent isn't as obvious as Geordie or Scouse. "Bloody (*'bloody'* - *yes!*) own goal, it was, so it means we've lost 2-1" he grunts angrily, not noticing my grin. What's all this "we" Kemo Saby? *We've* won. Ha ha ha. I've got a pocket radio in the car, which picks up Radio Nottingham, on which the commentators confirm the 2-1 win, the injury time OG, and the fact that Stockport didn't really deserve the win. Well, no but there you go. You don't always get what you deserve in football, do you? Ha ha haaa.

It's ironic, really, when I think how concerned I was about potentially missing something when I had to leave before the end at Wycombe back in October, and of the fact that I missed nowt. Here, I leave quite voluntarily, and miss not only a winning goal, but a winning *own* goal. And therefore, no doubt, an hilarious one to watch and celebrate. Not to worry. I open a can of orange, and enjoy a session of splendid belching.

The Peak District looks even more beautiful at dusk, with the sun burning a fiercely bright red, a scene spoilt only slightly by another burst of cow shit. It's the same one we had on the way in, I think - it's just lingered. I spend most of the journey back with my chin on my knees, so open-mouthed am I at the beautiful scenery. This is what people must mean when they say life is good. Even though I didn't see the last minute winner, I'm happy. I'm home at twenty to seven. The Ceefax says we're still seventh, but now only three points off the top, with at least one game in hand on everyone else. What a splendid day out.

March 25th 1997. Carlisle United (home) (AutoWindscreens Shield Northern Final Second Leg).

Well, I might not give a toss about the prestigious AutoWindscreens Shield, but clearly Carlisle do - there's absolutely thousands of the buggers here tonight.

I approach the ground, and lend an ear to a steward I vaguely know who seems busting to tell someone his news. Apparently, the information from the Carlisle police initially was that they were going to bring 2,000 fans - more than enough for the Railway End's 2,700 capacity. However, two hours before kick off, County got a call to say that - er, sorry - there would actually be nearer 4,000 coming. The police are thus reduced to knocking on the local residents' doors, asking them to shift their cars so that the 27 coaches the steward says are on their way have somewhere to park. Half an hour before kick off, there are already massive queues outside the Railway End turnstiles.

Whoops.

Thankfully, whoever decides such things is sensible enough to delay the kick off for fifteen minutes, which gives me ample time to reflect - and it's strange, but I almost tend to forget, with everything else going on - that there's a Wembley game at stake tonight, an outcome I have desperately wanted us to avoid ever since the second round game at Burnley back in February. Come half past nine, we could be at Wembley. No nooo NOOOO! Thank God we're 2-0 down.

The main news of the week for County is that just before deadline day, we signed Kevin Cooper, a winger from Derby on loan; Gordon Cowans - ex-England midfielder, but don't get excited because he's about 38 - on a free transfer from Bradford; and, most excitingly of all, Ken Charley from Peterborough. Despite him scoring two goals against us in the playoff final of 1992 - the second, heartbreakingly, thirty seconds or so after we had equalised in the 89th minute - I'm still heartened by this player, because he's got a hell of a record as a goalscorer - most importantly, in the Division we're aspiring to join. The downside of the frenzied transfer activity is that Birmingham also tabled a bid for Mike Flynn, although they were told to piss off (in so many words, I hope).

As kick off approaches, so the Railway End is inevitably filled to capacity.

County are reduced to accommodating the overspill in the closest two blocks of the Barlow Stand: another rare example of sensible thinking from the County hierarchy, as was the tannoy announcement giving details to the fans waiting outside. There are also Carlisle fans in the Main Stand seats where away fans normally sit - they seem to be encircling that end of the ground in a pincer-movement.

The teams emerge, and Alun Armstrong's presence confirms the report on teletext earlier, which stated that he was playing despite a groin strain - showing where Dave Jones' priorities lie. I'm sure it must be nice to lead a team out at Wembley - one of the highlights of a manager's career, I would expect - but surely he can see the folly of risking a player with an injury, when there's a promotion campaign resuming on Saturday?

I heard a few examples of the arrogance of their fans in the queues outside before the game, which were as distasteful as the Middlesbrough fans' superiority complex; I almost find myself wanting to beat the bastards. Almost. When the game starts, however, it's clear that there are quite a lot of angry, desperate people, who don't share my views, *genuinely* wanting County to win. Mr Intolerant, for example, sitting just behind me, with his frantic "for fuck's sake Marsden. Kick it! Who the fuck's that to, Gannon?" keeps up a constant moan for the whole game: "Come on Jones, sort it out! What kind of a ball's that!? Is there sugar in this tea!? Who the hell chose the curtains in that house across the road?!?" Alun Armstrong tries a skilful flick into space that's *just* intercepted: "take the bleeder with you!" he shouts, so, having had enough, I stand up, turn round, and thump him, hard, right on the end of his nose. Well, I mutter a bit, and think nasty thoughts about him, which amounts to much the same thing, really.

After an opening flurry, Carlisle find their rhythm, and set about defending what they've already got. Even early on, it doesn't seem like County have got the wit to break them down, and the first half ends without any score (I seem to be writing that an awful lot). The second period follows the same pattern, and I start to relax, as it becomes clear that we're not going to Wembley in the AutoWindscreens this season.

I still find it amazing how desperate and angry the County fans are, though. It helps the atmosphere, mind - people really want us to win. Armstrong, again, is on the receiving end of a disproportionate amount of criticism, on one occasion just failing to get a ball that a tremendous amount of spin takes away from him. "You're too fucking slow, man!" yells someone, with a descant of "which cunt set your alarm clock this morning?" from another. People become irrational when they're this desperate: good looking balls that just fail to reach the target become "fucking shit! what was that?!" *"This is just how it was at the beginning of the season"* cries one voice, pathetically. Is it bloody hell as like. County have still got all the pressure; Carlisle are just a very good side, especially at defending, and are simply proving impossible to break down. Let's face it, people, they've hardly had a shot in the second half.

With about ten minutes to go the ball goes into the Carlisle fans in the Vernon Stand, and, mindful perhaps of Mike Flynn's long throws, they keep the ball and won't give it back. It's a textbook timewaste: as soon as a replacement arrives and Flynn's about to launch it, the original comes sailing back onto the field. I have to laugh, although, those behind me don't get the joke: "you sad bastards" rings out, followed by something I've not heard at any football ground, let alone County, for many years: "you're going to get your fucking heads kicked in."

The frustration has seeped onto the field, it seems, and, following two bookable offences in quick succession, Tom Bennett becomes our second player to be sent off in this tie, adding to the away fans' enjoyment of the evening. I've had enough and leave a couple of minutes before the end. Although satisfied with the result, I don't particularly want to watch mass celebrating from the away fans. There's always the distinct possibility it could turn nasty as well. I go home with the most uniquely mixed feelings; we didn't lose, but it was as good as. And I feel satisfied. Strange.

March 29th 1997. Crewe Alexandra (home).

This is a match just loaded with potential irony - what's the betting we win the one that doesn't matter (AWS a few weeks ago), and don't win the one that does (today)? It's also the second successive home game against a fellow-promotion rival, and thus one imbued with all the tension and importance of the game with Bury three weeks ago.

Oblivious to the tension, and merely excited to be coming to County again, Julia's joined me once more. Feeling as edgy as I did for the Middlesbrough home game, I wish all *I* had to worry about was peripherals such as the finding the sweets my Nanny has bought me, pinching some chewing gum off my Grandad, and whether the bear mascot will be chucking sweets my way at half time. I always think it's quite appropriate that Julia comes with me to County games against Crewe, actually, as they were the team that provided the opposition on the first occasion both she and I went to County. Julia saw a 3-1 win a couple of years ago, and I saw a drab 0-0 draw on October 9th 1972; both games a summary of our County-watching lives. Julia has seen nothing but relative success in the couple of seasons since her début; I saw the 70s and 80s.

The snappy mood from midweek still seems to be prevalent, as an early missed header from Alun Armstrong brings an amazingly venomous cry from someone near me: "get him off, get him off! You overpaid, poncy twat!" Just when I think I can't be any more amazed at some County fans' attitudes, I hear something like this. You really couldn't blame Armstrong if, having heard that, he washed his hands of County and buggered off to join the big club he one day surely will.

The talk before the game was that, with games in hand, promotion is now in our own hands. This is true enough, but I'm always wary of such talk, for the obvious - and oft-stated - reason that it's difficult to actually win all those games in hand. Even though to do so would indeed take us into a promotion position, I'm convinced that we'll still have to rely on others slipping up. Thankfully, of late that's exactly what they have been doing.

The underlying logic behind speculation about games in hand, of course, it that you win the games not in hand, of which today's is one. The trouble is that despite it being an open, exciting game, with County having slightly the better of the chances, we once again approach half time scoreless. Charley, on his County début, is actually looking fairly sluggish, as though he was only required to play within himself for a doomed Peterborough team. Just as I think we're going to see another goalless first half, however, County take the lead. Chris Marsden plays a ball to Tom Bennett, who hits a superb diagonal pass into the path of Cooper, also making his (Stockport) County début. He takes the ball on a couple of strides before firing a shot beyond the Crewe keeper and into the corner.

Julia heads for the front of the stand at half time, to try and catch some of the sweets County's idiot mascot is throwing out. I'm so up at the goal that not only do I join her, ostensibly to keep an eye on her - that I almost dive into the mêlée myself. I'm not that stupid, though; there are absolutely chaotic scenes as the kids fight for toffees, and the dickhead inside the costume actually takes great delight in throwing most of the sweets over the heads of the kids, and into the faces of the adults, sitting reading their programmes a few rows back. The bear really is the most embarrassingly moth-eaten and threadbare of mascots, and I find myself wondering why the hell we've got a bleeding bear anyway? We've got no connection with bears. Why not some kind of a Mad Hatter character?

We head back to our seats, sweetless (although God knows she's been given enough by my mum anyway), ready for the second half. The atmosphere picks up a bit, although, strangely, the game itself quietens down. Julia joins in the chanting with gusto - she's far less self-conscious than me. I never joined in a chant as a kid, although that might have been because the games were so low key - due to County being crap - that there wasn't much chanting anyway. But I tend to think that had there been any, I wouldn't have participated, as, with the exception of once or twice, literally, when I was caught up in the excitement of a last minute equaliser in a big game, and indulged myself with a quick burst of "you're not singing anymore," I've never joined in chanting anyway.

The game continues in its fairly low-key manner, although as we approach ninety minutes, Crewe, realising that the game's almost up, in more than one sense, start to press frantically. We're then, once again, hanging on at the end, and, once again, we manage it, and the referee blows the final whistle to a huge cheer. This was an important win. We've now gone fourth in the table, three points off second place, with two games in hand on everyone else (and three on Brentford). I still think it'll be difficult to get automatic promotion, but April will, hopefully, decide it. We could do without having to win at Luton in our last game.

APRIL

NATIONWIDE LEAGUE DIVISION TWO

	P	W	D	L	F	A	Pts
BURY	38	20	10	8	56	34	70
BRENTFORD	39	18	13	8	54	38	67
LUTON TOWN	37	18	10	9	60	39	64
CREWE ALEXANDRA	39	19	5	15	49	42	62
WATFORD	38	15	17	6	39	27	62
STOCKPORT COUNTY	**35**	**17**	**10**	**8**	**50**	**36**	**61**
BURNLEY	39	17	9	13	61	42	60
MILLWALL	39	16	11	12	49	47	59
BRISTOL CITY	39	16	9	14	56	45	57
WALSALL	38	16	9	13	46	41	57
BLACKPOOL	39	14	14	11	50	40	56
WREXHAM	38	13	17	8	43	41	56
GILLINGHAM	39	15	8	16	47	52	53
BOURNEMOUTH	40	14	11	15	37	38	53
CHESTERFIELD	36	14	11	11	33	31	53
PRESTON NORTH END	41	15	6	20	43	52	51
BRISTOL ROVERS	40	13	11	16	42	43	50
PLYMOUTH ARGYLE	39	11	14	14	42	52	47
YORK CITY	38	11	11	16	40	55	44
SHREWSBURY TOWN	40	10	12	18	47	66	42
WYCOMBE WANDERERS	39	11	8	20	39	52	41
PETERBOROUGH UNITED	40	8	14	18	49	69	38
ROTHERHAM UNITED	40	6	13	21	34	59	3'
NOTTS COUNTY	40	5	13	22	27	52	28

April 1st 1997 Bournemouth (away).

A confession. Such is my determination to attend every game County play (at least this season) that I have spent Christopher's fifth birthday travelling to the south coast. My God, what a parent.

Look, we pretended it was yesterday. He's non the wiser. He had a great day; loads of nice presents. For God's sake, I even arranged for my sister Claire to buy a Buzz Lightyear in the States and send it over because the Disney shop in Stockport had sold out despite Anna queuing outside before they opened the other Saturday. If he'd've had his birthday on the correct day - today - he'd've had to go to school, whereas kidding him it was yesterday - a bank holiday - meant he had the whole day to celebrate. Honestly, *he didn't know any different.*

So why do I still feel like a shit?

Come to that, why the bloody hell did Bournemouth switch this game? It was originally scheduled for yesterday, and whilst a bank holiday away game would have been inconvenient for County fans, it'd've meant one less midweek game, and one less half day off work. Of course, we all know why it's been shifted - because since Leeds fans rioted there a few seasons ago on a bank holiday Monday, the local plods don't allow the team to play home games on such days. The fact that County will, at best, take a couple of hundred fairly mild-mannered regulars, and the chances of a riot breaking out in the town centre are about as likely as Elvis being discovered riding Shergar on the surface of the moon mean nothing of course. Bournemouth don't play at home on bank holidays. Never mind why, they just don't. Funny that - an inflexible police attitude; they're usually so accommodating.

I'm on the coach again today. I had originally considered the train, but the shift to Tuesday night (and the APEX fare of £45) meant that it's the club coach once more. Unsurprisingly, with a lunchtime start and an early morning return, there aren't many of us waiting outside the club when I arrive at ten to one. I've left my car outside my Aunt Lily's, who, conveniently from me, lives a couple of minutes from the ground in Edgeley

At the services, I succumb to a rush of blood and splash out on two CDs - the Lightening Seeds' new one, and Pulp's "Different Class". As I also buy Viz, a carton of Ribena and a packet of crisps, I wouldn't be surprised if the total is the highest the girl behind the counter has ever taken. Still, I've got one of those credit card things, so it hasn't cost me anything at all, really.

I listen contentedly to my new sounds, and, reading Viz, the time passes reasonably quickly. It's still arse-numbing, but surprisingly early, when we're approaching Bournemouth in what seems particularly appropriate weather - a lovely late evening sun. The ground also seems to be in a more salubrious part of town; all in all, it seems hard to imagine we're going to a football match.

The crowds approaching the ground soon confirm we are, however. It's going to be a big crowd tonight - after weeks of speculation that the club were going bust, there is going to be an announcement, it has been widely leaked, about the securing of its financial future. I have to confess to feeling rather guilty at this point. Although I would hate to see any club go under - and God knows we were as close as anyone on more than one occasion in the 80s - there would have been a rather bright personal silver lining for me, as I would have saved God knows how much money, and half a day's holiday, by not having to come all this way, and we would also have been able to celebrate Chris' birthday on the correct day.

We're early enough for me to have my usual wander before I go inside. As a result of the announcement, there are lots of people outside, not all merely fans. The local media interest is obviously high - local radio and TV vans are much in evidence. I also note more than one person arriving on a bike. You don't often see that at a football ground, but it is genteel Bournemouth after all. The crowd outside seem worryingly geed up for the game, but I'm fairly confident: County can party poop with the best of them.

I go inside, get my usual pastie, coffee (which is so hot it melts the plastic stirring tag, and keeps a group of us warm until half time) and Mars Bar. I sit on the terrace, at the quaintly named Brighton Beach End (which seems an odd place for someone to have written their memoirs), put on my headphones and contentedly watch the players warming up. About ten minutes before kick off, a group of self-important suits wander onto the pitch and congregate in the centre circle. After being fawningly introduced by the announcer, the leader grabs the mike and tells the home fans what it is they've been waiting to hear.

Well, if that's what they've been waiting to hear, they're very easily pleased, is all I can say. There's absolutely no detail at all, just a load of waffle about "lots of hard work still to do," quite a few "hopefully"s and "possibly"s and a singular lack of "yippee we've got the money - we're saved!"s. You can almost sense the unspoken "is that it?" from the press box. This was supposed to be a dramatic announcement about the future of their club, and you'll get more drama at the announcement of the half time draw winner. Still, at least the suits got their moment of glory on the pitch. I shouldn't be so cynical, I suppose. I'm here now, and we've already kidded Chris about his birthday, so there's absolutely no reason at all to wish Bournemouth any ill-will (apart from the fact that they beat us at our place with that brilliant goal, the bastards). Good luck to them, I say.

The teams emerge, and the game's ready to start, but "Disco 2000" - the track I actually bought the CD for - is playing, so I signal to the ref if he wouldn't mind just delaying the start a bit. I won't be long... Bastard! He's let them kick off. So it is that I watch the first couple of minutes, with Jarvis Cocker blasting "won't it be strange when we're all fully grown" into my head.

Apart from a shot from Alun Armstrong which hits the post in the first few minutes, the game follows a similar pattern to most in recent weeks - no bleedin' goals. Half time (more Pulp) comes and goes, and neither team seems able to break the deadlock. Armstrong is getting frustrated at his lack of goals in recent weeks (although he's still making a great contribution) - that much seems obvious. Trouble is, we've got a particularly fussy get of a referee today. With ten minutes left, Armstrong gets penalised for a bad jump in the area, and gives the referee a mouthful, which gets him a yellow card. He continues to vent his frustration, however, and the referee immediately flashes the yellow again, theatrically, and then gets out the red and waves that too. You get the impression that he takes so much pleasure in such brandishing, that he'd wave a purple, a green and a blue card if he had them.

It's arguable whether it was a second bookable offence, actually, as Armstrong didn't pause for breath. Okay, you could argue that a bad bout of swearing is itself enough to warrant dismissal, but where's the consistency? Not all players who swear at the referee even get booked. Where's the tact? Where's the referee's car so I can let his tyres down?

The game ends, inevitably, 0-0. It's a point, which will just about maintain our challenge, but we really needed three tonight. We troop out morosely to the coach and watch the home fans straggling away as we inch our way through them. The police stop the traffic again, and we're soon away and setting a course for the north. It's the kind of result you don't need after a trip of this length. I'm not saying I would have preferred a defeat, but such a nonentity of a game really does make you question why you do it - why you pay good money to come all this way for nothing.

To round the evening off nicely, whoever's controlling the video puts on a film that so fantastically inept, I can't even watch it ironically. It starts with Patrick Swayze standing on his head in a desert, and goes rapidly downhill from there. Thankfully, I do manage to grab some sleep on the double seat, but it's still one hell of a journey, punctuated by yet another depressing midnight service stop.

I finally arrive home just before twenty to three. It's the latest return yet, but with midweek jaunts to Plymouth and Gillingham still to come, the record is there to be broken.

April 5th 1997 Bristol Rovers (home).
Since our 1-1 draw at their new ground in August, Rovers have gone rapidly downhill, so that they're now hovering precariously over the relegation foursome.

Saturday Night and Thursday Morning

We should therefore be fairly confident of a win today. Well, to be more precise, we *are* fairly confident of a win today - or at least I am - whether we get one is, of course, another matter.

There's depressing news on the team front before this game. Brett Angell is going to have to have a cartlidge operation, and is expected to miss the rest of the season. Meanwhile, Armstrong will receive a ban for his sending off on Tuesday, meaning that Charlery - himself suspended against Bournemouth for a misdemeanour committed whilst still at Peterborough - had better start pulling his finger out and playing to his potential. Gordon Cowans is in midfield for Chris Marsden - suspended until about 2003 because of his various bookings and sendings-off - and Kevin Cooper starts on the wing. The side thus has a slightly unfamiliar air; something we haven't seen too often this season.

Early on, County seem to be struggling against a fairly strong wind, which is across the pitch, sadly, rather than end-to-end. We settle after ten minutes or so, however, and begin to dominate. Once again, however, all the domination in the world amounts to nowt if you can't score, and, once again, we can't. Rovers, who seem to have come today with one aim: a nil-nil draw, are halfway towards achieving their target.

Half time brings, amongst the usual birthdays, supporters club meetings and other half times, a bizarre announcement that the Grand National has been abandoned - but no indication why. Is it a starting cock-up again? The weather? What? You can't just tell us that the race isn't on and nothing else. I've not got a bet on myself, but I'm curious. Speculation behind me is that it's probably a bomb scare.

After an hour, Luis Cavaco makes an appearance, and immediately looks sharp, creating a number of chances, and causing the Rovers left back no end of trouble. County are being urged on by the crowd now, but still cannot seem to get the ball into the net. With five minutes left, however, Cavaco receives the ball on the right wing, directly in front of us in the Cheadle End. He cuts inside the area and suddenly has a chance. Skilfully, he lobs the ball over the head of the last defender, who stupidly jumps up and handles. Handball! Penalty! MUST BE! YES!!

The referee points to the spot - he had no option, really, it was that blatant. The only thing that remains is to decide who's going to take it. Armstrong's taken them before, but has been replaced by Mutch. No one else seems willing to volunteer, even Paul Jones, who scored the winner at Crewe from the spot after all. Jim Gannon - who has taken them before - half offers, but it's clear that not even he wants to take responsibility for such a vital kick. Eventually Kevin Cooper - presumably figuring that as he's only on loan, he won't have to stay and face the music should he make a cock of it, steps up and grabs the ball. He places it on the spot and, facing four thousand people who are all holding their breath, passes it into the corner. Yes! That's the winner. Three points. Where does that put us in the league?

It might well prove to be the winner, but the match is far from over. Bristol suddenly start to play, and County's nerves mean that the rest of the game is played out mainly in our half. It doesn't help that on a rare occasion that we do break away, Ken Charlery - who has once again been unimpressive - misses the easiest chance of the season, when he controls the ball in front of a completely open goal, steadies himself, and then hits it high into the Cheadle End.

There can only be seconds remaining when, with that jet engine revving up again, I move over to the exit gate. I've discovered previously that going out through the Cheadle End gate, running along the road outside for about twenty yards and re-entering through the Main Stand exit gate means I get to watch the last few seconds in an area with a relatively large amount of space, rather than trying to crane my neck for the last few seconds with the rest of the Cheadle Stand departees. I do this today, and am thus able to watch as County mount an attack down the right wing, in front of us. A Rovers defender goes in hard, and the ball balloons high into the air and straight down towards me.

At last. At last I'm going to re-enact one of my earliest memories, from when my dad used to bring me. We were once defending a 1-0 lead, in the days when the Vernon Stand was the Popular Side terrace, and the ball bounced into the crowd. A bloke near me grabbed it, held onto it for a few seconds, and then, with the opposition player angrily asking for it back, threw it back over his shoulders, further into the crowd. It was then almost immediately thrown back onto the field, of course, but I was mightily impressed by what I saw as a marvellously opportunist way of helping County, all the more so when we hung on for the few seconds left, to win the game.

And now I have the chance to emulate that unnamed hero of all those years ago. Yes, me. And all I've got to do is catch this ball. Easier said than done. It swirls away over my shoulder, and as I turn to smother it, bounces up and fetches me one in the face. I do manage to grab it however, a touch frantically, it has to be admitted, which is probably why the bloke near me, fearing I'm going to lob it straight back, shouts "hang onto it - hang on!"

"I am," I reply as best as I can through my fat lip, and do so. I sense hundreds of people looking at me, and it takes a massive amount of will power to hang on to the ball for what seems like hours - in reality, about ten seconds. Finally my will cracks, but I have just enough nous for a final attempt at wasting time. I turn away from the Cheadle End, towards which County will be throwing the ball when they eventually get it, and hurl the ball as far as I can back down the pitch. Bugger! I didn't see Sean Connelly ambling up from the direction of the dug-outs, and the ball goes straight to him, albeit with enough force to make him look a trifle surprised. Damn! It looks as though I was meaning to throw it to him, and perhaps even speed things up. Arse!

It doesn't matter, however, as we hang on to our one goal lead (that's known as déjà vu, incidentally), and the referee blows for another vital home win. We're still fourth, still with games in hand, and promotion gets ever nearer.

April 8th 1997 Plymouth Argyle (away).

Hell's bells. Turning up at the ground at quarter to twelve for the second week in succession brings it home to me what a sod of a three weeks I'm in for. Bournemouth last week, Plymouth this - and we haven't finished there, either. Next week we're all off to Gillingham.

It's the usual routine, one that I've played out far too often already this season - sandwiches, CD player with at least six CDs, four of which I won't listen to, book I won't read, and "Guardian." The faces are familiar, too, as I'm again on the club coach. It's getting so sad that I'm actually grunting greetings to one or two of them as we arrive outside the ground. Not that I feel in any way superior, or unfriendly - it's just that acknowledging them like this is a tacit admission that we're all extremely pathetic. I'd rather just pretend that what we're doing is not in any way out of the ordinary - there are people doing this all over the country, you know.

The journey down - the longest of the season - is slightly enlivened by a couple of young truants behind me, who are having a detailed conversation about Subbuteo. God knows why that game is so popular - I've always hated it, although today it provides a welcome diversion, as, to pass the time once I've finished the paper, I see how many table-top football games I can remember from my own youth, whilst listening to The Housemartins through the headphones. Including Subbuteo, I manage six.

The first I can recall, because I owned a copy myself, which was my pride and joy, was called "Striker," and, to my mind, it was the Rolls-Royce of table-top football games. It had everything: playability, realism, and one of the most absurd playing concepts you'll ever see.

The idea of the game was simple enough to grasp, although it seemed to be based, oddly enough, around indoor Recreation Centre five-a-side, complete with rebounding walls. Each player occupied a zone, and when the ball came to rest in that player's zone, he was deemed to have possession. Striking the ball, however, was the highlight. Each player stood on his own plinth, with right leg raised in readiness. When his head was pushed down sharply, the leg fell and struck the ball. Brilliant! Hell, you could even chip it (or so the blurb said, although I have to confess I never managed this art myself, preferring, as in life, to be master of the toe-end). Quite apart from the intrinsic enjoyment of the game itself, however, generations of small boys who weren't very good at football occupied themselves on the school fields of England by making their mates laugh pretending to be "Striker" characters: "Look Phil, guess what I am" (Presses own head down and makes kicking movement with right foot) "ESPLEY! GET DRESSED!"

The "Striker" goalkeepers were positioned in a state of cat-like alertness, and the ball was released by placing it between their legs and yanking the stick which held them violently to the side. This invariably led to slightly unrealistic goal kicks, the slingshot effect of which sent the ball pinging madly two or three times up and down the length of the pitch, and, eventually, broken goalkeepers. This was a sound marketing move, however, in view of the potential for supplying replacements - diving goalkeepers were available as add-ons. I remember saving up all my birthday money for a set of these. They were also on sticks, but had a diving action, caused by pressing down on a panel as you moved the keeper to the side. This made it immensely difficult to stop the ball, but at least the keeper made a superbly graceful dive as it whizzed past him. As this was the 1970s, and I was a County fan, I didn't consider it particularly unrealistic.

Stafford.

Bar football is the next one, probably catapulted into my conscious by the fact that, as it's only a game which can be satisfactorily played when pissed, it was the most popular game at Keele, knocking pools darts and space invaders into a cocked hat (assuming there was one nearby). Fiendishly difficult to master, yet, as it is best appreciated by playing with a group of similarly pissed friends (hence, perhaps, its particularly appropriate name), always a riot of laughs, especially when the ball rolls slowly into one of those all too many areas in the corner, where the players on sticks can't reach it, and the games becomes less a question of who can propel the ball into the goal using the handles, and more a question of which team can tip the ball into the goal by picking up the machine and using brute force. It's a game that has stood the test of time, although players must always watch out for the sad case who will insist on saying "oh come on, if we're going to play at all, we might as well play properly" and keeping score.

It's also available as a fairly spindly home version, which will, if used properly, be broken by the time Top of the Pops starts on Christmas Day.

Birmingham.

Casdon Soccer was probably the first table-top football game I ever owned.

Saturday Night and Thursday Morning

I first saw a copy of it in primary school; like most schools, the last day of the summer term was bring-your-toys-in-day, and St Bernadettes', Stockport, was no exception. I arrived, complete with Ker-Plunk, or Mousetrap, or some such, only to be greeted by a veritable phalanx of small boys clutching Casdon Soccer.

The game itself was simple to play and involved no installation. The "field" was a self-contained green plastic area, about three feet by two, but divided up into a number of craters, or troughs; at the bottom of each of these was a player. Whilst this may have made it seem as though you were playing on the surface of the moon, albeit a very smooth moon, it served its purpose in ensuring that the ball was always in reach, unlike the problems sometimes experienced with bar football. Each character was on a plinth, with a small sturdy tag-like affair sticking out to one side. The game was played by the use of two control knobs, each of which moved one half of your characters through 360° The object, obviously, was to flick the ball into the goal, an aim only slightly handicapped by the fact that the keeper's tag-like affair was about three times the size of an outfield player's, and took up about half the goal. Indeed, the only concession to reality was a small plastic keeper, in an unfeasibly dynamic diving position, slotted on to the top as an afterthought.

I managed to persuade my mum to buy me a set for the following Christmas, but it was out of date by then.

Tewkesbury.

A game which I can only identify as The One I Once Saw in Smiths is next up, so-called because I only ever saw it once, on display in WH Smith's in Stockport. It was a similar size to Casdon Soccer, with a similar playing surface. The difference was that the players were actually spring loaded, and the ball was propelled by bending each figure back to its fullest extent, and flicking it. Trouble was, the spring was so powerful that the ball flew forward at a speed which, to scale, would mean shots of around 600mph on a full size pitch, testing all but the most agile of goalkeepers.

The game never really caught on, presumably due to the potential it held for blinding the participants.

Gloucester.

Another title-less game - The One With The Magnets - although whether my inability to recall the title implies a direct correlation with how good the game actually was, I wouldn't like to say.

Extremely simple in concept, it was another game which employed the use of green felt as a pitch (thus predating its similar use at Preston, Luton and QPR by well over a decade). The plastic players sat on top of the felt, with strong magnets in their bases. A similar magnet, with opposite polarity, was placed on the end of a stick which each human player would then use, under the table, to manipulate the plastic players above.

The game was less memorable for its playability than for the sight it conjured up for spectators - two flushed adolescent boys, their arms pumping frantically backwards and forwards out of sight underneath a table. This led to the game fading from view, allegedly following pressure from the Boy Scouts Association Michael Wood Services.

Subbutteo's the last one I recall, although as we're just pulling into the services, I don't think about it for too long. This is useful, as it was the worst of the lot. Basically, it was a game for anoraks, completely unplayable, but with a collectible element. Most pathetic of all was that "stand" you could buy - a pathetic structure, the design of which would these days be rejected by a Unibond League club - with half its occupants permanently frozen in a state of ecstatic celebration. Probably because the Malmö (International Edition) replica team kit's just arrived in Toys 'R' Us.

At the services, I feel it's time for a spot of reflection. Most of the others seem happy and eager as they leap from the coach for refreshment. I, however, am weary. I'm beginning to understand the deep futility of all this travelling (10 bloody hours, today, for crying out loud) for a mere 90 minutes of football. Is it the event? Well no - it's not even as though it's a cup final. Dedication? Okay, there's probably an element of that, although whether that's an intrinsically admirable quality is open to debate. Stupidity? Definitely.

Following a few miles of patchwork countryside, we leave the M5 at ten to five. It's a lovely evening, with a beautifully low, deep red, setting sun - hell, I could almost be going on holiday (I suppose am, in a sense). I still want to be at home, however. I know what will lift my mood, of course - the game itself, when it kicks off, which rather gives the lie to my world-weariness. I'll be as excited as anyone else if and when we score.

We finally pull into the Plymouth car park at quarter to six - a full two hours before kick off. I know it's difficult to judge a journey from one end of the country to the other, through some of the most snarled-up motorway junctions in England, but this is really a bit early. The lunatic from the Bristol Rovers away game at the start of the season taps me on the shoulder, causing me to give a startled leap, and the headphones which are currently blaring The Lightening Seeds to snap from my ears. "They have a car boot sale here on Sundays" *Jesus! Don't do that again!* "Do they really?" I hope I sound suitably astonished. "Yes. They do." We don't talk again for the rest of the season.

There don't even seem to be any pubs nearby, although when I ask a steward, he points me in a particular direction confidently enough, so off I set, with only a slight nagging doubt as I wonder where the rest of the coach went. I've also got doubts about that steward, as, after twenty minutes walking in the only direction he could possibly have meant, I still haven't found a pub, although I did clock a chippy for the way back. Finally, after a false alarm that turned out to be a used car dealer's, and so much walking I'm probably in Exeter, I at last happen upon a tavern, set almost apologetically into a row of houses on the main road. Thank God. I go inside; there's only one other customer - a hairy, scruffy article who looks up and glares as he sees me. "And a good morrow to you, stout yeoman," I think. I approach the bar, but rather than accepting my order, the barman barks, "mythic sea monster" Eh? "Nine letters - L, something, something, something, H, A, N." I notice the opened tabloid on the bar. Oh, right, a crossword. Thankfully, after only a couple of seconds hesitation, I'm able to tell him, "Leviathan." He looks at me disgustedly then turns his attention to the other customer "and you a marine biologist," he says. I worriedly drink the quickest pint I've ever consumed and head back to the ground via the chippy. I think the pub was called the "King's Arms", although it could equally well have been called the "King's God-awful Pint," or "The Lunatics' Arms."

The pub was so far away that after I've eaten my chips and walked back leisurely, it's not far from kick off. I take a pleasant stroll through the local park - which, conveniently enough, is the way to the visitors' turnstiles anyway - and enter the ground. The away terrace is high up a flight of steps, punctuated every so often by flat bits with large signs for people descending, which say "10 Steps Start Here." Nice of them to point it out, but where's the sign saying "Look At Those Large Floodlight Pylons," or "Doesn't It Get Dark At Night?", or "To Enhance Viewing Pleasure, Patrons Are Reminded That They Should Face The Pitch"? I also notice loads of police inside, chatting to each other, discussing their overtime as they keep less than half an eye on the marauding hordes from Stockport. I sometimes feel like walking quietly up behind one of these groups - you see them often enough at away grounds - and shouting "boo"! Just to keep them on their toes, you understand.

Speaking of the marauding hordes, tonight must be the lowest turnout yet this season; I would guess there's not many more than a hundred County fans here tonight. The Fingerpost have brought a coach, as they always do, but even if they filled it - which I doubt - ours was half empty. I'm not complaining, mind - I managed to get a double seat with a good view of the video, and I should be able to spread out on the way back and grab a few winks, even if not forty. I wander over to an empty place on the far side of the terrace where my own company is waiting for me - I do like him - and lean against an ironically-named crush barrier.

The game starts, and County tear out of the traps, with the recalled Luis

Cavaco showing the benefits both of a lay-off, and the realisation that his place in the team isn't to be taken for granted. We almost take the lead when a brilliant first-time cross from Cavaco is headed against the underside of the bar by Armstrong. We don't score from our early pressure however, and, as Plymouth are allowed to get back into the game, we reach half-time with County slightly on top, but no score. I slump to the floor, and get out my CD player, and Pulp CD.

The second half starts, and Plymouth come more into the game. County start to warm up their subs, who immediately start to get stick from a group of lads behind me. It's good natured, and familiar banter, though, the reason for which becomes clear when I sneak a look round at who it is doing the cat-calling. It's actually the non-playing members of the County squad - Bound, Jeffers and Mike - who for some reason have wandered out onto the terrace to watch the second half. It's something you wouldn't necessarily expect from Man United, say - their players coming out to watch the game on the away terrace.

Plymouth have by far the better of the second half, and although, yet again, neither team looks like scoring, it's County who are hanging on at the end. The final whistle brings down the curtain on another midweek game at the far end of hell - and another bloody scoreless match. I wander back to the coach for the late-night marathon, but to add insult to injury, we can't leave straight away because the bloke who was sitting in front of me hasn't shown up. Silly old bugger. To add injury to insult, however, a copper comes on board to tell us that the guy's fallen and broken his nose; he's being patched up and won't be back for a few minutes - just what you need with God knows how many miles to go. It's nearly ten when he limps aboard (strange that a busted hooter should cause him to limp), with a massive bandage enveloping his conk, which he dabs at gingerly with a tissue. Presumably he didn't notice the four massive signs saying "10 Steps Start Here," or at least misinterpreted them to mean "Go Arse Over Tip Here And Break Your Nose If You Want."

By the time the coach pulls into Edgeley, five and a half hours later, at half past three on an echoey Thursday morning, the last throes of some formulaic Stallone/Van Damme futurewar crap thudding around inside my throbbing head, a broken nose seems like a fun time. I've got the worst trip over, but there's still Gillingham in a week's time to do before I can relax. I yawn my bleary-eyed way back to Lily's, get in the car and sleepdrive home. Six hundred miles for no goals - some people might say that was a rather pointless way to spend 16 hours. At the moment, I wouldn't disagree.

Saturday Night and Thursday Morning

April 12th 1997 Burnley (home).

We seem to have established a pattern for home games; it's another lovely hot sunny day today. It's also probably the most eagerly-awaited home game of the season, against the buggers from Burnley, eagerness made all the more intense by the ridiculous score at their place back in October.

Because of the rivalry, the police have decreed that today's game shall have an early kick-off. Rather than starting before the pubs open, however, they've settled on the compromise of one o'clock, which seems a touch odd, to say the least. Either start at a time which allows no drinking whatsoever, or kick off at three, but what's the point of simply making people drink faster?

Whether it's because people have been boozing or because of the opposition and the importance of the game to both teams, I wouldn't like to say, but the atmosphere inside the Cheadle End is unbelievable - probably the best of the season, including cup games against Premier League opposition. The stand isn't actually full, however, so I sit close to, but not actually on, my season ticket seat, ready to move there if I'm shifted. Once again, however, I'm in the middle of the moaning old bastards; they seem to have collared this whole area. Early on in the game, which the atmosphere has inspired County to start at a right old lick, a good move *just* doesn't come off; simply to annoy, therefore, I shout "good move - unlucky!" A bloke in front of me mutters, ostensibly to his mate but loud enough for me to hear, "it wasn't a fucking good move at all". Cheeky bastard. I'm not giving in to him, however - the type of person whose only reason for attending a football match, whatever's happening on the pitch, is to moan, and so I start playing it up, loudly and vocally applauding virtually every pass just for his benefit. More than one of my comments make him start muttering under his breath to his mate, so I do it all the more. The tutting woman seems to be back as well, although when I steal a look back during a quiet passage of play, I realise it's actually a bloke. Whether it was him doing the tutting the other week I wouldn't like to say

The trouble is, although the team as a whole are playing well, and pinning Burnley in their own half for long periods, there is actually at least one genuine reason to moan on the pitch - Ken Charlery, who is looking worryingly like a severe waste of money. I was genuinely excited by his signing - more so than that of Brett Angell, in fact - as he came to us with a genuinely good goalscoring record. Whether he's unfit, ill-prepared, or simply unused to County's style of play is debateable, but he cannot seem to put a foot right, and most of the time we're effectively playing with ten men.

Still, I'm cheered up by the chant of "Adrian Heath is a homosexual" - it's the first time I've heard it since it was utilised to taunt the old Arsenal player, Willie

254

Young, back in 1980. It's so old, however, that only a few seem to be chanting it - the diehards from the old days perhaps?

Half-time arrives, with the depressingly familiar tale of lots of County pressure and no goals. The football is soon enough forgotten, however, as, just after the teams leave the field, and amidst the usual inconsequential announcements, comes an event which completes my footballing education. For the first time ever, I witness something first-hand without which I would have gone to my grave an infinitely poorer person. A streaker.

Sadly for the majority of the crowd, he's a bloke - although as he came out of the Burnley fans at the far end, and my eyes aren't the best, I wouldn't actually put money on it. He doesn't get very far either, managing to dodge a couple of stewards at pitchside, but succumbing to reinforcements - whose enthusiastic pursuit might suggest to a cynic that they're rather taken with the prospect of wrestling with a naked man - just outside the penalty area. He's marched off with a steward's jacket held in front of his naughty bits, taking the salute from both sets of fans.

For the second half, I've spotted my dad and Martin, and so go and sit with them, leaving the moaners to mumble and mutter to their hearts' discontent. I'm not keen on the lower, wider perspective, but any view would beat the aural misery I suffered in the first half.

Burnley come back into the game with a gusto that is rather worrying, and Paul Barnes, the guy who scored all the goals against us at Turf Moor, looks livelier when attacking the away support. He's a bit of a whiner, however, and seems to be constantly reminding the referee of the rules, complaining about his treatment from the County defence, and generally winding us all up. It's thus the loudest cheer of the day, therefore, when he gets booked for moving the ball away at a County free-kick, and then gesturing that the only reason he was booked was that the referee was listening to the Cheadle End.

A couple of minutes later, Lee Todd, as he did at Bury, deliberately knees the ball back to Paul Jones. Barnes, the closest Burnley player to the action, at first doesn't react, but when the fans at the far end roar their protest, he realises he might be on to something and frantically appeals to the referee. "Now who's listening to the crowd, Barnes?" I shout, and get one of my rare laughs from folk in the vicinity.

Towards the end, with another 0-0 draw looming large, the thought occurs that it's a hell of a long time since we scored a goal from open play. Dave Jones, seemingly in agreement, sends Andy Mutch to warm up. As he approaches the Burnley fans sitting at the far end of the Main Stand, he seems to be barracked and booed.. A bloke sitting behind me elucidates: "He scored a fucking goal against these bastards in the playoffs once, didn't he? Go on Andy!" Mutch comes on a couple of minutes later and, with the scoreboard showing less than four minutes left, performs a footballing miracle to rank with his goal at Southampton. A ball is played into the area from deep, and the keeper, running out of the area to kick it clear, can only boot it against Luis Cavaco. I'm not sure exactly what happens then, but it seems the ball rebounds high into the air, where Mutch leaps, gets a foot to it, and scrambles it into the net. Arrrgh! It's got to be a foul, hasn't it? Is it a foul? Yes? NO! ARRRGH!! The referee's signalled the goal, Mutch is giving it plenty to the Burnley fans, and there's pandemonium in the Cheadle End. For my part, I'm jumping around and clapping above my head so energetically that I can feel myself fainting once again. I force myself to calm down, as the loudest chant of the season - quite possibly the loudest chant I've ever heard at County - rings out around Stockport: "You're staying down, you're staying down, you're staying... **BURNLEY'S STAYING DOWN!"**

There's no time at all for Burnley to get anything from this game - and in any case, as we know, County can defend a one goal lead against anybody this year; soon enough, to a cacophony of shrill reminders, the referee blows for time. The team celebrate as though they've just beaten, well, Southampton at the Dell, Blackburn at Ewood or West Ham at Edgeley Park. Eventually, they reluctantly drag themselves off the pitch, and we leave the ground.

No quick getaway today, of course, having stayed behind for the gloating, so in an attempt to beat the heavy traffic, I take the backroads past my aunt's house, but find the way as clogged down there as anywhere else. Doubling back, I decide to head back to the main road past County and simply put up with the wait. Oh, what a happy accident. As we emerge onto the side road which leads to the main road, what should we spy but the Burnley coaches, being escorted away from the ground to the M63, but caught up in the traffic, and stationary like everyone else. If that woman in front would just ease across to her right, and let me squeeze through on the left... oops, on the pavement... there! Past her. I zoom to the end of the road, and both Martin and me wind down our windows and indulge in a spot of gloating. 1-0 signs, and pointing at the floor to indicate where we feel Burnley will be next season compared to ourselves is the order of the day, we feel. Instead of studiously ignoring us - the best policy - one or two Burnley fans can't help rising to the bait, and make, hilariously, "5-2" signs. Brilliant! As if that matters now, you pillocks! We laugh uproariously at them, pointing, flicking the Vs, and generally making merry with their discomfort. What a game, what a day. Football, eh?

April 14th 1997 Watford (home).

Julia accompanies me tonight, as does Anna, interest rekindling as the importance of the matches increases. Julia wouldn't normally be allowed to a midweek evening game - her normal bedtime being midway through the second half - but her school was doled out some freebies for the original date (this game was scheduled for 28th December, but fell foul of the Siberian nonsense), so we're allowing her to come to an evening game as a one-off. I'm also able to do some reallocating of season tickets and spare freebies with my dad and Martin, with the result that we're all able to see the game for nowt. Stick that up your £18 Middlesbrough tickets, County.

Inside the ground, it's clear that there are other parents being as liberal as us tonight, as Julia meets up with a giggle of her schoolmates, including her Best Friend, Heather C. Trouble is, we're in the Barlow Stand, and fairly low down it too, with the result that there's not only little atmosphere, but the view's fairly crap as well.

As a result, it's also hard to feel motivated, despite the fact that this is an extremely important game. Four out of the last five games, including today, have been against sides pushing for promotion themselves. We've won the previous three (Bury, Burnley and Crewe), and if we were to make it four tonight, we'd be putting ourselves in a great position for promotion. The longer the season goes on with our fate still in our own hands, the less likely we are to slip up at the final hurdle. At this stage of the season, it's almost as though you can't enjoy the game - it's just the means to an end; the end being, hopefully, three points.

We start fairly confidently, giving reason for optimism. For Luis Cavaco, however, things couldn't get worse, as he recoils from an innocuous looking challenge after fifteen minutes or so, and lies still. It's one of those injuries that you know is bad immediately, from the reaction of the players, of both teams. Sure enough, after five minutes of treatment on the pitch, Cavaco is gingerly stretchered off, his left leg strapped and bound. It makes you feel a bit sick, does an injury like this; the reaction of the players showed, to me, that his leg must have been broken badly enough to be distorted. Poor sod. Cavaco was also playing better than ever since he was recalled. The last similar situation involving a County player was a couple of seasons ago, when Brian McCord's career was finished after a bad tackle at Swansea (McCord successfully sued for damages in the High Court, winning the case earlier this season).

I don't know whether the rest of the ground's any different, but there's no atmosphere here in the Barlow Stand, unless you count the shrieking and laughing of kids. There is the odd chorus from the Cheadle End, which leads to Julia, the old County hand, starting her mates off on one she's copied: "you're staying down, you're staying down, you're staying... Watford's staying down..." they shriek, before the chant peters out, leading to even more giggling and shrieking, and the other kids in the rows in front turning to stare in open-mouthed amazement, as children do.

Apart from watching the youngsters, there isn't really much else to hold my attention, apart from the Watford fans amusing themselves with a trick they've obviously perfected over the years. As Paul Jones shapes to take a goal-kick, there's a load of shushing, before, as he runs to strike the ball, a loud *OI!* The first time they try it, the keeper actually half turns in surprise.

Booing the keeper in this way is an all-time classic football fans' idiosyncrasy, which has developed and matured over the years. It was, of course, originally conceived as a genuine attempt to put the opposition goalkeeper off whilst taking a goal kick, and was therefore spelt "wooooaaahhhhh... AY!!" The juvenile supporters behind the goal would slowly build up noise level as the keeper placed the ball, reaching a crescendo as he approached to kick it. The poor sap was supposed to be so startled by the sudden "AY!" that he skewed his kick straight into the path of an opposing attacker. What was ignored was the fact that the element of surprise was somewhat lost when the climax was telegraphed by the preceding "wooooaaahhhhh... ". The Watford fans have obviously recognised this fact, with the result we've just seen. The strange thing is, however, that despite the chant never, ever, in any one of the tens of thousands of games at which it must have been deployed, succeeding in making a goalkeeper miskick by even half a degree, it continued to flourish and develop.

That said, once the realisation that the chant was useless in its intended capacity dawned, and the FIFA "no backpassing" mandate did the job of presenting the ball to the attacker far more effectively, the shout slowly transformed into simply being a jeer, usually expressed as "youuuu'rrrrre... shit! AH!", the only acknowledgement to its origins lying in the tempo and timbre.

Variations on the theme include "you're sheep... baaaa!", which is directed at fans from more "rural" parts. In this context "rural" is a definition so loose that it encompasses towns with conurbations denser than many cities, but which seem somehow as though they *should* be rural, as well as every single team from Yorkshire and Wales.

At half time, I go for a wander behind the back of the Vernon Stand, mainly to keep out of the way of the marauding tinies. When I get back to my seat, however, Anna's getting her ears bent by one of the mothers, who's come in and nicked my seat at half time, so I have to sit in front, even closer to the touchline. The mother's obviously here under duress, to keep an eye on her charges, unlike Anna, who's here to watch County. Anna keeps turning her head to watch the game as the other woman's talking, but to no avail. I think the woman can't conceive that a fellow mum would actually want to see the game.

Although many of the people around me probably don't appreciate it, County desperately need a goal. Thankfully, they get one, in the 53rd minute, and a hell of a goal it is too. Cooper makes good progress down the wing before cutting inside and finding Jeffers. He flicks the ball through the legs of the last defender, moves into the area and hammers a shot past the Watford keeper and into the far corner. Brilliant! Sod the fact that I'm surrounded by Julia's classmates, and their parents - I'm up and leaping around in a manner best described as frenzied. Ordinarily, a child would be intensely embarrassed by such a display from their father, but Julia's too busy going mad herself. That's my girl.

Immediately following the goal, Watford pour onto the attack. A six pointer for us, against a promotion rival, is, by definition, as important a game for the opposition. How they don't equalise I'll never know, as Paul Jones makes three fantastic saves, the middle one of which I doubt any goalkeeper in any league could have bettered. The noise from the Cheadle End now sounds good where I'm sitting, especially the chants of "we're going up" - sounding more justified by the game.

Following the saves from Jones, I'm far more confident that we'll now hang on and win, despite Watford trying as hard for an equaliser as Burnley, and Bristol Rovers, and Crewe, and Bury... Sure enough, the final whistle brings an end to yet another single goal home win, against yet another of our promotion rivals. We're now second, although there are others playing tomorrow. The only other game we've got left against a promotion rival, however, is the last game of the season, against Luton, and the way things are working out, it seems as though we might not need to get anything from that one. We could also probably get away with losing at either Preston or Gillingham, as long as we win the other one.

April 16th 1997 Gillingham (away).

Well, we're finally here - the last midweek marathon. I feel demob-happy as I leave work at eleven again, leaving the car at Lily's and heading to the ground. The fact that we've also got a fantastic record at Gillingham in recent years also helps lift my spirits - win tonight and we're looking good - and I mean *really* good - for promotion.

It's funny what a difference a week can make. My spirits couldn't be higher today, as I walk from my aunt's to the ground, watching people going about their normal workaday tasks on Edgeley. On the coach, too, where I grab another double seat, I'm mellow, relaxing as I gaze out of the window at the sunset.

Saturday Night and Thursday Morning

At the services - the last afternoon stop of the season, ha ha - it seems I can do no wrong, as I storm the fruit machines. I hit about three jackpots, and am left with so many tokens that I have to hurry to feed them back in before I can get back on the coach. Luckily, some of them turn into proper money, as I get enough small wins to turn about twenty quid's worth of tokens into a tenner, coming out about seven or eight quid up (notice the true gambler only relating tales of his wins? My kids didn't eat for three days after the Plymouth game. Only joking).

Underway again, we make reasonable time to the M25, and start to skirt London. I'm into provincial pleb mode again, as I think I can identify Battersea Power Station in the distance. I didn't realise you could see it from here. Oh, you can't; as we get closer, it becomes the Dartford crossing. The twinkly old Thames looks very fetching in the late evening sunshine, I must say - assuming that it is indeed the Thames. If I thought that was Battersea Power Station, this river could well be the Humber for all I know.

We leave the M25 and dive downhill towards Kent. We're soon off the motorway and looking for Gillingham. We pass a place called Thong, which seems to me to be a singularly unfortunate place to live - although not as bad as Bumhole in Suffolk - and are soon in Gillingham and looking out for the floodlights.

The driver hasn't a clue where the ground is, so we stop and get directions. It's easy to miss, mind, and sure enough we do. Stopping again, we ask a mother struggling with a couple of kids. She couldn't be more helpful, going into great detail, even when we've established where we should be heading. "Shut up big tits, you've told us enough" shouts a lad behind, thankfully not loud enough for her to hear. This is terrible, it really is. I have no doubt that I could strike up a conversation about County with any of these people in a pub, and pass an extremely pleasant hour or two in their company. Yet here's a local woman, struggling with her kids, yet still good-natured enough to offer us more information than we've asked for, and all those gits can do is get cheap laughs from their cronies by grunting scummy physical insults at her. I find that tremendously depressing. Thank God it's the last coach trip of the season.

Once again, we're here extremely early - five o'clock, although it's about 20 past when we eventually reach the ground and disembark. With well over two hours to kill, the pub beckons. Being fond of my own company, I set out walking, and find a local about half a mile away, complete with the ubiquitous early evening alcholics. There's a bloke and a woman propping up the bar, and, sure enough, despite my mental hate-waves, I'm enough of a stranger to be questioned incessantly. I suppose they mean well - the bloke even goes to the trouble of shaking my hand when I go in. He obviously thinks I'm ripe for conversational picking, so I pointedly read my paper, which stops him, although not entirely. "Leviathan," I say, which stumps him, and he eventually shuts up. After an hour or so, I take my leave of them. I'm sure at the end the woman thinks I'm playing tonight. I know for a fact the bloke thinks I'm from Scunthorpe.

Heading back to the ground, I see two separate election posters for the Monster Raving Loony party, posters which make me suspect we're in student territory. It's a deprived looking area - which again, could mean we're in student territory. The ground is tightly enclosed by the terraces, although my pre-match walkabout establishes that they're at least building on one side. Indeed, this site is covered by blue tarpaulin which is easy to move aside, giving a reasonable view of the pitch when I do so. I wonder whether anyone watches the game from here.

In the County end at a game like this, there're a lot of familiar faces, and I stand next to Louis from the Fingerpost, and behind Martin Frost and Jeff Lawrenson. Another predictable element of a north-south game is the chant of "dirty northern bastards" that go up when a County player goes in hard early on.

Chris Marsden's served his time by now (I wonder why I made that particular connection?), but is on the bench at the start; reasonable enough that Jones doesn't want to disturb a winning team, I suppose. We could do with him, though, as our first half performance is absolutely crap. Jones has been telling the press for weeks now that playing two games a week doesn't affect the players, but if he's honest, I'm sure he'll admit it does. County look lethargic, and it's no surprise when Gillingham's pressure is rewarded after half an hour with a goal. A corner is headed home by an unmarked striker at the near post.

Half time sees Louie fall short of his previous high standard when the best he can do is two jokes so old they're bald. The first is the one about why you shouldn't wear Russian underpants (Chernobyl fall-out), and the other about two buckets of sick walking down the road when one starts to weep. Come on, you *must* have heard it. You know, the one where the first bucket says what's up with you...? Come on - the second one then says I was brought up round here. Yes, that one.

Marsden still hasn't been brought on, although he is after the first five minutes of the second half see no change to the score. There is a thrill of anticipation as he comes on: "come on Chrissy lad," shouts someone, "sort them out!" A minute or two after he gets on, however, he loses the ball and someone to my left raises a laugh by shouting "come on Marsden, you've done fuck all since you came on." This is topped by someone behind, who adds, "you've done more than Charlery, though." Someone else tries "in four games," but only gets a few grins - that's too near the mark to be funny.

Bury and Brentford both won last night, which makes it important that we get something tonight, but despite a ten minute spell of concerted pressure, we're obviously not going to score. The game peters out to the sound of the Gillingham fans' delight as they put one over on the dirty northern bastards.

Back on the coach, some light relief is provided by listening to the Coca Cola Cup final replay; the biggest cheer County fans have raised all night is when Leicester's winner goes in. Following that, however, it's yet another fucking Jean Claude Van Damme film. I didn't know the bastard had made that many. Well, I suppose in a sense, he hasn't; he's just made the one, which keeps getting remade with a different title. Thankfully, my recent coach experience has made me a sleep expert, and I get a good couple of hours in, which makes the journey far less excruciating than it might otherwise have been; it's merely ghastly.

At three o'clock, I clatter back through the echoey streets to Lily's and pick up the car for the last time in this momentous season. Wouldn't you know it, for the first time, it struggles to start. It eventually fires when I've woken up the whole street, and I shamefacedly trundle home, for the last time in the early hours of Thursday morning.

April 19th 1997 Preston North End (away).

Having accepted that we could probably have lost one of the two - Gillingham and today - Wednesday's result makes a win today imperative. We're still third, but lost one of our games in hand against Gillingham.

It's a nice easy trip to Preston - straight up the M61 past Bolton's new stadium. This is a fantastic looking structure - as though a spacecraft has headed to earth, and chosen Horwich as a likely looking spot. Sadly, Bolton are already promoted to the Premier League, meaning I won't get to see the inside of the ground next year, even if County do go up.

Having set off at one, we arrive at Deepdale early enough to park in a side street close to the ground. Leaving Martin in the car and my dad looking for a pub, I take a wander around the ground again. Deepdale has changed since I was last here two or three years ago. The home fans are now allocated the Town End, behind the goal where away fans used to go; as a result, we're to be placed in a paddock in front of the old Main Stand - an area that I've heard is pretty crap at the best of times. I refer to the structure in front of which we will be billeted as the "old" main stand, because of the other main change to Deepdale since I was last here: the Tom Finney Stand. This is an absolutely marvellous new structure, opposite where we will be situated, which is based on the stadium in Italy where Ireland played that World Cup quarter final against Romania. Only one side of the ground has so far been built in this style, but the rest is apparently promised as and when Preston progress up the leagues.

The stand that has been built has been named after Preston's most famous player, Tom Finney, and - in a great touch - has the image of his face picked out with different coloured seats, rather than the usual "PNE FC", or "SCFC." I suppose the only negative aspect of this is that it might be considered slightly disrespectful to have the face of one of your favourite sons being covered by arses during the game - a statement which might well have caused alarm had a Preston doctor used it years ago: "Mrs Finney, I'm afraid it's bad news - your son's face is covered with arses". Continuing my wander, I actually see the great man himself arrive and head for the stand named after him. I presume he doesn't have to pay to get in, although it must still be an odd feeling, to sit in a stand named after you.

Eventually, I complete my tour of Deepdale, head back for the car, and meet the others. We head for what is now the away end, and go inside. Sure enough, the dire warnings I had heard about the view prove to be well-founded, as we're in a crappy little paddock, that fills to capacity with County fans. Luckily, ducking down under a crush barrier, we're early enough to grab a reasonable spot.

Preston start well enough, but after a bright opening, County have a great chance to score after ten minutes or so. Armstrong sets up Charlery brilliantly, but with an open goal in front of him, and a keeper deciding which way his token dive will have to go, Charlery, incredibly, miskicks, and bobbles the ball gently back to the keeper, who just about manages to stop laughing long enough to casually pick it up. This seems to be the final straw for the County fans, as far as Ken Charlery is concerned. It's hard not to sympathise. In the games he's played since his transfer, he's looked, to be frank, bloody awful. I suppose it's hard to slot into a side like this, that's had an amazing season before you arrived, but he is a professional. As the saying goes, my grannie could have scored that.

At least County take heart from the near miss, and start to dominate the game. Although half time is reached with no goals, it really does seem as though County are the only team that will score. The anger at Charlery's miss has dissipated, and the half time buzz is optimistic - win today and we're back on course.

The second half continues in the same vein, although frustration starts to mount as County's domination of possession isn't turned into goals. Alun Armstrong is guilty of a miss almost as bad as Charlery's, although as he makes the chance himself, playing a brilliant one-two with Tom Bennett before blasting his shot wide, he perhaps is not as deserving of criticism as Charlery - not that that stops the slag-Armstrong morons, who give full vent to their feelings.

Anger at Alun, however, is nothing to what erupts amongst the County fans with ten minutes left. Preston, who have hardly had a shot on target the whole game, move down the right, and the ball is fired into the area. As it's cleared, it falls to one of their midfielders, lurking outside the area, and he hits a fantastic first time volley into the corner. The home fans to our left in the Town End go absolutely ecstatic, their celebrations in direct contrast to our shocked silence. That's the winner - we won't come back from that, we realise, with mounting horror.

As the game meanders to its climax, anger builds on the away terrace. This might strike a neutral observer as particularly unreasonable - it is, after all, the team's fourth game in eight days - and I suppose they may have a point. What I think it is, however, is frustration, manifesting itself in anger. Following Monday's game, when we beat Watford to go second, promotion seemed almost assured. Two defeats - both away at sides with nothing to play for - have left our promotion hopes, whilst not in tatters, looking decidedly threadbare.

I head sullenly for the exit, pausing only to take a leak in one of the toilets - actually a portakabin near the turnstiles. As I'm standing there, I hear the most disgusting retching as someone in the ladies next door redecorates one of the toilet bowls (it could be the sink, or the floor, of course, but I'm assuming). I can't decide whether it's illness, or a comment on the game.

April 22nd 1997 York City (home).

I recalculated my bet last night. Rather than the three hundred and odd quid I was expecting if only County won the league (I've given up on Newcastle), I realise I would have actually picked up £420 had County not cocked it up for me.

We can still get second, though. After Saturday's débâcle at Preston, we're still fourth, and with one game in hand on everyone else. Even better, although we're seven points off the lead, we're only two points off second place.

There is a major boost before the kick off, when Brett Angell - thought to be out for the season, actually makes the bench. If ever we needed a goalscorer, it is now. We may well still be playing good football, but it's painfully clear that unless we start scoring, we're going nowhere, never mind Division One.

York should really present no problems today, and County start as if that's indeed the case, with a couple of early corners, and some good saves by York's keeper boding well. Inspired by this, County turn up the pressure, and the away goal leads a charmed life. So do the team, come to that. After twenty minutes in which they have hardly been able to get out of their own half, York take the lead with, of all things, a comedy goal. Their centre forward picks up the ball in his own half and a-bobbles and a-stumbles forward with it, Gannon and Flynn trotting alongside, but seemingly reluctant to get in a tackle, before he enters County's area. Unable to believe he's got this far, he then scuffs a shot, which seems to take deflections off both defenders, the keeper and one of the floodlights before trickling into the corner.

Although we've dominated, impatience at County's slow, deliberate style of play quickly turns to anger around me as a result of the goal. "Come on Charlery, fucking jump!" "Get on with it Gannon!" Thankfully, order is restored five minutes after York's opener, when County equalise with a great goal. The ball is worked out to the right, where Chris Marsden sends in a great cross. Tom Bennett - making up for being the one who lost the ball in the middle of the field to the York scorer - arrives at pace to thump home a header.

There is no more scoring in the first half, however, and the potential importance of the goal for York is brought home when a bloke nearby points out that the last time we scored more than one goal was a month ago, when we beat Notts County - with two own goals.

In the second half, County move down a gear; we seem to have run out of ideas. We still have the majority of the play, but clear cut chances are conspicuous by their absence. Of course, if we hadn't gifted York a goal, we'd now be in our favourite position of all: defending a one goal lead, and against a team, moreover, who hardly seem likely to score a "proper" goal.

We need something desperately, and with this in mind, Jones brings Brett Angell on. His reception is that you'd expect to be given to a miracle worker, but then again, in a football sense, he is. With fifteen minutes left, Tom Bennett, determined to do what it takes to atone for his earlier cock-up, finds space on the edge of the area. He shoots, and the ball is deflected up off a defender and across the box, where Angell is waiting to head it in. Absolutely fantastic. He might look ungainly - and he does, to be honest - but who gives a toss if he scores goals? Goals, moreover, none of the other players look like scoring most of the time. The relief is so great that the chant of "Oh now you've got to believe us, the County's going up" is the loudest it's been all season. It even drowns out the Borussia Dortmund fans who are in the Cheadle End, taking in a game before going to Old Trafford tomorrow night, and singing their German songs. In deference to them, a chorus of "we only hate Man Utd" is aired.

York are never going to score, and we hold on for one of the more comfortable of our "defending a one-goal lead" wins. Outside the ground, word quickly gets around that Luton and Bury drew with each other 0-0, and, a bloke tells me, Brentford beat Blackpool. Shit! Oh no, sorry mate, Blackpool beat Brentford, 1-0. Whoo-hoo! We're now second on merit, and still with a game in hand. Surely now we're in with a great chance of going up?

265

Saturday Night and Thursday Morning

April 26th 1997 Wycombe Wanderers (home).

Amazingly, although I knew on Tuesday that results elsewhere had been good for us, I didn't know precisely how good until Wednesday morning's papers. The almost incredible situation is that two wins out of our final three games will mean we are promoted. Simple as that. We're at home to Wycombe today, and should really win, which will mean that we could get promotion by beating Chesterfield next Monday, in another rearranged game.

Such is the requirement. What it has meant, practically, is that tickets for next Monday are suddenly at a premium - so much so that when I went down on Wednesday morning at what I thought was probably a ridiculously early ten past eight, there was already a fair old queue. I eventually got my hands on the piece of paper which will guarantee my attendance at what could well, at quarter past nine next Monday, have been the most unforgettable County game in living memory.

I was depressed, though, by a conversation I heard behind me in the queue; a group of fans were discussing how much admission would be next season if County were to go up. The consensus seemed to be £12, and, even worse, there seemed a resigned acceptance of such a price. Were we to get promotion, I would hope against hope that the County Board would show a bit of common sense and not charge so much. Whilst they would have no problem in filling the ground for a game against Manchester City at those prices, a Tuesday night game against Grimsby wouldn't draw the punters in, no matter which division the teams are in. What's really worrying is the fact that even the consideration of such prices is enough to depress me; it could even reach the stage where I would have to ration the games I attend myself. This would have been barely credible even a few years ago; after a season in which I have attended every game, home and away, it's unthinkable.

The atmosphere inside is appropriate for such a game. The Cheadle End had already sold out before today, so the decision was made - sensibly - to give County fans the Railway End as a one-off, with Wycombe fans accommodated in two blocks of the Vernon Stand. I feel sorry for them, having to pay a quid extra, until I remember that we were ripped off at their place, paying a tenner, never mind nine quid, for a behind the goal view that was seven quid the year before. Bollocks to 'em.

Anna and Julia are here today, for hopefully County's last home game in Division Two for at least a season. Alun Armstrong is Julia's favourite player, and after twenty minutes, he's mine too, when he gives us the lead, ending a personal goal drought that dates back to the game with Shrewsbury on February 15th. He controls the ball on the corner of the six yard box as though it's stuck to him, turns and fires into the bottom corner. I know, as do most other fair-minded fans, that his contribution to the team goes beyond mere goalscoring, but there are always those arseholes who can't see beyond players finding the net. Okay, one goal will hardly shut them up, but it'll help his confidence, and hopefully there'll be more to follow. The euphoria, both on and off the pitch, is tangible, and I even shout "that's how to control the ball, Charlery!", for the benefit of the Armstrong detractors around me, rather than Charlery himself (who probably wouldn't have heard me anyhow, if I'm brutally honest).

It gets even better ten minutes later, when a Flynn long throw causes panic in the Wycombe box, and a defender heads into his own net. It's now looking like that game on Monday will indeed be the clincher. Although Wycombe aren't as bad as York (probably because they're still not safe themselves at the bottom of the league, and are thus fighting for the points), they still don't look dangerous, and the mood amongst County fans changes from ecstatic to frivolous, illustrated best when a Wycombe player, warming up, heads over to the Cheadle End. His shorts are not the most voluminous ever made, and a couple of cries immediately ring out: "Get some shorts that fit, you bastard!" is quickly followed by "Look at that arse!"

The flippant mood continues into the second half, even affecting the scoreboard operators, who announce the arrival of substitutes "Super Mutchy" and "JJ" (John Jeffers). The scoreboard operator is obviously having a field day, as the word "penalty!" suddenly appears for no apparent reason. Either that or he's psychic, as, a few minutes later, Wycombe do get a penalty, when Flynn handballs.

They score, and suddenly the air of gaiety is transformed. Suddenly all is tense, as the visitors sense a point to be gained, and County, for all their experience in this situation, start to crap themselves. For the first time all afternoon my heart starts pounding, especially as Jones has brought off Kieron Durkan, a winger, for Tony Dinning, a defender. He might as well have instructed the scoreboard to say "Please Attack Us, Wycombe".

The tension turns to abuse, which gets personal "Who had that baby, Marsden, you or your girlfriend?" shouts someone, alluding to a newspaper story of the other day which announced the birth of Chris Marsden's first child. All of a sudden, the game's unbelievably tense as Wycombe press. They are probably no more likely to score than any of the other teams have been in this position, but there's always a first time, and this is the last game of the season, after all - one half of a potential promotion winning double. Incredibly, so late in the game that I've moved away to the exit, Lee Todd clears off the line. Hearts are pounding all around the stadium when the referee finally blows the whistle.

Saturday Night and Thursday Morning

County do a lap of honour at the end. Throughout the 70s and 80s, we always used to pour onto the pitch and salute the players as they re-emerged from the Main Stand after the last home game. Strangely, despite twenty years of almost total lack of success, such occasions were always good-humoured, with the exception of one particularly crappy season when something collectively snapped, and chants of "sack the board" rang round the ground. In these sophisticated days, the team does laps of honour - maybe this year there'll actually be something to honour?

More important than any celebrations, however, premature or not, is the fact that we've just achieved our seventh successive home win. Whilst we didn't, as I feared, win all those games in hand, other teams did, as I hoped, slip up. Today might have been tense, but we've done it. We've won the first game in the double that could see us promoted. As I walk slowly away from the ground, I force myself to take in the enormity of what today's win, lucky though it was in the end, means. After such an incredible season - and the turnaround in the league would warrant such a description in itself, let alone any cup heroics - we're down to the most simple of equations. Win at Chesterfield on Monday, and we're up.

April 28th 1997 Chesterfield (away).

I've got a particular image of tonight implanted firmly in my conscious, where it will probably remain, at the risk of sounding melodramatic, until the day I die - or at least until the day my faculties go and I'm left to dribble custard into my cardigan. The image is that of Alun Armstrong - young, talented, pilloried by some ignoramuses, yet as honest and dedicated as they come - hearing the final whistle and immediately, *instantly*, turning and running ecstatically, at full pelt, surfing the crest of a huge wave of adrenaline, not to the players' tunnel, not to any of his team mates, not to his manager, but to the fans. It's a mutual explosion of euphoria, both on and off the pitch, and in those few moments, as I watch this young lad race to express his absolute, unequivocal joy with the people who have supported him and his team mates, through thick and thin, downpour, fog, frost and traffic, spending hundreds, even thousands, in the process - in those few moments, and in that image - a young lad running at full speed towards the fans, then the delight, the sheer bloody joy of what being a football fan can sometimes mean, is encapsulated. Christ, my eyes are prickling as I write this, three weeks after the event.

Six hours earlier, as I leave work at quarter to four, such joy is far from my mind. It's absolutely pissing down with rain as I make my way home. It's ironic, I suppose, in this season of precipitation, that the match which might well see our season climaxed takes place on such a day. Sod irony, though - what I'm more concerned about is how such weather will affect our chances. The rain is absolutely heaving down - so heavy, in fact, that I'm half wondering if the match is at risk.

Knowing Saltergate as I do, I've got some sympathy for those in the open end tonight. I would normally have been amongst them, but such is my paranoia about perhaps getting there late and ending up with a crap view, that I decided to get a ticket for the seats tonight, a decision made slightly easier by the fact that it's only a quid extra at Chesterfield. My dad is also sitting down, although Martin has stuck with the terrace. Anna was also planning to come tonight, but cried off after the Wycombe game - so tense was that particular afternoon that she doesn't think she'll be able to cope with tonight. I'm not so sure myself - if I'm going to be tense, I'd rather be there in person rather than listening on the radio, which I always find frustrating anyway - and often extremely tense.

What I could really do without tonight is heavy traffic. Heavy traffic that causes traffic jams. Bloody traffic jams that start just after Disley, and, when you pass the traffic lights that heralds the turn off for New Mills, and thus what you thought was causing you to queue, continue on the other bloody side. Most screamingly annoying of all is the fact that the holdups are caused by a sodding great tree-stump that some clever swine thought it would be a wheeze to fell today and leave in the road overnight, thus causing the blood pressure of the thousands of Stockport people heading over the Peaks to Chesterfield tonight to go through the roof. Aren't people who decide when roadworks are to take place, when drains are going to be replaced, and when bleeding tree stumps are going to be felled supposed to take into account things such as football matches? If they aren't, then they bloody well should be.

Luckily, I set off ridiculously early (bless that paranoia), and so am past the bloody stump in enough time to still be well on schedule for a seven o'clock arrival; I'm soon renewing acquaintances with my old friends Perryfoot, Smalldale, Wormhill, Chuffpiles and Knobwaggle (okay, okay, same joke, but it still works, though, doesn't it? Well, I laughed). We also pass through the rather literally named village of Stoney Middleton - literally named because it's next to a quarry ("waall, our village be stoney, aand it be in the middle o'things, so whaat should we caaaall it? Newtown?")

Once we climb over the Peaks, the torrential rain eases off somewhat, and we can even see clear sky ahead, so any fears about the match being called off are abandoned. We make good time to Chesterfield, and park up on the main road at the bottom of the hill that leads to Saltergate. I'm due to meet the guy who's having Anna's ticket, so I lurk around in the rain that's restarted with a vengeance, and watch the County fans stream in. It's in this position that I hear the home announcer thank the County fans for the support Chesterfield got on their way to the cup semi final the other week. Apparently, as they came in through Stockport on their way to Old Trafford, County fans were out with banners wishing them well. It was a nice touch by the County people, and an equally nice touch by the home announcer to acknowledge it.

The coaches have obviously been delayed by the treestump, and so don't arrive until just before kick off, along with the guy who wants the ticket. In the meantime, I hear from a copper that the home ends have sold out as well, which disappoints a number of County fans who didn't realise the game was all-ticket. It's pitiful to see their faces as they realise - if it'd've happened to me, I'd have gone straight down the home end and paid to get in there, but even that's not an option tonight. The lad who wants my ticket shows up and pays me the nine quid that Chesterfield charge for their seats, and I hurry away through the rain to the stand.

I use the facilities before finding my seat, and am amused to discover that the ancient old bogs inside the stand are just like those outside, albeit with a roof - punters actually have to step over the trough to get in. No wonder the seats are only a quid more than the terrace.

I move up into the stand just as the game kicks off. I'm rather surprised to see my dad, however, sitting in the aisle. When I ask him why, he indicates some people to his left - they're apparently in our seats and won't shift. No, sorry, I'm not having this, not tonight of all nights. The stand is full, obviously, and I want to sit next to my dad. I'm buggered if we're going to scrabble around for two odd ones apart from each other that have been left over because these ignorant sods - staring fixedly ahead even though they *know* they're in our seats - won't shift. I call over a nearby steward - the one who my dad says he has already tried to get to help, without success because the steward wants an easy life. Well, he ain't gonna have one. Do something useful for once. "These people are in our seats," I tell him, showing him the tickets, "can you move them please?" He moves over to them and I squat in the aisle next to my dad. They're obviously arguing the toss, as he starts to debate it with them. I lose interest, however, because on the pitch, County are building a move down the left wing. Todd has found Alun Armstrong, who is shaping to cross. As he fires in a perfect ball, the whole stand rises, arguments about seats forgotten for a moment. In the middle is Brett Angell, and Alun has sent over the perfect ball. A man of Angell's size couldn't really miss, so good is the cross. Sure enough, he doesn't, heading it down, under the keeper's desperate dive, and in. For probably the most important game in the memories of the people here tonight, we've taken an early lead. The old wooden stand shakes with the reaction of the County fans.

In the midst of the celebrating, however, I'm angry. I should have seen that goal from the seat I paid for, not the fucking aisle. The steward moves back towards us, "do you actually want to sit in *those* seats?" he asks. Jesus! "I'm with my dad, and we want to sit together - why can't you tell those fucking people to sit in the seats they bought, and we'll sit in ours, for God's sake?" I'm hyped up by the goal; perhaps not the best frame of mind in which to debate the issue. Suddenly, a bloke has appeared at the side of us, "I don't want a scene," he says. Eh? "Neither do I, but *they're* in the wrong - they're in our seats."

"Well why don't you sit there?" he says, indicating two seats in front which I hadn't noticed before. It's a matter of principle now, though. I want these bastards, who haven't said a word, or indicated in any way why they won't shift, moved.

"Look, why don't you just sit in those seats," says the bloke, and I suddenly realise I'm talking to John Rutter, County's commercial manager, who is also an ex-player - one whose singular lack of talent didn't prevent him being a fixture in the County side for most of the late seventies and early eighties. "Because they're someone else's," I say, "they're just late - what's going to happen when *they* arrive?"

"No one's going to come late," he says, managing to sound both scornful and patronising at the same time. "*I* got in late there's been traffic on the road and there's loads still late for God's sake" I blurt, anger making me incoherent. I'm painfully aware that we're blocking the view of people behind, not that any of them are actually moaning about it. I also realise that it'll probably take coppers to shift these ignorant bastards, and rather than taking a further fifteen minutes or so sorting it out, and blocking the view of people behind all the while, we decide that we'll have to sit in the two empty seats. I still want to know why Rutter thought it necessary to stick his oar in, though. "What's your problem," I say to him, "you're a club official!"

"I'm not a club official" he says, strangely, because I know he is. He's set me up for the winner, though: "so what the fuck's it got to do with you, then?"

I don't wait for his answer; me and my dad struggle past the occupants of the row in front, and fall into the two empty seats. It's then that we discover the reason they're empty - there's a whacking great post in the way of the far goal. It's too late now, though - we're lumbered. I manage to salvage some consolation, however. I realise that if we stand up whenever the action's down that end, we'll both see better, and block the view nicely of the idiots in our seats. Just let them try and protest. I grow more convinced as the game goes on that they are the people who should be sitting in these seats, and, knowing they had a restricted view, wouldn't then move back to them.

Luckily, there's quite a lot to be standing up for, as County seem to be wanting to put the game out of sight in the first ten minutes. Angell bursts through a few minutes after his goal, and lobs the keeper, who just manages to touch the ball on to the bar and over. Then someone has a shot which is kicked off the line. Chesterfield, however, still trying to get a playoff spot, *and* prevent County beating them four times in a single season, come back into the game. They don't look much like scoring, however, and half time arrives with our lead intact.

We stand up for a stretch, and as I glance around, I recognise a few familiar faces - one of the directors' sons in front; a couple of County fans I saw in the players' seats at Bury. There's also another club official - some kind of lottery honcho - sitting right next to me. I suddenly realise with a flash of inspiration that we're sitting in the freeloaders' seats. *That's* why Rutter was involved - being commercial manager, he had probably got the seats for those arseholes behind us, and having told them to sit in our seats, was desperate to ensure that they weren't kicked out to the restricted view ones. It all becomes clear.

I'm not that bothered now, though. County being in the lead and only 45 minutes from Division One is far more important; we're also now attacking the goals that I *can* see. Behind it, the terrace is packed with soaking wet County fans. I remember the last time we were in a similar position - potentially clinching promotion at an away ground. It was the first full year under Danny Bergara, and our last game of the season was away at Halifax. It wasn't made all-ticket, and around four thousand County fans made the trip across the Pennines to take over The Shay, in absolutely blazing hot weather. If we won and Southend lost, we were up. At half time, Southend were reported as being 2-0 up, and we were 0-0. Even worse, after an hour, Halifax scored. Then Bergara brought on substitute Ian McInerney - still one of my favourite ever County players, simply because of what he did that afternoon. He set up an equaliser with about fifteen minutes left, and then, five minutes later, scored the winner himself following a fantastic run. I think I became the most demented I have ever been on a football ground that afternoon, because, with the score 1-1, some complete twat in the County end started a rumour that Southend had been pulled back and were now losing 3-2. The final whistle signalled a pitch invasion by ecstatic County fans starved of success for twenty years. I had a radio to my ear in the centre circle at the Shay when I heard that Southend had actually won. Coming down from that high was the worst feeling I've ever experienced at a football ground. The players thought they were up too, which was probably a contributory factor to the way that they then went and lost the playoff semi final 6-0 - to Chesterfield, ironically. We were promoted the following year, though, so that was okay.

There are no opportunities for evil rumour-mongerers tonight. Apart from the fact that we know exactly what we have to do - win, without relying on results elsewhere - there are no other games taking place.

The second half starts, and seems to pass surprisingly quickly. That's probably because Chesterfield seem determined to make a game of it, and are actually giving us some real problems. Sensing this, the County fans pinch the ball and ape the Carlisle fans of the other week, waiting until the keeper is about to kick the replacement before heaving the original back into play. It's amusing, as ever, but something I think we don't need tonight. All that lost time is going to be added on.

My nails are bitten to bleeding - literally - when, with fifteen minutes left, the police take up their positions in front of the away support: another sign that promotion's near. Once again Chesterfield surge forward, and put the shits up the County fans. My heart's pounding worse than it has at any stage this season. County have a period of pressure, but don't seem that keen to score. We're just defending a lead again, something we're excellent at, but surely 2-0 would finish the game now?

In the old wooden stand, the desperate atmosphere is just like Southampton; we're full of the same excitement and tension. By now, we're well into injury time - how much is the ref going to play? And why the fuck did those idiots hang on to the ball? Wind a referee up and see how far it gets you; he'll add on twice as much. We've made all our time-wasting subs, one of whom, Ken Charlery is finally starting to perform - holding the ball up well in the home team's half, and frustrating their players. Then they rob the ball and surge forward. See? I told you we should have gone for the second! They force their way into our penalty area and score. NO! Tony Dinning has kicked the ball off the line. Can you believe it - he's kicked the fucking ball off the fucking line!

Over to my left, I can see the Sky camera trained on the dug-out. They're not covering the game live, but they need the standard celebratory pictures for tomorrow's sports bulletins, of course. Those standard celebratory pictures that you see so often, and tonight they'll be *our* manager, *our* players, *our* fans - *us*. I hope to God they've got it right, however - there won't be much of a reaction at the final whistle if Chesterfield equalise.

Eyes flicking from the referee to play and back again. Someone behind me says, frantically, "Six minutes! Six bloody minutes!" Eyes back to the referee. Blow, you bastard, blow. He blows. The final whistle, the one that indicates we are promoted, gets blown, and we all leap up as one, my mouth open wide, like everyone else's, in an ecstatic roar as Alun sets off on his run. Suddenly nothing else matters - the rain, Rutter's small-mindedness, nothing. We're promoted.

Saturday Night and Thursday Morning

I watch Alun start to take off his kit and heave it into the crowd - his shirt is followed by his boots, one then the other, and his shin pads. I wonder what else might follow, but he collects himself just in time. These pictures are going to be all over the press tomorrow, remember - better not get snapped in your undies, Al.

The pitch is full of club hangers-on and arse-lickers, embracing the players. I normally dislike these people, whose prime aim in their life sometimes seems to be to frustrate the fans, but I wish to God I was one of them tonight.

Jim Gannon is wiping away tears on the sleeve of his shirt; I'm blinking back tears myself. The players are cavorting in front of the fans, playing piggy back, forming a team picture with that stupid bouncing up and down that Liverpool pioneered a few years ago. Someone has thrown on a huge inflatable champagne bottle, and Lee Todd is posing with it for tomorrow's papers. There are a few home fans staying behind to watch the spectacle. I know how most of them feel: envious, yes, but not bitter - I've done it all too often myself at Edgeley Park, when a team has come to beat County and get promoted. Chesterfield have already showed themselves to be magnanimous to a fault, and the bitter fans have already sloped off home. Those that remain are, like me in 1986 (Southend), 1982 (Port Vale) and 1979 (Port Vale again), simply enjoying the sight of mass happiness; enough of a reason in itself to stay behind and watch.

The players finally leave the field, and we dash back to the car as quickly as we can. We've done the celebrating; there's no need to get caught in traffic. I'm glad we hurried when we get underway, though, as we drive up to a roundabout and back towards home. For the first time in my footballing life, I can make like an Italian, and lean on my horn. I'm not the only one, as Chesterfield is suddenly turned into Milan. The County fans respond, as I jab the horn: Da Da Da-da-da Da-da-da-da.. COUNTY!

The drive home seems longer than normal. Don't ask me why - it just does. Thank God it was a reasonably local team and we didn't clinch promotion at one of those south coast jobs. Most will actually be back home in Stockport for last orders if they want. Not me, though. I drop my dad and Martin off and go home. I tell Anna all about it and she goes to bed. I'm too hyped up to sleep, I think, but I'm wrong. Channel-surfing, trying to find some mention of the news, I'm suddenly very, very tired. I wander upstairs and sleep the sleep of the First Division football fan.

MAY

NATIONWIDE LEAGUE DIVISION TWO

	P	W	D	L	F	A	Pts
BURY	45	23	12	10	60	38	81
STOCKPORT COUNTY	**45**	**23**	**12**	**10**	**58**	**40**	**81**
LUTON TOWN	45	21	14	10	70	44	77
BRENTFORD	45	20	14	11	53	42	74
BRISTOL CITY	45	21	10	14	69	49	73
CREWE ALEXANDRA	45	22	6	17	55	46	72
BLACKPOOL	45	18	15	12	59	45	69
WALSALL	45	19	10	16	54	51	67
WATFORD	45	16	19	10	44	34	67
WREXHAM	45	16	18	11	52	49	66
BURNLEY	45	18	11	16	67	54	65
CHESTERFIELD	45	17	14	14	41	39	65
GILLINGHAM	45	18	10	17	58	59	64
MLLWALL	45	16	13	16	50	53	61
BOURNEMOUTH	45	15	14	16	43	45	59
PRESTON NORTH END	45	17	7	21	47	55	58
BRISTOL ROVERS	45	15	11	19	46	48	56
PLYMOUTH ARGYLE	45	12	17	16	47	58	53
WYCOMBE WANDERERS	45	14	10	21	49	56	52
YORK CITY	45	13	12	20	46	67	51
SHREWSBURY TOWN	45	11	13	21	49	72	46
PETERBOROUGH UNITED	45	10	14	21	54	73	44
NOTTS COUNTY	45	7	14	24	33	58	35
ROTHERHAM UNITED	45	6	14	25	37	69	32

May 3rd 1997 Luton Town (away).

What a week. What a bloody week. Promotion to Division One on Monday after sixty years; Labour landslide on Thursday after eighteen. It's particularly appropriate that we're playing Luton today, in fact, as their Chairman used to be David Evans, the loudmouth MP who was in the news a few weeks ago for displaying his mindless bigotry to a group of sixth formers, who released the tape of his rantings to the press. (I'm not sure if he is still the Chairman, and frankly I couldn't give a toss. Come to that, I'm not even sure he's still an MP; I could definitely give a toss about that). I'd love to see him today, actually, and have a good gloat, or perhaps poke him in the eye with a sharp stick. That said, he's probably lying low with the rest of the Tories.

It was under the Chairmanship of Evans that Luton imposed an almost universally-reviled away fans' ban at Kenilworth Road (which would have buggered me up this season had it still been in existence) a couple of seasons ago. Today, however, around 1,900 County folk are expected to make the trip; the tickets sold out quickly, before promotion was confirmed at Chesterfield, and whilst it was still thought this match might matter.

It does matter, in fact, in that we could still win the championship. Apart from anything else, Monday's result at Chesterfield moved us level on points with Bury, although we've scored a couple of goals fewer. If we win, therefore, and Bury either lose or draw, we are champs, and I relieve Mr Hill of 420 quid. We can also finish top by scoring three more goals than Bury do, even if they do win. As this would require a minimum victory for us by four goals, I think we're really hoping that Bury don't win. As they're at home to a Millwall team that have been in freefall since we stuffed them 5-1 at Edgeley Park, it has to be said that it's unlikely we will win the title, but then again, Jim Gannon was 28-1 to score the first goal at Sheffield United...

I had considered the train today (into and out of London), but was persuaded by a friend, Phil Brennan, to join the trip he had organised, largely because he had arranged an early start and a lunchtime buffet at a pub in Towcester. So it is that the party starts outside the Sir Robert Peel in Edgeley at 8.30, with the landlord serving ale to those people whose constitutions allow it.

As both teams are nicknamed "The Hatters," *The Tea Party* has declared a hat day, and so I have spent much of the previous week searching for suitable headgear. This caused more of a problem than it might otherwise have done, because I possess - and there's really no delicate way of putting this - a bleeding enormous head. I distinctly remember going down Stockport with my mum when I was about 10 and looking for a hat to take to the summer camp I was about to attend. As a kid, I was immensely proud (roughly about as proud as I am ashamed today) that the only size hat we could find to fit me was a gents' extra-large. Yesterday, then, I eventually managed to find an adjustable white baseball cap in Burtons, which, on the largest setting, just about perches ridiculously on top of my dome.

We make good time to Towcester, and are in the pub just after 12. It's a pleasant enough place, ancient and low-beamed, with original wooden floors; just the kind of place, in fact, that those idiots who pronounce both the "e"s in the phrase "olde worlde" refer to as olde worlde. I don't bother trying to get served in the initial surge off the coach, preferring to grab a seat for me, Martin, and Jack and Dave Oldham. It's a squeeze, but we just about manage to sit on the one seat. Soon enough, the queue at the bar is only about six or seven deep, so I go to get served. I notice a pump serving Courage Directors' and whilst I'm not one of those ale bores, I do know that this is a nice pint; it's the drink I tend to have in a nearby pub whenever Anna and I go out for a curry. As I sip this one, however, it seems rather flat and watery; for subsequent rounds, I join Martin in having Fosters lager (yes, he's not only got a kid's ticket for today, he's indulging in a spot of underage drinking too).

Soon enough, after two pints and a tremendous buffet, it's time to go, and forty minutes or so later, we're pulling up outside a row of terraced houses that I know must be near the ground because I've seen the floodlights. Oops, silly - my mistake: the row of terraced houses *is* the ground. The away end is so tightly up against the back of the terrace that the club, at some point in their history, have obviously bought a couple of the houses, and knocked through the living room to form turnstiles (not something you'll see recommended in your average DIY book). Above this bizarre entrance, the top floor of what was previously a house is now still inhabited, as a flat. Inside, you walk through what was once the back garden, and up a tight iron staircase to enter the back of the away end.

Quaint, maybe, but the seats that Luton have sold for £12.50 stretch my sense of humour somewhat. Bolted onto the old terracing, the leg room is so narrow that sitting comfortably is well nigh impossible; I have to settle for a kind of semi-stooping perch on the edge of the seat. Packed in with 1,900 other fans like this also means that it's absolutely boiling hot; what doesn't help is that the first, flat pint I had back in the pub seems to be griping away, leaving me feeling just a touch nauseous.

The game starts and County storm onto the attack. They go close a number of times in the early stages, and it's no injustice when, after ten minutes or so, Alun Armstrong shows great skill in taking the ball past the last line of Luton's defence, and thence round the keeper, who upends him. It's definitely a penalty, but the referee decides, probably correctly, that as Armstrong had taken the ball wide, he was probably not in a clear goalscoring position, and so the keeper can stay on. Nevertheless, Kevin Cooper steps up to place the ball into the corner of the net, and we've got the early goal that kindles unrealistic hopes of trumping Bury, no matter what happens at Gigg Lane.

The County fans celebrate the goal in the usual manner, and taunt the home supporters in the main stand in the usual manner. The self-belief that the goal gives the County players causes them to play the ball around confidently, and heralds the arrival of a new chant, to the tune of "Blue Moon": *"Braaa-zeeell - It's just like watching Brazil."* In response, the best the Luton fans can do - and there are a lot of them, as the game's a sell-out, because home fans also thought there may be something at stake when the tickets went on sale - is "you all support Man United," which receives the contempt it deserves.

There is, in fact, quite a bit of taunting, defiant from Luton fans disappointed that this is a meaningless game for them, and celebratory from County fans who know they're up already. The home support have another reason to make noise about five minutes before half time, however, when they equalise. A long ball is punted forward and finds the County defence in some confusion. One of the Luton strikers, seeing an opportunity, nips between Mike Flynn and Paul Jones and lobs Flynn's weak back-header over the keeper and into the net.

Somewhat unsurprisingly, a defiant "we're up - we don't give a fuck" is the response from the County fans, although I sense disappointment from people, like me, holding out a genuine hope that we could nick the title today. There's been a lot of talk that today will be a party, but I rather think all the celebrating has been done on Monday night and most of the rest of the week; the implication that you have to wait until the next game to celebrate promotion seems a strange one to me. "Fuck all - you're going to win fuck all," is directed at us, following which comes an immediate response: "What division are you in?" (surely "which", I think, pedantically)

Whilst all this has been going on, I have been feeling more and more sick. I'm not the only one suffering from the heat, as I have heard comments to that effect from the people around me. By the time the whistle sounds for the break, however, I am feeling really bad. I watch for a few minutes as County officials try and help the party atmosphere by throwing into the crowd ancient replica shirts, and other crap they can't get rid of in the club shop. Incredibly, fully grown men are fighting frantically for this tat; I watch two of them directly in front of me in the aisle almost come to blows over a child-sized three year old goalkeeper's jersey. Somewhat surprisingly, the stewards, who for all of the first half were using threats, intimidation and physical force in order to keep their yellow painted aisle nice and free of people, are now standing blankly watching a virtual riot develop in the same area. Inconsistency from stewards - now that's something you don't see very often.

In an attempt to stop my stomach churning, I wander back out to the exit steps, and pause, breathing in through the nose and slowly out through the mouth, and listening to a young mother getting some disgusting barracking from the morons around me as she brings her washing in from the line in the garden below. It's no good - I realise that I'm going to have to chunder, and make my way down the steps to the toilets. They're busy, however, and as there's no way I'm going to go in there and chuck up with dozens of spectators hardly able to believe their luck (a young woman we could shout "get your tits out" to *and* some poor sap puking - is it Christmas?), I sit down on the floor outside, and slump against the wall, moaning gently.

After five minutes or so, I can hear that the second half's started, and so judge it safe to struggle to my feet and enter the toilet. Sure enough, there are only a couple of stragglers shaking off the drips, so I dive into the nearest trap and bolt the door. Adopting the traditional position, I make a couple of loud retching noises, but nothing happens other than my stomach contracting and groaning. Pizza. Bacon. Chip fat. Marmite. Nappies. Mustard. A marmite and bacon butty spread with extra lard and dipped in grease... ohhh Godddd.... With a terrifying "YYYAARRLLLGLLPPHLLLLLLLLLMMMPPPFFFFH!!!" most of the beer-saturated buffet leaps back out through my mouth and impacts against the seat, the floor, the walls and, I wouldn't be at all surprised, the ceiling. A couple of heaving spasms later, and, with my body trembling gently with the aftershocks, I dare to open my eyes.

Oh dear.

Oh dear, oh dear.

The toilet block was hardly the most salubrious of conveniences - indeed, it would have given Rotherham and Chesterfield a run for their money in the disgusting facilities stakes (and now over to Newmarket for the 3.45 - the Disgusting Facilities Stakes) - but there was clearly no need for this.

. Oh dear, oh dear, oh dear.

I have seemingly managed to do the impossible and make the place look worse than it did before I entered. Infinitely worse. I will spare the gentle reader's sensibilities by not giving further details; suffice to say that even though I used up all the available toilet roll (bizarrely for a football ground, there was a fairly full roll still in place), I was not quite able to rid the seat of all the regurgitated precipitate. I shuffle slowly back to my seat, feeling alternately nauseous and shamefaced. I also manage to make myself giggle slightly hysterically when I picture the face of the poor YTS lad on toilet cleaning duties when he opens the door of trap one on Monday morning.

Thankfully, ridding myself of the awful beer in this way has made me feel a lot better (although I bet it doesn't do the same for the YTS lad on Monday), although I start to develop a headache which carries on getting worse as the day drags on. I say "drags," as the second half is something of an anticlimax. I've heard from someone with a pocket radio that Bury are winning 2-0, which hands them the title; we'd now need to score another five. In the event, it's Luton who come closest to scoring, and only a final three remarkable saves from Paul Jones give us the draw.

Luton do a lap of honour at the end; a dangerous presumption with the playoffs still to negotiate. There's lots of mutual clapping - we applaud the Luton players as they go past, and their fans applaud ours. Once the players have finally left the field, the fans applaud each other. How nice. I bet you there wouldn't have been any of this had the final promotion place been decided today; "you're gonna get your fucking heads kicked in" would have been likelier.

I wander back out to the coaches. They are all parked along the street which contains the turnstiles, and ours is, conveniently, the closest. I step gingerly on board, my head hammering, and watch hundreds of hyperactive, pissed County fans making complete and utter twats of themselves. Primary object of their barbed wit is the young girl who was bringing in her washing at half time, and is now leaning out of her front room window with her baby son, watching the world go by. Of course she is simply asking for shouts of "slapper, slapper," isn't she, in the same way as young girls who dress attractively are asking to be raped. I'm gratified to see she fights back verbally, although she doesn't stand a chance against the massed ranks of morons. Pity she didn't have a high-pressure hosepipe to hand, or a machine-gun.

One of the females on our coach gets back on, saying, incredulously, "what a horror she was, eh?" to the coach in general. "What the hell do you expect," I say, quite loudly, ostensibly to Martin, but using him as the conduit for making a point to this silly cow. I needn't have bothered, as she didn't hear me. I'm suddenly immensely glad the season's over. I know these people are kindred spirits in one sense, but I'm sick to the back teeth of small-minded, moronic, bigoted, offensive pricks, of the type, sadly, that seem to make up a significant portion of the genus football fan *(canbe completeus moronicus)*.

At the end of the game, quite a few County fans ran onto the pitch to offer their congratulations to the players. Luton, as the scene of the infamous riot by Millwall fans in the mid-eighties, are hardly the type of club to overlook such behaviour, harmless though it is on one level. Sure enough, when it comes to head counting, we're one short, and a lad admits that his missing mate was one of those dragged off the pitch. He goes to see the police who take great delight (I'm making an assumption here, but you have to admit I'm probably right) in telling him that it'll take about an hour and a half to "process" his pal. ("Yes, your honour, the bruises on the accused occurred when he was unfortunately processed down a flight of stairs"). The consensus on the coach ("bollocks to him") is that we shouldn't wait, so, pausing only for his mate to take him his wallet so he can make his own way home, we're away, bidding farewell to the 37th away ground of the season.

The journey back is like so many others - uncomfortable, with bland motorway and snatched sleep. After four hours and a fifteen minute stop, we pull into Edgeley just before nine. I drop Martin off, and make my final journey of the season from football ground to home. It's over. No playoffs, no finals, just promotion. To Division One. It's finished. This season has ceased to be. It is an ex-season. After sixty-seven games, there are no more (I used to be a student, can you tell? You should hear my word-perfect rendition of the "Lumberjack Song").

I get home, head pounding, and let myself in. Julia is still awake, having been allowed to stay up and watch the Eurovision Song Contest with her mum; she's still at an age where she finds it genuinely exciting. It's all I need, however. After lying on the settee for ten minutes or so, I can't take any more. I wish them both goodnight, and go to bed.

AFTERWORD

NATIONWIDE LEAGUE DIVISION TWO

	P	W	D	L	F	A	Pts
BURY	46	24	12	10	62	38	84
STOCKPORT COUNTY	**46**	**23**	**13**	**10**	**59**	**41**	**82**
LUTON TOWN	46	21	15	10	71	45	78
BRENTFORD	46	20	14	12	56	43	74
BRISTOL CITY	46	21	10	15	69	51	73
CREWE ALEXANDRA	46	22	7	17	56	47	73
BLACKPOOL	46	18	15	13	60	47	69
WREXHAM	46	17	18	11	54	50	69
BURNLEY	46	19	11	16	71	55	68
CHESTERFIELD	46	18	14	14	42	39	68
GILLINGHAM	46	19	10	17	60	59	67
WALSALL	46	19	10	17	54	53	67
WATFORD	46	16	19	11	45	38	67
MILLWALL	46	16	13	17	50	55	61
PRESTON NORTH END	46	18	7	21	49	55	61
BOURNEMOUTH	46	15	15	16	43	45	60
BRISTOL ROVERS	46	15	11	20	47	50	56
WYCOMBE WANDERERS	46	15	10	21	51	56	55
PLYMOUTH ARGYLE	46	12	18	16	47	58	54
YORK CITY	46	13	13	20	47	68	52
PETERBOROUGH UNITED	46	11	14	21	55	73	47
SHREWSBURY TOWN	46	11	13	22	49	74	46
ROTHERHAM UNITED	46	7	14	25	39	70	35
NOTTS COUNTY	46	7	14	25	33	59	35

Phew! When I took the decision last June to go to every game in a lower division club's season, and to write about it, little did I expect what I've just experienced.

In an average Second Division season, I'd probably expect County to play around 52-53 games (46 league, 1 AutoWindscreens Shield, 2 Coca Cola Cup and 1 FA Cup are the minimum, and although they'd be very unlucky to go out of all the cup competitions in the first round, you wouldn't expect many semi-finals). But, as we all now know, this was not an average season. 67 games was exceptional, and very probably (I'm not quite sad enough to do the research) the most County have ever played in a single season. This book was originally conceived as a chronicle of the highs, the lows, the pleasure and the inconvenience of following a bog-standard lower division club throughout a given season; what it ended up as is a first-hand account of Stockport County's most successful season ever. Like many other County fans, I genuinely expected the team to do well this year - yes, even to be promoted - but you could say a major cup semi-final and three wins on Premiership grounds were something of a surprise.

So would I do it again (with the dangling carrot being the fact that no future season can ever, surely, represent such a feat of endurance)? Sadly, probably not. Apart from the fact that any other season could simply never live up to the glories of this one, the cost - at least in Division One - is simply prohibitive.

County's admission prices have just been announced for 1997-98, and, true to form, our idiotic Board (is there another kind?) have decided to impose 33-40% increases, simply because we're in "The First Division". It remains to be seen whether County fans, who in 1995/96 were paying £7 to watch Swindon, Oxford, Bradford and Crewe will roll up in their thousands to pay £12 to watch the same teams two years later, simply because the game is taking place one division higher. It's also doubtful that the neutrals will come and see (with due respect to all these teams) Reading, Bury, Charlton, or Portsmouth. It doesn't help, either, that early applicants for season tickets at Maine Road were charged £200, compared to County's £228.

The price rises took some of the gloss off promotion for me. Not because I can't afford it, but because the deep malaise that is the Manchester United plc syndrome, I now see being mirrored at my club. There is a whole swathe of supporters - unemployed or on poverty wages - for whom the idea of watching County is now a pipe dream. Yet these people have always been, until recently, the lifeblood of a football club. It's no easier for families, either, even middle-class families like mine. At next year's prices, it would cost Anna, me and the kids (assuming the boys were old enough to be interested) a staggering thirty-nine quid to go to a game - and in five years or so, when the boys *will* be interested, God knows how much it'll be. When I think about what alternative entertainment I could offer the kids with that kind of money, then, frankly, I wouldn't inflict County upon them (and were they to be aware of the treats they could have instead of watching certain games at Edgeley Park, "inflict" would probably be the correct word). And I'm a third generation fan, who experiences genuine pleasure at seeing *my* kids enjoying supporting the team.

Yes, the price rises genuinely took away some of the gloss. I console myself, however, by thinking "stuff the Board," and remembering the highlights, of which this season contained an inordinately high number - after a start that ranks with the worst I can remember in my twenty four years of watching the team. The win at Millwall, for example, followed by the absolute annihilation, on their own ground, of a Sheffield United team destined for the First Division playoff final. The fact that we were undefeated on four Premiership grounds, winning three times. Beating West Ham at Edgeley Park. Putting Stoke out of the FA Cup in the last such tie ever to be played at the Victoria Ground. And then the run of the mill wins, that were far more significant in their own way: the comeback at Wrexham, the 5-1 victory that gave us a double over Millwall, and, most gloriously of all, the home defeat of Burnley, at such a crucial time, and in such a manner.

In one of those average seasons I referred to above, you'd expect two or three of the above memorable events. To have so many, and in a season which I had already decided to watch in its entirety, almost beggars belief. I'm glad in a way that I can't afford to do it again, because it will never happen again. Rather like the sportsman who retires at the pinnacle of his career, it's probably better to accept that 1996-97 was, and will remain, County's best ever. It'll never be repeated, so why bother repeating the feat of attendance?

Anyway, I must be off - I need a rest. I've also scrapped the Fiesta, and I've got a couple of cars to see. And some decorating to do. And a holiday to arrange. And a garden to sort out. And I think I've got three kids around here somewhere...

STOCKPORT COUNTY FIXTURES 1996-97

1995

				F-A	Scorers
Aug	17	Crewe Alex	A	0-1	
	24	NOTTS COUNTY	H	0-0	
	27	BOURNEMOUTH	H	0-1	
	31	Bristol Rovers	A	1-1	Jeffers
Sep	7	Watford	A	0-1	
	10	WREXHAM	H	0-2	
	14	PLYMOUTH	H	3-1	Gannon (2), Armstrong
	21	York City	A	2-1	Angell (2)
	28	GILLINGHAM	H	2-1	Armstrong, OG
Oct	2	Millwall	A	4-3	Durkan, Armstrong (2), Gannon
	5	Burnley	A	2-5	Angell, Mutch
	12	PRESTON NE	H	1-0	Angell
	15	LUTON TOWN	H	1-1	Angell
	19	Wycombe	A	2-0	Angell (2)
	26	Walsall	A	1-1	Durkan
	29	CHESTERFIELD	H	1-0	Dinning
Nov	2	BRISTOL CITY	H	1-1	Bennett
	9	Brentford	A	2-2	Angell, Cavaco
	19	BLACKPOOL	H	1-0	Bennett
	23	Shrewsbury	A	2-3	Angell, Marsden
	30	WALSALL	H	2-0	Angell (2)
Dec	3	Rotherham Utd	A	1-0	Durkan
	14	PETERBOROUGH	H	0-0	
	21	Bury	A	0-0	
	26	Wrexham	A	3-2	Armstrong, Gannon, Dinning (pen)

1996

				F-A	Scorers
Jan	18	MILLWALL	H	5-1	Mutch, Armstrong (pen), Flynn, Cavaco (2)
Feb	1	BRENTFORD	H	1-2	Cavaco
	8	Bristol City	A	1-1	Armstrong
	15	SHREWSBURY	H	3-1	Angell (2), Armstrong
	22	Blackpool	A	1-2	Mutch
Mar	1	ROTHERHAM	H	0-0	
	8	BURY	H	2-1	Mutch, Jeffers
	15	Peterborough	A	2-0	Cavaco, Marsden
	22	Notts County	A	2-1	OG, OG
	29	CREWE ALEX	H	1-0	Cooper
Apr	1	Bournemouth	A	0-0	
	5	BRISTOL ROVERS	H	1-0	Cooper (pen)
	8	Plymouth	A	0-0	
	12	BURNLEY	H	1-0	Mutch
	14	WATFORD	H	1-0	Jeffers
	16	Gillingham	A	0-1	
	19	Preston NE	A	0-1	
	22	YORK	H	2-1	Bennett, Angell
	26	WYCOMBE	H	2-1	Armstrong., OG
	29	Chesterfield	A	1-0	Angell
May	3	Luton Town	A	1-1	Cooper (pen)

Cup Competitions

Coca Cola Cup

Aug 20	CHESTERFIELD	H	2-1	Mutch (2)
Sep 3	Chesterfield	A	2-1	Ware, Mutch
Sep 17	SHEFFIELD UTD	H	2-1	Flynn, Bennett
Sep 24	Sheffield Utd	A	5-2	Gannon, Armstrong (2), Bennett, Angell
Oct 22	Blackburn	A	1-0	OG
Nov 27	West Ham	A	1-1	Cavaco
Dec 17	WEST HAM (replay)	H	2-1	OG, Angell
Jan 22	SOUTHAMPTON	H	2-2	Armstrong, Cavaco
Jan 29	Southampton (replay)	A	2-1	Angell, Mutch
Feb 26	MIDDLESBROUGH	H	0-2	
Mar 12	Middlesbrough	A	1-0	Connelly

FA Cup

Nov 16	DONCASTER	H	2-1	Flynn, Mutch
Dec 7	Mansfield	A	3-0	OG, Durkan (2)
Jan 15	Stoke City	A	2-0	Durkan, Armstrong
Jan 25	Birmingham	A	1-3	Angell

Auto Windscreens Shield

Dec 10	Doncaster	A	2-1	OG, Cavaco
Feb 4	Burnley	A	1-0	Nash
Feb 11	Bury	A	2-1	Dinning (pen), Angell
Mar 4	Crewe	A	1-1	Marsden (County won 5-3 on penalties)
Mar 18	Carlisle	A	0-2	
Mar 25	CARLISLE	H	0-0	

Scorers

	Lg	FA	LC	AWS	Tot
Armstrong	9	1	3	-	13
Mutch	5	1	4	-	10
Angell	15	1	3	1	20
Jeffers	3	-	-	-	3
Ware	-	-	1	-	1
Gannon	4	-	1	-	5
Flynn	1	1	1	-	3
Bennett	3	-	2	-	5
Durkan	3	3	-	-	6
Dinning	2	-	-	1	3
Cavaco	5	-	2	1	8
Marsden	2	-	-	1	3
Nash	-	-	-	1	1
Connelly	-	-	1	-	1
Cooper	2	-	-	-	2
OG	4	1	2	1	8
Totals	60	8	20	6	94